⊞ ESPIONAGE/INTELLIGENCE LIBRARY ⊞

FROM GEORGE WASHINGTON TO
COL. ELIAS DAYTON,
26.7.1777

"The necessity of procuring good Intelligence is apparent & need not be further urged—All that remains for me to add is, that you keep the whole matter as Secret as possible. For upon Secrecy, Success depends in Most Enterprizes of the Kind, and for want of it, they are generally defeated, however well planned and promising a favorable issue.

> I am Sir
> Yr. Most Obed. Sev."

THE BALLANTINE ESPIONAGE/INTELLIGENCE
LIBRARY

is the first cohesive collection of true chronicles of the greatest, most important, and most intriguing events in the history of international espionage and intelligence gathering. The series offers astonishing new information for the professional and an exciting introduction for the uninitiated. The books delve deeply into the people, events, and techniques of modern espionage—the puzzles, wiles, ruthlessness, romance, and secrets of this endlessly fascinating world.

Written by eyewitnesses or experts, they read "like fiction." But they are undeniably more powerful, because they are *true* . . .

⊞ ESPIONAGE/INTELLIGENCE LIBRARY ⊞

CODEWORD: DIREKTOR

Heinz Höhne

The Story of the Red Orchestra

Translated from the German
by Richard Barry

ESPIONAGE ★ INTELLIGENCE ★ LIBRARY

BB

BALLANTINE BOOKS • NEW YORK

Published originally under the title
Kennwort: Direktor
by S. Fischer Verlag, Frankfurt am Main

© S. Fischer Verlag GmbH,
Frankfurt am Main, 1970

Library of Congress Catalog Card Number 79-154774

ISBN 0-345-30241-9

This edition published by arrangement with
Coward, McCann & Geoghegan, Inc.

Manufactured in the United States of America

First Ballantine Books Edition: August 1982

For My Wife

Contents

Organization of Rote Kapelle

Resident Director Western Europe—Leopold Trepper

Belgium

"Kent" Group
Brussels
(liquidated Dec.
1941)
Victor Sukulov-
Gurevich
(the "Petit Chef")
|
Michail Makarov
(radio operator
and coding)
|
Anton Danilov
(liaison with other
espionage groups)
|
Konstantin Yefre-
mov (later head of
the "Bordo" group)
|
Rita Arnould
(in charge of the
Brussels office)
|
Sophie Posnanska
(cipher expert)
|
Abraham Richman
(passport forger;
later with "Bordo")
|
Malvina Gruber
(courier)
|
Isidor Springer
(industrial informer;
later in France)
|
Augustin Sesée and
Hermann Isbutsky
(radio operators;
later with "Bordo")
|

Otto Schumacher
(radio operator;
later in France)
|
Simone Phelter
(liaison with
France)
|
Maurice Peper
(liaison with
Holland)

"Bordo" Group
(Brussels—
liquidated
July/August 1942)
|
Konstantin
Yefremov
(Head—previously
with "Kent")
|
Abraham Raichman
(previously with
"Kent")
|
Johann Wenzel
(head radio operator,
Western Europe)
|
Augustin Sesée and
Hermann Isbutsky
(previously with
"Kent")
|
Franz and Germaine
Schneider
(couriers)

France

"Gilbert" Group
Paris
(liquidated autumn
1941)
Leopold Trepper
(the "Grand Chef")
|
Leon Grossvogel
(founder of French
and Belgian cam-
ouflage firms em-
ploying (among
others) Alfred
Corbin and
Robert Breyer)
|
Hersch and Myra
Sokol
(radio operators)
|
Vassily and Anna
Maximovich
(agents)
|
Käthe Voelkner
(informer in Sauckel
organization)
|
**Comintern agents
under "Gilbert"
group**
Henry Robinson
(chief courier)
|
Valentino Escudero
(radio operator)
|
Pierre and Lucienne
Giraud
(assistant radio
operators)

Germany

Marseille Group
(from August 1942)
Viktor Sukulov-
Gurevich
(formerly head of
"Kent" group,
Brussels)
|
Marguerite Marivet
and Alepée
(agents)

Lyon Group
(from August 1942)
Head:
Esekiel Schreiber
Isidor Springer
(industrial informer;
previously with
"Kent")
|
Otto Schumacher
(radio operator;
previously with
"Kent")

"Choro" Group
Berlin
(liquidated Sept.
1942)
Head: Harro
Schulze-Boysen
|
Hans Coppi
(radio operator)
|
Oda Schottmüller
Kurt Schumacher
Erika von Brock-
dorff (assistant
radio operators)
|
Horst Heilmann
(informer in
Signals Security)
|
Johann Graudenz
(informer, aircraft
production)
|
Walter and Martha
Husemann
Anna Kraus
Walter Kuchen-
meister
(agents)

"Arwid" Group
(liquidated Septem-
ber 1942)
Head: Arvid
Harnack
|
Adam and Greta
Kuckhoff
(couriers and cipher)
|
John Sieg
(agent)

"Arier" Group
(liquidated Septem-
ber 1942)
Ilse Stöbe
(liaison with
Moscow)
|
Rudolf von Scheliha
(informer in Foreign
Ministry)
Kurt Schulze
(radio operator)

Holland	*Reserve Circuit in Switzerland*
"Hilda" Group	**"Dora" Group**
Amsterdam (liquidated August 1942) Head: Anton Winterinck	(Geneva, Lausanne) Head: Alexander Rado (forced to evacuate in November 1943)
Johann Wenzel (Comintern agent; trainer until 1940; then in France)	Rachel Dubendorfer (succeeded Rado in 1943)
Wilhelm Voegeler (radio operator)	Alexander Foote (radio operator— "Jim" in Lausanne)
Johannes Luteraan (liaison)	Edmond and Olga Hamel (radio operators— Geneva)
Daniel Goulooze Adam Nagel Hendrika Smith (agents)	Margaret Bolli (radio operator— Geneva)
Jakob and Hendrika Rillboling (liaison with Brussels groups)	Rudolf Rössler (informer)
	"Pakbo" Group Head: Otto Pünter Christian Schneider (informer)

Author's Acknowledgments

I wish to thank all those people, institutes and authorities who have assisted in the production of this book by furnishing information, material and advice. They are so numerous that I cannot mention them individually. I am especially indebted, however, to the editorial office of *Der Spiegel*, to whose generosity I owe the fact that I have been able to use documents hitherto forbidden to historians. My very special thanks go to my wife who throughout the work on this book has given me every encouragement and shown unending patience. Production of this book was only made possible by the fact that for months she gave up all her spare time to it. The book is therefore dedicated to her.

Prologue

THE MESSAGE SPELLED disaster. Dr. Otto Pünter (code-name "Pakbo"), organizer and cryptographer of a Soviet espionage circuit in Switzerland, ran his eye over the text, still in clear. Then he reached for a travelogue, *From Pole to Pole* by the Swedish writer Sven Hedin, which he used for enciphering his radio messages.[1] He opened a page, wrote down ten letters from it and turned them into columns of figures. The figures added up to a tale of woe for Soviet espionage headquarters in faraway Moscow:

> "To Direktor. Through Pakbo. A large-scale organization providing information to the Soviet Union was discovered in Berlin in September. Many arrests have already been made and more are imminent. The Gestapo hopes to be able to uncover the entire organization."[2]

It was late September 1942. No sooner had Pünter's message been deciphered in the headquarters of the Soviet Secret Service than Moscow's espionage chiefs[3] became uneasy. On 5 October Colonel-General Ivan Terenchevich Peresypkin[4] radioed to the "Dora" circuit in Switzerland:

> "To Dora. Pakbo's last message about discovery of a large-scale organization in Berlin is important. Pakbo should try and establish who has been arrested and what has actually been found out. When did discovery take place and when did arrests begin?"[5]

1

But Pakbo could not help his Moscow masters. His intelligence lines to Berlin were dead. Not even a hint came to show which members of the Berlin circuit had fallen into the hands of the Gestapo. In vain Moscow searched for the whereabouts of their German informers. In vain the Soviet Secret Service tried to establish whether information still being radioed from Germany was genuine or an intelligence gambit on the part of the enemy. In vain Colonel-General Peresypkin admonished on 20 November:

"To Dora. It is of great importance that Pakbo should find out exactly who has been arrested so far. Who is in charge of the investigation?"[6]

Pünter-Pakbo was forced to discontinue his inquiries with nothing achieved; Moscow went on working in the dark. Hitler-Germany's counter-espionage authorities had taken the strictest secrecy precautions and they succeeded in concealing the fact that the largest circuit of agents in the history of international espionage had been put out of action.

Only a few of the high priests in German Military Intelligence and the Gestapo knew how extensively Soviet espionage had sabotaged Hitler's war machine. Stalin's agents had passed on Luftwaffe strength returns, secret statistics of German arms production, the Nazi hierarchy's political secrets and details of Military Intelligence's sabotage operations.[7] As early as 7 May 1942 Adolf Hitler had said to one of his personal staff: "The Bolsheviks are ahead of us only in one thing—espionage."[8]

They had spied in German military headquarters, profiting from the loquacity of officers and secretaries. Their leaders in Berlin, Luftwaffe Lieutenant Harro Schulze-Boysen and Dr. Arvid Harnack, a senior civil servant [Oberregierungsrat], knew many of the secrets of the Reich Ministries of Aviation and Economics; their agents had infiltrated Military Intelligence [the Abwehr], OKW's [Oberkommando der Wehrmacht—High Command of the Armed Forces] decoding section, the Propaganda Ministry and the Nazi Party's Racio-political Office.[9]

In Belgium, Holland and France was another espionage organization, closely linked to the Schulze-Boysen/Harnack group and ready to try to discover anything which the latter did not know; it was led by two Moscow-trained secret service officers, a Pole named Leopold Trepper (the "Grand Chef") and the Russian, Victor Sukulov-Gurevich alias Kent (the "Petit Chef").[10] Under cover of communist-run firms these two had established business connections with Wehrmacht agencies and come to know of many troop movements in the West and many personnel changes in German staffs.

Nevertheless, even the Kremlin's octopus-like espionage organization had its Achilles' heel. No sooner had the Abwehr detected the first secret transmitters of the Trepper-Kent circuit than one Soviet spy after another went over to the German side. Many a Moscow agent betrayed his comrades; in a comparatively short time the entire organization was rolled up.[11] Worse still, on behalf of the Gestapo the "converted" Soviet agents carried on a "Funkspiel" [radio "playback" game] with Moscow, this time passing false information.[12]

But the enemy must not perceive that this game was being played; he must continue to believe that his agents were still at liberty. In fact for weeks he thought that they were still going full blast, as the German end of the game proved, for whenever, via the "converted" spies, the Gestapo asked Moscow for money, information or even men to be dropped by parachute, the Soviet Secret Service hastened to comply. But this game could obviously only proceed provided no word were allowed to reach the outside world about the destruction of the spy ring.

Even the peculiar codename—"Rote Kapelle" ["Red Orchestra"]—with which the Abwehr christened the Soviet circuit had to remain secret. The name was not in fact invented by the Gestapo to insult Hitler's communist enemies, as suspicious anti-fascists later maintained; it sprang from the terminology used by the dispassionate counterespionage professionals of the Abwehr.[13]

The word "orchestra" had long formed part of the Abwehr's vocabulary. Admiral Wilhelm Canaris' officers described any enemy espionage circuit as an "orchestra"; its short-wave transmitters were "pianos," its radio operators "pianists" and its organizers "conductors." With the appearance of innumerable secret allied radio sets it became normal to refer to the "orchestras" either by their area of operations ("Maritime Orchestra" or "Ardennes Orchestra," for instance); so when the first Soviet transmitter was located, using the call sign PTX Moscow, the title "Red Orchestra" was coined.[14]

The name became synonymous with a secrecy such as only totalitarian systems can impose. Not even the smallest hint was allowed to give away the secret of "Red Orchestra." No one was allowed to know anything—the German people must not know that Soviet spies and anti-Nazi resisters had been obstructing the regime's war effort for years; the Soviets must not know that their spy ring had long since been uncovered.

The case was declared "Top Secret." The spectators' seats at the Reich Court Martial on the members of the Berlin espionage circuit were nearly empty; only the most senior officers, under whom the spies had worked, were informed.[15] The accused were only told of the Court Martial's decision at the last moment. When Frau Marie-Louise Schulze, Schulze-Boysen's mother, presented herself at the prison on 27 December 1942 with a parcel for her son, she was given a rough reception by Dr. Manfred Roeder, the senior military Judge Advocate-General who had prosecuted at the Rote Kapelle trial. "No need for that. Your son was hanged five days ago by order of the Führer." Beside herself, the mother wailed: "No! It can't be true! You can't have done that! I'll never forgive you." To which Roeder replied: "I refuse to do business with you while you're so overwrought."[16] Roeder then handed Frau Schulze and Dr. Jan Tönnies, the sociologist who was with her, "a piece of paper to sign recognizing that we and our families must anticipate the most severe punishment if we said even a word about the death of our children. Thereupon I inquired of him [Roeder] what I was to say if people asked after Harro. He replied: 'Who will ask after Harro anyway?' I said: 'All our friends and relations.' He answered: 'Tell them your son died for you.' "[17] Similarly he threatened Falk Harnack, the communist agent's brother who had been called up into the Wehrmacht: "Forget your brother! You have never had a brother! If you breathe a word about the trial, as a soldier you will be summarily shot. The matter must remain top secret."[18]

Everyone signed the declaration; everyone held his tongue. The secrecy decree applied even to the Gestapo and the Abwehr. The Rote Kapelle affair was an "Eyes only" matter; only officers in the highest positions and the experts immediately concerned with espionage were allowed to know what the words meant.[19] Both OKW and the RSHA [Reichssicherheitshauptant—Reich Central Security Department] demanded the strictest observance of the "Basic Order" of 11 January 1940 by which Hitler had decreed: "1. No one—no agency, no officer—is to be informed of any secret matter unless it is absolutely essential that they have knowledge thereof for reasons of duty. 2. No agency and no officer may learn more of any secret matter than is absolutely essential for the execution of their duties. 3. No agency and no officer is to learn of any secret matter or of the essential part thereof earlier than is absolutely necessary for the execution of their duties."*[20] The Rote Kapelle experts insulated themselves both from their equals and their superiors. Captain Harry Piepe, the Abwehr officer responsible for France and Belgium, was allowed to inform only the Heads of the Abwehr offices;[21] Heinrich Reiser, a senior Gestapo officer [Kriminalkommissar] and SS-Hauptsturmführer [Captain], was instructed to inform neither the Commander of the Security Police in France nor the Head of his Desk IV (Gestapo).[22]

The counter-espionage sleuths succeeded in reducing even Hitler to silence. On 22 December 1942 Himmler, the Reichsführer-SS, was alerted by Heinrich Müller, the Head of the Gestapo, who had heard "that the Führer and the Reich Marshal [Göring] are toying with the idea of publicizing the sentences on Schulze-Boysen and the rest." This would obviously have jeopardized the radio game with Moscow. Müller warned: "I beg to point out that in this event the lines we have built up to Moscow would be lost once more." Even Hitler held his tongue.[23]

The secret was kept to the end of the war. Only after the collapse of the Third Reich did the world learn of Rote Kapelle's triumphs and defeats. Sensationalist writers set to work to reveal the history of the Second World War's most remarkable espionage organization. West Germany's illustrateds and periodicals bounded on to the subject with their usual wealth of imagination. First in the field was Axel Springer's *Kristall* in 1950,[24] but it was soon followed

* Von Schramm is incorrect as regards content, date and title of this Hitler order; what he calls "Führer Order No. 1" was in fact the "Basic Order" issued on 11 January 1940; it did not, as Schramm assumes, include a threat of severe punishment.

by revelations and so-called factual accounts in other periodicals and newspapers. The titles alone show that most were cases of pure sensationalism—"The Cat in the Kremlin,"[25] "The Secret of Rote Kapelle,"[26] "Red agents in our midst,"[27] "Women in the Reds' Game,"[28] "Treachery kills an army."[29]

Even the more serious authors, however, produced accounts of Rote Kapelle. As early as 1946 Fabian von Schlabrendorff, one of the conspirators of 20 July 1944, gave some information in his book *The Secret War against Hitler;*[30] a year later appeared Rudolf Pechel's *Deutscher Widerstand* [German Resistance];[31] in 1948 the Central Research Office of the "Association of Victims of the Nazi Regime" [Vereinigung der Verfolgten des Naziregimes—VVN] in East Berlin published a monograph on "The Schulze-Boysen/Harnack resistance group";[32] in 1956 came the Russo-American writer David Dallin with his *Soviet Espionage*[33] and in 1967 the Frenchman Gilles Perrault with *L'Orchestre rouge.*[34]

Remarkably enough, the stories both in the illustrated papers and the majority of these books produced confusion rather than information. The story of Rote Kapelle soon proved itself to be a lucrative field for the more inventive authors. From the "betrayal" of the Stalingrad army to Stalin's Fifth Column in Hitler's headquarters—nothing was too fanciful for the imaginative genius of the spy-ring sensation-mongers.

On 5 September 1950, for instance, the German Press Agency informed its readers that Rote Kapelle had been "a resistance group, the nucleus of which had already been destroyed in 1936" and that "a large number of younger officers of the Seeckt school" had belonged to it.[35] Roeder, the ex-prosecutor, maintained that the Soviet author Ilya Ehrenburg was the *éminence grise* of Rote Kapelle;[36] other authors promoted Rado, the organizer in Switzerland, to the position of head of the spy-ring[37] or gave his name a Russian twist and turned him into Comrade Radow born in Hungary.[38] In their monumental work *Thirty-three Centuries of Espionage* Rowan and Deindorfer state that "Caro" and "Agis" were the Soviet secret service codenames for Schulze-Boysen and Harnack.[39] One writer describes Rote Kapelle as a creation of the Gestapo;[40] the journalist Fallen de Droog maintains that it was a codename for the Moscow espionage headquarters;[41] yet another thought it a nickname used because Schulze-Boysen had many musical friends.[42]

Faced with such chaos, the Board of the Hamburg Association of Journalists advised editors in West Germany to expunge the words "Rote Kapelle" from their vocabulary: "There was no such thing as 'Rote Kapelle' and consequently no one can have been a member of this 'Rote Kapelle.' "[43]

The imaginative capacity of the literary amateur detectives was inexhaustible. The British author, Gerald Reitlinger, discovered that the Germans had never laid hands on the leaders of the organization;[44] Pechel apparently knew that Hitler had increased the death sentences pronounced by the Reich Court Martial from 50 to 100.[45] The Nazi writer Karl Balzer even unearthed a whole series of new spy cells—a "Libs Group," a "Dancer Group" and an "Engineer Group."[46]

Such baseless tales could not, of course, have circulated had not all documents and witnesses vanished at the end of the war. The records of the Rote Kapelle trial were added to Nazidom's funeral pyre by the demolition squads in early summer 1945. Their last hiding place was Gamburg Castle in the Taubertal, where SS-Hauptsturmführer and Kriminalrat Heinz Pannwitz "burned and pulverized everything until there was nothing left."[47] Everything else (records of agencies not subordinate to the Gestapo, for instance), scattered though they were, were pocketed by the Allied secret services which, with the Cold War beginning, were interested in any clues as to methods used by the Soviet Secret Service.

Toward the end of the 1940s West German Public Prosecutors and the US Army's war crimes investigators recorded every word about the activities of Rote Kapelle when checking whether the Nazi lawyers had committed crimes against humanity in dealing with Soviet spies; but the press had no access to the records of these investigations.[48] The former German counter-espionage experts too were removed from the public gaze; they were in the victors' interrogation camps, subjected for months at a time to questioning and alluring offers from the Allied secret services.*[49] Reiser, the ex-Police Commissar, for

---

* The post-war adventures of the leading Gestapo officials were not in fact as colorful as many authors think. Perrault, for instance (op. cit., p. 374), says that Horst Kopkow, desk officer of IV A-2

instance, recalls: "The French once even made me an offer that I should work for them. They were prepared to let me out if I would get going and discover for them the various senior officers who had been concerned with Rote Kapelle and who had disappeared."[50]

The majority of those in a position to know continued to hold their tongues. Ex-Gestapo officials were afraid that they would be accused of extorting confessions; the survivors of Rote Kapelle observed a discreet silence since they hoped to be accepted as legitimate democratic opponents of Nazi tyranny rather than be regarded as Soviet spies.

For a short time it seemed as if the Rote Kapelle survivors might be prepared, according to their lights, to shed some light on the mystery. Immediately after the war Schulze-Boysen's and Harnack's former friends, now released from prison and penal servitude, banded together and demanded reparation for the injustice done to them. Among them were Greta Kuckhoff, a communist party functionary and widow of Dr. Adam Kuckhoff, Schulze-Boysen's assistant who had been executed, Günther Weisenborn the playwright and Dr. Adolf Grimme, the last social-democrat Minister of Culture in Prussia.[51] Their quarry, passionately pursued, was (in Grimme's words) "one of the worst criminals of the travesty of justice of those years,"[52] Dr. Manfred Roeder, the ex-Luftwaffe Judge-Advocate and prosecutor at the Rote Kapelle trial. These three were determined to have their old enemy severely punished and, in Greta Kuckhoff's words, "would not rest until the stain left by men such as Roeder was erased from the face of Germany."[53] On 15 September 1945 Grimme filed a case with the Judge-Advocate of British Military Government in Hannover; shortly thereafter Frau Kuckhoff

in the RSHA, was officially registered as dead by the British Secret Service but was in fact allowed to return to West Germany in 1949 and assumed the name Kopkow-Cordes in 1954; he also says that SS-Standartenführer Friedrich Panzinger, Kopkow's old head of section, hid in a monastery and committed suicide in 1961 when discovered by the West German legal authorities. It now transpires that Kopkow was released by the British in the autumn of 1947 and then assumed the name of Cordes; Panzinger, who had been a prisoner of war in the Soviet Union, returned in 1955, was listed as an accessory to murder in August 1959 and on 9 August took poison before his first interrogation. (Letter dated 4 April 1968 from Horst Kopkow-Cordes, *Neues Deutschland*, 13 December 1955, and *Münchener Abendzeitung*, 12 August 1959.)

and her two associates submitted to the International Military Tribunal in Nuremberg that Roeder should be called to account for crimes against humanity.*[54]

In her submission to the Military Tribunal Greta Kuckhoff said: "I am convinced that the most stringent investigation is necessary in this trial of Judge-Advocate Roeder. His pitiless and prejudiced attitude during the Schulze-Boysen/Harnack trial resulted in the destruction of the most unequivocal and stable resistance group; it had soberly and realistically considered the possibility of overthrowing the Nazi regime from within and had come to the conclusion that the only prospect of success lay in cooperation with the democratic and socialist peoples."[55]

The three plaintiffs submitted that Roeder had extorted evidence, had treated witnesses and relatives of the accused with brutality, had brought pressure to bear on the court and had used his close connections with Hitler to extract sentences of death.[56] Frau Kuckhoff called for evidence both through the VVN and the newspapers in Berlin and the Soviet-occupied zone;†[57] anyone who had any complaint against "this beast" was asked to come forward.[58]

The American prosecution in Nuremberg investigated the case but found the evidence insufficient to justify bringing Roeder to trial.‡ Roeder's three enemies persisted, however. When the Americans released him in 1947 Frau Kuckhoff demanded that the Berlin Public Prosecutor issue

* The three plaintiffs based their cases on the Allied Control Commission's Law No. 10 prescribing investigation of all crimes against humanity committed by Germans. Falk Harnack, who strongly supported the case against Roeder, argued as follows: The Allied Tribunal in Nuremberg had declared the Reich government to be a criminal organization; consequently any action against it was self-defense; there could be no counter-claim of self-defense and therefore any counter-action was criminal.

† Responsibility for the collection of evidence against Roeder lay with the "Victims of Fascism" Committee of the Municipality of Berlin (Desk officer Frau Lippold) and a Special Commission of the Soviet Zone VVN (Desk officer Klaus Lehmann, author of the monograph *The Schulze-Boysen/Harnack Resistance Group*, already mentioned); written evidence was first checked by Weisenborn. See exchange of letters between Professor Heilmann and the Secretariat-General of the VVN and Berlin Municipality—in Heilmann's private papers.

‡ "The Americans thought that they could learn something from him. Evidence against Roeder was scanty and was insufficient to justify a trial for crimes against humanity. In addition his brazen attitude won him the respect of the Americans."[59]

an arrest warrant for him.[60] Finally she took the case up
with the West German judiciary and the file ended up on
the desk of the Public Prosecutor of Lüneburg, now the
responsible authority since Roeder had meanwhile taken
up residence on his wife's property at Neetze near Lüneburg.[61]

No sooner had the Lüneburg Public Prosecutor begun
has investigations, however, than he found that his main
obstacle was Greta Kuckhoff herself. Perhaps she had received a hint from the Soviet Secret Service that they had
no wish for a Rote Kapelle trial in the West; perhaps she
had qualms lest the trial should discredit her story that
Rote Kapelle was a political resistance movement. In any
case Frau Kuckhoff now suddenly demanded that Roeder
be handed over to an eastern bloc country.[62]

This was a plan near to the Russians' heart. In January
1948 the Berlin Public Prosecutor told Dr. Robert M. W.
Kempner, one of the US prosecutors, that he heard "that
the Russians were demanding to sit in judgment on the
accused."[63] The American authorities, however, refused
to hand Roeder over to Moscow.

Then Frau Kuckhoff had another idea. On 7 June 1948
Horst Heilmann, father of the Horst Heilmann who had
been executed as a friend of Schulze-Boysen, was told by
the Secretary-General of the VVN that: "Comrade Kuckhoff considers it absolutely necessary to apply for Roeder
to be handed over to a Polish court and has taken the
necessary steps to this end."[64] Based on a vague rumor
that in late September 1939, when President of the Luftwaffe Military Court in Bromberg (Bydgoszcz), Roeder
had passed death sentences on Poles, Greta Kuckhoff now
urged the Polish government to demand Roeder's extra-
dition.[65] Heilmann did not in fact think that she had much
prospect of success, saying that "Roeder stands very well
with the American occupation authorities."[66]

Later even Comrade Kuckhoff was left wondering why
her Warsaw friends did not follow up her suggestion. The
Lüneburg Public Prosecutor knew the reason and told her
so: there had never been a "Bromberg trial"; some Polish
hostages had been shot by German soldiers at the time but
Roeder had not taken part in any legal proceedings.[67]
Greta Kuckhoff insisted, however, that former military
legal officers had written to her describing the savagery of
Roeder's action in Bromberg.[68] When the Public Prosecu-

tor asked her to produce the letters, however, she refused. Greta Kuckhoff was by then a director-level official of the Ministry of External Affairs in East Berlin and later became chairman of a bank (the Notenbank) in the German Peoples Republic. She refused to record her statements and broke off all relations with the West German judiciary. A Roeder trial in West Germany, she wrote on 12 December 1949, would be "completely meaningless" since "conditions in West Germany are such that no equitable outcome can be expected."[69]

Her two co-plaintiffs, Grimme and Weisenborn, also lost interest in the case which they had once pursued so industriously. Grimme had meanwhile (summer 1949) become Director-General of the North-West German Radio and, after perusing his statements to the Public Prosecutor, became afraid that he and Weisenborn would be "at the muddy end of this case" and that as a result their position "would probably become untenable."[70] Weisenborn too was worried that after the trial "all the members of Rote Kapelle would be branded as traitors."[71] He thought he knew a way of escape from this distressing situation. He inquired whether it would be possible "to annul the case if someone suggested to the witnesses that they fail to put in an appearance."[72] The Public Prosecutor replied with a warning against so crude a manipulation of evidence and ultimately came down on Roeder's side: in 1951 investigations into the case were suspended.[73]

From this time on the ex-leaders of Rote Kapelle took refuge behind a curtain of silence. In the majority of cases Frau Kuckhoff refused to answer inquiries from the West—after all she maintained that only a Marxist could pass fair judgment on the Schulze-Boysen/Harnack group.[74] Günther Weisenborn took refuge in the fairy tale that Rote Kapelle had been a resistance group whose sole purpose was political reform.[75] Finally, Adolf Grimme, who knew little of his friends' espionage activities, continually tried to explain that "in fact there was no such thing as Rote Kapelle. The 'Rote Kapelle' idea was invented by the Nazi propagandists as a term applicable to a whole series of more or less unconnected instances of resistance."[76]

No sooner had these people been silenced than the other side demanded to have its say—self-righteous anticommunists like Roeder and liquidators of the past from the old Abwehr. Many of these used pseudonyms for the men they were describing. Unfortunately, both the press and the historians fell for the cover-name game. *Mittag,* for instance, published a photograph of Rote Kapelle's chief radio operator in Western Europe; his name was given as "Wilhelm Schwarz."[77] The readers were not to know that "Schwarz" was a pseudonym arbitrarily invented by Piepe; the photograph, however, did in fact show the real radio operator, the communist agent Johann Wenzel.[78] The fictitious Schwarz promptly appeared in various books; even the ex-Abwehr author Paul Leverkuehn accepted Piepe's ghost figure.[79]

Another of these fictitious personalities was Colonel-General Feodor Kuznetsov, who was presented as the Red Army's supreme intelligence chief.*[80] Ever since he has been a shadowy figure in books and on the radio. Many authors have accepted this super-spy without checking in Soviet sources whether a Colonel-General of this name ever served in the Soviet secret service. The secret service expert Dallin, for instance, believes in him,[81] as does Wilhelm Ritter von Schramm, the chronicler of Rote Kapelle.[82] As late as June 1968 listeners to the German radio were told what a menace Colonel-General Kuznetsov had been to the soldiers on the German Eastern Front.[83]

The reticence of the ex-Abwehr and Gestapo functionaries almost forced historians to invent even further pseudonyms. Dallin's book, for instance, was the first serious account of Rote Kapelle, but even this is full of false names such as Kalthof, Hofmann and Weber;[84] the Frenchman Perrault too was forced to introduce misleading names for people already referred to under some other title—equally false.†

---

* Kuznetsov's biography shows that he never worked in the Soviet Secret Service. He was born in 1904, volunteered for the Red Army in 1921, was a student at the Lenin Military Academy in the 1930s, and before World War II entered the political administration of the Soviet Army (information from the Research Institute for the USSR, July 1968). In fact the Director of the Central Office for Information was Colonel-General (later Marshal) of the Signals Service Ivan Terenchevich Peresypkin (see Hans Koch: *5000 Sowjetköpfe,* p. 636; *Who's Who in the USSR* 1961/62, p. 584; *Biographic Directory of the USSR,* p. 484; personal file on Peresypkin in the Research Institute for the USSR, April 1960).

† For instance, he calls Dr. Wilhelm Vauck, the German decoding expert, Kludow, whereas Flicke had already introduced him as Vauth.[85]

The result of this confusion has been that in the Federal Republic history does not yet really know what Rote Kapelle was. In 1951, for instance, the historian Hans Rothfels could not make up his mind how far the Schulze-Boysen/Harnack group was "in touch" with the Soviet Union;[86] ten years later the young historian Helmut Heiber considered that "it could not yet be finally established" whether Rote Kapelle was not "an invention of the RSHA."[87] What the historian does not know, the people cannot be expected to know either. Rote Kapelle remains a mystery.

Such uncertainty is doubly deplorable since it enables demagogues both of the Right and the Left to twist history for their own ends. Rote Kapelle is no ordinary affair of espionage; for Germans the case is charged with all the emotions born of failure to come to terms with their past.

"Treason," in the sense of betrayal of one's country, is the explosive word used, and many Germans find it irksome for it raises the whole question of their attitude to the regime known as the Third Reich. Even the terms in which the history of Rote Kapelle has been written are indicative of the Germans' attempt to put a gloss on their Nazi past and make one wonder whether the Germans have yet learned to discount the patriotic and ideological catchwords which obscure rather than illuminate this chapter of German history.

It is now more than a quarter of a century since this espionage organization was broken up, but a true history of Rote Kapelle remains an essential feature of Germany's political housecleaning—and the story can now be told, unvarnished by false names or self-justificatory statements by the participants. Hitherto unknown documents have been discovered; vital interviews have been held with participants on both sides; all published sources, both in the East and the West, have been sifted. So I have been able to write a true history of this spy-ring. It is a story of spies, of traitors and idealists, of the hunted and the hunters, as exciting as any spy novel. But it is more than that; it is a history lesson showing the lengths to which men can be driven when their State no longer recognizes the principles of law and humanity.

There is need of such a history because of the existence in Germany of two vocal groups which prevent the Germans realizing the scope and significance of Rote Kapelle.

Right-wing extremists have made the case their own because they see in it the "treason" which they would like to lay at the door of any group whose object was internal resistance to Hitler; their left-wing opponents, on the other hand, present Rote Kapelle unequivocally in the guise of a democratic resistance movement; this they do to justify an ideology whose anti-fascist exterior cannot conceal the fact that its official practices bear an ugly resemblance to those of National Socialism. Both sides understand each other perfectly. One form of extremism begets another—as so often happens when ideological romancers play fast and loose with history.

Many (far too many) Germans find the right-wing arguments plausible because they cannot reconcile themselves to the fact that the Schulze-Boysen/Harnack group bore little relation to the standard picture of the Soviet spy. The leaders of the Berlin spy-ring regarded themselves as resisters fighting the Third Reich; they wished to replace the Nazi dictatorship by their concept of a socialist republic, inseparably linked to the Soviet Union.[88]

So improbable a blend of resistance and espionage, of treason in the sense of subversive activity against one's own government and treason in the sense of betrayal of one's country, of democratic propensities and communism, was bound to excite the wrath of all the unthinking superpatriots. Violent anti-communism offered them an excuse for failure to reflect on their own shortcomings during the Hitler period; they were now Cold War crusaders and so they condemned the Rote Kapelle survivors as a form of ideological vermin. As if the Third Reich with its system of oppression, its persecution of the Jews and its warlike adventures had been a normal State with, therefore, a normal claim to the loyalty of its citizens, these right-wing extremists clubbed together during the early post-war years to hunt down the Rote Kapelle "traitors." Their own guilt complexes and exaggerated notions about the effectiveness of espionage gave rise to a ghoulish indictment: the Soviet spies in Berlin had condemned thousands of German soldiers to death, had been the cause of German defeats in the East and had delivered the Reich over to bolshevism.

"Betrayal of Germany" was the least which ex-SS-Untersturmführer [2nd Lieutenant] Erich Kernmayr, alias Erich Kern, could find to say.[89] The *Deutsche National-*

Zeitung, always on hand to vilify opponents of Hitler, considered that "traitors like Schulze-Boysen, Harnack and others" had the lives of "hundreds of thousands, probably even millions, of German soldiers on their conscience."[90] The *Reichszeitung* proclaimed: "The entire German High Command was riddled with Stalin's agents; no one can win a war if the enemy is sitting in his own headquarters."[91] Karl Balzer, who thought that "practically everything betrayable was betrayed,"[92] said sarcastically: "It is easy to wage war when one knows beforehand not only the enemy's every move, but in most cases also his troop strengths and the equipment he will use."[93]

Even more balanced authors, however, such as the ex-Nazi diplomat Paul Schmidt, alias Paul Carell, took part in the anti-Rote Kapelle campaign. In his book on the Eastern campaign, *Scorched Earth,* he maintained that Rote Kapelle's treachery had largely contributed to the Soviet victory in the battle of the Kursk salient in 1943.[94] The *Hausfreund für Stadt und Land* believed that the "German invasion plan for the East" had been given away and that "treachery had been decisive in the battle for Stalingrad and in the Caucasus offensive."[95]

The journalistic persecutors of Rote Kapelle came to believe in their own ghost stories. There could be no clearer illustration than the campaign against Adolf Grimme. As a devout socialist he had for a time taken part in the Harnack group's discussion evenings—nothing more.[96] Even he was accused by the self-appointed prosecutors of responsibility for the death of German soldiers. The Reich Court Martial had acquitted him of any suspicion of espionage and had only sentensed him to three years' hard labor for "failure to disclose a treasonable intent";[97] he himself protested that "even the Nazis admitted that I had betrayed nothing to communist Russia."[98] But none of this was any use; the old charges were repeated over and over again; even in 1952 Keller, speaking for the SRP,* was still saying: "He betrayed brave German soldiers to Moscow."[99]

The patent camouflage tactics adopted by the Rote Kapelle survivors, however, provided unintentional assistance to the right-wing extremists' campaign of vilification.

---

* Sozialistische Reichspartei—an extremist right-wing party banned in the 1950s.

They tried to minimize the espionage aspect of the activities of Schulze-Boysen, Harnack and their friends. Privately and when off their guard the defenders of Rote Kapelle such as Greta Kuckhoff and Günther Weisenborn would boast about the allegedly decisive wartime successes of their former organization;[100] in their public utterances, however, they were careful to avoid giving any details of their collaboration with the Soviet Secret Service.

Frau Kuckhoff maintained that Schulze-Boysen's group intended to "rouse resistance against oppression" by means of a "vast poster campaign," "leaflets and pamphlets" and "work with transmitters."[101] These sinister "transmitters" were apparently to be used only for propaganda purposes; they were "resistance transmitters" as in Weisenborn's play on Rote Kapelle *Die Illegalen*.[102] Even as late as 1965 Weisenborn sidestepped any suggestion that the group had been engaged in espionage, merely saying that Schulze-Boysen's people had apparently had a "secret transmitter" and had "maintained radio contact with the USSR as the Gestapo's final report says," but that it was "hardly possible to say how far this went."[103] Such statements were intended only for a gullible public. Privately, however, both Frau Kuckhoff and Weisenborn were quite open about Rote Kapelle's espionage activities. Years earlier Weisenborn had written a history of Rote Kapelle which he never published; it showed that he knew a great deal—"The transmitters were kept moving. One was with Countess Erika von Brockdorff-Rantzau, one with Harnack and one, passed on by the Kuckhoffs, with Graudenz on the Alexanderplatz." He knew the radio operators too: "Walter Husemann was the link between Kurt Schulze, the operator whose set went 'dis' in 1942, and Hans Coppi who wanted to become an operator; Husemann also passed on to Schulze information from his armaments firm."[104]

Greta Kuckhoff also knew all about spying. In a confidential report she said: "I collected the first radio set from Alexander Erdberg (the Russian organizer) about a week before the outbreak of war. We had it for a day or two and it then moved on. It weighed eight pounds and fitted into a small suitcase."[105]

But the outside world was still given an idealized picture. In the East Berlin paper *Weltbühne* Frau Kuckhoff told her public that Harnack's "weekly reports," based on secret information from the Reich Ministry of Economics, were intended for anti-fascist "work in the factories."[106] Privately, however, she admitted that the destination of these reports was very different—the Soviet Embassy in Berlin.[107]

On another occasion, when asked why Rote Kapelle had only looked eastward, Frau Kuckhoff replied with an indication that it had been in contact with resistance groups in France and Belgium also.[108] She did not, of course, explain that she was referring to Trepper's and Kent's espionage organizations.

Frau Kuckhoff and Weisenborn apparently did not realize that such dubious circumlocutions merely added fuel to the fire of the right-wing extremist campaign. They evidently did not notice that the close connection between the Schulze-Boysen/Harnack group and the Soviet espionage organization, which their ambiguous statements were intended to conceal, had long been a subject of public self-congratulation in the East.

From 1960 onward the Soviet Union began to pay public tribute to spies whom they had officially ignored for decades; from Richard Sorge to Kim Philby all were now heroes of Socialism. Moreover, they were no longer resistance fighters; they were "agents." On 6 October 1969 the Presidium of the Supreme Soviet of the USSR gave a posthumous award of the Order of the Red Banner to the most important members of Rote Kapelle including Schulze-Boysen, Harnack and Kuckhoff,* and laudatory articles in the Russian press concentrated upon their espionage activities. *Pravda* wrote: "During the early years of the Great Patriotic War the German anti-fascists collected and transmitted to Moscow much valuable information revealing the situation in fascist Germany's homeland and the war plans of the Hitlerite fascists."[110]

For a long time—far longer than in the Soviet Union—the East German press and authors had drawn a veil over the Schulze-Boysen/Harnack group's intelligence activities; in the book on the German Labor Movement from 1933–45, published by Laschitza and Vietzke in 1964, and in Tomin's and Grabowski's *Heroes of the Berlin Underground,* published in 1967, there was no word of spies,

---

* Harro Schulze-Boysen, Arvid Harnack, Adam Kuckhoff, Ilse Stöbe and Hans-Heinrich Kummerow were awarded the Order of the Red Banner. Günther Weisenborn, Karl Behrens and Albert Hössler the Order of the Great Patriotic War, First Class.[109]

only of resistance fighters. Not until the end of 1967, the twenty-fifth anniversary of the execution of Schulze-Boysen and his friends, did the East German public learn from *Neues Deutschland*, the official Party newspaper, that the resistance group had transmitted "most important information to Soviet agencies by radio and other means."[111]

Junge Welt, the East German youth newspaper, knew what this information was—"information on current war production, planned offensives and other important events."[112] The East Berlin women's periodical *Für Dich* was even more accurately informed.[113] It translated a series of five articles from *Pravda* on Ilse Stöbe, a fringe figure of Rote Kapelle—codename "Alta"; in the circumspect anti-facist jargon of East German journalism it said that "people should now know in what a vital sector she had fought against the Nazi regime."[114] The article contained hitherto unknown details—"Alta's" radio messages to Moscow, her overall task, her informers, her meeting points and her organizer, "General Petrov." The conclusion was obvious: information on "Alta" must have been released by the Soviet Secret Service.

So the story of Rote Kapelle ends where it began—in Soviet Secret Service headquarters. Rote Kapelle was born in Moscow in the 1930s when the Soviet espionage chiefs saw the collapse of the mightiest intelligence organization ever maintained in a foreign country by a secret service. However successful Rote Kapelle may have been, it was only a pale reflection of the fine-spun network spread over Germany by Moscow's intelligence after the First World War.

Without its precursor, Soviet espionage in Germany in the 1920s and 1930s, Rote Kapelle cannot be understood. That was the formative period for the habits of thought and behavior followed by German communists of the Hitler period. The story begins in the autumn of 1918 when the first Soviet agents infiltrated into Germany, thus opening one of the most dramatic chapters in the history of international espionage.

1

The Jungle of the "Apparats"

THE STORY OF Soviet espionage in Germany starts with a piece of luggage. It belonged to the recently installed Soviet Embassy in Berlin and was on a porter's barrow amid the hustle and bustle of the Friedrichstrasse Station. The trunk fell off the barrow and split open; thousands of leaflets carrying a call to revolution fluttered all over the platform. The German police took action and a few days later Adolf Joffe, Soviet Russia's first Ambassador to Berlin, was politely requested to leave Germany together with his staff.[1]

This was the first case of Soviet espionage on German territory and it took place in October 1918.[2] No one, of course, then used the word espionage; at the time there was officially no such thing as a Soviet Secret Service. Nevertheless, ever since the formation of the Soviet Republic bolshevist agents had been at work in Germany and their purpose was that which Russian espionage had long served: to obtain information on the country whose armies at that time were still deep in the Ukraine, the Caucasus and the Baltic provinces.

Germany had been the main target for Russian espionage ever since the beginning of the twentieth century. When defeat in the Russo-Japanese war of 1904–5 halted Russian expansion in Asia, the Imperial Russian General Staff's secret service concentrated upon Germany (and her ally Austria-Hungary), the power which blocked Russian ex-

19

pansionism in the Balkans and Eastern Europe.[3] Before
that a Russian spy had been an apparition almost unknown
to Germans; the traditional spy was a Frenchman. For
years the old-established friendship between the service
chiefs of Berlin and St. Petersburg had made military
espionage unnecessary. When the two Emperors were each
Field Marshals of the other's country, when the two armies
used each other's field service regulations, there was hardly a need for secret intelligence; the two sides knew each
other. If perchance a Russian spy was discovered in Germany, he was sure to be an agent of Section Three of the
"All-highest Chancellery of His Imperial Majesty" or its
successor organization the "Okhrana" (Security); he would
be on the hunt for anti-Czarist bomb-throwers and so be
entitled to every assistance from the Imperial German
authorities.*

The Russian setback in the Far East, however, put an
end to this idyll. The Russian General Staff despatched to
Germany a swarm of agents, directed by the Military Attachés in Berlin and Vienna. They were particularly successful in the German frontier zone which was kept under
observation by a team of ten secret service officers in each
western Military District of Russia.[5] Their main informants
were clerks in German fortresses and higher-level staffs of
German frontier formations.

The star organizer was Colonel Batyushin, head of the
intelligence section of the Government-General in Warsaw.[6] Across his desk came papers revealing the enemy's
most closely-guarded military secrets—plans of the German fortress of Thorn (Torun) handed over by its Chief
Clerk,[7] information from the Königsberg garrison provided
by a regimental clerk,[8] the entire mobilization plan of the
Austro-Hungarian army sold by Alfred Redl, a Colonel in
the Austro-Hungarian Secret Service.[9] Finally, through a
corrupt agency of the German General Staff, the Russians

* The "All-highest Chancellery" was a special agency of the Czar
dealing with matters which the imperial autocrat did not wish to en-
trust to his Ministries. Section One checked all reports addressed to
the Czar by the authorities; Section Two was responsible for the
drafting of legislation; Section Three was the headquarters of the
Secret Police; Section Four dealt with the Czarina's welfare institutions. Section Three was formed after the Decembrist rising of 1825,
was disbanded for incompetency by Czar Alexander II in 1879, re-
constituted with the title "Okhrana" and placed under the Ministry
of the Interior.[4]

obtained plans of practically all the German fortresses. The deal was discovered in time, however, and the purchaser, the Russian Military Attaché in Berlin, was expelled from the country forthwith.[10] Walter Nicolai, head of the German Secret Service, lamented: "The Russian espionage agencies in Germany were so brazen that they demanded German police protection against the plainclothes officers (who were only watching them, not acting) and against the general public which was becoming increasingly suspicious."[11]

The First World War, however, put an end to Russian espionage successes. The Imperial General Staff's Secret Service vanished in the chaos of the Russian collapse. In March 1917, after the fall of the Czar, it was abolished as an instrument of oppression and counter-revolution.[12]

But the secret service holiday could not last long. After the signature of the Russo-German Peace Treaty at Brest-Litovsk in March 1918, the young Soviet Republic found itself beset on all sides. From north, east and south White Russian armies were advancing with troops of the Entente behind them; in the West, the Peace Treaty notwithstanding, the Germans were moving forward. As a measure of self-preservation it was essential to know the enemy's every move beforehand. The most dangerous were the Germans; they were occupying large stretches of Russia.[13]

At the end of 1918 a new secret service was formed in the Peoples Commissariat for War; it was initially known as the "Red Army Registration Section."[14] Early in the 1920s this became the "Fourth Department" of the General Staff and five years later turned into "Razvedupr," short for Glavnoe Razvedyvatelnoe Upravlenie—Chief Intelligence Administration.*

Its first head was Jan Karlovich Berzin, an Old-Guard bolshevist and later General, a long-standing comrade of Lenin who had several times been condemned to death and life-long exile.[16] Henri Barbé, the French communist leader, describes him in 1931 as "a man of about fifty, in military uniform, on his tunic two Red Banner decorations . . . about 5′ 8″ tall; his skull was shaved."[17] He became cordially loathed by non-Russian communists because he

---

* "Razvedupr" is used here instead of the more usual "GRU" since it was the current term in the 1930s and 1940s. Even German police files of this period refer to Razvedupr.[15]

blatantly placed Russian security interests above those of the world communist movement.

Berzin had studied the methods of the Czarist Secret Service; he both copied and improved them. In process of time he built up a headquarters with a "Director" (Upravlyayushchy) at its head,[18] assisted by a First Deputy whose official title ("Commander") showed that he was responsible for the technical and administrative running of the secret service.[19]

Berzin organized the headquarters into six Divisions: 1. The "Agentura" dealt with the employment and direction of agents abroad. 2. The "Operations Division" acted as headquarters for military intelligence, subversion and espionage. 3. The "Information Division" was responsible for collecting, evaluating and distributing information received. 4. The "Head of Agents' Training" Division controlled the selection and training of agents and informers. 5. The "Head of External Traffic" Division supervised the intelligence briefing of Military Attachés. 6. The "Intelligence Communications Assistants" Division (added later) dealt with radio intelligence.[20]

The most important Division was Operations. It consisted of six sections, the first three organized geographically: Section I dealt with Western Europe, Section II with the Middle East, Section III with America, the Far East and India; a fourth section was responsible for procurement of technical intelligence equipment (radio sets, secret inks, photographic apparatus, etc.), a fifth handled terrorist operations abroad, and a sixth dealt with "misinformation" or enemy deception. During the Second World War sections were added for codes and ciphers and enemy intelligence in the West Russian Military Districts.[21]

Direct lines linked the headquarters at the Kropotkin Gate, Moscow,[22] with Soviet diplomatic missions abroad. The majority of these included a Military Attaché[23] who was the representative of the headquarters, received his instructions from Moscow and passed them on to the Resident Director. The latter was the real chief of the agents in the country concerned.[24]

The Resident Director lived outside the Embassy or Legation, was usually a Soviet citizen and ran two or three groups of informers.[25] He passed his information to the Military Attaché who was his sole channel of communication to headquarters. The Resident Director and his agents only operated independently in the event of war; before the outbreak of hostilities the Military Attaché had to deliver to him the radio sets stored in every Embassy, together with a code and money;[26] from then on the local man's only contact to headquarters was via an anonymous being, the Director's head radio operator in Moscow.

The work of the Military Attachés and Resident Directors was subject to an intricate control system. Visiting inspectors would appear unannounced from Moscow[27] and check all the Military Attaché's files, for headquarters demanded painstaking precision. The Military Attaché had to keep a "log book"[28] in which was recorded every contact with persons of importance from the secret service point of view; standard expressions had to be used—whether it was a "contact," "normal contact" or "urgent emergency contact."[29]

Visiting inspectors also noted whether the Military Attaché kept himself adequately aloof from the rest of the diplomatic staff. In every embassy the Attaché worked in a secret area reserved for Moscow's special employees, a secret world with sound-proof walls, electrically operated steel doors and loopholes in the passages. On the third floor of the Soviet Embassy in Berlin, for instance, a 100-room building on the fashionable Unter den Linden, a series of rooms housed a photographic laboratory, an armory, radio transmitters and receivers, and facilities for forging passports.[30]

Visiting inspectors checked to see whether the conspiratorial rules were being observed. Every member of an espionage circuit had a cover name and a number, both allotted by headquarters.[31] It was strictly forbidden to inquire as to real names. Words in frequent use were translated into a special secret service jargon; a passport, for instance, was a "shoe," a forger of passports a "cobbler," a revolver a "camera" and enemy counter-espionage personnel "hounds."[32]

Strict rules were laid down for contacts between agents. They might not visit each other in their homes nor refer to cover names, addresses or organizational details in letters or over the telephone; written messages were to be destroyed at once and diaries were not to be kept.[33] The Russians insisted on extreme punctuality; when agents met in a "safe house" their first action was to agree on precautions in the event of the contact being interrupted by the police.[34]

In a spy circuit hardly anyone knew anyone else. According to Cookridge the rule was that A, the Resident Director, "knows the identity of B1, B2 and B3 under him, but that B1, B2 and B3 do not, at any rate in theory, know each other. B1 knows C1, C2 and C3, who work under him, although probably he only actually meets C1, who in turn may be in touch with D1 and so on for each group. Only A knows the names of all the men and women in all the different groups, but they do not know each other."[35]

But where was Russia's military secret service to recruit its foreign agents? Berzin could think of only one source of supply: local communist parties. He could not conceive that any foreign communist could be unwilling to assist Soviet espionage. Headquarters' pressure for the maximum number of foreign communists to enter their service became even greater.*

Here came the first sign that the "Director's" authority was not unlimited. Another agency laid claim to the pool of communist agents abroad—the Soviet Secret Police under Felix Dzerzhinsky.[37] He came of a landowning family, was close to Lenin and had been a savage competitor of Berzin ever since the formation of the Soviet State, for the Secret Police wished to confine Razvedupr to purely military intelligence. Such rivalries are no peculiarity of the Soviet Union, however; secret police and secret service have always been at loggerheads, whether they be called SD and Abwehr as in Hitler Germany, or FBI and CIA as in the United States. In Soviet Russia's case, however, there was a further factor: Dzerzhinsky's organization, formed in 1917 with the title "Extraordinary Commission for the Fight against Counter-Revolution and Sabotage" and known as "Cheka" from its Russian initials, was given complete control over all State security.[38] In 1922 it was renamed GPU (short for "Political Police Administration") and lost some of its absolute authority;[39] nevertheless, Dzerzhinsky retained his seniority over his secret service rivals.

Razvedupr found itself shorn of its prerogatives by the GPU. Enemy intelligence and counter-espionage in the

---

* Henri Barbé, the French communist leader, protested against Razvedupr's ruthless recruiting campaign among members of his Party and quarreled with Berzin as a result.[36]

Red Army and frontier Military Districts were handed over, not to Division IV of the Secret Service, but to Division III of the Commissariat for War, and this division was staffed solely by GPU officers;[40] it was under the Special Division (Osobyi Otdjel—OO) of the Secret Police.[41]

The existence of this Special Division signalled a further loss of authority by the Secret Service, since the OO was responsible for the entire cryptographic service. The cipher section was located at 6 Lubyanka Street, Moscow, a GPU building in which a mere couple of rooms were reserved for a group of military cipher clerks under Colonel Kharkevich.[42] He was subordinate to Gleb I. Boki, the head of the OO, although he was permitted to report to the General Staff of the Red Army.[43]

Another competitor of Berzin's spy organization was the Foreign Department of the GPU, formed in 1921 and known as INO (Inostranni—Foreign Countries).[44] Its original purpose was surveillance of White Russians who had fled to the West but it soon developed intelligence ambitions. INO maintained resident organizers with their own informers abroad and was later represented in every Soviet diplomatic mission, the cover appointment usually being that of Secretary of Embassy. This official had a watching brief over the orthodoxy of every member of the Embassy including the Military Attaché, and noted everything which, by the elastic GPU standards, could be classified under "Fight against Counter-Revolution."[45]

The Secret Police were also in close touch with the communist underground abroad, primarily in those countries which Moscow thought ripe for revolution. The GPU smuggled weapons into the country concerned, formed terrorist groups and trained foreign communists in the art of subversion.[46]

As far as espionage abroad was concerned, Berzin did contrive to confine his rival Dzerzhinsky to strictly "defensive" tasks; the Central Information Division of the Politburo of the Communist Party, which dealt with disputes between the Secret Service and the Secret Police, decided that offensive enemy intelligence was the sole prerogative of Razvedupr.[47] Nevertheless, the Secret Service had to be continually on guard against further invasions of its territory by the Secret Police, for the latter now began to work with another of its rivals abroad—the Comintern.

Comintern, short for "Communist International," was the worldwide Communist Party organization formed in Moscow in March 1919 under the leadership of the highest Soviet functionaries.[48] Its formation was a reflection of the hopes of European communists for worldwide red revolution; the thirty-two founder members of Comintern believed that, by means of their organization, bourgeois capitalist society would be replaced by communism, which alone could prevent imperialism instigating another, even bloodier, war.[49]

Since world revolution failed to materialize, however, the Comintern increasingly developed into an instrument of Soviet policy. It had been formed in Moscow, its headquarters was in Moscow and its orders came from Moscow. Soviet functionaries presided over the more important agencies of the Red International, in particular its Presidium's Executive Committee (EKKI) with its various departments.[50] A Russian was Chairman of EKKI; the basic Comintern decisions were taken by the Politburo of the Soviet Communist Party, only the executive instructions being left to EKKI.[51]

The conspiratorial dreamworld in which Comintern headquarters lived was Russian-inspired. At the Second World Congress of the Comintern in July and August 1920 the Russian leaders forced through the decision that, in addition to their legal agencies, communist parties should form underground organizations to prepare for armed revolt.[52] The official reason given was that the bourgeois capitalist governments were determined "to murder communists in all countries"; "by systematic illegal efforts," therefore communism must prepare "for the moment when bourgeois persecution will come out into the open."[53]

As a result of this decision, alongside the Secret Service and the Secret Police, there was now a third agency concerned with conspiratorial machinations. EKKI's emissaries carried on skillfully concealed underground warfare against non-communist states; its "international instructors" supervised the formation of illegal communist party organizations;[54] they armed and financed them; they set up workshops for the forging of passports and they organized a courier system linking the illegal Party agencies to Comintern headquarters.[55]

In this unseen world of underground politics the man who directed the empire remained a shadowy figure even to the conspirators. He was Osip Piatnitsky, the Comintern's *éminence grise*, the head of its organization and its treasurer.[56] He worked primarily through a department to which no communist might openly refer, the OMS. The letters stood for "Otdel Mezhdunarodnoi Svyazi"—International Liaison Department.[57]

This apparently innocent title concealed the fact that Piatnitsky and his OMS had a finger in the pie of every communist party and in practice decided their policy. He was the master of the mighty Comintern "international instructors," his department maintained established offices abroad and had representatives in Soviet diplomatic missions. OMS representatives abroad were frequently more influential than their rivals from Razvedupr or the GPU.[58] With such powers the head of OMS was clearly a central figure in Soviet espionage. Neither the Secret Police nor the Secret Service could do their work abroad without agents from the local communist parties or the help of the Comintern's passport-forging shops. So both Razvedupr and GPU kept in close touch with the Comintern. Representatives of the Secret Service were included in Piatnitsky's Military Division, which promoted revolutions abroad;[59] senior GPU functionaries were members of Piatnitsky's International Control Commission, which maintained a much-coveted secret registry including the personal files of all international communists of note.[60]

So at the end of the First World War three separate branches of the Soviet espionage machine—Secret Service, Secret Police and Comintern—set out to cover Europe with an invisible network of informers. As before, the target which seemed to them most important was Germany.

The Soviet leaders had never ceased to hope for a "German October," communist seizure of power in Germany. Without a German revolution Lenin could not see how he could change the structure of Russian society; the intelligence and education of the German working class, he thought, would relieve the Russian revolutionaries of the almost intolerable burden involved in setting up the classless society in a country where brutality and ignorance were rife.[61]

Initially the methods used by Soviet espionage in Germany were governed by this anxious expectation that their

German comrades would follow their lead. So it was the Comintern which set up the first intelligence circuit in Germany. Chance also played its part: when Joffe, the Soviet Ambassador, was expelled at the end of 1918, only the Comintern functionaries were left to represent the interests of the new Russia.*

In the summer of 1919 two bolsheviks, J. Thomas and M. G. Bronsky, set up a modest propaganda office in Berlin which they called "West European Bureau" (WEB); they offered its services to the Executive Committee of the Comintern.[63] WEB was later to develop into the largest Comintern intelligence and operations headquarters next to Moscow. Initially, however, its two founding fathers merely edited two small newssheets, the *Rätekorrespondenz* and the *Russische Korrespondenz,* and painted the German public glowing pictures of bolshevist Russia's new Eldorado.[64]

Thomas and Bronsky were left to their own devices for months; they did not even have a telephone line to Moscow and their only occasional contact with EKKI was through a couple of couriers.[65] Not until after the Second Congress of the Comintern in the summer of 1920 did Moscow become more enthusiastic. As a result of the Congress decision to form underground communist organizations in all countries a group of Russian Comintern representatives was sent to Germany; the most important was Yelena Stassova, codename "Herta," an Old-Guard bolshevist and daughter of a Czarist Governor.[66] With the help of Soviet funds and advisers she formed a German communist underground organization, known in the Party jargon as the "Apparat," a name borrowed from a gang of thugs formed in 1919 by the left-wing socialist, Richard Däumig.[67]

Däumig had been a sergeant-major with the German forces in Africa and then editor of *Vorwärts;* he belonged to the left wing of the Independent Social-Democrat Party, which worked closely with the German Communist Party (KPD), formed in December 1918.[68] Like so many communists, he thought that the revolution could be brought about by technical and terrorist methods alone. In

---

* Soviet Russia's official diplomatic representatives, Joffe, Bukharin and Rakovsky, were expelled in November 1918; in February 1919 Radek, the official representative of the Soviet Communist Party, was arrested.[62]

his view small armed fanatical assault squads should liquidate policemen, murder politicians and blow up public
buildings. These assault squads were to work underground
and emerge on D-Day with the precision of automata—
hence the curious name "Apparat" (machine).[69]

Däumig, the terrorist, had soon collected one or two
resolute revolutionaries and a gang of suburban toughs.
He allied himself with a similar group from the communist
party, and the "apparat" was in business. But Party headquarters soon found his daredevil terrorist exploits wearing to the nerves and disowned the refractory "Apparat."[70]
In 1920 Däumig was forced to disband his organization
and, as Erich Wollenberg the ex-"Apparatchik" says, most
of his thugs "more or less returned to crime."[71]

To fulfill Moscow's order to form a communist underground Yelena Stassova looked to this organization. From
the debris of the Däumig group together with some youthful communists a secret communist self-defense formation
was constituted known as M-Apparat (military); as its
head Yelena nominated Hugo Eberlein, the Spartacist.[72]

Shortly thereafter Piatnitsky, the manager of the Comintern, despatched further reinforcements of experienced
infiltration technicians to Berlin. As Deputy Head of the
Press Section the Russian communist Mirov-Abramov arrived at the Soviet Embassy together with twenty-five assistants and couriers;[73] their job was to supervise the
German Communist Party's preparations for civil war.
Mirov-Abramov became the German Party's treasurer;
Wilhelm Pieck, a Communist Party functionary and later
President of the German Peoples Republic, reported to
him regularly in order to draw the Party's pay.[74]

Simultaneously WEB was building up its courier system.
In Berlin "safe houses" were organized where communists
on the run could escape from the police.[75] Within a few
months WEB had blossomed out into a headquarters for
agents; several sections were formed (including one for
counter-espionage) and they directed a whole army of
informers, infiltrators and nihilists, all of whom were ready
at any time to play their part in fomenting the long-
awaited revolt.[76]

Early in 1923 Moscow's prophets of revolution saw the
"German October" approaching. In January, French and
Belgian troops occupied the Ruhr and shortly thereafter
passive resistance spread like a forest fire among the Ger-

mans.[77] This resistance, however, was bound very soon to bring a Germany crippled by war and by the Allies to the edge of economic ruin, and so, thought the communists, here was a unique chance of turning nationalist bourgeois resistance into revolution against the ruling classes.

Moscow seized its moment. The Comintern's Personnel Department asked Berzin's Secret Service for five or six officers capable of injecting some military precision into the German preparations for revolution.[78] Berzin collected a team, including Walter Krivitsky, the future espionage General, and in January 1923 the group set forth for Germany.[79]

From the pool of manpower provided by the communist "M-Apparat" they formed three separate groups. The M-Apparat as such was restricted to those members fit for military service, whom Berzin's officers regarded as the future leaders of a German Red Army; an intelligence section (N- [Nachrichten] Apparat) was formed to keep the political enemy under surveillance, while a "Subversion Service" (Z—Zersetzung) infiltrated agents into the police and the army.[80]

The Russian Secret Service professionals being primarily interested in enemy intelligence, the lion's share of the one million dollars allotted by Moscow for this German adventure in 1923 was devoted to the intelligence organization and the "Subversion Service."[81] Berzin's minions found an eager helper in Hans Kippenberger, son of a Leipzig clergyman; they judged him capable of forming and directing an effective agents' circuit.[82]

Kippenberger was then a young communist of 25 and he turned out to be a fanatical and resourceful organizer. His entry in the Gestapo's list of suspects later said: "Kippenberger, 15.1.98, journalist, head of the GPU."[83] He soon became a leading figure in the communist student movement; Dallin says that "he retained to the end the traditional outward traits of an idealistic student";[84] it was not long before he had become a key man in the communist underground in Hamburg. He commanded the Red "Hundreds" in the Hamburg workers' quarter of Barmbek,[85] where he had been discovered by Krivitsky's people. Kippenberger remained faithful to Barmbek but at the same time he formed the "subversive service" which his communist masters wanted. He soon had an effective circuit of agents available.[86] Ruth Fischer, the ex-communist, says that they "infiltrated enemy organizations, pretending to be supporters, became influential and so obtained private information. Connections between the Party and agents in the army or the police were kept most strictly secret."[87]

Men of Kippenberger's stamp assisted the Russians to form the first civil war brigades. Many of the activist members were ordered to leave the communist party and join one of the three "apparats." They moved into "safe houses" and severed all contact with their friends. They were provided with hand grenades and revolvers and trained for civil war in backyards and remote forest areas.[88]

Once the first cadres had been formed Moscow despatched a second wave of Soviet instructors. A politico-military organization (MP) had been constituted meanwhile to include all communists fit for service,[89] and the key positions in this were occupied by hundreds of Russian officers. The MP was directed by a Reich headquarters in Berlin, under which were six "regions"; the latter were commanded by trusted German communists but real power was in the hands of Soviet officer "advisers."[90]

On 11 September 1923 the Soviet Politburo decided to risk an uprising in Germany.[91] German resistance to the French occupation of the Ruhr had collapsed, the Reich's economy was an almost total wreck and the unity of the Republic was imperiled. The Comintern hastened to despatch the man who was to lead the revolt; Peter Alexei Skoblevsky, Reich leader of the MP, assumed command of the red underground.[92]

Skoblevsky, an ex-mechanic and civil war General,* alerted the "apparats" and opened the secret armories. The "apparatchik" Adolf Burmeister recalls that "Saxony and Thuringia were to strike first, followed by Hamburg, Berlin and the Ruhr. It was a plan, drawn up with complete professionalism, for a military *putsch.*"[94]

But the revolt failed. In Saxony and Thuringia the communists, together with left-wing Social-Democrats, did succeed in setting up Popular Front governments; only in Hamburg, however, did the red revolutionaries march—

---

* Peter Alexander Skoblevsky was born on 16 June 1890 in the South Russian town of Tambov. His real name was Rose. He commanded a Red Army division in the Russian civil war and, while in Germany, used the codenames "Alex," "Helmuth," "Gorev," "Pavel," "Kirlov," "Wolf" and "Goldmann."[93]

early on 23 October.[95] They were so miserably armed that the revolt collapsed in barely 48 hours.[96] Kippenberger, commanding in Barmbek, fled and was smuggled to Mossow by his Russian friends.[97]

Skoblevsky did not abandon hope of a Red victory, however. He let loose a new "Apparat," the most futile and criminal in the history of German communism. This was the T-Apparat (Terror), known by its opponents as the "German Cheka" because it was trained for its sinister role by experts from the Soviet Secret Police.[98] Early in October, acting on Skoblevsky's orders, Felix Neumann, a typesetter described by one of his contemporaries as "a miserable pasty-faced creature with a sour wrinkled expression,"[99] had collected a mobile gang of thugs and political fanatics. These would-be executioners were to square accounts with deviationists in the KPD and liquidate prominent anti-communists.[100]

No. 1 on their list was Hans von Seeckt, the Reichswehr General and Chief of the Army Staff, the most powerful man in Germany at the time. With two crack revolver shots Neumann slipped into the Tiergarten to lie in wait for Seeckt on his morning ride. The three crouched in some bushes and waited. A few yards from them, however, Seeckt's horse suddenly shied; Neumann lost his nerve and rushed away with his terrorists.[101]

Neumann then had another idea: he would destroy his class enemy by means of germ-infected rabbits.[102] He doused some cabbage leaves with cholera germs, fed them to a rabbit and then waited for days to see the result of his experiment. But the rabbit apparently lacked proper revolutionary fervor; it grew fatter and fatter. One day it was gone; a hungry comrade had eaten it.[103] The mystery was finally solved; the alleged cholera germs came from a chemist who, pestered by Neumann, had given him some harmless substance in a horrific wrapping.[104]

The ridicule of his comrades spurred Neumann to further exploits. In Berlin he and some of his apparatchiks attacked Rausch, a communist barber whom Party headquarters suspected of being a police informer; they wounded him so severely that he died.[105] This act of bravery, however, spelled the doom of the murder brigade. Neumann fled to south Germany; there he was rounded up by the police during a drinking bout and suddenly, during his interrogation, he began to boast about his exploits.[106]

In one of Neumann's pockets the police found the address of a "safe house" in Berlin where he was to meet Skoblevsky. Detectives went there and found their man—Neumann's Russian master.[107] Alexei Skoblevsky tried no more. In 1925 he and his leading terrorists appeared before the Court for the Protection of the Republic; Skoblevsky, Neumann and a third terrorist were condemned to death—which they managed to escape;* their minions were sent to prison.

The terror machine was dead and Moscow's dreams about a "German October" finally dissipated, but the framework of the communist spy system still remained—invisible. Elements of the M, N and Z apparats were untouched by the German police and on the remnants of these Razvedupr built up "a brilliantly functioning intelligence service" which General Krivitsky thought was the "envy of all other nations."[109]

The Secret Service was now in the lead as far as espionage in Germany was concerned, for the failure of the "German October" had administered a severe blow to the prestige both of the Comintern and the Secret Police. Though the Soviet espionage monster was still three-headed, Berzin's people now dominated the field. Germany was clearly recovering her strength and was once again a factor in Moscow's power politics, so Russia's secret service was given back its traditional role. The order of the day now was no longer revolution but intelligence about Germany's industrial and military potential.

Razvedupr's first concern was to get the leaders of the unsuccessful October revolution back into safety and make use of them in a new Soviet espionage organization. For this purpose an M (Military) school was set up on the outskirts of Moscow where German communists were taught all the tricks of the espionage trade.[110] It was under the exclusive control of the Secret Service[111]—as opposed to the Lenin School, formed in 1926, where foreign communists were taught civil war strategy and tactics by the

* In order to liberate Skoblevsky the Russians arrested three German students in Moscow and accused them of plotting the assassination of Stalin; they were condemned to death. The Russians then offered Berlin an exchange of prisoners and the Reich Government accepted. Neumann's death sentence was commuted to one of life imprisonment and then to 7½ years; in prison he became friendly with some Nazis with whose assistance he escaped in 1928.[108]

Comintern (though with considerable assistance from Razvedupr).[112]

The M-School was set up in 1924.[113] It was an espionage academy where the Red Army trained selected German agents. Berzin crammed into his pupils the rudiments of communist "conspiratoria"; they learned how to use invisible ink and how to give pursuers the slip; they practiced radio and coding; they were initiated into General Staff procedures and given shooting practice. Finally they were distributed to special Red Army units where they received basic military training and on maneuvers were taught the importance of secret service information to the fighting troops.[114] Finally they took an oath to the Red Army.[115]

Practically every one of the M-School graduates entered the Secret Service and practically every one of the 1923 German leaders was on Razvedupr's list.* All the old faces collected in the M-School—Hans Kippenberger, the Z-Apparatchik, Wilhelm Zaisser, the MP leader, Arthur Illner, head of the MP in East Prussia, and Joseph Gutsche, his counterpart from Berlin, Oskar Müller, head of the MP in Frankfurt, and Albert Schreiner, another MP leader.[117]

Some of them went off to China where Moscow spied fresh revolutionary prospects;[118] most of them, however, prepared themselves to go back to Germany. They found well-camouflaged positions awaiting them prepared by the Soviet Secret Service.

Razvedupr set about creating a new espionage organization in Germany immediately after the Skoblevsky trial in 1925. German industry was the secret service target, for its productions were of the highest importance both for the Soviet economy and defense. Attention was concentrated on the iron and steel, chemical, electrical and aviation industries.[119]

Razvedupr made use of every Soviet institution having contact with the German economy. The most important was the Soviet trade delegation at No. 3 Lindenstrasse (later No. 11 Lietzenburger Strasse), Berlin.[120] The most

---

* One of the few exceptions was Wollenberg, who had been leader of the MP in South-west Germany and had issued orders to the Terror Apparat. Though he served in the Red Army for a time and rose to be battalion commander, he never joined Razvedupr and later broke with Stalin.[116]

senior secret service agents were carried on its books;[121] Berzin's people were also prominent in the delegation's branches in Hamburg, Königsberg and Leipzig.[122]

The trade delegation was the product of the increasing commercial traffic between Germany and Russia; it was supposed to facilitate on-the-spot decisions and maintain contact with the major German firms interested in business in Russia. At the same time, however, it became the headquarters of Russian espionage; it had its own coding department for radio communications with Moscow;[123] its most important section—the Technical Department—was run by the Military Attaché;[124] a photographic laboratory was installed so that stolen secret papers could be quickly copied.[125]

The layout of the building itself gave away the fact that it was a nest of spies; the backyard abutted on to a building, giving on to the Ritterstrasse, occupied by two jewellers, the brothers Löwenstein, who were in Razvedupr pay.[126]

Secret lines linked Razvedupr's observation posts with Russo-German companies; the latter included the "Russo-German Transport Company" (Derop-oil), the "Russo-German Aviation Company" (Deruluft) and the "Guarantee and Credit Bank for the East Ltd." (Garkrebo).[127] The Berlin office of the Soviet news agency "Tass" was also wound into the espionage organization.[128]

German communists made good whatever the Russians lacked in Germany. Informers from the KPD's central committee watched every move by the German counter-espionage authorities and kept an eye on the German employees in the trade delegation. The Party rented houses where Soviet agents could go to ground and bought businesses in which new arrivals could be covered as employees.[129] The KPD also allowed Razvedupr to use their passport-forging establishments, although strictly these were under the Comintern.

The KPD functionary Leo Flieg ran a veritable false passport empire employing 170 people whose sole job was to provide communist agents with false papers, "stories" and money.[130] Two thousand passports and 30,000 rubber stamps were always to hand.[131] Flieg had six workshops possessing in all 1.7 tons of various kinds of type and there were branches in practically every European capital.

Almost the entire communist movement worldwide made use of his products.[132]

The Soviet espionage headquarters in Germany were now ready for action and the technical equipment was available, but the army of indigenous informers was still lacking. This was the moment for the M-School graduates. In 1927–8 Berzin's pupils, led by Hans Kippenberger, returned to Germany determined to create a Soviet spy system which in its own way would be unique.[133]

Kippenberger collected the remains of the old 1923 underground "apparats" into a new organization which he termed the "AM" (anti-militarist) apparat.* Its members' orders were to infiltrate the police, the Reichswehr and opposition parties, and sabotage any action directed against the Communist Party. Simultaneously the "counter-espionage" Department of AM was to prevent the infiltration of police informers into the Party and purge it of unreliable elements.†

The most important section was the reports or "BB" [Betriebsberichtsterstattung] which soon became an indispensable part of the Soviet Secret Service.[136] In 1932 Kippenberger divorced it from AM and raised it to the status of an apparat; at its head he placed an old crony of the Hamburg days, Friedrich Burde (codenames "Edgar" or "Dr. Schwarz"), who had been chief of BB since 1929.[137] Until it was finally broken up BB remained Razvedupr's main instrument for the penetration of even the most obscure German firms and enterprises.

The BB was not unlike the "Rabcor" organization, a worldwide communist movement formed in Russia in Lenin's time. Since initially the Soviet press was without trained journalists, the editors hit upon the idea of recruiting volunteers from factories, offices and organizations to report on events within their concerns; these uneducated helpers were known as "raboch korrespondenti" (Rabcor for short)—"workers' correspondents." Russian edi-

---

* "Anti-militarism" was the name of an international communist movement, the aim of which was to prevent an Anglo-German anti-Soviet crusade, the Soviets' bogey in 1927–8. At the Sixth World Congress of the Comintern in July–August 1928 all communist parties were called upon for "systematic anti-militarist work."[134]

† The purpose of the AM was to subvert and demoralize the enemy. It was divided into sections dealing with the police, the Reichswehr and opposition organizations, a "counter-espionage section and a reports section."[135]

torial offices were soon flooded with a stream of reports which produced an unexpected and unvarnished picture of Russian conditions.[138] The attention of the GPU was soon drawn to these reports, for they revealed abuses in the factories, opposition to the Party and the regime, and corruption among officials. Editors were accordingly ordered by the Secret Police to forward to them any reports containing denunciations. The "workers' correspondents," therefore (in 1930 there were some two million), more or less involuntarily entered the service of the GPU.[139]

Since Europe's communist parties habitually copied any Russian innovation, the Rabcor movement spread to the West. From an instrument of internal political thought-control grew a method of espionage—instead of the GPU the Secret Service, instead of political denunciations reports on tank production, arms deliveries and new processes in the armaments industry.[140] This form of espionage was almost unassailable since no authority could forbid a worker to tell his newspaper or his party about events in his factory.

With German thoroughness Kippenberger and Burde brought the BB (Betriebsberichterstattung = works reporting), their form of the Rabcor system, to a fine art. BB agents would talk to their mates in a factory and pledge them to help; each agent was kept continuously *au fait* with what he was required to find out—at one moment it would be the state of the order book in a certain factory, at another whether factory equipment for Russia was made of first-class material, at another arms deliveries to potential enemies of the Soviet Union, at another the production of smoke shell or poison gas.[141]

There was literally nothing which Razvedupr's German organizers did not wish to know. At one moment they were after the plans of "Battlecruiser A,"[142] at another aircraft-engine drawings from the Aviation Research Establishment.[143] The author of one of BB's printed questionnaires wished to find out: "Has your firm a special service of watchmen? How many are there? What are their shifts? How closely are the doors guarded (a) by day, (b) by night? Are the watchmen armed? If so how? If with firearms give make and caliber."[144]

Almost imperceptibly the BB's masters turned their queries and instructions more and more towards the armaments industry. A written instruction from Party headquarters, probably about 1932, included among "tasks coming inrceasingly into the forefront" as top of the list "strategic questions: the Reichswehr's movement and operational plans, those of the police and defense formations, concentrations, tactics, state of training and equipment."[145]

Though the BB's questions were on matters of interest to Russia, no Russian was ever seen. The informers in the factories dealt only with the German who had recruited them; they had no idea that all the information found its way either to Burde's BB headquarters or to Kippenberger,[146] who meanwhile had been elected a Reichstag deputy, nor that these two passed it on to their Soviet masters, initially the Mashkevich brothers* and from 1929 the resident director Boris Bazarov.[148] Kippenberger and Burde thought it wiser to conceal the Soviet interest in their work from the 3,000–4,000 members of the BB.† Informers were merely told that their reports would be of use primarily in preparing the struggle for the dictatorship of the proletariat and were therefore in the interests of the Party. Later came the additional argument that it would all be useful in the fight against fascism.[150] For the more anxious comrades, who might be hesitant to take the final plunge into treasonable activities, the apparatchiks had a more involved story. The informer was told that his work would assist the Soviet Union to reach Western industrial standards; anyone who refused to the Soviet Union western industrial secrets was sabotaging the efforts of the proletarian fatherland and doing a disservice to peace.[151] A note attributed to a BB man under arrest read: "We call it industrial assistance, not espionage."[152]

Little by little many comrades lost their horror of espionage; industrious agitators set out to convince them that treason was an obsolete idea. In factories and laboratories, firms and agencies, shipyards and workshops thousands upon thousands of German communists began to spy. It was as if a whole party had entered the service of a foreign espionage organization. Reichstag deputies like Jonny Scheer collected agents' reports and held parcels for Soviet couriers;[153] provincial deputies like the Bavarian Eugen Herbst recruited informers;[154] the secret party cadres formed themselves into armies of Soviet agents.

---

* The Mashkevich brothers came from Baku and were in charge of Soviet industrial espionage from 1928 to 1934.[147]
† Dallin gives the number as "several thousands" in 1928.[149]

The German Communist Party comprised a quarter of a million members, 27 newspapers, 4,000 cells and 87 auxiliary organizations,[155] but above all it had its underground apparats and its special services. All this became no more than "a foreign section of the Soviet Secret Service" and was "at the exclusive service of the aims of the Soviet state" in the words of Wollenberg, the ex-communist.[156] Ruth Fischer says that the Party cadre no longer "felt themselves to be representatives of an international workers' party but of the official Russian Party; they were secret agents of a foreign power."[157] Every German communist felt himself called upon to join in the underground struggle on behalf of the Soviet Union, to engage in "systematic anti-militarist work," as the Sixth World Congress of the Comintern had described espionage in 1928.[158] Heinrich Schmid, a BB man arrested in 1931, put it even more clearly. The Party, he admitted to the court, recognized two forms of industrial espionage: academic espionage which every communist ought to undertake in his own factory, and practical espionage, for which only particularly intelligent and reliable comrades were used.[159]

Germany was the arena for a mass espionage system such as the world had never known. Every year brought fresh espionage trials, the courts dealt with communist agents practically every month. In October 1930 a circuit of communist agents was broken up in the Gruson Works, Krupp's Magdeburg subsidiary; its leader was an engineer named Kallenbach.[160] In December 1930 the Russian engineer Volodichev and his two German assistants were arrested at Siemens & Halske for espionage on behalf of the Soviet trade delegation.[161] In January 1931 an engineer named Wilhelm Richter was convicted by the works police of the Polysius Cement Works, Dessau, of the theft of secret papers for the benefit of the Soviet Union.[162] In April 1931 a 25-strong circuit of informers led by Karl Dienstbach, a BB agent, was discovered in Ludwigshafen; they had been passing information to Russia from numerous chemical works in Southern Germany.[163]

The network of German agents of the Soviets was drawn ever tighter, the spies infiltrated with increasing audacity. According to the *Bayerische Staatszeitung,* in April 1931, 134 serious cases of espionage had been detected in a single German firm between 1926 and 1930.[164] In 1927 alone the courts dealt with 3,500 serious cases of industrial espionage, the majority for the Soviet Union.[165] Between June 1931 and December 1932, 111 cases of treason were filed—again the majority were concerned with espionage for the Soviet Union.[166]

Despite a number of setbacks, Berzin had every reason to be satisfied with the output of his German agents. German industry and defense potential held fewer secrets for Soviet intelligence than ever before. David Dallin says: "The German contribution to Soviet espionage during its first decade was enormous, exceeding in quantity the contribution of all the other non-Russian components of the apparat abroad; in quality it exceeded even the Russian core itself."[167]

Berlin became headquarters No. 2 for Soviet Russia's worldwide espionage system; orders to Soviet secret service agents all over the world issued from Berlin. Berlin was the headquarters for Soviet espionage in France, Holland and Belgium;[168] there was the communist passport-forging workshop. Berlin was "the field headquarters for the entire Communist International; all lines ended in Berlin which maintained a single channel of communication to Moscow" —thus Richard Krebs, a Comintern courier.[169]

Such achievements, of course, were only possible in a state verging on disintegration which, though putting up a desperate defense against the totalitarian forces of the period, could no longer rely on the loyalty of its citizens. Moreover, the republic's liberal laws were inadequate to deal effectively with Soviet espionage.

The main target of Russian Intelligence was industry but the German criminal code recognized only military espionage; the only provisions to which the red industrial spies were amenable were the elastic paragraphs on unfair competition and so the maximum penalty a spy had to fear was one year's imprisonment. Not until March 1932 did the "Decree on the Defense of the National Economy" prescribe severer punishments for communication of industrial secrets to unauthorized persons; an industrial spy could then be sentenced to three years' imprisonment.[170]

Frequently, however, the Foreign Ministry advised against too vicious a pursuit of the Soviet spies. In post-Versailles Europe Soviet Russia was one of the few states for whose sympathy Weimar Germany could hope. Whenever the German counter-espionage authorites wished to follow the tracks of some known spy into the Soviet trade delegation, the Wilhelmstrasse diplomats intervened; moreover, the trade delegation invariably reacted to the discovery of a spy-ring with a flat denial, saying that they had never been in touch with the agents in question.

The sleuths of Berlin Police Headquarters were unlikely to forget that they owed to the intervention of the Foreign Ministry their worst defeat in their battle against communist agents. The case occurred in the spring of 1924. A communist named Hans Bozenhardt, a member of the Terror Apparat and employee of the Soviet trade delegation, had been arrested in Stuttgart and two Württemberg police officers were ordered to conduct him to Stargard in Pomerania. They had to travel via Berlin where they missed their connection to Stargard.[171] The prisoner proposed to his two guards that, to while away the time, they should take some refreshments; he knew a nice little place in the Lindenstrasse, he said. The policemen, who did not know Berlin, had no idea that Bozenhardt's "nice little place" was in fact the Soviet trade delegation.[172] Hardly had they entered the alleged café when Bozenhardt shouted: "I am Bozenhardt and am employed here. These are two Württemberg police officers who have arrested me for treason and are taking me to Stargard." He tore himself away from them and rushed off, while Russians hurried along, seized the two policemen and locked them in a room.[173]

At last Berlin Police Headquarters saw an opportunity of penetrating the Soviet espionage fortress. On the pretext of searching for the fugitive Bozenhardt police forced their way into the trade delegation on 2 May 1924 and occupied the building. Room after room was searched, safe after safe opened and papers confiscated.[174] Hurriedly Starkov, the head of the trade delegation, alerted the Soviet Embassy;[175] Krestinsky, the Ambassador, drove straight to the Foreign Ministry and protested against this violation of the delegation's extra-territorial status—and at once the Foreign Ministry called the police off.[176] The raid had to be stopped and any Soviet officials arrested were released.[177]

The Lindenstrasse debacle illustrated yet once more the impotence of the German police in matters of counterespionage. The law was inadequate, government backing was halfhearted only and they were deprived of practically any opportunity of penetrating the Soviet espionage network. From Moscow's point of view, therefore, Berlin's counter-espionage was hardly an adversary to be taken seriously. In addition both the authorities responsible for counter-espionage in Germany, the police (Abwehrpolizei —counter-espionage police) and the Abwehr (Military Intelligence), suffered from a shortage of money and personnel.

As a result of the left-wing democrats' aversion to the aura of power and mystery associated with a political police, the Abwehrpolizei could only go about their business furtively. With the abolition of the pre-1918 political police the Abwehrpolizei had no further official existence, though in fact it continued unofficially in the form of Section IA in every police presidency.[178] This was where the police officers responsible for counter-espionage were to be found.

They labored under difficulties, however, since there was no overall organization covering the counter-espionage desks or commissariats in the various police headquarters. No central agency existed to evaluate information received and exploit it by coordinated action; it had merely been agreed that Section IA of the Berlin Police Presidency should constitute a sort of information clearing house— but it had no established authority.[179]

The military sleuths were in little better case. After much hesitation and in defiance of the Versailles Peace Treaty ban on a German military secret service, a small secret service group under Major Friedrich Gempp had been formed in 1920 to deal with enemy espionage.[180] It formed part of the Reichswehr Ministry but even so was not allowed to appear under its real name; it was called "Abwehr" (Counter-intelligence) to underline its defensive intent.[181] Its office on the Berlin Tirpitzufer housed in all only three General Staff officers and seven retired-officer employees;[182] this meager staff was hardly likely to strike much terror into a foreign espionage service of the gigantic size of Razvedupr.

So neither the Abwehr nor the Abwehrpolizei were in any position to halt the onrush of Soviet spies. They were in fact so helpless that they were forced to leave the formation of factory security services to the resources and initiative of private industry.[183] The Abwehr's most important office in East Germany, that in Königsberg, was manned by a solitary retired cavalry captain[184]—and he was so occupied with Polish espionage that he left that of the Soviets untouched.

From the outset the Abwehr resigned itself to inability to penetrate the Soviet Secret Service;[185] nor was the Abwehrpolizei ever able to probe the communist network of agents. Dallin considers that "the German police were surprisingly ignorant concerning the activities of the various Soviet apparats."[186] They knew neither the addresses nor the personnel of the communist underground organizations; they had no conception of the BB's informer system; they knew nothing of the Soviet Secret Service lines within Germany.

In 1932 the Berlin Police Presidency on the Alexanderplatz sent to the Moabit criminal court a 500-page report on the KPD's underground organization; it did not observe that on its way the report disappeared for a short time into the Soviet trade delegation and was there photographed.[187] For years the police thought that the headquarters of communist espionage was the KPD office in the Karl Liebknecht Haus, Berlin;[188] they passed innocently by the "Führer" publishing house at 131–2 the Wilhelmstrasse without suspecting that it concealed "a dozen Comintern sections and a whole army of shorthand typists, couriers, translators and security guards."[189]

Seldom had a counter-espionage service been so helpless in face of the assault of enemy spies. Then, however, appeared an extremist political movement which offered the frustrated policemen and soldiers their release; it promised radical changes in Germany and, above all, freedom from what they called the "bolshevist menace." Adolf Hitler's cohorts seized power in the Reich.

Many of the police, naturally prone to authoritarianism, succumbed to the siren song of the new potentates; many of the soldiers were tempted by the new regime's nationalist overtones. The Nazis promised what the Republic's policemen had always been asking for: more money, greater prestige, improved methods of dealing with crime and espionage, centralization of police work, freedom from public criticism and diplomatic interference.[190]

Moreover, Germany's new masters showed that they meant what they said. In a matter of months they had constructed a police machine unparalleled in German history. The political police with their counter-espionage desks, only surreptitiously and reluctantly tolerated under

Weimar, were removed from the police administration and concentrated into a special agency under centralized command—the Secret State Police or Gestapo.* Now they were the servants of one man only and they served only a single purpose—maintenance of the Führer dictatorship's system of tyranny.

The Gestapo at No. 8 Prinz-Albrecht-Strasse, Berlin, became the headquarters of the hunters both of political fools and of spies. From the summer of 1934 the actual Gestapo formed Department II and the Abwehrpolizei Department III.[192] Henceforth they were inseparable, twin guardians of the regime; they spread a finespun web over the entire country, sharing offices and sub-offices in every province; they kept spies and enemies of the regime under surveillance; they controlled the Reich frontiers and kept watch on public opinion.

No German police force had ever maintained such a system of control. An intricate scheme of lists and card indexes was designed to register every possible opponent of the regime and every potential spy; a carefully calculated tracking system was supposed to guarantee that no fugitive could escape the Gestapo's all-seeing eye.[193] The primary task of the frontier police, now part of the Gestapo, was to apprehend traitors on the run or spies trying to infiltrate.[194] Authority over the concentration camps gave the Prinz-Albrecht-Strasse an additional weapon: undesirable aliens could be incarcerated in a concentration camp pending deportation.[195]

Anyone who slipped through the Gestapo's net had to run the gauntlet of another array of Nazi guardians of the regime, the SS Sicherheitsdienst [Security Service—SD]. With its headquarters in Berlin and its Sectors, Sub-Sectors and Outposts distributed all over the country, to the outward eye the SD resembled the Gestapo; with its army of unknown informers in every sphere of the nation's life,

* Section IA of the Berlin Police Presidency was the germ of the Gestapo. In April 1933 it moved to No. 8 Prinz-Albrecht-Strasse and became the Secret State Police Office [Geheimes Staatspolizeiamt—Gestapo]. It took over all the political sections of the Prussian police and from 30 November 1933 formed a separate branch of the administration. The political police were similarly divorced from the administration in the other German *Länder*. The individual political police forces were concentrated under command of the Reichsführer-SS, Heinrich Himmler, in practice in spring 1934 and formally in 1936 when Himmler became "Chief of the German Police."[191]

however, it proved both more effective and more dangerous; in the words of one of its leaders it was "the versatile
instrument for use against all opposition circles and in all
spheres of life, the people's sense of touch and feel."[196]

As the years went by the Nazi police state's own apparat
expanded. Step by step the triumphant police enlarged the
borders of their empire: in 1933–4 the political and counter-
espionage police combined to form the Gestapo;[197] in
1936 the Gestapo and Criminal Police were merged to
form the Security Police [Sicherheitspolizei—Sipo];[198] in
1939 the Sipo and SD were concentrated into the Reich
Central Security Department [Reichssicherheitshauptamt
—RSHA].[199] The expansion of the police had thus reached
its peak.

Meanwhile, however, many professional police officers,
brought up in the tradition of legal norms, had realized
that the new rulers were not interested solely in the
customary protection of the State against agents and saboteurs. Somewhat enviously the police observed that Military
Intelligence (the Abwehr) on the Tirpitzufer, though given
the resources for material expansion by the regime, largely
held aloof from the new potentates' ideological vagaries—
there had already been sharp disagreement between the
heads of the Abwehr and the Abwehrpolizei over methods
of dealing with their opponents.* The military adhered to a
certain code of conduct in secret service matters, whereas
deliberate abandonment of all scruple was the order of
the day in the Prinz-Albrecht-Strasse.

Alongside the old-established police officials came the
fanatical youngsters of the Führer dictatorship trained in
Nazism's cadet colleges and schools to execute like robots
any order, however criminal, issued by their leaders. Most
significant was the fact that these newcomers wore the
black death's-head uniform of the SS whose leaders had
annexed authority over the police and who wished to trans-
form the police into a master caste independent both of
Party and State.

Heinrich Himmler, the Reichsführer-SS, Chief of the

---

* Relations between the head of the Abwehr, Captain (Navy)
Conrad Patzig, and that of the Abwehrpolizei, Dr. Günther Pat-
schowski, a senior civil servant [Oberregierungsrat], became so
strained that in 1934–5 both had to be replaced by more diplomatic
characters. Captain (Navy) Wilhelm Canaris took over the Abwehr
and SS-Oberführer [Colonel] Werner Best the Abwehrpolizei.[200]

German Police from 1936, together with his diabolical assistant, SS-Gruppenführer [Major-General] Reinhard Heydrich, Chief of the Security Police and SD, inoculated the police with the poison of blind totalitarian thinking, and many traditionalist police officials were corrupted by it. The SS police chiefs were obsessed with crazy ideas of neo-Germanic paganism and anti-Semitism; they were continually preaching to their State Protection Corps pitiless hatred of all enemies of the state and of spies. The police found themselves in a world of brutality in which any political opponent was considered a fiend. Whether he were a Jew or a freemason, a communist or a democrat, any enemy of the regime was fit only to be banished from the "popular community."

The worst fiend of all, however, was the communist, labeled as "bolshevist" or "Jewish bolshevist" in Nazi terminology. A Gestapo internal instruction of 1937 laid down that the communist was an "enemy of the people" and "nothing but an instrument of Jewry which has thus found a method of reaching its goal—world domination."[201] In the police training courses the communist and his underground organizations were increasingly presented as the depersonalized "enemy"; communism was caricatured as an abomination. Endlessly Himmler hammered into his policemen that in the struggle against communism "there can be no truce; there are only victors and vanquished and defeat in this struggle means death for a people."[202] Heydrich proclaimed: "Years of bitter struggle will be necessary finally to drive the enemy back on all fronts, to destroy him and to safeguard Germany, both racially and spiritually, against renewed enemy incursions."[203]

So the Nazi regime entered the battle against Soviet spies in Germany inflamed with all the emotion stemming from a crusading ideology. What the KPD's dilettante Terror Apparat had once tried to do, the Gestapo and SD now practiced on their communist enemy with Teutonic thoroughness. Germany became the battleground for two totalitarian engines of power.

The first Nazi blows against the communist party and its organizations, however, were unproductive. Immediately after the seizure of power the police and the Party activists set forth to administer the *coup de grâce* to communism; the Reichstag Fire during the night 27–8 February 1933 was followed at once by the emergency Ordinance "For

Protection of People and State" and this was the signal for a witch-hunt after communist functionaries.[204] On 3 March 1933 Göring, Prussia's Minister of the Interior, told his policemen: "It is the aim and object of this decree that the wider powers which it gives should primarily be used against the communists, but also against those who work with the communists and who support or further their criminal objectives."[205] Using the pretext that the KPD was planning an armed rising, the Gestapo and other police formations smashed the communist Party organizations. All communist deputies to the Reichstag or provincial parliaments who had not already fled were arrested;[206] every communist functionary was removed. Meanwhile other police squads were disbanding the communist organizations and forcing their way into the local KPD offices. .

At the end of February the police had already carried out a surprise raid on KPD headquarters in the Karl Liebknecht Haus with its network of secret passages and complicated alarm system; it had long been a high-priority target for the Berlin sleuths.[207] Thousands of communists vanished behind the barbed wire of the concentration camps, insulted and frequently maltreated, without a case against them and with no official warrant for their arrest. In April 1933 there were 30,000 concentration camp prisoners in Prussia and of these at least 80 per cent were almost certainly communists.[208] Simultaneously, German-Soviet firms and agencies suspected of harboring Soviet spies were occupied by the police. In late March police in many cities searched the offices of Derop, the oil syndicate; early in April they raided the Leipzig branch of the Soviet trade delegation.[209] The offices of the transport firm Derutra and Soviet ships were also searched.[210]

From the counter-espionage point of view, however, the results of this campaign, widespread and violent through it was, were meager; hardly a single spy came to light. A police officer told Dallin, the historian: "We were unable even to identify a person; today she is Klara, tomorrow Frieda and in another section of the city her name is Mizzi. We were often at a loss."[211] Privately even Himmler admitted: "We had to undertake the most laborious and detailed work lasting months, if not years, before we could gradually roll up the communist underground organization, for its ranks were always being refilled."[212]

The KPD agents remained so difficult to find that Nazi

opportunists began to invent secret communist organizations and then belabor perfectly innocent people. Police Inspector Lothar Heimbach, executive head of the Gestapo office in Dortmund, recalls the activities of a trio of Party fanatics in his anti-communism section who continually fabricated red conspiracies.[213] "At some restaurant during the night," Heimbach says, "these people would think up the idea of blowing skyhigh some 'apparat' somewhere and then make a series of arbitrary arrests of 'enemies of the State.' Later, when they could really find no communist agents or functionaries at all, they used *agents provocateurs* and constructed some 'apparat' in order to be able to destroy it afterward, thus producing satisfying statistics to be reported to higher authority."[214]

Such industry was rewarded by Himmler until even he perceived that the alleged discoveries of secret organizations were in fact imaginary. Only by degrees did the Gestapo realize that they had missed Moscow's espionage and informer organizations; in a subsequent confidential report they had to admit that the police had "more or less no knowledge" of the KPD's secret organization.[215]

In fact the red apparats had made meticulous preparation for the Nazi assault. In early summer 1932 Burde, the head of the BB, and his successor Wilhelm Bahnik, had been instructed by Moscow to prepare their organization for a fascist seizure of power.[216] Part of the informer network was put in cold storage, alternative accommodation was prepared and the most important members were provided with false papers.[217] Leaders were told to weed their files and forward any unwanted papers to Moscow. Kippenberger, the head of the AM, looked out reliable men through whom he could continue to work even in a Nazi Germany.[218] The Party as a whole reduced its cadres to groups of three or five, sufficiently unobtrusive to survive the enemy's wave of terror.[219]

Savage and ruthless though it was, the regime's campaign failed to deal the communist party a mortal blow. When Ernst Thälmann, the Party chairman, and his successor Jonny Scheer were arrested,[220] Wilhelm Pieck and Walter Ulbricht with the leading members moved to Prague, where they formed a new Central Committee and resumed the underground struggle against the Nazis.[221] So-called "senior advisers" infiltrated back into the Reich to reorganize the Party's district system, now in disarray;[222] by the end of 1933 the Party leaders considered the situation in Adolf Hitler's Germany so calm that they allowed the senior comrades in Berlin (Rembte, Maddalena and Stamm) to form a "nation-wide KPD headquarters."[223]

Kippenberger too carried on as before. While in exile in Prague he had quickly built up a courier system to those members of the AM and BB who had remained behind, and had put his diversified organization to work once more.[224] Bahnik, the head of the BB who had also escaped to Prague,[225] placed his informers primarily in the west German industrial area: one BB circuit under Heinrich Fomferra covered the Krupp works in Essen, a second under Hermann Glöggler the IG-Farben factory in Hoechst, and a third under Hans Israel, the senior BB functionary in west Germany, the Düsseldorf area.[226]

The SD was forced to register "an increase of underground subversive acticity."[227] In summer 1934 its security section reported to Himmler: "Those Marxists still active are experienced operators in underground tactics. It is becoming increasingly difficult to keep their activities under constant surveillance, increasingly difficult to discover and raid their courier 'post-boxes,' their distribution points for equipment and their duplicating establishments, increasingly difficult to penetrate their organization."[228]

Nevertheless, gradually the Gestapo succeeded in perfecting their surveillance and tracking system and in drawing the net tighter around their enemy. Communist agents found themselves facing an increasingly sophisticated crime-detection machine: every Gestapo office had to maintain an "A" card-index giving a complete survey of all known enemies of the regime; Group A1 comprised "in addition to the most dangerous traitors to the government and the country, primarily saboteurs, functionaries and agents of the BB or AM apparats."[229] The communist did not exist who was not included in some Gestapo card-index. If a known communist went to ground, his name automatically appeared in the Gestapo's "Register of fugitive communists."[230]

If the fugitive was thought to be still in Germany, he became the quarry of an octopus-like tracking system. Every police station had to join in the hunt, as prescribed by a whole range of official applications for and aids to search, such as the "German Criminal Police Review"

(Register of crime committed),[231] the "German Criminal Police Register" (list of persons for whom arrest warrants had been issued),[232] the "Residence Inquiry List" (persons whose place of residence was to be discovered),[233] and finally the "G" card-index (list of persons to be kept under unobtrusive observation).[234] The sleuths' most important reference book was the "Secret Register" issued monthly by the headquarters of the counter-espionage police; it gave full details of all agents being sought—personal description, profession or trade, examples of handwriting, photographs, list of acquaintances.[235]

The methodology of the anti-communist spy-hunt was the work primarily of a plump thickset Bavarian who brought to his task an unusual combination of cunning, capacity for detail and brutality. Even before 1933 Kriminalinspektor Heinrich Müller, now an SS-Hauptsturmführer [Captain] and head of the "Communism" desk in the Gestapo, had had the reputation of being a fanatical anti-communist.*

As a young criminal police officer, an assistant in Police Headquarters, Munich, he had had to investigate the murder of Munich citizens by communists at the end of the Red Republic in Bavaria; it was an experience which he had never forgotten.[237]

Detection of underground communist intrigue became his speciality and for years he worked as head of the "Communism" desk in Section VI of Munich Police Headquarters.[238] This work stood him in good stead in 1933 when, as a Catholic and right-wing democrat, he was in urgent need of some clearance certificate to enable him to continue his professional career under the Third Reich. Diligently he dictated for his new masters "a series of long

* Heinrich Müller was born in Munich on 28 April 1900; after a primary school education he became an apprentice aircraft mechanic; in World War I he rose to Sergeant Pilot, being demobilized in 1919, when he joined Police Headquarters, Munich, as a junior assistant. His subsequent career was as follows: passed first-year examination and appointed police officer; 1929 police secretary specially concerned with the communist movement in Section VI of Police Headquarters, Munich; 1934 transferred to the Gestapo, Berlin; 1935 head of Department II (Gestapo); 1936 head of Gestapo Office in headquarters Sicherheitspolizei; 1937 promoted Kriminalrat [senior police officer]; 1939 promoted Reichskriminaldirektor [Police Director]; 1941 appointed SS-Gruppenführer [Lieutenant-General in the SS] and Lieutenant-General of Police. Member of the Nazi Party from 1939.[236]

reports on the structure of the communist party, beginning with the Spartacus League and ending with the Central Committee in Moscow." His secretary Barbara Hellmuth recalls that in these reports "he set out all he knew about the aims of the communist party, its recent underground activity, its methods of running agents from the East, etc."[239]

As a result of these reports Heydrich's attention was drawn to Müller and the man who had once been a dedicated anti-Nazi soon became one of the most unscrupulous and subservient members of Heydrich's staff. When the SS took over the Gestapo, Heydrich took his staff with him to Berlin; Müller was given increasingly responsible jobs until he eventually became head of the Gestapo Office in Headquarters Sicherheitspolizei, thus acquiring the notorious nickname "Gestapo Müller."[240]

As time went on Müller gathered around him the gang of anti-communist sleuths destined later to put an end to the Rote Kapelle. Friedrich Panzinger, Müller's friend and contemporary, was head of a division,[241] Karl Giering from Mecklenburg was a senior officer [Kriminalkommissar] in the "Communism" desk,[242] Horst Kopkow, an ex-chemist from Allenstein, set up his own office in the Gestapo to deal with communist saboteurs,[243] the Berliner Johann Strübing specialized in Soviet radio operators and parachutists.[244] The nucleus of the anti-communist spyhunters was taking shape.

One of the Gestapo's innovations produced the decisive breakthrough in the battle against the network of red agents. Müller's office set up a sub-desk N [Nachrichten—intelligence] represented in every Gestapo agency,[245] and N had its own agents who infiltrated the communist underground organizations. Of particular importance was the fact that some of these agents operated abroad, primarily in Czechoslovakia and France where they worked their way into local communist headquarters.[246] The system soon proved itself effective.

Gradually Moscow's spider's web unfolded itself before Müller; he began to see the whole empire of communist agents—the courier posts, the "safe houses," the organizers, the "post-boxes." The Gestapo knew, for instance, that Reinhold Martin, born in Novgorod-Volinsk, was "a Soviet-Russian courier who had crossed the German frontier illegally on 6 August 1936,"[247] that Leo Roth, the AM apparatchik, "almost invariably" traveled "second class by express train" and carried "a strikingly yellow leather suitcase."[248]

The Gestapo knew who and what "Hugo" was—"organizer of an underground communist intelligence circuit in Prague, 5′ 8″–5′ 9″ tall, 30–32 years old, jet-black hair parted on the left, medium forehead, strikingly light-blue eyes, nose medium size and slightly hooked, fairly full lips, feminine complexion."[249]

With such precise information the Gestapo was hardly likely to take long in sweeping up Moscow's underground spy organization. Early in 1935 the BB circuit in the Krupp Works was blown,[250] in March the entire communist party headquarters was rounded up,[251] in May they netted Israel, the BB local organizer, Karl Tuttas, head of the AM in Lower Rhineland,[252] and later Holzer, the BB functionary in Magdeburg.[253]

The KPD's and Comintern's passport-forging organization was no longer safe from the claws of the Gestapo. The police uncovered two large workshops and Richard Grosskopf, Karl Wiehn and Rewin Kohlberg, the head operators, were consigned to a concentration camp.[254] The Prinz-Albrecht-Strasse was forced to admit, however, that "the assumption on the part of the police that they had destroyed the entire passport forging organization was wrong. In two places two sets of counterfeit stamps, false passports, genuine passport forms and other material were seized in large quantities. It was not known, however, that a similar number of false passports, etc. were stored at a third location."[255]

The rank-and-file communist members were in danger too. The Gestapo had hit upon the idea of following up the distribution system for communist literature entering Germany from abroad and discovering who the addressees were.[256] "As a result of this measure," the Gestapo reported, "major communist organizations were paralyzed and their members sentenced to long terms of imprisonment. The remaining communists, who had not been caught, were intimidated."[257]

Moscow and the exiled communist leaders drew their conclusions. At the end of October 1935 the German Party leaders met for the Fourth Party Conference of the

KPD in the Moscow suburb of Kuntsevo; for camouflage purposes it was known as the "Brussels Conference." They decided to disband the existing circuits of agents in Germany[258] and replace them by small groups directed by "instructors" (collective leadership in each sector was established in January 1937). The "instructors" worked from abroad and were each responsible for a specific area of the Reich.[259] The "Center," located first in Prague and then in Stockholm, dealt with Berlin and central Germany; "North," located in Copenhagen, was responsible for the Baltic coast and Silesia, "South" in Switzerland for southern Germany, "Saar" in France for the Saarland, "South-West" in Brussels for the Middle Rhine, and "West" in Amsterdam for the west German industrial area including Bremen.[260]

Kippenberger protested against this destruction of his life's work,[261] but Ulbricht, the Party boss who was coming increasingly to the fore as the Soviets' agent No. 1, insisted. The Russians were anyway losing confidence in Kippenberger and his AM; in Amsterdam its Dutch section had been in touch with the British Secret Service[262] —a deadly sin in Soviet eyes. In November 1935 Ulbricht despatched to Amsterdam Wilhelm Knöchel, a Lenin School graduate and a member of the Zr. Apparat [subversion] whom he trusted and dismissed the "traitors," including the "instructors" Erwin Fischer, "Heinz" and "Martin."[263]

The Russians took their cue from Ulbricht; even the Soviet Secret Service must have realized that effective work in Germany was no longer possible. About the time of Ulbricht's conference Dr. Gregor Rabinovich, a "visiting inspector," left Moscow with the object of liquidating the once proud Soviet espionage empire in Germany. He disbanded the BB's industrial espionage circuit and put the entire apparat in cold storage; even the name BB was expunged from the vocabulary. In addition Rabinovich closed down Razvedupr's bases in Germany.[264]

All that remained of the mighty structure of apparats and secret organizations was 25 agents and contact men, whom Rabinovich distributed across the country and pledged to continue working for the Soviet Secret Service.[265] Before returning to Moscow early in 1936 he met the leading members of this forlorn hope—but in Copenhagen, for he did not think Germany safe enough.[266] Then he gave the signal for the greatest evacuation in the history of Soviet espionage.

It was a melancholy withdrawal. Razvedupr's Germany teams moved to Holland and France whence they could observe the Third Reich's increasing arms program;[267] the West European Bureau of the Comintern moved to Copenhagen and Paris;[268] the false papers organization, or what remained of it, had already taken refuge in the Saarland, still under international control.[269] But they were not left long in peace in the Saar; the documents organization moved on to France, where it was joined by Razvedupr and Comintern agents and the Prague exiles.[270]

The catastrophe of the Soviet agents became total, however, when their masters were sucked into the internal power struggles in Russia. A bare eighteen months after Rabinovich had made his clean sweep, the communist espionage aristocracy came to an end in the death-mills of Stalinism.

The struggle for power in the Soviet Union led to an explosive revival of the old antagonism between Secret Police and Secret Service. Joseph Stalin used ever more brutal methods to safeguard his personal dictatorship and eliminate any actual or supposed opponent in Party, State and Army; to this end he made increasing use of the Secret Police as a deadly weapon. It had meanwhile been rechristened and given extraordinary plenary powers; originally the GPU, in July 1934 it became the GUGB (Glavnoe Upravlenie Gosudarstvennoe Bezopastnosti—Supreme Administration for State Security), forming a special section of the Peoples Commissariat of the Interior (NKVD).[271] With Nikolai Yezhov at its head it drowned any opposition in a conformist self-criticizing wave of terror.[272]

The Yezhov terror descended also on those three traditional opponents, the Secret Police, Razvedupr and the Comintern; the mistrustful misanthrope in the Kremlin suspected their leaders of plotting against him. Soon the "head suspicion-mongers" of the GUGB prepared to strike their deadly blow: in June 1937 Marshal Tukhachevsky, the most powerful man in the Red Army, fell;[273] Zinoviev, the Chairman of the Comintern, had by then already appeared in court.[274] With them they carried down almost their entire underground organization.

One after another the espionage chiefs fell before the

Secret Police firing squads—Berzin and his successor Uritsky,[275] Piatnitsky, organizer of the Comintern,[276] and his deputy Mirov-Abramov,[277] General Putna, the Soviet Military Attaché in London,[278] Ignaz Reiss, head of Razvedupr in Switzerland.[279] Hundreds of secret service men were ordered back to Russia and shot; thousands were arrested. ·

The heads of the German apparats did not escape. Kippenberger was accused of being a German spy, arrested and shot.[280] Moscow had the same fate in store for Flieg, head of the passport apparat, Roth, Kippenberger's deputy, and Eberlein, head of the old M-Apparat.[281] Burde, the head of the old BB, was typical of many of the apparatchiks; he was running a Razvedupr espionage group in Scandinavia when the order to return to Moscow reached him; he said: "I am now going to my death, but I have no choice." He too was executed.[282]

Only those who had the courage to escape to the West could save themselves from the Yezhov terror—temporarily. General Krivitsky, Resident Director for Western Europe, fled to America,[283] General Orlov of the Secret Service did likewise,[284] Agabekov, who had been Resident Director in Turkey, hid in Belgium.[285] But the GUGB trackers patiently followed their quarry: in March 1938 they kidnapped Agabekov;[286] in February 1941 Krivitsky died under suspicious circumstances (allegedly suicide) in a Washington hotel room.[287]

The Soviet espionage organization had committed harakiri. The rump of Razvedupr was taken over by the GUGB and became subordinate to the Commissariat of the Interior. The Gestapo could now cross the names of their most important enemies off their list.

As early as 22 March 1937 the Gestapo noted a "somewhat reduced tendency to open, but of course illegal, communist activity in Germany." Comment: "Germany is no longer the main target of Comintern and Soviet policy. The Third International lacks adequate trained personnel to be equally active in all countries simultaneously."[288] Razvedupr had shot its bolt in Germany—at least for a time.

2

The "Grand Chef's" Circuit

THE RUSSIAN SECRET Service organization in Europe lay in ruins; Russia's espionage elite was languishing in the death cells of the Secret Police. Exhausted by the bloody struggles for power within the Soviet hierarchy, deprived of her military leadership, paralyzed by fear of the dictator Stalin and the efficiency of his liquidation squads, Russia was an easy prey for her enemies. There was no secret service to guard her against the machinations of her foreign foes, no Soviet spy-ring to act as outpost and gather in the signs and signals of approaching danger.

But the war in the shadows went on. Even the ogre in the Kremlin began to perceive that he could not go on for ever celebrating his triumph over the "treacherous" Secret Service. The Soviet Union was in more urgent need than ever of an efficient espionage machine. Stalin proclaimed: "Our army, our punitive organs and intelligence service no longer have their sharp edge turned to the inside of the country but to the outside, against external enemies."[1]

In fact Joseph Stalin had good reason to wish to know the plans of foreign powers. In the East the Japanese Generals, who had been planning the conquest of Siberia for years, were in the ascendant; in the West the leaders of National-Socialist Germany were pursuing their program of conquest with vigor. Germans and Japanese had already come together in the Anti-Comintern Pact—clearly directed against Moscow; many of the barriers holding the

Germans away from Russia were already down—Austria had been overrun, Czechoslovakia robbed of the Sudetenland and Poland (apparently) enlisted on the side of Adolf Hitler's eastern crusade. Moreover, the British conservative politicians were by no means hostile spectators of Hitler's eastward advance; inevitably the Munich capitulation of September 1938 reinforced Stalin in his old suspicion that one day the British imperalists would let loose the German dogs of war to achieve that which they had been unable to do themselves during the Russian civil war—eliminate the Soviet system.

In face of such dangers reconstruction of the Soviet Secret Service was the order of the day. A further development contributed to the rejuvenation of Razvedupr, which, as we have seen, had been placed under control of the Secret Police in 1937;[2] this was the reform of the Soviet State Security system. Early in 1938 Lavrenti Pavlovich Beria, a Georgian like Stalin, was summoned to Moscow and commissioned by the Dictator to reorganize the Secret Police, the GUGB.[3] Stalin had crushed all internal opposition; he had no further need of executioners; his object now was to consolidate his dictatorship by more subtle methods.

Beria put a stop to the terror and purged the GUGB of its more murderous thugs. The Cheka brutes were replaced by experts in police surveillance, the denouncers by collectors of secret information.[4] Information was the new watchword. Beria set up a whole series of schools and academies to train a new type of secret policeman, the scientifically trained observer, the expert eavesdropper and ferret, schooled (in the words of the historian Levitsky) "as professionals to penetrate all strata of Soviet society."[5]

The introduction of professionalism into the Soviet Secret Service world liberated Razvedupr from its GUGB fetters. Beria realized that espionage could not be conducted by police methods; moreover, in view of the German and Japanese threats, the military star was rising rapidly and so it was obvious to him that direction of the secret service could no longer be withheld from the Red Army. By the end of 1938 Razvedupr was master in its own house once more.[6]

A new generation of Soviet officers took their places in the spy headquarters on Kropotkin Square, Moscow; like their liquidated predecessors they were determined to sacrifice all to the good of the Russian state. Admittedly the new leaders of Razvedupr did not carry the political guns of a man like Jan Berzin. They were military technicians, initially hardly conversant with the rules of underground warfare. Most of them came from the Signals Service which was apparently thought best qualified to fill the holes in the Secret Service ranks left by the Secret Police bullets.

So the Signals Service provided the man who was to figure in the history of Rote Kapelle as the mysterious "Direktor"—General Ivan Terenchevich Peresypkin, Military Commissar at the Signals Scientific Research Institute since 1937.[7] Like many Soviet officers of the time he had had a versatile career. Peresypkin had joined the Red Army as a volunteer during the civil war, had then become a miner, had found his way back to military life through the All-Union Lenin Youth League and had then risen rapidly on the political side of the Red Army. In 1932 he entered the Technical Military Academy for Electronics and, on passing the final examination in 1937, ranked as the radio specialist in Army headquarters.

It is not possible to say whether, when the Soviet Secret Service was revived, Peresypkin took over direct from Uritsky, the head of Razvedupr who had been murdered. The official Soviet biographies show him in 1939 in the Central Administration for Intelligence of the General Staff; after the outbreak of World War II, however, he left the Secret Service for a time and was succeeded by General F. I. Golikov, commander of Sixth Army. Peresypkin did not finally take over as head of Razvedupr until summer 1941, by which time he was Colonel-General and Deputy Peoples Commissar for Defense.* From the outset he was the "Director," the ubiquitous Chief. He and his officers brought to their job the self-assurance of Stalin

---

* Details of Peresypkin's career are as follows: born 1904, volunteered for the Red Army in 1919, three years a miner in the Donetz Basin, course at the Red Army politico-military school in 1923, employed on the political side of the Army 1924–32, at the Technical Military Academy for Electronics 1932–7, Military Commissar at the Signals Scientific Research Institute 1937–9 followed by service in the Central Administration for Intelligence, Peoples Commissar for Civil Communications 1939–41, Head of the Central Administration for Intelligence and Deputy Peoples Commissar for Defense 1941–5, member of the High Command from 1942, by the end of the war Marshal of the Signals Service.[8]

loyalists, against whom the Secret Police had had nothing even in the worst days of the purge. Slowly they drove the Secret Police out of the military secret service field once more.

In 1939 the GUGB was forced to evacuate its oldest-established bridgehead in military territory, Section Three in the Peoples Commissariat for War; it had been manned by Secret Police officers and had been solely responsible for counter-espionage in the Red Army.[9] Henceforth the military had their own counter-espionage agency, the RO (Rasvedky Otdjel—espionage section); enemy intelligence in the frontier military districts also became Razvedupr's responsibility.[10]

Razvedupr also gained entry to the most secret science of all, hitherto the preserve of the Secret Police—codes and ciphers. The Soviet Secret Service officers were only too well aware that espionage work in war would be primarily a battle of secret transmitters and radio operators; hence the rapid development of a "Special Radio Section" (Osobiye Radio Division) camouflaged as an Institute for Gold Research and housed in the Lenin Hills near Moscow;[11] hence the institution of special courses at the School for Radio-telegraphy in Moscow.[12] Without its own codes and ciphers, however, the Secret Service was bound to lose the coming radio war. Razvedupr was therefore given its own cipher section, headed by Lieutenant-Colonel Kravchenko.[13]

Technical innovations alone, however, were not enough to win a future espionage war. What Razvedupr lacked were trained secret service officers, radio operators and cryptographers. The headquarters on Kropotkin Square therefore combed the Red Army for officers interested in secret service work and enlisted them for service in the underground. The newcomers were not lacking in good will but this was not enough; they had to be trained to be masters of the spy's trade.

Here too Razvedupr had to start from scratch; even the Red Army's Secret Service schools had been "purged" by Yezhov. Early in 1939 the Intelligence School, closed by the Secret Police, was reopened and given the status of a Military Academy.[14] The Signals School in Sokolniti was amalgamated with another army institution and expanded into a central secret service training establishment;[15] the Red Army's spy trainers even had the entrée into the General Staff Academy.[16]

But the Second World War was looming ever nearer and Razvedupr clearly had little time to prepare itself for the conflict. Peresypkin and his staff had their whips out. They instituted intelligence courses in which hurriedly recruited officers were trained for secret service work in three to six months.[17] Only the Central Intelligence School was allowed the luxury of eighteen-month courses and in 1940 even these were cut to six months.[18] The espionage professionals grumbled that no secret service officer could be trained in so short a time—three to four years was normally required; nevertheless, the medium-level and junior positions were quickly filled with new men. A Young Guard of Soviet espionage functionaries had arisen—enthusiastic, courageous, but inexperienced and only superficially trained.

Such were the officers who manned the initial centers of Soviet espionage abroad. A glance was enough to show that the prospects for Russian enemy intelligence were bleak indeed: in Germany Razvedupr's work had been brought to an almost total standstill; in Switzerland and Western Europe the espionage machine had lost both its leaders and its drive; in many other countries intelligence work was paralyzed by the ideological schism between Stalinists and anti-Stalinists.

Only in a few places was the outlook more promising: in 1937 the old Razvedupr had succeeded in setting up a widespread sabotage organization in northern and western European ports with lines running back to the German communist apparatchik Ernst Wollweber in Oslo.[19] At about the same time Rudolf Herrnstadt, a Razvedupr agent in Warsaw, reported that he had recruited Rudolf von Scheliha, First Secretary at the German Embassy there and a major land owner in Silesia, to work for Moscow;[20] the Soviet Secret Service was thus enabled to read many of the communications exchanged between the Embassy and the Wilhelmstrasse in Berlin. Another Soviet spy had the entrée to the German Embassy in Tokyo—Richard Sorge, Far East correspondent of the *Frankfurter Zeitung* and a confidant of the Ambassador. Eugen Ott.[21]

Razvedupr even possessed underground channels into some of the Ministries of the Third Reich. Ever since the establishment of the Nazi tyranny Dr. Arvid Harnack, a senior civil servant in the Reich Ministry of Economics, had been passing to Soviet Intelligence all the Ministry secrets accessible to him;[22] the anti-fascist furor of the Spanish Civil War had inspired Harro Schulze-Boysen, an Air Force Reserve Lieutenant, to do likewise with the contents of the safes in the Reich Ministry of Aviation.[23]

Despite these isolated successes the new leaders of Razvedupr took a pessimistic view of the possibilities of work in Germany. Their representatives in Berlin were indeed told to coordinate the work of the Harnack and Schulze-Boysen groups of informers, but nobody in Moscow thought that they would achieve a major breakthrough thereby. Espionage work in Adolf Hitler's Reich was too dangerous, the supremacy of the Gestapo too deadly. As far as the German war machine was concerned observation and intelligence-gathering must take place from neighboring countries, the democratic states of the West which would not place too great obstacles in the way of Soviet spying on the Third Reich.

Belgium was the ideal observation post; there the law of treason attached only lenient penalties to espionage, provided it was not directed against the country itself.[24] Parts of the old Comintern circuit working in Weimar Germany had withdrawn to Belgium; from Belgium Razvedupr could set up an informer network in France and Holland, possibly also in Denmark.[25] Moreover from Belgium it was possible to observe, not only Germany, but also Great Britain whose leaders Moscow still suspected of planning an anti-Bolshevist crusade in alliance with the Nazis.[26]

A further point in Belgium's favor was the fact that it was the only country with which the Moscow headquarters maintained a smooth flow of radio traffic. Starting in 1934 the Comintern, assisted by the Secret Service, had set up a radio network linking Moscow with its local offices and certain communist parties in Western Europe;[27] the main Moscow transmitter used the call-sign WNA—hence the reference in the Abwehr files to the "WNA circuit."[28]

The construction of this radio network was primarily the work of an East Prussian communist whom his comrades considered a genius in the radio game—hence his nickname "the Professor."[29] This was Johann Wenzel, born in 1902, No. 3140 on the Gestapo register and "Hermann" to Razvedupr; he came from Niedau near Königs-

berg, was a member of the BB and even before 1933 one
of the key figures in communist industrial espionage.[30]
Even after 1933 he had done some successful spying for
Moscow: late in 1934 he had recruited a group of informers in Düsseldorf for use in the German armaments
industry; a circuit of his agents in the Krupp Works in
Essen obtained plans of guns and tanks which he then
smuggled abroad.[31]

When the BB was broken up by the Gestapo early in
1935, Wenzel was recalled to Moscow. There he attended
the Red Army's Politico-military School (a development
of the old M School).[32] He showed such brilliance in
espionage and radio work that even seven years later two
German communist functionaries arrested in Slovakia
could still remember their fellow pupil Hermann and put
the Gestapo on his trail.[33]

Wenzel entered the service of Razvedupr and went to
Belgium in 1936.[34] The idea was that he should set up a
small circuit of agents in Brussels and at the same time
place his radio expertise at the disposal of the Comintern.
Wenzel soon became the Comintern's chief radio operator
in Western Europe; he himself worked a radio transmitter
in Belgium, he kept in close touch with the radio operators
of the Dutch and French Parties and began to train communist radio operators.[35] Whenever a set went "dis," whenever some comrade failed to decipher the complicated
Soviet code, "le professeur" was always on hand to re-
establish severed communications.

Meanwhile, from communist émigrés Wenzel had collected a miniature intelligence apparat, subsequently known
to the Gestapo as "Group Hermann."[36] The circuit collected information, prepared false passports and arranged
mailing addresses. It consisted of five people: Wenzel the
organizer, his mistress Germaine Schneider, a Swiss who
had been working for the Comintern ever since the 1920s
and who acted as courier for the group using the codename "Schmetterling" ["Butterfly"],[37] her ex-husband
Franz Schneider,[38] a Polish forger named Abraham
("Adash") Raichman[39] and his Czech mistress Malvina
Gruber, née Hofstadyerova.[40]

The most important member of the group was the
"cobbler" Raichman, whose forgeries later became indispensable to every Soviet espionage circuit in the West. His
past is highly obscure; Perrault, the French author, states

that Raichman was thrown up by the Comintern's passport forging apparat in Berlin;[41] ex-Gestapo officials, on the other hand, consider that this "tough and devilishly clever Polish Jew" (as André Moyen, the Belgian ex-Abwehr officer, describes him)[42] was one of the leaders of an erstwhile ring of completely non-political gangsters specializing in forgery and smuggling.[43] All agree, however, that "the manufacturer" (Raichman's codename) was a master forger, had worked in Palestine and had been providing the communist underground in Western Europe with his wares ever since 1934.[44]

Thanks to these experts Wenzel gradually attracted the attention of his Razvedupr masters, although from the intelligence point of view the value of his organization was small. From 1938 onward the tiny apparat proved increasingly useful.[45] Finally it seemed to offer such prospects that the Moscow headquarters decided to expand it. Unwittingly Johann Wenzel had laid the foundation for Rote Kapelle.

The little flags on the situation map in Russian Secret Service headquarters were now building up into a solid ring of agents. Brussels was the center of a web of Soviet informers spread over Western Europe and strong enough to be used simultaneously both against Germany and the Western Powers. A team of Soviet Secret Service officers was now ready to take over the leadership.

After a short period of acclimatization in the West, Captain Victor Sukulov-Gurevich was ordered to set up a circuit of agents in Copenhagen for infiltration into Germany.[46] Michail Makarov, an Air Force Lieutenant, was placed in charge of radio operations in the new expanded organization in Belgium;[47] 2nd Lieutenant Anton Danilov was responsible for liaison between the Soviet Embassy in Paris and the groups in Belgium and Holland.[48] Finally, Engineer Third Grade (equivalent to Captain) Konstantin Yefremov was given the job of keeping the armaments industries in Western Europe under observation.[49]

Headquarters took great pains to give these four key agents good cover. Each received a new identity with well-prepared papers. Passport No. 4649 issued in New York in 1936 turned Sukulov-Gurevich into Vincente Sierra, a citizen of Uruguay born on 3 November 1912 and living at No. 9 Calle Colon, Montevideo;[50] Makarov was now Carlos Alamo, also from Montevideo, born on 12 April

1913.[51] The other two agents were given a Scandinavian background. Danilov became a Norwegian, Albert Desmet born in Orschies on 12 October 1903;[52] the Ukrainian Yefremov turned into Eric Jernstroem, a Finnish student born in Vasa on 3 November 1911.[53]

Every form of subterfuge was adopted to cover the tracks of the four Soviet agents. Sukulov-Gurevich actually flew to Montevideo in order to start his journey to Belgium from there;[54] Yefremov, the pseudo-Finn, took an even more roundabout route; he started from Odessa whence he took a ship to Rumania; he then went on to Belgrade and from there into Switzerland; via Paris he reached Liège where he studied chemistry for a term at the university, and so finally arrived at his destination, Brussels.[55]

Industriously though the four studied their new roles, however, their devotion to duty could not conceal the fact that they were inadequately trained for their job. They were typical products of the short Razvedupr courses; none of them had had a basic training in secret service work. The Rote Kapelle legend built up by the anti-communists later presented them as sophisticated super-spies, but the truth is much more prosaic. Makarov, the airman from Kazan, was particularly unsuited to espionage work;[56] he was a jovial extrovert who liked fast cars (anathema to the espionage professional since the inevitable accidents attracted police attention), wine and pretty women.[57] He was an attractive showman, said to be a nephew of Molotov, the Soviet Foreign Minister,[58] but he was oblivious of the rules of the conspiratorial game, averse to discipline and longed for warlike adventure; during the Spanish Civil War, although only a member of the ground staff and without training as a pilot, he had flown a bomber single-handed against Franco's troops, saving his own side from catastrophe thereby.[59]

Sukulov-Gurevich too, vain and a sartorial eccentric, was no more than a caricature of the traditional spy.[60] Wherever he went he left a broad trail of luxury living and amorous entanglements. Some aspects of his career as a spy were almost pathetic; he was the son of a Leningrad workman, educated at a good school and with a gift for languages; during the Spanish Civil War he had fought in the International Brigade as an officer;[61] in his young days he had read Smirnov's novel *Diary of a Spy* and had become so absorbed in the hero, a British agent named Edward Kent, that he called himself Kent for ever after[62]—his fellow-officers in the army knew him as nothing else. In one respect, however, he differed from Makarov: when in a tight corner he proved himself a cool calculating spy despite all his braggadocio.

The other two agents, Danilov and Yefremov, were little better prepared. 2nd Lieutenant Danilov had been seconded to the diplomatic service immediately after military training;[63] Captain Yefremov, on the other hand, had a successful career as a technical officer behind him. He was a specialist in gas warfare, had studied chemistry in Moscow and served for years on the Soviet-Manchurian frontier in a technical section of the Far Eastern army.[64]

The short training which all these four had received in Moscow's spy schools was hardly adequate for the ambitious task allotted them by Razvedupr. Makarov could barely use a radio set (he was only taught by Wenzel);[65] Yefremov, though supposed to be a Finn, could not carry on even the most elementary conversation in Finnish,[66] though the Gestapo later credited him with cover "so excellent that it extended even to every button on his clothes and underwear."[67]

Rote Kapelle would indeed have got off to a bad start had not the man arrived who, more than any one single person, was responsible for the success of Soviet espionage in Western Europe. He was known by his underlings—and with good reason—as the "Grand Chef," or Big Chief, for he proved both in victory and defeat that he was schooled and experienced in every trick and every subterfuge of the conspiratorial trade. He was called Leopold Trepper and was a very different proposition from the others in his future circuit; he did not come from the Red Army; he was not even a Soviet citizen, but a Pole, a Jew and a professional revolutionary.[68]

Trepper brought into the story of Rote Kapelle an entirely new ingredient. His four Soviet colleagues were officers, accustomed to carry out any order from their superiors; the only subordination acceptable to Trepper, however, was voluntary submission to an idea, uncompromising discipleship. Orders from above might suddenly change the aim or direction of a conflict, but the fanaticism of the lone-wolf revolutionary permitted no deviation from his charted course—and Leopold Trepper's course had long been charted; his guiding stars were communism and Polish Jewry.

Trepper was a shopkeepers' son, born in Neumark near Zakopane on 23 February 1904; owing to the early death of his father he was brought up in poverty and misery; for lack of money he was forced to abandon his studies at Cracow University where he was reading history and literature;[69] he took up casual work, first as a mason, then as a locksmith, then as a miner, and during this period became a communist.[70] In 1925, with others of his ilk, he engineered a strike in the Galician town of Dombrova; it was suppressed by the Polish army. Apart from the memory of eight harsh months under detention this adventure left him with a new name—henceforth he called himself Domb, the first four letters of Dombrova.[71]

As a communist and a Jew, however, Trepper was now a doubly marked man and the change of name did not prevent him being harried by the semi-fascist Pilsudski regime. He thought his position so dangerous that he joined the Zionist organizations and with their assistance emigrated to Palestine in 1926.[72] He became a farm laborer in a kibbutz and then an apprentice in an electrical firm, but the lure of illegal communist work was still strong. He joined a communist organization known as "Unity"[73] and there made the acquaintance of the woman who later became his wife, a school-teacher named Broide Sarah ("Luba") Maya (divorced—married name Orschitzer); she had been born at Drohubucz, Poland, in 1908, was on the police books as an accessory to political murder and had fled to Palestine.[74]

Trepper thus became one of a small circle of Polish-Jewish communists united by a common fate. Most of them had studied at Polish universities, had become involved in revolutionary intrigue and had then gone to ground in Palestine. The Jews' Promised Land had no attraction for them. The middle-class Leon Grossvogel,[75] the clerk Hillel Katz,[76] the workman Alter Ström,[77] and the secretary Sophie Posnanska[78]—none of them wished to remain in Palestine, all of them longed to return to Europe, to the revolutionary battlefield.

But how were they to get out of this burning, parched strip of desert known as Palestine, which none of them liked? An avenue was open—entry into the service of the Comintern or the Soviet Secret Service. One of the circle,

Isaia Bir, a mechanical engineering student, showed his friends the way.[79] He opted for Razvedupr, went to France and started up as an informer in a chemical factory. Later he collected a Rabcor circuit providing the Soviets with information on French industry; his instructions came via the editorial office of the communist newspaper *L'Humanité* or through local Communist Party groups in France.[80] By 1929 Bir was so well established in the Soviet espionage underground that he summoned his old friend Alter Ström from Palestine. Ström became Bir's senior organizer[81] and in his turn called his friends from Palestine and incorporated them into Bir's intelligence circuit. Trepper arrived in 1930.[82] He soon discovered that he was a born agent and quickly rose to be one of Bir's most successful associates.

Trepper lapped up Bir's teaching which was later to turn him into an expert at covering his tracks; he learned the art of disguise, how to deceive his opponent and how to escape from a tight corner. Bir's nickname among the sleuths of the Paris Sûreté (Security Police) was "Phantomas"[83]—and for good reason, for he would bob up and disappear again like a ghost. He seemed to know the back door of every house in Paris, every cellar hideout; he was continually escaping his pursuers and to the very end they were puzzling as to who "Phantomas" really was. When they finally caught him in June 1932[84] they were almost disappointed; instead of the standard super-spy whom they expected, they found themselves confronted by an unassuming student who ran a sort of spy youth club (at 28 years old Trepper was the oldest).*[85]

While under arrest, Bir and his agents talked to "Charles Faux Pas Bidet," an official of the Sûreté, and it was made clear to them that their organization had fallen victim to the main malady of communist spy circuits, treachery within their own ranks. A member of the circuit had betrayed Bir's address to the police and had arranged a meeting, as a result of which "Phantomas" was arrested.[86] At the end of 1933 Bir, Ström and five other agents were sentenced to three years' imprisonment by a Paris court.[87] Only one of the leaders escaped the clutches of the police —Trepper.

* Dallin (op. cit., p. 54) states that Bir was the elder but he was clearly unaware of Trepper's date of birth.

He went to Berlin where the Secret Service office responsible for France, and reported there. The Razvedupr people put him on a train for Moscow with instructions to remain in his seat on arrival until everyone else had left and someone from headquarters had made himself known.[88] Trepper, alias Leiba Domb, did as he was told and thus started his career in Razvedupr. But his moment did not come for years; it almost seemed as if headquarters had no use for him. He whiled away the time with studies and temporary work: he attended a high school in Podrovsky, he edited the cultural section of the Yiddish newspaper *Emeth* and he went to the intelligence lectures at the Moscow War Academy.[89] Then his chance came.

In 1936 the members of the Bir apparat were released from prison; they demanded asylum and maintenance in the Soviet Union.[90] It was still a mystery who had blown the spy-ring in 1933. Riquier, a journalist, editor of *L'Humanité* and member of a six-man committee of the French Communist Party, was under suspicion; he had been the channel of communication between the Bir organization and its Soviet masters.[91] On the other hand it was not impossible that Alter Ström or some other agent in the group had betrayed it. To establish who the guilty party really was, headquarters despatched Trepper to France.[92] He brought all his detective ability to bear in order to clear his friends.

After laborious research he found the answer: Riquier had not been the traitor. Trepper discovered that the police had been informed by a Dutch communist who had belonged to a spy-ring in the United States and on his arrest had acted as a double agent for American counterespionage.* The unsuspecting Moscow headquarters had transferred the Dutchman to France, he had informed the Americans and they had passed his information to the Sûreté. When Trepper presented his report, headquarters demanded proof. Trepper went back to France and returned with irrefutable documents—the letters written by the stool pigeon to the US Military Attaché in Paris.[94]

Trepper's voyage of discovery to France convinced his masters on Kropotkin Square that he was a talented agent. After the liquidation of the Razvedupr elite and the flight

* Dallin still clings to the theory that Riquier was guilty but Perrault's later researches show that this was not the case.[93]

of General Krivitsky, the Resident Director for Western Europe, no one seemed better qualified than Trepper to take over leadership of the planned Western organization. He knew the French arena, his Polish friends of the Bir apparat were either still in France or had gone to ground in Belgium. He spoke French like a Frenchman and could also speak German, the language of the principal enemy and the future lingua franca for Soviet radio operators in the West.

So Leopold Trepper was nominated head of the Western Europe circuit. His orders were to collaborate with Makarov and Yefremov (the latter remaining in the background) in building up Wenzel's circuit in Belgium, then to set up further groups of agents in France and Holland and later gain contact with the Berlin group centered on Harnack and Schulze-Boysen. Wenzel was to place his Brussels group under Trepper, at the same time expanding his network in Holland and becoming technical radio head of all circuits in Western Europe.[95]

The best cover for this operation, Moscow thought, was that of a business concern. Makarov and Kent appeared as rich South Americans interested in the export trade;[96] Trepper chose the role of a well-to-do merchant from Canada.[97] A Canadian passport, No. 43 671, issued to a certain Michael Dzumaga born in Winnipeg on 2 August 1941, which had fallen into the hands of the Soviet Secret Service during the Spanish Civil War, was altered in the name of Adam Miklas, trader. Trapper had acquired his new identity.[98]

Unlike Yefremov, Trepper took minute pains to make himself acquainted with his Canadian background. An ex-Gestapo official, who had obviously interrogated Trepper after his capture, says: "He had briefed himself most carefully on the Canadian official and business world and on life in Canada in general; he had even obtained detailed reports on Canadian industry, economy, food supply, agriculture, forestry and every conceivable item."[99]

Thus prepared, in the spring of 1939, the "Grand Chef" departed on his great adventure.[100] His Canadian passport could obviously not show a Soviet visa, so for his round-about journey to Belgium he used a series of false papers: one passport took him to Finland and Sweden and with another he traveled to Denmark and Antwerp; there at last he received his Canadian passport from a representative of the Soviet Trade Delegation; its stamps proved that the holder had just arrived from Canada.[101]

Step by step Soviet espionage headquarters despatched their leading agents to Western Europe. Trepper installed himself in Brussels on 6 March 1939;[102] Makarov arrived in April;* Kent came in on 17 July, though (at any rate according to the plan) he was due to remain only a few months.[104] Finally in September Yefremov too reached Brussels.[105] Danilov, on the other hand, went no further than Paris, where he was absorbed by the Soviet Consulate;[106] in fact he belonged to the Embassy but was forbidden to enter it, since no one was to know that he was working with Captain Karpov, Assistant for Special Services to General Susloparov, the Soviet Military Attaché.[107]

Before his leading Soviet agents were ever established in Belgium and France, however, Trepper had arranged suitable cover for them. Immediately on arrival in Brussels he had contacted Leon Grossvogel, his old friend from Palestine, who had meanwhile established himself in the Belgian textile industry.[108] He owned a firm, "Au Roi du Caoutchouc," which dealt in raincoats and had branches in Ostend and Antwerp.[109]

Trepper hinted to his friend what business had brought him to Brussels and invited Grossvogel to become the spyring's financier. Grossvogel, who was still a communist, agreed. With 10,000 dollars from Trepper's secret espionage funds the two friends formed a raincoat export firm in Brussels, the "Foreign Excellent Trenchcoat";[110] as one of its directors they appointed an unsuspecting but respectable Belgian, Jules Jaspar, an ex-consul.[111] The new firm set up branches in Belgian, French, German and Dutch ports, ideal observation posts for England and Germany.[112]

When Makarov reported to Trepper, therefore, the initial cover organization was ready. But the "Grand Chef" was too cautious to allow his radio operator to become connected with "Trenchcoat." The conspiratorial rules laid down that agents should know each other as little as possible and so he urged Grossvogel to sell the Ostend branch of "Caoutchouc," hitherto run by Grossvogel's wife.[113] Simultaneously he aroused Makarov's interest in the busi-

---

* Dallin's date (September 1939) is obviously wrong; the Gestapo Final Report shows Makarov as arriving about April 1939.[103]

ness. The deal was concluded; Makarov paid 200,000 Belgian francs and became the owner.[114] With a radio set in his suitcase he moved to Ostend.

Grossvogel increasingly turned into Trepper's assistant No. 1; via him Trepper regained contact with his old Palestine companion Hillel Katz, who entered the service of the Soviets as Trepper's secretary;[115] later they were also joined by Sophie Posnanska, another old friend from the Holy Land; she now called herself Anette or Anna Verlinden in Moscow and was allotted to Trepper's organization.[117] The four Poles formed the hard core of the spy-ring which, thanks to Grossvogel's excellent contacts, occupied an increasingly strong position in the Belgian business world.

Grossvogel had a friend named Isidor Springer who worked in the Antwerp diamond exchange and who introduced Trepper into a new circle of communist informers. Springer had been a KPD functionary but had broken with the Party; nevertheless, he was willing to take a hand in Soviet espionage.[118] He brought along other friends: Hermann Izbutsky the courier,[119] Augustin Sesée, a merchant marine radio operator,[120] Rita Arnould, a German émigré and Springer's mistress,[121] and Simone Phelter, a girlfriend of Grossvogel and employee in the Franco-Belgian Chamber of Commerce.[122]

Meanwhile the members of Wenzel's circuit had joined Trepper and Wenzel himself had started technical radio training for the organization. Thanks to his foresight the circuit had four workable sets in Belgium, all ready for use; one Wenzel kept in his Brussels apartment,[123] a second was with his assistant Raichman,[124] the third was with the "Ostend musician" as Sesée called himself,[125] and the fourth was kept under lock and key by Makarov.[126] Makarov's "musical box" was first in line; if that failed Wenzel's set was to take over; the other two sets were to be held in reserve.

Wenzel then extended his network into Holland where further sets were installed. Early in 1939, via Daniel Goulooze,[127] a Dutch communist radio operator and an old comrade from the Comintern days, he had gained contact with a circle of communist functionaries in Amsterdam.[128] Shortly thereafter Moscow instructed him to proceed to Amsterdam for a rendezvous with Winterinck,[129] a Comintern man selected by Razvedupr to head the Dutch group. Winterinck, known in the Party as the "Big Man" because of his enormous girth,[130] had previously worked for the Comintern organization "Red Aid"; he had postal and courier communications to Germany, later used by the secretariat of the KPD-in-exile in Stockholm under Herbert Wehner, when it attempted to regain a foothold in Nazi Germany.[131]

Wenzel taught Winterinck the rudiments of radio work, gave him the codename "Tino,"[132] and set him to work. Winterinck had soon collected a small group of agents, twelve in all including couriers and informers.[133] Goulooze, the radio operator, already had a set and two further sets arrived later.[134] Wenzel also trained the communist Wilhelm Voegeler as a radio operator.[135] By the end of 1940 "Hilda" (the codename of the Dutch group) was in radio contact with Moscow.[136]

Trepper's organization was now really starting to work and permanent contact between the organizations in Belgium and Holland was maintained by Jakob and Hendrika Rillboling, a husband-and-wife combination representing "Hilda,"[137] and the Belgian agent Maurice Peper.[138] The Belgian circuit still kept quiet; Trepper thought it more important to recruit informers and organize contacts with the business world, the diplomats and the military than to send information over the air. The time for output had not yet arrived; the Hitler-Stalin Pact had just been concluded; Moscow and Berlin were still doing business under its false colors. Trepper would only really start work in the event of a Russo-German conflict.

The German conqueror's victory march, however, forced the "Grand Chef" out of his reserve. Adolf Hitler's armies compelled the Soviet espionage organization to change its plans and reduce its barely established commitments in this invisible war.

Hitler's warlike adventure in Poland had upset Razvedupr's plans for a stealthy advance in the West. The outbreak of war in September 1939 prevented the establishment of an apparat planned for Denmark, since Kent, who was still in Brussels and destined to be head of the Danish organization, was ordered by headquarters to remain in Belgium and join Trepper.[139] In addition Great Britain's entry into the war necessitated a revision of the organization in the Atlantic ports of Western Europe which had been primarily designed for observation westward. There was no longer any doubt where Britain stood and so gradually Trepper's organization directed its efforts exclusively eastward.

Trepper had hardly adjusted himself to the new situation, however, when the German armies, tanks and bombers demolished one of the most important strategic assumptions on which the Soviet espionage campaign was based. Its strategic principle had been that the intelligence assault on Germany must be directed from neighboring neutral territory, out of range of the Third Reich's counterespionage agencies. As a result of the German western campaign of May/June 1940, however, Moscow's agents were confronted by the physical proximity of Hitler-Germany; the hunted and the hunters were now next-door neighbors; in Brussels, for instance, the Abwehr office tracking down Rote Kapelle was in the same building as the head office of one of Trepper's pseudo-firms, separated literally only by a wall.[140]

The German military operations on the Channel coast made it abundantly clear to Trepper that he must change front quickly. Makarov's raincoat business in Ostend was destroyed by a German bomb,[141] and Trepper could count himself lucky that he had previously ordered Makarov to conceal his radio set in Knokke-le-Zoute, east of Ostend.[142] Makarov was so shaken that he refused to leave the arms of his mistress, the wife of Guillaume Hoorickx, the artist, and was most unwilling to obey Trepper's order to bring the set to Brussels.[143] Trepper had to go to Knokke himself and fetch the set, forcing his way through the advancing German tanks. He dressed Makarov down and threatened to send him back to Russia the next time he disobeyed orders.[144] The threat was not very seriously meant, however, since the "Grand Chef" now needed every one of his agents. For the first time Moscow was making use of its new network of informers, for, like every other staff in the world, the Soviet General Staff had been taken by surprise by the Wehrmacht's blitz strategy and was now demanding rapid and detailed information from its spies.

Trepper alerted his circuit. In both Belgium and Holland agents and informers set out to discover the secret of the German Western offensive. During his enforced trip to Knokke Trepper had noted down anything which struck him about the Germans as they drove by.[145] Fresh reports came in daily and little by little the picture built up. Early in June Trepper was able to send the Director in Moscow an 80-page report, transmitted via the Military Attaché of the Soviet Legation in Brussels.[146]

This was the last service Trepper could render the Military Attaché, however. On the occupation of Belgium by the Germans the staff of the Soviet Legation was withdrawn and the Military Attaché with them.[147] The organization now had to rely on its radio sets; they were the sole means of contact with the Director.

The first radio team was installed in a villa in the Avenue Longchamp, Brussels.[148] It was intended only to pass messages to Moscow occasionally, primarily in order to check the equipment and keep in continuous touch with headquarters; the informer network itself remained silent. Marakov worked the set, Sophie Posnanska did the encoding and Springer's girlfriend Rita Arnould, somewhat unwillingly, acted as courier.[149] She was driven into the service of the Soviets only by extreme economic necessity (her husband, a Belgian businessman, had died a few weeks earlier), and by fear of her German fellow-countrymen (she was a Jewish ex-communist).[150]

As head of the group Trepper made increasing use of Captain Kent. He was living a gay life on the fourth floor of No. 106 Avenue de Emile Beco; its gaiety was increased by the fact that, during one of the German air attacks, he had met and fallen in love with the blonde occupant of one of the other apartments in the building, Margarete Barcza, widow of a Czech millionaire.[151] The pair later moved into a 27-room house in the Avenue Slegers, where they became the center of an exclusive society of conservative and right-wing Catholic fops.[152]

Trepper had great difficulty in keeping the Soviet would-be gentleman's mind on his duties. Little though he liked the small unattractive Kent, however, Trepper needed him, for he was the only Russian capable of taking over the Belgian circuit.[153] Trepper's own days in Belgium were obviously drawing to a close; the increasingly strict German occupation regime was leaving him less and less elbow room. He could no longer appear as a Canadian businessman since Canada was at war with Germany; Raichman had already forged him fresh papers in the name of Jean Gilbert.[154] Many of his most intimate Jewish friends were in danger; the occupation authorities were preparing anti-

Jewish legislation which made it certain that Grossvogel would shortly lose all his possessions.[155]

It was high time to evacuate to France. Of course the German military were in control there too, but they did not know Belgians like Leo Grossvogel. Moreover, an intelligence circuit had to be set up in France also. In August 1940 Trepper together with his mistress Georgie de Winter (he had sent his wife Luba and the children back to the Soviet Union)[156] and Grossvogel moved to Paris. Kent became the "Petit Chef" (Little Chief) and Trepper's Belgian circuit turned into the "Kent Group."

With his two assistants, Grossvogel and Katz, Trepper began to form a new espionage circuit in Paris. The three were joined by an old hand in communist conspiracy with experience in work both for the Secret Service and the Comintern—Henry Robinson. Born in 1897, son of a Frankfurt businessman, he had fought in the Spartacist movement, been a Comintern "instructor" in Paris, and early in the 1930s had become the officer responsible for industrial espionage on the staff of "General Muraille," the Resident Director; he had finally become head of OMS for Western Europe.[157]

Robinson brought into Trepper's embryo French organization an intelligence circuit whose informers worked in numerous government agencies—they even had links to the Vichy cabinet and the French Army's Secret Service.[158] The Robinson circuit was also in close touch with the French communist party and Razvedupr's Swiss organization.[159] On the private and more romantic net Robinson was even in contact with the Berlin group, for Klara Schabbel, an old-guard communist, was his ex-mistress and mother of his son, now serving as a Lance-Corporal in Adolf Hitler's army.[160]

A second group of agents, initially regarded with some suspicion by Trepper but finally accepted, brought him into contact with another section of French society—the church, the aristocracy and the Russian émigrés. Heading this group were two children of a Czarist general from Chernigov, Vassily Pavlovich Maximovich, a mining engineer, and Anna Pavlovna Maximovich, a nerve specialist.[161]

They had initially belonged to the Young Russia movement, an association of White Guard émigrés in France with somewhat fascist tendencies, but had drifted into Soviet service since the money enabled Anna Maximovich to open a private clinic.[162] This clinic became a repository of highly important information, since it was frequented not only by the Russian émigré leaders, who lived largely off Anna Maximovich's money,[163] but also by Monsignor Chaptal, Bishop of Paris,[164] and Darquier de Pellepoix, Commissar-General for Jewish Affairs in the Vichy government; the latter's brother was the clinic's head doctor.[165]

Trepper was primarily interested in the Maximoviches because of their relations with the German occupation authorities. As a General's son Maximovich was on good terms with officials in the German military administration, particularly since he had formed a liaison with a secretary of the Womens Service, Anna-Margaret Hoffman-Scholtz ("Hoscho").[166] She was in fact no normal secretary; she came of a good family and had a relative serving as an officer in the Western occupied territories.* Her first job as secretary was in the office of Hans Kuprian, a senior military administrative officer and specialist on refugee questions.

Immediately on the occupation of France the Head of Military Administration, the administrative branch of Military Government as distinct from the fighting troops, formed a special detachment to repatriate the seven million refugees in France made homeless during the fighting. Von Pfeffer, a senior government official [Regierungspräsident] serving in Military Administration, was appointed commissioner for refugees and he despatched his officials into the refugee camps to organize their transportation. On one of these inspection trips Kuprian and his secretary met the refugee Maximovich.†[168]

The secretary, no longer in her first youth, took a liking to the Russian baron and was only too ready to be wooed. Their friendship continued when the Refugee Office was

---

* Perrault (op. cit., p. 192) says that Hoscho came of a good Hanover family. In fact her home was in the neighborhood of Potsdam (Wendisch-Buchholz).[167]

† Perrault's statement (op. cit., pp. 195, 204) that Maximovich belonged to a sort of resistance group of senior German officers, including "General" von Pfeffer and "Colonel" Kuprian, is presumably only speculation; at the time in question (after the outbreak of the Russo-German war) neither Pfeffer nor Kuprian was serving in Paris. Pfeffer left Military Government, France, early in 1941; Kuprian was seconded to District Headquarters [Feldkommandantur] 758 in April 1941 and on 1 September 1941 became Head of Administration in the Bordeaux District.

the Schulze-Boysen/Harnack group in Berlin.[183] There is proof that he went to the Leipzig Fair in the spring of 1941.[184] A few months later he journeyed to Leipzig again and, as the Gestapo later established, was to "hide 1,000 marks in each of two oak trees and radio the precise position of the trees to Moscow."[185] Who the money was intended for is unknown.

Kent managed to combine intelligence duties with his business trips to Simexco's branch in Prague. His destination on one such journey was the art repositories belonging to the Czech agents Frantishek and Woyachek, where he was to meet an agent named Rudi and hand him 2,000 marks. The operation was a failure, however, because both the Czechs had been arrested by the Gestapo shortly before.[186]

Kent displayed such energy that the Germans later thought that he had been the real head of Soviet espionage in Western Europe. Meanwhile Trepper, the actual Chief, had been appointed Resident Organizer for Western Europe.[187] He must have viewed Kent's promotion with mixed feelings, for he had great difficulty in controlling the "Petit Chef." Trepper insisted that he come to Paris and report every week.[188]

These meetings encountered opposition from an unexpected quarter, however—that of Kent's jealous mistress. She knew nothing of Kent's espionage activities and suspected that his regular meetings with Trepper were a front for some new love affair.[189] Since finding in Kent's coat pocket a signed photograph of Nila Cara, the cabaret artist, she had taken to interrupting Trepper's and Kent's meetings by hourly telephone calls. Margarete Barcza now admits that "this put him [Kent] in a towering rage every time."[190]

The suspicious Trepper frequently went to Belgium to supervise Kent's work; a room in Kent's flat had to be permanently reserved for him.[191] The spectacle of Simexco's office in Brussels stimulated in Trepper a desire to form a similar camouflage firm in Paris under his direct control. Grossvogel set to work once more.

The new firm, named Simex, was a faithful copy of Kent's concern. This time, however, Grossvogel saw no reason to introduce a neutral businessman as cover; the three principal Soviet spies in occupied France joined the firm quite openly. Trepper ("Gilbert") was the manager of Simex,[192] which had an initial capital of 300,000 francs;[193] he nominated Katz, his amaneuensis, as Chief Secretary;[194] Grossvogel figured as a partner;[195] the head of the secretariat was a French communist, Suzanne Cointe, a general's daughter.[196]

The business was entered in the register of the Paris Chamber of Commerce in summer 1941[197] and the four agents set up shop in the Lido building on the Champs Elysées.[198] None of the employees had an inkling that all the threads of the greatest Soviet espionage organization in Western Europe centered on the luxurious office of the manager, Gilbert; in the rear of this office was a small room in which the codebooks and address lists of Trepper's circuit were kept.[199]

The cover was perfect. Like most of his colleagues in Simex, Emmanuel Mignon, the assistant to Katz, the Chief Secretary, merely thought that Simex was "an amusing outfit; everyone was always in good form. We dealt exclusively in black-market business."[200]

The German authorities too were completely unsuspecting and were only too happy to accept Simex deliveries. Monsieur Gilbert was ready to provide anything and was often to be seen in the company of German officers; he was given a privilege vouchsafed to few Paris businessmen—a special pass allowing him to cross the demarcation line into occupied France.[201] The business made fantastic profits. Mignon says: "We made a lot of money, but not a sou remained in the office. As soon as the safe was full Katz or Grossvogel would descend and remove the lot."[202]

But before the new firm could spread its net wider, Adolf Hitler let loose the catastrophe which Trepper and his agents had been expecting for months: the German war machine charged into Russia. The moment had come for Trepper's organization to prove its worth, the moment which he had been continually predicting, although Moscow's reaction had merely been one of incredulity. Trepper's reports had been ignored by the Soviet leaders, as had the warnings of Richard Sorge and the Czech agents who had reported the Germans moving up to the western frontiers of Russia.[203] On the latter messages Stalin had written in red ink: "This information is an English provocation. Find out who is making this provocation and punish him."[204]

On 21 June 1941 Trepper had gone to unoccupied France

to present an urgent report to Susloparov, the Soviet Military Attaché, who had moved from Paris to Vichy. Gist of the report: All indications were that the Germans would attack Russia that very night. General Susloparov's reaction was: "My friend, you're completely out of your mind," and at first he refused to forward the report. Then, however, his attitude changed[205] and Trepper returned to his hotel satisfied. The next morning the hotel-keeper woke him shouting: "Monsieur, it's happened; they've attacked Russia!"[206]

It had indeed happened. This was the moment for which they had all been waiting in their various concealed positions; this was the moment they had longed for, since all doubt was now swept away. The standstill order no longer applied; Trepper's submarine raised its periscope in a sea of field-gray uniforms. The mortal struggle was on.

Ironically, however, at exactly this moment the "Grand Chef" found himself deprived of any method of maintaining permanent contact with his Moscow headquarters. Trepper's French organization possessed no radio set.[207] For months Susloparov had promised his Resident Director to hand over one or two sets in the event of emergency; yet, when the Soviet Embassy in Vichy closed its doors and its staff departed for Moscow, the Military Attaché was forced to admit that he possessed not a single set.[208] Trepper was left without radio communication to Moscow.

Could not headquarters have instructed at least one of the groups operating in Western Europe to lend Trepper a set? The idea occurred to no one; everyone was clearly too jealous of his prerogatives. Every group had its own job and was only in distant touch with its neighbor. But what about the local communist parties? Could not they have made a set available? This might have been possible, but headquarters looked with disfavor on contacts with the communist party; each leading organizer was only allowed to meet a delegate from his local communist party once a year and then only on direct instructions from Moscow.[209]

So this was what the much-trumpeted planning and system behind the Soviet Secret Service amounted to; this was what passed as preparation for silent warfare against the most ferocious military machine in Europe. For years the Soviet espionage academies had taught that the coming war would be decided in the ether but, when eventually

war came, the most productive circuit of agents had not
even a single set. And this was no isolated instance: the
Moscow headquarters hoped that its most important information would come from its Berlin group, but had omitted to provide that group with a trained radio operator.[210]
Radio communications were, and remained, Rote Kapelle's
Achilles' heel.

The "Grand Chef" had no alternative but to look for a
set somewhere and meanwhile pass messages for Moscow
via Kent's set. This turned the "Petit Chef" into *the* central figure of the Soviet espionage organization in the West.
The more desperate the situation of the Russian armies
facing the German invasion, the shriller became Peresypkin's calls for information, analyses and statistics. But the
only one who could answer was Kent, for he possessed
the best radio communications to Moscow.

For weeks Kent's operator, cryptographer, agents and
couriers never took off their clothes. Kent and his gang
left the villa on the Avenue Longchamp in Brussels and
occupied new quarters in a three-storied house, No. 101
Rue des Atrébates.[211] There the team continued to work
at their old jobs (operator—Makarov, coding—Sophie
Posnanska, courier—Rita Arnould); from autumn 1941
they were reinforced by Danilov who had evacuated from
Vichy.[212]

From now on Kent's radio team was working almost
non-stop. Informers collected their information, couriers
hurried to the "post-boxes," the two organizers, the Big
Chief and the Little, sifted the reports. Then the material
was encoded in the Rue des Atrébates and made ready for
transmission. At midnight Makarov would hurry along
and work his set for five hours at a stretch.[213] Using the
call-sign "PTX," every important scrap of information had
to be transmitted to Moscow at once, every request from
headquarters met forthwith.

The General Staff of Russia's hard-pressed armies seemed
to issue a new request or a new mission every minute:

10 August 1941: "Kent from Director. Schneider's
source seems to be well informed. Check through him
total German losses to date, showing type and campaign
separately."[214]

29 August 1941: "Information required on possibilities
of production of chemical warfare material in German
factories. Prepare for sabotage in works concerned."[215]

10 August 1941: "Require report on Swiss army in view of possible German invasion. Strength of army in event general mobilization. Type of fortifications. Quality of equipment. Details of air force, tanks and artillery. Technical resources by arms of service."[216]

There was literally nothing which the Director did not wish to know—the Wehrmacht's strategic plans, details of German air operations, information on relations between the Nazi leaders and senior officers, changes in the location of the Führer's headquarters, strengths of German Army Groups, troop movements in the western occupied territories[217]—Moscow was interested in every detail bearing on the war. All this was accompanied by continuous exhortations from the Director to report quicker, better and more. As an instance:

"You should learn from the Lille incident. Check all your contacts with political circles. Remember that such contacts may endanger the work of the entire organization. Keep a strict watch on your people's acquaintances."[218] On another occasion:

"Your organization must be divided into a number of self-contained groups, communicating with each other only through you. The loss of a group must neither affect nor endanger the work of the others. The radio network must be decentralized as quickly as possible. Remember that your work is of the utmost importance."[219]

"Kent from Director"—"Kent from Director"—"Kent from Director"—Moscow messages left the "Petit Chef" not a moment's peace. He was forever dictating messages, information reports and tidings of gloom.

October 1941: "From Pierre: Overall strength of the German army 412 divisions. Of these 21 in France at present, mostly second-line divisions. Their strength varies owing to continual drafts. Troops which were near and south of Bordeaux . . . are on the move to the East; they consist of some three divisions."[220] A further message:

"From Emil. Two new German gas formulae have become known here: 1. Nitrosylfluoride. Formula: NOF. 2. Cacodylisocyanide. Formula: $(CH_3)_2$ AsNC."[221] Yet another:

"From Jose. Near Madrid, six miles west of the city, is a German intercept station for British, American and French (colonial) traffic. It is camouflaged as a business organization with the cover name 'Stürmer.' Spanish government is *au courant* and supports the station."[222]

And finally: "Source: Jacques. Germans have lost the élite of their forces on the Eastern front. Superiority of Russian tanks not disputed. General Staff discouraged by Hitler's continual changes of plans and objectives."[223]

Every message demonstrated that Trepper's and Kent's agents were producing what was expected of them. Undoubtedly the western organization had proved its worth. Nevertheless, Kent was in danger of being submerged by the flood of information; unaided, his group had to deal with all messages originating from Belgium and France, whereas the small Dutch circuit "Hilda," which was well provided with sets, was by no means overworked.[224]

The messages piled up on Kent's desk to such an extent that he demanded additional sets and codebooks from Moscow.[225] At first there were no further sets available but the Director nevertheless tried to help: Kent and the "Grand Chef" were temporarily authorized to make use of the reserve network which Razvedupr had set up in Switzerland.

After the Yezhov purges a Razvedupr agent, Ursula-Maria Hamburger, had revived a small informer circuit in Switzerland and at the end of 1940 this had been taken over by Alexander Rado (codename "Dora"), a long-standing Hungarian communist.[226] Rado expanded the circuit so rapidly that he soon had fifty informers at his disposal.[227] More important than all from Trepper's and Kent's point of view, he possessed three radio sets: one ("Station Jim") was in Lausanne and was worked by the British operator Alexander Foote; a second was held by the husband-and-wife combination, Edmond and Olga Hamel, in their villa in Geneva; the third was worked by Rado's girlfriend, Margaret Bolli.[228]

The Swiss network was intended to come into action should the spy circuits in Western Europe and Berlin be blown; only in that case was Rado really to begin work. As a result of the shortage of sets and the workload on Kent, however, the Director decided to bring Rado's sets temporarily into play at this point. For a time his messages became as important as that of Kent.

On 6 September 1941 Moscow was told: "Germany agrees that, after the capture of Leningrad, Finland should conclude a separate peace; this would shorten the German front, thereby releasing German troops and easing the transport and supply situation."[229] On 20 September Rado passed on the following: "The next German objective is to cut Russian communications to the Anglo-Saxons by the capture of Murmansk."[230] On 22 October: "As a result of their losses the majority of German divisions on the Eastern front have lost their homogeneity. Apart from some fully trained personnel they consist of men with four to six months' training and others who have only had one-sixth of the necessary training period."[231] And again: "On 17 October the German High Command issued instructions for a possible prolonged siege of Moscow. For some days heavy coastal and naval guns have been on the move to the Moscow front from Königsberg and Breslau."[232]

Kent was just beginning to feel some relief from the pressure of incoming information when the Director gave him a new task. On 10 October 1941 Makarov took down a message from Moscow and Kent read: "Go forthwith to the three addresses in Berlin given below and find out why radio communication is always failing. If these failures continue, you should take over transmission of radio messages. The work of the Berlin groups and the transmission of information is of the utmost importance. Addresses: 19 Altenburger Allee, Neu-Westend, third floor right—Choro; 26a Fredericiastrasse, Charlottenburg, second floor left—Wolf: 18 Kaiserallee, Friedenau, fourth floor left—Bauer. Remember 'Eulenspiegel.'* Password in each case: 'Direktor.' "[233]

A week later a further message from the Director told Kent, who had not yet left for Berlin, that communications between Moscow and the Berlin group had broken down once more owing to the amateurishness and inefficiency of Hans Coppi, a young communist whom Schulze-Boysen, the organizer, had installed as radio operator. Kent was ordered to hand over a new set to the Berliners and teach Coppi to work it.[234] Kent departed for Berlin.

On 19 October Kent met Schulze-Boysen and Harnack, the two leaders of the Berlin circuit, and impressed upon them the absolute necessity of maintaining radio communications with Moscow; should Coppi fail again, he said, a courier system was available which would enable

* See p. 179.

the Berlin messages to be transmitted to Moscow via Brussels.[235] The two Germans promised to do better. On 20 October Kent went on to Prague, where he had something else to do for the Director.*

On return to Brussels, however, he found bad news awaiting him: Coppi had resumed contact with Moscow but a day or two later (on 21 October) had gone silent again.[237] So Kent now had to pass Berlin's messages to Moscow, since the Director thought them of the utmost importance and was particularly pressing on the subject.

Only gradually did Kent realize why Coppi had so suddenly gone off the air. He had stopped transmitting because the intercept detachments of the German radio counter-espionage service had worked their way to within a few yards of him. Trepper and Kent were not slow to grasp the significance of the Berlin message of doom. The Germans were on their tracks. The German radio counter-espionage was girding its loins for a counter-stroke.

---

* Kent's mission was to re-establish communications with the Soviet espionage group in Prague, "Oskol", and to pass on the wavelength laid down by Moscow, on which the "Oskol" set was to work.[236]

3

Alert on the Hot Line

THE APPEARANCE OF Soviet agents inside Adolf Hitler's empire caught the German counter-espionage services totally unprepared. Helplessly the Third Reich's radio experts listened to their enemy's traffic; direction-finding squads from the Wehrmacht and police searched in vain for the hideouts of the Red spies. The Germans were faced by an apparently insoluble mystery.

Radio message after message demonstrated the impotence of the German defenses. OKW's* intercept stations industriously transcribed the invisible enemy's coded reports; the address groups of the mysterious messages were carefully registered in the list of call-signs maintained by Counter-espionage—but the spies' secret language remained unintelligible to the Germans.

The first Rote Kapelle message was heard about 3:58 a.m. on 26 June 1941 by the intercept station at Cranz near Königsberg.[1] "KLK from PTX 2606.03.3032 wds. No. 14 qbv," the operator wrote; there followed thirty-two five-figure groups ending with the signature "AR 50385 KLK from PTX." Even the most highly qualified experts could not decipher it.[2] The appearance of the unknown transmitter put the entire German radio counter-espionage system on the alert. Only a few hours later the teleprinters

* Oberkommando der Wehrmacht—High Command of the Armed Forces.

were tapping out an order to the Wehrmacht's direction-finding stations: "Essential discover PTX schedule. Night frequency 10 363. Day frequency unknown. Priority 1a."[3]

No sooner were the Germans sure that this strange transmitter with call-sign PTX was in communication with Moscow than further stations were reported. By 8 July 1941 the intercept service had seventy-eight Comintern transmitters on its books and by October there were a further ten.[4] (By July 1942 there were 325 clandestine Soviet sets working in German-occupied Europe,[5] the majority admittedly on the Eastern Front.)

For the Abwehr* and Gestapo sleuths these bleeps in the ether seemed like a mocking reply to their fruitless efforts to penetrate the secrets of the Soviet espionage machine. For years Admiral Wilhelm Canaris' Abwehr had been thrashing over the problem how to break into the Soviet Secret Service and stop the advance of the red spies.

In 1935 Group III F had been formed in the Abwehr under Captain (Navy) Protze to deal with counter-espionage;[6] it was to recruit informers to keep suspected spies under surveillance; it was to defeat or penetrate enemy espionage services and feed them misleading information ("playback" material). But neither Captain Protze nor his successor, Lieutenant-Colonel Joachim Rohleder,† who took over in 1938, succeeeded in penetrating Razvedupr.[7]

The Abwehr approached its task in a realistic frame of mind. It agreed with Heinrich Himmler, who secretly admired the Russian police state and had said: "Russia is indeed hermetically sealed; no sound reaches the outside world from behind its walls; nothing from the hostile outer world can penetrate into Russia."[8] A frontal assault clearly offered no prospects; infiltration into Russia's vast empire was only possible from the periphery.

Fortunately the Abwehr office in Königsberg was on good terms with certain senior officials in the Lithuanian Secret Service; the Lithuanians, the Abwehr thought, would

---

* Military Intelligence.

† Lieutenant-Colonel Rohleder, who took over Group III F in the Abwehr on 22 January 1938, was born in Stettin on 29 April 1892. He attended the Cadet College in Oranienstein and the Senior Cadet College, Berlin-Lichterfeld and joined 8 Life Guards Grenadier Regiment in 1911. He retired in 1930 and joined the Secret Service in 1935 as a desk officer, becoming head of a section in 1938—from *Der Spiegel* archives.

assist in passing agents across the Soviet frontier.[9] But the Lithuanians disappointed their German friends; action against their mighty neighbor was too risky for them. "They would not lift a finger against the Soviet Union," ex-Lieutenant-Colonel Reile of the Abwehr recalls.[10] The Abwehr then thought that the Hungarians might do what the Lithuanians would not. In 1935-6 the Abwehr office in Munich contacted the Hungarian Secret Service and they did promise to help the Germans gather intelligence in Russia. But the Honved spies also proved incapable of slowing the Abwehr's dilemma.[11] Then I M, the naval desk of secret intelligence in the Abwehr, had a new idea; they proposed to place informers on ships calling at Soviet ports and infiltrate into Russia that way.[12] The plan proved as impracticable as did another, to use German tourists in Russia for intelligence purposes.[13]

Only one method remained: to espouse the cause of the Russian émigrés and exploit their contacts with their old homeland. In 1937 the Abwehr contacted a group of exiles known as OUN (Organization of Ukrainian Nationalists) whose leader, Colonel Eugen Konovalets, had been working with the Germans ever since 1921.[14] Konovalets was murdered by Soviet agents but his successor, Colonel Andrei Melnik, was only too willing to help the Abwehr set up an informer network in the Ukraine.[15] His promises proved deceptive, however, and the Abwehr had to content itself with a plan to use the Ukrainians for sabotage operations in the event of war against the Soviet Union.*

Every attempt to infiltrate Russia had failed. The Abwehr could see no loophole into the secret Soviet world. Colonel Ernst Köstring, the German Military Attaché in Moscow, gave up the struggle, saying: "An Arab with a flowing white burnous would be more likely to pass unnoticed in Berlin than would a foreign agent in Russia."[17] The Soviet Union remained a blank space on the Abwehr's situation maps. The problem therefore became more and more the preserve of the RSHA under SS-Gruppenführer Reinhard Heydrich.

The Abwehr's failure provided its power-hungry rivals, the Gestapo and SD [SS Security Service], with an opportunity to score points off the "reactionary" Abwehr. In

---

* Before the Polish campaign Abwehr II did form a regiment of OUN members with the cover name "Mountain Peasants Help" to carry out espionage and sabotage activities in rear of the front.[16]

the mid-1930s they had succeeded in destroying the illegal German communist apparats—why should the Soviet Secret Service be a tougher nut?

In fact no organization in the Third Reich had put such prolonged and strenuous effort into observation of the communist espionage services as had Himmler's and Heydrich's police machine. The Gestapo and SD were indoctrinated with the spirit of the Nazi Party's anti-bolshevist crusade; they had the drive inherent in the highly developed machinery of a police state; so they had explored every possibility of penetrating the Soviet Secret Service. On paper these guardians of the regime had every prospect of outwitting their rivals on the Tirpitzufer, Abwehr headquarters.

The mere layout of the files in Gestapo headquarters shows how meticulous their enemy-surveillance was: Series 20^{01} included all reports from "Soviet representatives"; Series 20^{02} registered "entries and exits of Russian nationals"; 20^{10} dealt with "international communist agents," 20^{12} with "Soviet-Russian spies" and so on.[18] A memorandum by Heydrich's staff (Security Police and SD) gave the duties of the "Soviet-Russian affairs" desk as: "detection and observation of Soviet Russians in the Reich, their residences, lodgings, etc.; detection and observation of the movements of Soviet Russian diplomats worldwide; handling and observation of Soviet Russian ships in German ports; treatment and evaluation of all information from or about the Soviet Union."[19]

Nothing was left to chance; the Gestapo engine of surveillance and intelligence processed, investigated and noted every aspect of Soviet espionage activity. The office responsible was Section IV of the RSHA (Gestapo under Reichskriminaldirektor Heinrich Müller); within this Desk IV A2 under Kriminalrat Horst Kopkow dealt with sabotage and the forging of political papers, Desk IV C1 under Polizeirat Matzke was responsible for "evaluation, card index, surveillance of foreigners," Desk IV E1 under Kriminalkommissar Lindow handled "general counterespionage matters, prosecutions for treasonable activities" and Desk IV E5 under Kriminalrat Walter Kubitzky was "Counter-espionage East," the real opponent, therefore, of the Soviet Secret Service.[20]

The Russian division of Section VI of the RSHA

(Head: SS-Brigadeführer Heinz Jost, succeeded by SS-Oberführer Walter Schellenberg in 1941), the SD's foreign intelligence service, was equally specialized.[21] SS-Sturmbannführer Karl-Otto von Salisch, head of Desk III (East), coordinated the intelligence effort into the Soviet Union of the SD Regions in eastern Germany; SS-Sturmbannführer Rudolf Seidel of VI A3 directed informers located abroad and SS-Sturmbannführer Dr. Gräfe headed the "Eastern" Group (VI C).[22]

So specialized a machine was bound to be superior to the military Abwehr, materially at least. The Gestapo and SD had a number of successful infiltrations into Russia to their credit. The Ausland SD [External SD] had contacts with White Guard officers in Paris under the ex-Civil War General Nikolai Skoblin;[23] during the Tukhachevsky affair Heydrich even managed to get into direct touch with the Soviet Secret Police. Representatives of Yezhov, the head of the GUGB, negotiated with Heydrich's agencies concerning the delivery of and payment for certain incriminating documents forged by the SD proving that the Soviet Marshal had been an accomplice of Western imperialism.[24] (Heydrich never realized that, Stalin having decided on the elimination of Tukhachevsky weeks before, he was doing no more than running errands for Yezhov.)

The SD even succeeded where the Abwehr had failed. On 23 January 1940 Section VI reported to Heydrich that it had acquired "valuable sources of reliable information from Russia" in Estonia and Lithuania; "it might even be possible to penetrate into Russia itself, in particular from Poland; certain emissaries are always traveling into Soviet Russia from there to reconnoiter the situation, general atmosphere, etc."[25] During the Russo-Finnish war in the winter of 1939–40 the SD maintained useful contacts with the Finnish Army; the SD reported that it received "impeccable reports from the Russo-Finnish front, particularly on the quality and strength of the Red Army."[26]

Successful though the Gestapo and SD might appear in some respects, however, Nazi political fantasies frequently led the RSHA sleuths to adopt theories which, for a professional policeman, were pure self-deception. The secret papers of the RSHA show that these guardians of the regime harbored some quite astonishing beliefs about the Soviet Secret Service. Himmler stated quite seriously that the "bolshevist General Staff, the Jewish leadership" of the

Soviet Secret Service was to be found in (of all places) New York. At a closed session of the Prussian State Council, the Reichsführer-SS and Chief of the German Police divulged to the senior dignitaries of Party and State that the headquarters of the Russian Secret Service were located "either in Germany in the extra-territorial enclave of the Russian Embassy or on foreign territory largely in the guise of the communist leadership in . . . Holland and Denmark, or, going still higher up the scale, in the Kremlin . . . and finally at the very top level reaching the Jewish cabal in New York."[27] Looking at the world through those spectacles he had no difficulty in convincing himself that the internal Soviet struggles for power were nothing other than devilish machinations by Jewry.

In a "Strictly Confidential" report issued by the SD Information Office in 1937 the Stalin purge was attributed to the struggle between two power groupings in the Soviet Union: "One can be generally labeled as "western and freemason,' the other as 'eastern and ghetto-Jewish.' "[28] Accordingly Stalin's critic, Marshal Tukhachevsky, belonged to "the Western-Jewish-freemason forces and, although he acted cautiously, this was the direction in which he was tending, like other Trotskyists."[29] Some effort of imagination is required to picture Tukhachevsky and Trotsky as puppets of freemasonry!

Before the start of the Russian campaign, the RSHA did not know even the most elementary details of the Russian espionage organization. In the memoranda of Section IV E1, OMS (the Special Services section of Comintern headquarters) is thought to signify a radio training establishment;[30] the RSHA insisted that the GPU was responsible for the increase in Russian espionage activity, although that organization had been dissolved years before. SS-Oberführer Schellenberg informed his Reichsführer that the GPU was a "Special Espionage Section" in the Peoples Commissariat of the Interior and was the same as the Soviet Secret Service—no mention of Razvedupr.[31]

Widest of the mark were the analyses and reports in which the RSHA's Russian experts sought to explain where the mastermind of Soviet espionage in Germany was to be found. They thought that he was in the Soviet Embassy in Berlin; Vladimir Dekanosov, the Ambassador appointed at the end of 1940, was said to be "a confidant of Stalin," formerly "head of the Intelligence Section of the NKVD," and therefore a sort of super-spy. His arrival in Berlin had "heralded an unwelcome intensification of Russian Secret Service activity in Germany," Schellenberg said.[82]*

All of it was wrong. The RSHA could not be expected to know that, as a Foreign Ministry diplomat in Moscow,[33] Dekanosov had been at daggers drawn with Razvedupr ever since the beginning of 1939 because he had written off their (perfectly correct) reports about German intentions against Russia as pro-British provocations.[34]† The word might have reached them, however, that the mastermind of Soviet espionage was traditionally located in the Soviet Trade Delegation, not in the Embassy.

The omnipotent machine of the Gestapo and SD was therefore no better able to cope with Soviet espionage than the Abwehr. Heydrich, Müller and Schellenberg built up for themselves an entirely unjustified superiority complex *vis-à-vis* the Abwehr, the only result of which was to hamper the battle against Soviet espionage. The struggle between the two agencies even threatened to affect efficiency in the only field in which the Germans could match, if not outstrip, Razvedupr—radio counter-espionage.

Both Germans and Russians had discovered the importance of short-wave radio in espionage work at about the same time. At the end of the 1920s Russia had begun going over to radio for internal diplomatic, secret service and military communications. The Navy had been first in the field for communications between ships on the high seas and the naval staff; it had been followed by the Air Force and by 1927 short-wave radio was accepted in all important spheres in the Soviet Union.[35]

In Germany too radio had been introduced by the Navy. The Abwehr quickly realized that, for secret service work, short-wave radio could produce a technical revolution and they made increasing use of this new weapon. Germany and Russia were the only powers to enter the

---

* Actually, during the early years of the revolution Dekanosov had been one of the leading Cheka men in the Caucasus; early in the 1930s he became Deputy Minister-President of the Georgian Republic and entered the diplomatic service in April 1939. In the Peoples commissariat for External Affairs he was in charge of the Consular, Administrative and Personnel Sections (International Biographical Archive 12/54).

† Dallin's account is somewhat suspect here since he accepts without question or criticism the Gestapo's picture of Dekanosov.

Second World War with radio-directed circuits of agents. Desk Ii (Agents' radio communications and traffic) in the Abwehr commanded a shadowy army of informers equipped with portable transmitters which, in spite of their low power (20–60 watts), could "work over really incredible distances."[36]

In parallel with the Abwehr's increasing use of radio as a weapon, however, went the development by the Germans of a counter to it—signals security. The rapid evolution of radio technology enabled the Abwehr, not only to intercept enemy radio traffic, but also to track down and eliminate enemy agents' transmitters in wartime. The first job was that of the Intercept Service, the second that of Signals Security or radio counter-espionage.

The Intercept Service was the child of Lieutenant-Colonel Buschenhagen who, with a small cipher staff, had formed an "Evaluation Office" in the Friedrichstrasse in 1919; in 1920 he and his staff of twelve were transferred to the Reichswehr Ministry,[37] where they subsequently became Section II (Codes and Intercept Service) of the Abwehr.[38] By 1926 the Section was running intercept stations in six of the major German cities;[39] for defense against Soviet espionage the most important was the permanent station in Königsberg under command of Major von Richthofen which kept radio watch on the entire eastern area.[40]

Abwehr II's intercept service monitored the diplomatic and secret service traffic of foreign powers, while on the lower tactical level the armed forces intercept services dealt with their neighbors' military traffic; the Army maintained Radio Intelligence Regiments to intercept foreign armies' traffic, the Luftwaffe had its Radio Intelligence Service and the Navy the B Service [Beobachtungs—monitoring] to do likewise in the case of foreign air forces and navies.*

Signals security was the responsibility of another section of Canaris' organization, Abwehr desk IIIK under Lieutenant-Commander Schmolinski.[42] The section made good use of the progress in radio-location technique which made it possible to situate unknown transmitters by means of direction-finding.

---

* The intercept service was able to identify all units involved in 35 out of the 52 major maneuvers carried out in Europe between 1931 and 1937.[41]

In this case too it was the Navy which showed the counter-espionage authorities the way. It was important for the Navy to be able to determine the course and position of far-distant ships and this was the genesis of direction-finding; if two land-based stations with direction-finding antennae could take a bearing on a ship's transmitter, the point at which the two beams crossed (the "intersection") was the position of the ship. Radio counter-espionage had been born.

Desk IIIK began, at least on paper, to have some idea of what the future war against enemy radio operators would be like. With portable direction-finding sets, the Abwehr officers thought, it should be possible to pick up transmissions from the enemy sets and so locate them rapidly. This direction-finding equipment did not, of course, exist, but one day, they were sure, the technicians would be found who could construct this tracking equipment.

Many of the more conservative Abwehr officers, however, did not realize how valuable a weapon radio counter-espionage could be to them. Right until the outbreak of war they maintained that the radio spy was a mere figment of the spy-story novelist's imagination. Nothing else can explain the complacency with which the Abwehr allowed control of the emergent signals security service to be wrested from them.

This time it was another part of Himmler's empire which attempted to snatch one of the Abwehr's prerogatives—the Ordnungspolizei [regular police—Orpo] under SS-Obergruppenführer [General] Kurt Daluege. The law of 24 November 1937 on "black transmitters" had given the Orpo some claim to participate in radio counter-espionage;[43] these "black transmitters" were of no interest to the military, since they were merely sets working without an official license and generally owned by radio amateurs. But Daluege's people now set up a pseudo-military organization and began to compete with Canaris' office in radio counter-espionage: an "Intelligence Communications Agency" appeared in Orpo headquarters under Colonel of Police and SS-Oberführer Robert Schlake;[44] it consisted of no fewer than 2,000 men and had seven static direction-finding stations and a number of short-range sets.[45]

Heydrich, the head of the RSHA, however, was not prepared to tolerate this access of power on the part of

Daluege who was his bitterest rival in the SS. He was determined to have his own radio surveillance organization. In September 1939, therefore, he ordered the formation of a monitoring service to keep under observation something which hitherto only the Abwehr had watched, "the operational transmitters of enemy intelligence services."[46] Formation of a Security Police and SD radio training school gave notice that Heydrich was laying claim to radio counter-espionage.[47]

The rivalry between the senior SS leaders carried on down into the lower levels of the police machine. Heydrich had initially laid down that, within the RSHA, Section III (the Inland SD) should be in charge of the radio network,[48] but Müller, the head of the Gestapo, and Schellenberg, head of the Ausland SD, soon began to dispute Section III's title. Each was doing his own empire-building; Müller was continually trying to place Schulz, his own expert, in charge of the RSHA network, whereas Schellenberg maintained that radio counter-espionage was one of his responsibilities.[49]

Gradually, however, the military perceived that they were in process of losing a battle in the internecine struggle between the German power groups. On the outbreak of war the place of the "black transmitters" was taken by enemy clandestine radio operators, but the Orpo maintained that it was their prerogative to deal with them. This put the soldiers on the alert.

The Wehrmacht was able to halt the advance of the SS radio sleuths in time. The inefficiency of the radio-location sets used by the Orpo provided OKW with a pretext to demand sole responsibility for radio counter-espionage.[50] In late summer 1940 Hitler agreed and gradually there began to take shape a new clandestine force which was ultimately to bring Rote Kapelle to its doom.[51]

An operational staff was formed in OKW consisting of radio experts from the Wehrmacht, mostly ex-amateurs; at the same time officers and men who were radio enthusiasts were seconded from the monitoring sections of the three services and formed into Radio Monitoring Companies.[52] As units they remained with their arm of the service; initially (until early 1942) the army maintained two monitoring companies in addition to a static direction-finding station at Köge in Denmark; the Luftwaffe formed

one monitoring company and a flight of nine Fieseler-
Storch aircraft equipped with direction-finding gear; the
Navy merely seconded a few specialists to the monitoring
service.[53] On 10 September 1940 the Bavarian Lieutenant-
Colonel Hans Kopp, an experienced signals technician
with an engineering degree, assumed command of the new
force.[54]

Within a very short period what officially became known
as the radio Abwehr or Signals Security became an established service. The title was to some extent misleading
since, although the personnel were military, they were not
subordinate to the Abwehr.[55] Here was another example
of the intrigue and struggle for authority characteristic
of the Nazi Führer state: the Abwehr was not allowed
responsibility for radio counter-espionage, although without it any effective action against the Soviet spies was in-
conceivable.

Admiral Canaris, the head of the Abwehr, was a critic
of the regime and his opponents in the Security and
Regular Police took care to insure that no increase of
authority came his way. In fact he was forced to give up
his desk IIIK to Kopp, the head of Signals Security,
though he was allowed to retain Desk Ii which dealt with
the Abwehr's own clandestine transmitters and radio operators.[56] The retention of Ii showed how specious was
the reason given for the removal of Desk IIIK—that
Canaris' office was unable to supply the Monitoring Companies with adequate sets and spare parts.[57]

This same reason was held to justify subordination of
Signals Security to a senior military authority which had
already robbed Canaris' office of many of its responsibilities. In 1937 Canaris had had to make over his entire
coding and intercept service to a new division in Wehrmacht central headquarters, "Wehrmacht Intelligence
Communications" [Wehrmachtnachrichtenverbindungen—
WNV]; from 1940 this formed a separate office within the
OKW Operations Staff.*

Spheres of authority within the higher levels of the

---

* The "Division for Wehrmacht Intelligence Communications" was
formed within the Wehrmacht Office of the Reich War Ministry in
October 1937. When the Wehrmacht Office turned into OKW in
1938, the Division formed part of the operational branch. In spring
1940 the Operations Branch became the OKW Operations Staff of
which WNV formed a division.[58]

Wehrmacht were in fact extremely complex as far as WNV was concerned. Six days before the outbreak of war OKW had appointed General Erich Fellgiebel, an anti-Nazi, as head of WNV.[59] He was to supervise communications between the individual services and be responsible for those between OKW and the various theaters of war.[60] But Fellgiebel, who was an army officer, was an impotent potentate; he had no staff of his own, "nothing but a sonorous title, since I had no authority over the Luftwaffe or the Navy."[61] He could in fact have done nothing, had he not, in addition to being head of WNV, also been Army Chief Signal Officer.[62] For his secondary job in WNV Fellgiebel made use of his deputy, Lieutenant-General Fritz Thiele; under Fellgiebel's instructions he was the effective head of WNV.[63] In effect Thiele's division was the OKW Operations Staff's signals branch;[64] it was in a strong position vis-à-vis the three services since, from a technical signals point of view, it possessed a virtual monopoly within the Wehrmacht, as the titles of its four sections showed: the "Telecommunications Section" maintained contact with the Post Office and represented the wishes of the military on behalf of all three services;[65] the "Radio Section" [Funkabteilung—Fu] was in charge of the Wehrmacht's main radio stations and allotted frequencies to the three services;[66] the "Codes and Ciphers Section" [Chiffrierwesen—Chi], the old Abwehr II in Canaris' office, deciphered foreign governments' secret radio traffic;[67] the Section "General Authority for Technical Signals Resources" [Generalbevollmächtigter für technische Nachrichtenmittel—GBN] controlled the maintenance, distribution and replacement of all radio equipment.[68]

Only through Thiele's powerful organization could Fellgiebel do his three jobs: within the army he was in charge of the Army Signals Service, in OKW he was head of the Wehrmacht's communications and in addition, as "General Authority for Technical Signals Resources," he had to insure that all German radio communications functioned smoothly.[69]

OKW now introduced the newly formed signals security service into this jungle of military authorities. The old Desk IIIK of the Abwehr and Lieutenant-Colonel Kopp's monitoring force were merged into Thiele's office, where they formed Group III of the Radio Section or, in the Third Reich's official jargon, an agency known as OKW/

WNV/Fu III.[70] The radio counter-espionage officers installed themselves in the WNV office on the Matthäikirchplatz, Berlin.[71].

The deal between OKW and the SS/Police was consecrated by a Führer order. In June 1941 Hitler laid down that the Wehrmacht was the competent authority in all questions of radio monitoring.[72] The order had barely been signed when the first messages from the Soviet spies issued their challenge both to Signals Security and to the police.

However sharp the dissensions between the German rivals for power, however great the mutual distrust between the Nazi hotheads in Heydrich's empire and the conservative anti-Nazis on Canaris' staff, the assault of the Soviet spies and their radio operators was equally wounding to both the warring organizations. Shoulder to shoulder they set out to pursue their invisible enemy, with the military initially in the lead.

At first the hunters saw little prospect of tracking down their quarry. Fu III's direction-finding sets were inadequate. The Luftwaffe did indeed possess more powerful tracking sets in East Prussia, Silesia, Hungary and Rumania,[73] but they were denied to Signals Security so long as Fellgiebel and Thiele refused to grant Göring his dearest wish—to transfer the codes and ciphers section, "Chi," to Göring's telephone-tapping organization.[74] Initially Signals Security had to do without the Luftwaffe's long-range direction-finders.[75]

At the outset, therefore, Fu III had only short-range direction-finders and these could obviously only work once the locality from which the enemy set was transmitting had been established. The short-range sets had a further serious disadvantage: they were too large to approach a clandestine set unnoticed. The Wehrmacht had developed a so-called mobile direction-finder, but it could be carried only on a truck. The circular aerial, 3 ft. in diameter, had to be mounted on the roof of the truck and so was only too visible to any watcher whom the operator might post on the street during his time on the air.[76]

But the German counter-espionage had nothing else with which to discover the Soviet spies' invisible network. The intercepted messages were in so complicated a code that the WNV's decoding experts gave up the struggle.[77] Communications Security could only penetrate the spyring if they could detect that which constituted both the strength and weakness of modern espionage—the actual transmitter itself.

Though short-wave radio had undoubtedly made the transmission of information rapid and almost undetectable, this new form of espionage nevertheless had a chink in its armor which could lead to its own detection. As soon as the operator had written down his messages and had to start transmitting, he was fair game for the monitoring detachments of the enemy counter-espionage. His only chance of survival was to transmit from some hideout and for so short a time that his transmission would be at an end before his pursuers arrived on the scene.

The operators therefore took minute precautions to guard themselves against the enemy detection squads. The sets were housed in thickly populated quarters of towns and impenetrable built-up alleyways; they had to change their location frequently and vary their schedules; address groups of messages were continually being changed and new frequencies used. Watchers were posted to give warning of the enemy's approach. The operator usually worked in the top floor of a house, so that in emergency he could escape across the roofs at the last moment.

Theoretically location of a transmitter was easy. When the unknown operator came on the air, two monitoring detachments, each equipped with direction-finding gear, set off to determine the direction of the radio-waves. The two detachments posted themselves at two points some distance from each other and each took a bearing on the transmitter through their sets' directional aerials. The resulting data were reported to the detachment's commander who, with a street plan in front of him, transferred them to two transparent set-squares to each of which was attached a silken thread; placing the squares on the known position of each monitoring detachment and stretching the threads across the town plan along the bearings reported, the point where they crossed was the position of the transmitter; a glance at the map was enough to show the part of the town, or even the street, in which the transmitter was working.

This was the theory, but in practice there were almost insuperable obstacles to detection of an agent's set. The silk threads could only indicate its approximate location; when the monitoring detachments reached the part of the town concerned, they were faced with a bewildering conglomeration of houses, in one of which somewhere must be a radio set. They therefore had to take further bearings —and here the difficulties began. The approach of the truck with its aerials on the roof alerted the enemy operator's outposts and, before the detachment could get its direction-finder into position, the set had long since gone dead.

This difficulty defeated Signal Security's first attempts to track down the communist agents. Three months after the first signals from PTX had been heard,[78] Fu III thought it had an opportunity to carry out a coup against the unknown transmitter. The inadequate direction-finders in Cranz and Breslau were still searching for the location of the first set they had detected—that of Kent with the call-sign PTX; the monitoring experts were still puzzling whether it was working in North Germany, Belgium, Holland or France.[79] Then came a report to the Matthäikirchplatz that three transmitters had been located for sure—and they were in Berlin, barely two miles from counter-espionage headquarters.[80]

That honest signals officer Kopp could not believe that enemy agents were sitting and using their radios in the very center of the Greater German Reich. He checked and cross-checked the data, but it was all correct—three transmitters were working in Berlin and they were continually changing their call-signs, frequencies and schedules.

Kopp ordered to Berlin the direction-finding platoon of a Luftwaffe radio monitoring company, since Göring's men still possessed the best equipment.[81] Cautiously these sleuths stalked their way toward their enemy; as camouflage they wore Post Office mechanics' uniforms; in their street shelters, under which their equipment was hidden, they looked like Post Office cable mechanics carrying out repairs.[82] They worked under difficult conditions. One of them, the technician Leo Liske, recalls that the bearings were taken "mostly from the tunnels of the Underground and in some cases from anti-aircraft positions on the roofs. The Underground tunnels were not ideal places for us, but it worked nevertheless and indeed better than we expected."[83]

Street by street two detachments, each equipped with a direction-finder and a receiver, worked their way toward the clandestine transmitter. But their unknown opponent was on the air for such short periods that they frequently had not time to take their bearings. In addition, for days at a time, transmissions would cease altogether and sometimes they would come from an entirely new direction.

Nevertheless, by 21 October 1941 the detection squads had reached their target[84] and had discovered the approximate location of the transmitters; one set was near the Bayrische Platz, a second in north Berlin near the Invalidenpark and a third on the Moritzplatz in the southeastern part of the city.[85] Fu III ordered short-range direction-finding to start; in a few days, they thought, they were bound to know the actual houses from which the sets were being used.

A small but decisive error, however, now checkmated Kopp's radio detectives: the vehicles transporting the bogus Post Office workers' direction-finding gear did not carry Post Office markings and in fact their number-plates bore the letters WL (Wehrmacht/Luftwaffe).[86] While out for a walk Hans Coppi, the communist radio operator, noticed the WL plates, became suspicious and immediately alerted his chief, Schulze-Boysen.[87] On 22 October the Berlin transmitters relapsed into an abrupt silence.[88]

Following this failure in Berlin, Fu III was compelled to pay increased attention to the hitherto neglected trail of the set with the call-sign PTX which was working in the West. Further bearings had been taken and it was now established that the set was operating in Belgium; the experts' guess was the coastal area around Bruges.[89] Time was pressing, however, for it was becoming ever clearer that PTX was using schedules and frequencies similar to those of the Berlin sets and possibly might even be the master set of the four.

The radio sleuths turned for assistance to their old friends of the Abwehr. Abwehr Group IIIF, the counterespionage specialists under Colonel Rohleder, ought, they thought, to know where in Belgium PTX was to be found. Since the outbreak of war Section III of the Abwehr had collected the largest staff in the German Secret Services; there and in its outstations were the best Abwehr officers, covering the whole of German-occupied Europe with an anti-spy network.[90] They worked closely with Section IIIN (censorship) and hardly a single suspicious movement throughout occupied territory escaped their notice; at this point Rohleder's office was more influential even than the Gestapo and SD.[91]

Group IIIF's experts joined in the hunt for PTX. Over the "Adolf circuit," the direct scrambled telephone net linking the OKW Abwehr office in Berlin with all its agencies both in the Reich and occupied territory,[92] Rohleder alerted his IIIF officer in Ghent.

At first, however, "our man" in Ghent had no idea where to look in neighboring Bruges. He was Harry Piepe, Captain on the reserve, born in Uelzen in 1893, a cavalry lieutenant during the First World War and later commander of an anti-tank company during the French campaign; he had only been seconded to the Abwehr at the end of 1940.[93] He was a chairborne officer, at home with files and administrative arrangements; he came from the legal profession, the branch which dealt with official and assessor courts; he had risen to the rank of Senior State Attorney and was about to become head of the administrative branch of the legal profession in Harburg[94] when called up.

As an experienced interrogator he had been posted to counter-espionage and because of his knowledge of French had been appointed to the Abwehr office in Ghent.[95] For a long time he did not feel at home in the world of espionage and counter-espionage; as an ex-lawyer he was temperamentally inclined to quick action, but counter-espionage is a laborious, frequently frustrating, game of patience, the object of which is not the arrest of some individual, as in crime detection, but the unearthing of whole groups of evil-doers.

In addition Piepe was devoid of the necessary knowledge of the methods adopted by communist agents. Innocently he despatched his agents into the Bruges taverns to look for Soviet agents, searching where no knowledgeable person would have looked—among the Belgian communists.[96] Piepe recalls: "Our agents reported that all was quiet; the communists were frightened and passive."[97] Proudly he reported to Berlin that there were no spies in the Bruges area. But Signals Security was not satisfied with his report.[98] Fu III's direction-finders had now worked out a new location for PTX—Ghent. Piepe searched in Ghent.[99]

When the reluctant detective once more sent a negative report to Berlin, Rohleder became angry. The Colonel told Piepe kindly to leave his desk and place himself at the head of the hunt.[100] Piepe woke up and set off on the trail of the radio spies with all the pertinacity of the trained investigator.

The search in Ghent still yielded nothing, but Berlin now indicated Brussels as the probable location of PTX.[101] The short-wave monitoring station "West" was so sure of its ground[102] that Fu III despatched to Brussels Captain (Dr.) Hubertus Freyer, commanding the radio company of OKW headquarters, with a section of experienced operators and new direction-finding equipment.[103]

Piepe and Freyer started their joint search at the end of November.[104] Piepe had done some good preliminary work. He had moved into an apartment in the Boulevard Brand Witlock in Brussels, posing as a businessman.[105] He had flown over the city many times in a Fieseler-Storch equipped with direction-finding gear and had listened to PTX transmitting.[106] He was convinced that the set was located in the quarter of Brussels known as Etterbeek.[107] Prospects for action were favorable. The enemy operator had clearly been ordered to work without regard to his own security, for he transmitted for five hours at a stretch and always at the same time, midnight to 5:00 a.m. In addition the German occupation authorities in Brussels had decreed a night curfew, so the operator could not protect himself by posting someone to keep watch.[108]

Better still, Freyer's men brought with them a new short-range direction-finder. It was housed in an unobtrusive case into which the aerial was built; from the case a thin connecting wire led to the operator's ear.[109] So there was no engine noise, no truck with a telltale aerial on its roof to give warning of the approach of the radio detectives; the enemy was unlikely to guess that the innocent stroller with a miniature microphone in his ear was in fact a member of the German security forces.

Freyer's people set to work. Two weeks sufficed to locate PTX with some accuracy.[110] Freyer had set up a reception center in the courtyard of the Leopold barracks; there his specialists stuck a pin into the Brussels town plan, and it marked the Rue des Atrébates.[111] At the point marked Piepe's scouts reported, were three houses numbered 99, 101 and 103. No. 103 was empty; a Flemish family lived in No. 99; No. 101 was occupied by South Americans who worked for the German authorities.[112]

In which of the three houses might the transmitter be

The empty house seemed suspicious to Piepe, but he was taking no risks. He installed himself in a villa occupied by members of the Todt Organization which backed on to the three houses and had further bearings taken from there.[113] Freyer's experts were now in no doubt: the set was in No. 101, the house of the alleged South Americans.

Zero hour was the night 13/14 December 1941.* Piepe cordoned off the three houses with twenty-five men of a garrison battalion and ten men from the Secret Field Police, all with socks over their boots. Torches, axes and even fire hoses were held in readiness. Piepe gave the signal to attack and his men rushed the three houses, Piepe at their head. He himself with two Security Police made for the empty house,[115] but then he heard a soldier shout from No. 101: "Here! Here they are!"

Then came a fusillade of shots in the night. By the light of his torch Piepe saw the police chasing a man trying to escape. Meanwhile he had reached No. 101, brushed past a barking dog and cannoned into a dark-haired woman in a dressing gown. Piepe and his men rushed up the stairs and on the first floor found a room in which the set had been working only a few minutes before. The set itself was on a table and beside it lay papers with endless columns of figures. The operator's chair, on which the fugitive had obviously been sitting, was empty.[116]

Piepe hurried on. He reached the second floor. There he found another woman, lying in bed weeping. Before he could deal with her, however, came shouts from below: "We've got him! We've got him!" Piepe stumbled down the stairs again. Soldiers and policemen were holding a man who stared calmly at Piepe. It was the radio operator.

The man refused to give any information apart from his personal details: name—Carlos Alamo, Uruguayan citizen, born in Montevideo. Only later did Piepe learn that he was Michail Makarov, the Russian radio operator. The woman in the dressing gown, who was the group's cipher-

---

* There is some doubt about the date of this action in Brussels and official evidence is no longer available. The majority of authors (Dallin and Flicke for instance) give the night 13/14 December 1941; Perrault, on the other hand, basing himself on verbal information from Piepe, mentions the previous night. However, Piepe himself, in his accounts in *Mittag* and the *Harburger Anzeiger und Nachrichten*, states that action took place on the night 13/14 December.[114]

ine, called herself Anna Verlinden, concealing the fact that she was really Sophie Posnanska. The visitor too, who knocked on the door an hour or so later and was immediately arrested, gave his name as Albert Desmet; it was Anton Danilov. The only one to give her real name was the woman in bed—Rita Arnould, housekeeper and courier for the Brussels spy-ring.[117]

Rita apparently had confidence in Piepe who says that she was "very ready to talk";[118] she gave away what the others had concealed. "Have a good look downstairs," she whispered to Piepe. "What for?" Piepe asked. Rita Arnould's reply was cryptic: "You'll find it all right." Piepe signaled to his men and instituted a search of the room in which he had met Sophie Posnanska. The police tapped round the walls and soon discovered a secret door leading to a dark room; it was a complete forger's workshop containing passports, official forms, invisible inks and official stamps. Among the papers were passport photographs of two men unknown to Piepe.[119]

Rita Arnould enlightened her fellow countrymen: one photograph was of a man whom her associates had always called the "Grand Chef," the other of his deputy, the "Petit Chef"; the latter had been a frequent visitor to the Rue des Atrébates and had given them their orders.[120] Neither name meant anything to Piepe. Had he been quicker on the uptake, he might have captured the leader of the entire organization.

Hardly had the Germans left the house, leaving two Field Security Police behind, than there came another knock on the door. The police found themselves facing a ragged individual with a basketful of rabbits; he always sold his animals to the lady of the house, he told the two Germans. The Germans shooed him away,*[121] little suspecting that they had been talking to Leopold Trepper, head of Soviet espionage in Western Europe. Piepe admits today: "Well now, we were still amateurs; we still had to learn our trade."[122]

Gradually, however, even Harry Piepe grasped the fact that he had made a major breakthrough into the Russian espionage organization in Western Europe. He could now

---

* An ex-Gestapo official, writing under the name of John Nemo (*Das Rote Netz*, p. 4), gives another version. According to him Trepper appeared as a traveler and inquired of two policemen after a family living next door.

hope that one day he would be able to finish off the "Grand Chef" and his widespread organization. The papers discovered in the Rue des Atrébates and Rita Arnould's statements opened up new avenues which must somehow lead to the center of the enemy's web.

On the afternoon of 14 December 1941 Piepe reported to Lieutenant-Colonel Dischler, head of the Abwehr office in Brussels, that he had successfully completed the operation against PTX.* Dischler ordered him to report forthwith to Berlin, since a major operation against the Soviet spies would have to be initiated by the Berlin headquarters. But what should they call the "orchestra" (Abwehr jargon for an enemy secret service radio network)? Someone had the idea of "Rote Kapelle" [Red Orchestra].† A name had been found for the greatest espionage enterprise of the Second World War.

Even before Piepe had left for Berlin, however, the "Grand Chef" had begun to re-form his organization. He realized only too well that it had suffered an almost mortal blow. Rote Kapelle's master set was now no longer in operation and, with the simultaneous silencing of the Berlin sets, Moscow was to all intents and purposes cut off from its sources of information in the West—and all this at a moment when the Red Army General Staff had more urgent need than ever of the reports from its spies in the enemy camp. On 5 and 6 December 1941 the troops of the Soviet Western Front, the left wing of the Kalinin Front and the right wing of the Southwestern Front, had initiated the first Russian counter-offensive of the Russo-German war.[123]

Moscow now reaped a bitter harvest for the failure to provide its French circuit with radio sets in good time.

* Piepe states that the head of the Abwehr office in Brussels was Colonel von Servaes. Captain André Moyen, formerly of the Belgian Secret Service, however, who checked the German Abwehr documents after the end of the war, stated on 13 June 1968 that Servaes only served in Brussels from 1942; his predecessor was Lieutenant-Colonel Dischler.

† Piepe maintains that he coined the title "Rote Kapelle" in conversation with the head of the Abwehr office in Brussels. I have not accepted this story; as far as people and dates are concerned, Piepe's memory has proved highly unreliable (hardly surprising in view of the lapse of time). The Belgian André Moyen, who interrogated the Abwehr officers in 1945, states that Piepe never said a word to claim authorship of the title "Rote Kapelle." The probability is that it was a codename originating in the Abwehr office in Brussels.

With the loss of Kent's set in Brussels, Trepper was deprived of all radio communication with Moscow. Without the Director's authorization, however, he could not move a muscle to guard against future attempts at penetration; he could not appoint a new organizer for Brussels, he could not activate one of the other radio sets concealed in Belgium, he could not even ask the local communist party to pass on his messages to Moscow.[124]

The "Grand Chef" could do nothing other than await a signal from Moscow and meanwhile move the imperiled agents of his Belgian circuit into safe areas. He summoned Kent and his girlfriend Margarete Barcza to Paris and at the end of December allowed them to go to ground in unoccupied France; Kent was to form a new circuit in Marseilles.[125] He despatched Isidor Springer, the diamond merchant and Rita Arnould's lover, to Lyon on a similar mission.[126]

The "Grand Chef" had to wait more than two months for his message from the Director.[127] By mid-February 1942, despite stubborn German resistance, Soviet forces on the Eastern Front had advanced 250 miles[128] and recovered 50 Russian towns.[129] But they had to operate without Rote Kapelle's assistance. The General Staff in Moscow knew neither the number nor designations of the fresh divisions thrown in by the Germans; it did not know the plans for the forthcoming German spring offensive; it knew nothing of the disagreements between Hitler and his generals about the strategic objectives of the Russian campaign.

It took Trepper until February to establish contact with the French Communist Party.[130] He met an agent of the Party who called himself "Michel" and confided to him his difficulties; though the Party set was kept strictly separate from the espionage circuit, he asked Michel to use it to transmit to Moscow the messages which had piled up and to place a set at his disposal.[131] The communist comrades permitted the "Grand Chef" to communicate with Moscow and so at last Trepper could once more receive orders from Colonel-General Peresypkin. They were: Yefremov, who was still in Brussels, was to take over the Belgian circuit with Johann Wenzel as his radio operator;[132] the French Communist Party was authorized to use its transmitters for a limited number of Trepper's messages (some 300 cipher groups per week),[133] pending being able to place a set at the "Grand Chef's" sole disposal.

The French Communist Party was in fact so short of sets that Ferdinand Pauriol, its radio expert, had to rig up a set himself for Trepper's organization.[134] It proved to be too weak to work to Moscow. Its wattage was only just sufficient to reach the Soviet Embassy in London, whence messages were passed to Moscow.[135] The possession of even Pauriol's set, however, made Trepper happy; from the end of February Rote Kapelle once more began to transmit information to Moscow through Trepper's own operators, the Polish husband-and-wife combination Hersch and Myra Sokol.[136]

Trepper's German pursuers, however, had no conception of their unseen opponent's difficulties. They thought they were confronted with a super-organization of master-spies working with smooth uncanny precision; to deal with this would require the combined efforts of the entire police and Abwehr machines. Captain Piepe had gone to Berlin in mid-December 1941 to tell his most exalted masters about Rote Kapelle.[137] His report set Berlin by the ears: Abwehr, Signals Security, Police and Gestapo all set forth on the hunt for the "Grand Chef's" organization.

The RSHA was well aware that the sinister word "Gestapo" made Abwehr officers feel uneasy and so initially it kept somewhat in the background. To assist Piepe, the solid German citizen fighting for his country, Gestapo Müller selected a policeman of the old school, a man well versed in the art of helping conservative soldiers to overlook the more murderous manifestations of the Nazi dictatorship.

Kriminalkommissar and SS-Hauptsturmführer Karl Giering, born in 1900, son of a magistrate in Pechlüge near Schwerin, was a circumspect Mecklenburger, skilled at adapting himself to military ideas and ways. He could even lay claim to a modest military career, though it had carried him no higher than NCO: he had enlisted in 1918, had joined the Lüttwitz Free Corps in 1919 and in 1920 had transferred to the Reichswehr Ministry, from which he resigned three years later for health reasons (he suffered from a tumor). He spent two years as a watchman with the electric light bulb firm "Osram" and, when his health improved, started a new career in 1925 with the Berlin Criminal Police; he had already moved over to the

Political Police during the Weimar days and was taken on by the Gestapo in 1933. For a police official he had joined the Nazi Party astonishingly late—not until 1940.[138] This did not prevent him being one of the sternest guardians of the regime in the Gestapo, however. He played an active part in investigating the attempt on Hitler's life in the Munich Bürgerbräu in November 1939, earning the good will of his Führer thereby; in the Prinz-Albrecht-Strasse he had long been regarded as one of the most astute interrogators of Desk IV A 2 (Counter-Sabotage).[139]

Giering, the old-style policeman, seemed to his Gestapo masters to be the right man to take up the trail of Rote Kapelle alongside Captain Piepe. He comported himself discreetly—Piepe still calls him a "nice chap"[140]—thereby making it easier for himself to take refuge in the comforting tale that nothing was more abhorrent to Abwehr officers than working with the Gestapo.* (Perrault accepts this story implicitly, saying that Piepe was just as horrified by such insinuations "as any other gentleman of the Abwehr would have been.")[141]

In fact cooperation between Abwehr and Gestapo was standard practice in the Third Reich, particularly where communist espionage was concerned, a subject unlikely to lead to differences of opinion between the two rivals. Details were laid down in an Abwehr/Gestapo agreement of 21 December 1936, known as the "Ten Commandments": cases of espionage and treason were the Abwehr's business so long as "the interests of the Secret Intelligence Service and of counter-espionage" were affected; the Gestapo might only initiate investigations if "in the judgment of the Wehrmacht Abwehr office, neither Military Intelligence nor counter-espionage has any further interest in the case." When the Gestapo took over a case, the Abwehr could participate in interrogations, could itself interrogate Gestapo prisoners or apply for Gestapo interrogation files. In the reverse direction similar provisions applied.[142]

It was therefore perfectly normal and by no means the "astonishing decision" which Perrault thinks it,[143] that the Gestapo should become involved in Harry Piepe's investigations. Piepe and Giering became inseparable twins. The Captain and the policeman in concert followed up every

* In his introduction (dated 30 September 1967) to his series of articles on Rote Kapelle in the *Harburger Anzeiger und Nachrichten* Piepe said that he had "never worked with the Gestapo."

clue linking the nest of agents discovered in the Rue des Atrébates with other Soviet spy circuits in Western and Central Europe.

Rita Arnould gave away a great deal—Kent's addresses in Brussels (though of course he had now vanished), details of links with the Brussels Bourse, information about Abraham Raichman, the forger whose products Piepe had discovered in the spies' house, and news of Makarov's mistress, Suzanne Schmitz.[144] The remainder of those arrested in the Rue des Atrébates were incarcerated in the German military prison at Saint Gilles;[145] they refused to say anything, Makarov and Danilov in particular;[146] Sophie Posnanska preferred to kill herself rather than betray her comrades; later, in autumn 1942, she did in fact commit suicide.*

Giering attempted to break the conspiracy of silence. With considerable acumen he selected the weakest of the Rote Kapelle prisoners, the radio operator Makarov, who was still calling himself Carlos Adamo. Giering took the Russian to Berlin, installed him in his private apartment (telephone number 93 78 18),[148] and began to interrogate him in friendly conversation. Over coffee and cakes the Russian opened up and divulged many clues.[149] When he returned to Saint Gilles he had discarded his pseudonym and was once more calling himself Makarov.[150]

Step by step, therefore, Giering and Piepe pried open the "Grand Chef's" circuit. Marakov's mistress, Suzanne Schmitz, was arrested and quickly released again;[151] Goddemer and Vrankx, two of the agents, were interrogated;[152] Raichman, the forger, was placed under surveillance and induced through cut-outs to arrange meetings with members of Rote Kapelle still unknown.[153] Gradually the Germans gained a picture of the continental scale of the organization.

At the same time, however, Piepe and Giering realized that their enemy's Belgian circuit had been placed in cold

---

* Perrault and Dallin both state that Sophie Posnanska committed suicide shortly after her arrest, but this is probably incorrect. According to the telegram of 3 September 1942 (already referred to) from the Gestapo office in Düsseldorf to Kopkow, she was still alive at that date. The telegram says that "according to information from the office of the Sipo and SD representative in Brussels, sentence and execution" were to "take place soonest." From this it may be inferred that Sophie Posnanska committed suicide shortly before her trial.[147]

storage and that the "Grand Chef" was trying to carry on
from Paris. Early in 1942 Giering went to Paris,[154] where
the Gestapo had laid hands on the most comprehensive
secret police records in western occupied territory, the
personal files of the Paris "Sûreté Nationale" and the files
of other French police authorities, all captured in 1940.*
The Gestapo office responsible for counter-espionage was
Desk IV A under Kriminalkommissar Heinrich Reiser,
housed in the old Sûreté building in the Rue de Saussaies;[156] unfortunately for Giering it was very short-staffed
(six officials and a few secretaries only),[157] otherwise he
would undoubtedly have stumbled on the trail of Leopold
Trepper in the files dealing with the Phantomas case in
1932.

Giering did not institute a search in the Sûreté files. He
took counsel of his fellow-members of the RSHA working
in Paris, primarily Reiser and his superior, Kriminalrat
Beumelburg.[158] He asked them to look for any clue, however insignificant, to the existence of Soviet espionage and
radio groups. Reiser was ordered, in the event of any
suspicious clues coming to light, to telephone at once to
the Security Police office at 453 Avenue Louise, Brussels,
where Giering had installed himself.[159]

While informers lay in wait and the Wehrmacht and
police direction-finding squads searched for new clandestine sets, the counter-espionage decoders were attempting
to unravel the messages captured from the red spies. The
papers seized in the Rue des Atrébates in Brussels gave
them a tiny glimpse into that bizarre world which no
German cryptographer had yet entered—the world of
Soviet cryptography.

The Russians had always been regarded as unexampled
experts in the art of codes and ciphers. Ever since the
Soviet Union had been born its Secret Service had had the
reputation of possessing the most complex coding system.
Throughout the 1930s no one had been able to unravel
the Soviet codes.[160] Not a single great power had been able
to read the Soviet diplomatic traffic and even the apparently innocent figure-groups used by the Soviet Trade Dele-
gations abroad had proved unbreakable. In 1930 Hamilton
Fish, the American congressman and chairman of a com-

---

* The files were transferred to Berlin and incorporated into the
RSHA central card index early in 1942.[155]

mittee investigating communist activities, had managed to lay hands on 3,000 coded telegrams from the Soviet Trading Corporation "Amtorg" in New York. He handed them over to the US Navy's code and signal section which, after vain efforts to decipher them, reported: "The cipher used by the Amtorg is the most complicated and possesses the greatest secrecy within their [the Navy crpytanalysts] knowledge." Fish then called in the War Department, but eventually he gave up: "Not one expert—and they had had them from six months to a year—succeeded in decoding a single word of those cablegrams."[161]

The Japanese pursuers of Richard Sorge, the Soviet master-spy, met with no greater success. Since 1938 four Japanese agencies had been intercepting Sorge's radio traffic from the Tokyo area. Each year they noted the number of groups sent by the spy—in 1939 23,139 figure-groups, in 1940 29,179; but no Japanese could translate the mysterious figures.[162] The secret was eventually betrayed by one of Sorge's agents;[163] in no other way could Sorge's code be broken.

The Russian system of codes, though simple, was extremely puzzling. It originated from the numerical scheme adopted by the Bolshevists' social-revolutionary predecessors, the Nihilists. While in the Czarist prisons, they had worked out a code enabling them to talk to each other through the prison walls. They laid out a chessboard, each square of which represented an individual letter; the upper horizontal column and the left-hand vertical column were filled with figures; letters were transmitted by the number of taps on the wall corresponding to the figures given by the system.[164] The arrangement of letters and figures, known as the chessboard cipher, looked like this:

	1	2	3	4	5
1	a	b	c	d	e
2	f	g	h	ij	k
3	l	m	n	o	p
4	q	r	s	t	u
5	v	w	x	y	z

Each letter was represented by the figure from the vertical column followed by that from the horizontal, in other words w = 52, a = 11, r = 42 and so on.[165] If, for instance, the prisoners wished to signal "Warning," they would tap

on the wall: 52 11 42 33 24 33 22. When the warders
rumbled the system, the prisoners introduced a refinement;
they began to encode their messages by means of a previously agreed key word.

The message was first translated into the chessboard
figures and the key word equally turned into figures; finally
the two sets of figures—those of the message and those of
the key word—were added together. If, for instance, the
word "warning" was to be encoded using the key word
"Paris," the result was as follows:

Text in clear:	w	a	r	n	i	n	g
Chessboard figures:	52	11	42	33	24	33	22
Key word:	35	11	42	24	43	35	11
Encoded text:	87	22	84	57	67	68	33

The Soviets took over the Nihilists' chessboard system
and continually introduced more and more complicated
combinations. They used fresh sequences of figures in the
top row of the chessboard, for instance; in the second row
they would place the key word and fill the remaining
squares with the letters of the alphabet not included in
the key word. Then they introduced letters represented by
a singleton figure, so that their opponents could not tell
whether they were dealing in singleton- or two-figure
letters. In a 1937 code, for instance, the word "España"
(Spain)[166] was represented by: 8281 15 125—to all intents and purposes indecipherable; the initiated, however,
knew that this should be written: 8 28 11 5 12 5. Subsequently the Soviets started to arrange their texts in five-
figure groups.

Yet even this system did not seem secure enough. In any
numerical code there are rules governing the frequency
with which certain groups appear and, based on the regular-
ity with which certain letters occur, the expert can unravel
the code's structure. Tables are available showing the letters most frequently used; in German, for instance, the
commonest letter is "e" with 18.7%, followed by "n" with
11.3% and "i" with 7.9%.[167]

Moscow accordingly began to re-encode its coded messages, usually using words from books not easily obtain-
able such as novels or scripts of plays. Otto Pünter, the
Soviet ex-agent, explained how the system worked:[168]
Suppose that he had to report to Moscow that the SS Leib-

standarte Adolf Hitler had arrived in Warsaw, to encode his message he used the travelogue *From Pole to Pole* by the Swedish explorer Sven Hedin; he wrote down a sentence from page 12: "Documentary films are withheld but will shortly be released again." Since he only required ten letters for his key word, he used part of the first word—"Dokumentar" (in German). Pünter wrote down the key word in capitals and below it, on two lines, the letters of the alphabet not included in the word "Dokumentar"; in the left-hand margin of the three lines and along the top of the key word he put down a series of figures, so that each letter was represented by a two-figure number—A by 14, for instance, B by 26 and C by 76:

```
   2   7   4   0   5   3   6   9   1   8
4  D   O   K   U   M   E   N   T   A   R
6  B   C   F   G   H   I   J   L   P   Q
1  S   V   W   X   Y   Z
```

Pünter could now encode his message. He reduced it to the briefest telegraphic form: "Hitler Standarte in Warsaw" (in German "Hitlerstandarte in Warschau"), turned these into the figures indicated by the key word and arranged them in groups of five. The result looked like this:

```
56369   49634   84219   41464   24148
49434   36644   11484   21765   61404
```

Then came the re-encoding. Pünter wrote down the whole sentence "Documentary films are withheld but will shortly be released again" and turned this also into figures but on a system differing from that used for the original encoding in that letters were represented by singleton figures, not two-digit numbers. The second digit was simply dropped, A thus becoming 1, B 2, C 7, and so on. Finally Pünter added together the figures of the initial coding and those of the re-encoding. The message was now coded twice over.

At the end of the message Pünter added a final group destined for the addressee in Moscow, who of course had to know where to find the codeword in Sven Hedin's book, which he also had in front of him. The final group of the message about the Leibstandarte was "12085," meaning "page 12, line 08, word 5."[169]

With messages doubly encoded in this way the Soviet cryptographic maze was almost impenetrable. Yet it had a weak spot: should a key word from the book concerned, or even the book itself, fall into the enemy's hands, then it was only a question of time before his cryptanalysts succeeded in reading the coded messages.

This was precisely what Fu III's cryptanalysts were trying to do early in 1942 when they began to work through the papers contained in Harry Piepe's haul in the Rue des Atrébates. Signals Security on the Matthäikirchplatz had meanwhile collected a group of cryptanalysts headed by a highly intelligent man, Dr. Wilhelm Vauck, Reserve Lieutenant, in civil life a secondary schoolmaster;[170] he later became master for mathematics, physics and chemistry at the Wilhelm-von-Polenz High School in Bautzen. He was one of the most valuable specialists in "OKH/In7/VI/12," which hieroglyphics indicated the Radio Office of the Signals Inspectorate of the High Command of the Army; he was only on loan to Signals Security.[171]

Vauck assembled a number of students of mathematics and languages who had been conscripted into the Army and Air Force Signals services and concentrated them in his new cryptanalysis section in Signals Security Headquarters; they were young intellectuals dressed as soldiers, experts in the preparation of comparative tables and probability calculations. In their enthusiasm they did not observe that the enemy could listen in to everything they did—for one of Vauck's staff was Corporal Horst Heilmann from the Luftwaffe Signals Service and he was an associate of Schulze-Boysen, the chief Soviet agent, who had infiltrated him into the cryptanalysis section as a decoder for English, French and Russian radio messages.[172]

Lieutenant Vauck in fact had no cause for suspicion, since the auspices for his youngsters' work were good. A quick look through Piepe's haul had given Vauck to hope that this time he really would succeed in breaking the Soviet code.

Among the captured papers was a half-burned sheet which Piepe's policemen had found in the fireplace of 101 Rue des Atrébates. It had clearly been thrown into the fire by the radio operator Makarov as he fled. What remained of it showed a number of columns of figures. Vauck immediately suspected that this half-burned sheet of paper might belong to Makarov's encoding table.[173] Since at this time the Russian was still refusing to say anything, Vauck had to try to work it out himself.

For six weeks the Matthäikirchplatz cryptanalysts tried every known mathematical combination in order to unearth Makarov's encoding plan. But all in vain; they succeeded in reconstructing only one word: "Proctor."[174] The problem therefore was now to find Proctor. Meanwhile, however, the Germans had learned that the Russian Secret Service habitually took their key sentences from works of fiction; Proctor was therefore most likely to appear in a novel or play. But in which?

Captain Carl von Wedel, one of Fu III's senior evaluation officers and head of the desk "Contents Evaluation," set out for Brussels.[175] His object was to discover what books the Makarov circuit had used. Wedel interrogated Rita Arnould, the only inmate of the Rue des Atrébates who was willing to talk.[176]

Rita could remember seeing a number of books on Sophie Posnanska's desk, but Piepe had omitted to take the apparently harmless novels with him; Wedel searched the house in vain. Rita continued to cudgel her brains for the titles of the vital books. Von Wedel was able to find some of the books she mentioned in Brussels; he read them through at once, but none contained the name Proctor.[177]

Wedel's last hope was a novel published in 1910, *Le Miracle du Professeur Wolmar* by the French author Guy de Teramond. Wedel went to Paris and hunted through one secondhand bookshop after another. The book had never been on sale; it had been a free issue to readers of the Paris illustrated, *Le Monde illustré*.[178] Von Wedel was in luck; on 17 May 1942 he found a copy—and there the cryptanalysts found their Proctor.[179]

From now on Vauck's people could decipher Makarov's messages, but it was slow work. They did indeed possess the master book, but every one of its 286 pages had to be searched each time[180] to establish the passages which fitted the 120 messages (this was the number which counterespionage had captured with Makarov's set).[181] By June the cryptanalysts were going somewhat quicker; each day they were able to decipher two or three of the Makarov messages.[182] Message by message the true extent of Soviet espionage unfolded itself before Vauck's eyes; there was information about military establishments, armaments statistics, secret diplomatic reports and strengths of divisions.

His cryptanalysts' success, however, brought no great satisfaction to Lieutenant Vauck. Moscow had long since changed its coding system and so the deciphered Kent/Makarov messages to Moscow were only of historical interest. More important still, the fact that they could now be read did nothing to answer the vital question: who were the agents behind it all? Vauck therefore started working in the reverse direction and had all Moscow's messages to Brussels deciphered. Perhaps this would give some clue to the red circuit of agents.

The whole matter was still shrouded in mystery for Vauck's intellectuals when Giering and Piepe came to the rescue once more. Their listening posts in Brussels and Paris had again intercepted messages from the Soviet spies.

The first to get some indication that the spy-ring broken up in Brussels was continuing its work in France was Major Schneider of the Ordnungspolizei. He had a police direction-finder unit on a farm near Garches, west of Paris, and located an unknown transmitter in the Paris suburb, Maisons-Laffitte. "That's a Russian set," Schneider ruminated, and let his radio sleuths loose on Maisons-Laffitte.[183] On 10 July 1942 he alerted Beumelburg, the top Gestapo official in occupied France, and the latter in turn alerted his specialist on communism, Kriminalkommissar Reiser.[184]

Schneider reported: "For some days we have been keeping our eye on an enemy set which must be located north or northwest of Paris. So far we have not been able to pinpoint it, but today we've got it. We have now cornered it and put the short-range sets into action." To Reiser he said: "You'd better come along if you want to catch these people." Reiser collected one or two of his men, put on mufti and drove after Schneider's direction-finder truck. "It looked like a small delivery van," he reported; "nothing visible from outside. Our car was also well camouflaged of course."

Suddenly the truck halted in the Grand Avenue of Maisons-Laffitte. An orderly jumped out of the police car and pointed to two villas on either side of the street. Reiser's men charged up to both houses; he himself, with drawn revolver, forced his way into the left-hand house and snatched a man out of bed, but then realized that he was wrong. From the other villa, however, a policeman shouted: "We've got them!" In an attic room of the villa the Gestapo officials overpowered a dark-haired man who had been working his set at that very moment; other policemen brought along a woman who had been trying to escape through the garden with a packet of papers. They were Hersch and Myra Sokol, the two radio operators of the "Grand Chef's" French circuit.[185]

The coup in Maisons-Laffitte brought Vauck well on his way; the captured papers gave new clues to Rote Kapelle's coding system. Only the Sokols could have cleared up the final riddles, but the two Poles refused to speak.

Sokol was badly beaten up by the enraged Gestapo functionaries; he was tortured by submersion in ice-cold water.[186] Today Reiser denies ever using such methods, saying: "For my part I never did anything like that. It would have been too stupid to imagine that one could obtain information by such methods."[187] Nevertheless, when the Gestapo threatened Myra Sokol that they would shoot her husband, she gave away a lot—the subjects of the radio messages, lines to other members of the Trepper circuit and even the "Grand Chef's" cover-name, "Gilbert."[188] Trepper could count himself lucky that he had never given the Sokols his address.

Trepper hurriedly ordered a withdrawal and regrouped his shadow army. But his agents were already so demoralized by the precision of the German counter-espionage onslaughts that many of them were reluctant to continue. Once more Trepper's circuit faced disaster due to the tiresome problem of communications. Kent in Marseilles had a set but he was always finding technical faults as an excuse for inactivity.[189] Robinson, the organizer, also had a set but refused to place it at the "Grand Chef's" disposal.[190]

In desperation Trepper searched for some means of re-establishing radio communication with Moscow. After prolonged negotiations the French Communist Party came to the rescue once more and lent him a set.[191] But who was to work it? Two communists, Pierre and Lucienne Giraud, offered to house and work the set in their apartment at Saint-Leula Forest near Paris. Full of good will though they were, this did not solve Trepper's problem, since they did not know how to use it.[192] They themselves now looked for a radio operator and found one in Valentino Escudero, an exiled Spaniard. This proved an unhappy choice, however, for, after working for a short time, Escudero was picked up by the police for possessing a return ticket to Franco Spain and betrayed the whole group to the Germans.[193] While the "Grand Chef" was still searching for a way out of his dilemma, his pursuers were girding their loins for a further, and this time decisive, blow against Rote Kapelle. This was the coup which was the beginning of the end for the Soviet espionage organization in Western Europe.

The Belgian circuit had been in cold storage since December 1941 but it had not escaped the notice of Signals Security's direction-finders that, even before the coup in Maisons-Laffitte, it had been reactivated. From March/April 1942 a new transmitter had been working in Brussels; the Germans assumed that Kent, the "Petit Chef" who had fled, had been succeeded by a new man. In fact, as we know, it was Yefremov.[194]

Fu III's vast direction-finding aerials picked up signals from the enemy who had unexpectedly reappeared in Brussels. The direction-finding platoon of a monitoring company was accordingly once more despatched to Brussels and in a short time they were certain where the new set was located. By the end of July 1942 all the indications were that it was in the Brussels suburb of Laeken, to be more precise in an isolated house near a railway.[195]

Piepe struck on 30 July. With twenty-five men from the Field Security Police and a Luftwaffe barracks nearby he surrounded the house and a few minutes later the police were in occupation; it proved to be partitioned into small rooms. They found a radio set still warm, but the operator had fled. As Piepe stuck his head through a skylight, he saw a man running across the roof, revolver in hand. The man charged on, firing shot after shot, tore open a skylight and disappeared; pursued by the Germans he took refuge in the cellar and hid there. The Security Police discovered him and beat him up.

A few moments later he was standing bleeding in front of Piepe. He was reluctant to give the Captain his name, since he knew only too well that he had been one of the prize candidates on the Gestapo's black list for years—

Johann Wenzel.* But the name meant nothing to Piepe; he ordered Rote Kapelle's chief radio operator in Western Europe simply to be carted off to the military prison. Not until he received a teleprint from the RSHA did he realize that he had caught one of the most intelligent and active of Moscow's agents.[197]

By the time he received the teleprint, however, Piepe already knew that chance had dealt him a trump card. Early in the morning of 31 July the weary detective had taken home with him the papers captured from Wenzel and, as he sat on his camp bed, had had the surprise of his life.[198] The papers proved to be messages which Wenzel had received or was to send; the majority were in code, but some were still in clear. "There were precise details of German aircraft and tank production, of our losses and our reserves," Piepe recalls.[199]

Thumbing through the messages Piepe came on one which riveted his attention; it seemed at last to provide a clue to one of the Rote Kapelle agents. He says: "In one of the telegrams there was mention of a Berlin address which was of special importance and must on no account be discovered by the Germans."[200]

The existence of this telegram is confirmed by another Captain in the Abwehr, head of Desk F 1 (France, Belgium and Luxemburg) in Section III F of the Berlin headquarters. He says: "One day a decoded message from 'Rote Kapelle' arrived on my desk for evaluation. In it an agent was told to report to 'Schubo' whose address, with number of house and name of street, was given. I at once asked for a list of those living in this house. It included the name Schulze-Boysen."[201]

No sooner had Piepe realized the significance of the Wenzel papers than he reported to the new head of the Abwehr office in Brussels, Colonel Habs-Karl von Servaes.[202] Von Servaes immediately passed the news on to Abwehr headquarters on the Tirpitzufer, Berlin, and then he had another idea: "Herr Piepe, you must go to Berlin."[203] The next aircraft was already full, so Piepe climbed

---

* The Gestapo Report gives the date of the capture of Wenzel's set as 30 July 1942. This means that all the dates given in other sources are wrong; Perrault and Dallin give 30 June; Piepe in his series of articles entitled "Harburger jagte Agenten" in the *Harburger Anzeiger und Nachrichten* of 4 October 1967 says that the night 19/20 May was the vital date.[196]

into his old Chevrolet and drove like the wind to Berlin with his revolver and a briefcase full of the Wenzel messages beside him. On arrival he seemed to be in a great state of excitement and the duty officer at the Tirpitzufer refused to let him in until he had a look into the briefcase. Drawing his revolver, Piepe refused to comply. The duty officer thereupon shut him into the waiting room, from which he was rescued by Rohleder, the head of Counter-Espionage, who had been informed.[204]

The contents of Piepe's briefcase proved so important that Rohleder informed Colonel von Bentivegni, head of Section III in the Abwehr. The two Colonels immediately reported to Admiral Canaris and told him what Piepe had discovered during his Brussels coup.[205] Momentarily the military hesitated whether to hand the case over to the Gestapo. Within the Reich, Group III F of the Abwehr had its own set of agents, known in Abwehr jargon as the "Private Orchestra"; it was perfectly capable of shadowing suspected persons and infiltrating a foreign spy-ring. The Private Orchestra would quickly have been able to tell III F/1 who was the man in Piepe's message to be protected from the Germans: it was Lieutenant Harro Schulze-Boysen, a desk officer in the Reich Ministry of Aviation.[206] Should they carry on on their own without letting the Gestapo into the secret?

The idea was in fact impracticable anyway, for the Gestapo already knew too much. On 14 July 1942, a fortnight before Piepe's coup in Brussels, Vauck had deciphered Moscow's old message of 10 October 1941 ordering Kent to visit three of the leaders of Rote Kapelle in Berlin.[207] This message was even more explicit than that captured by Piepe; it gave all three addresses and the cover-names of the inmates: "19 Altenburger Allee, Neu-Westend, third floor right—Choro; 26a Fredericiastrasse, Charlottenburg, second floor left—Wolf; 18 Kaiserallee, Friedenau, fourth floor left—Bauer."[208]

Signals Security also had doubts about passing the message on unchecked. Was it conceivable that Soviet Russia's Secret Service, otherwise so sophisticated, would hand all its most important agents over to its German opponents simultaneously on a silver platter? But there could be little doubt; Vauck had encountered the name Choro over and over again in the messages; now it was clear why German names and the German language had played so large a part in Soviet radio traffic.

But who were Choro, Bauer and Wolf? Captain von Wedel soon found out. Signals Security having no "Private Orchestra," he called the RSHA and asked them to establish the names.[209] The Gestapo had the answer by 16 July 1942 at the latest. "Choro" was none other than Schulze-Boysen; "Wolf" was the cover name for Dr. Arvid Harnack, a senior civil servant in the Reich Ministry of Economics, and "Bauer" stood for Dr. Adam Kuckoff, the writer.[210] It was as simple as that. No more was necessary to track down Moscow's leading agents.

The Abwehr and Signals Security were now obliged to inform the Gestapo officially, since in the interior of Germany only the Gestapo was allowed to make arrests. Piepe was authorized to go to the Prinz-Albrecht-Strasse together with his Gestapo partner Giering and place himself at the disposal of Oberregierungsrat [Senior Government Counsellor] Friedrich Panzinger, head of Group IV A in the RSHA, who was in charge of the Gestapo campaign against Rote Kapelle.[211]

Early in August the soldiers and the policemen reached agreement on the highest level. Admiral Canaris, General Thiele, Colonel von Bentevegni and Gestapo Müller's representative, SS-Oberführer Schellenberg, laid down that the RSHA would be solely responsible for dealing with Rote Kapelle agents operating within the Reich; the Abwehr and Communications Security, on the other hand, with the assistance of the Gestapo, would pursue the campaign against Rote Kapelle circuits in the Western occupied territories.[212] Schellenberg records that "more than fifty persons in Berlin were thereupon placed under surveillance."[213]

Telephones were tapped, letters from abroad were opened, suspects were shadowed. The result astonished even the Gestapo experts. Adolf Hitler's guardians of the regime found themselves watching and listening to one of the strangest espionage organizations in German history.

4

"Choro" Calling Moscow

ON THE SECOND floor of No. 8 Prinz-Albrecht-Strasse, Berlin, in the office of Kriminalkommissar and SS-Unter-sturmführer Johan Strübing,* there was near-panic. Strübing, a 35-year-old Berliner, was in charge of "Enemy Parachutists and Radio Operators" in the Gestapo's counter-sabotage desk and for some hours a blue folder had been lying on his table, sent over from Headquarters Signals Security on the nearby Matthäikirchplatz.

Signals Security's reports left no further doubt; the Soviet radio messages deciphered by Fu III proved it: in the very center of Adolf Hitler's totalitarian state, under the noses of the omnipotent Secret State Police, a vast Soviet espionage organization was at work. The Russians must have innumerable agents and informers; they must have good contacts to firms and official agencies; their network of informers might well cover the entire Reich.

The deeper Strübing dug into the file, the more fantastic did he find what he read there. Germany's vital war secrets had been betrayed to Moscow; more than 500 messages had been radioed to Soviet headquarters.[2] But who were

---

* Johann Strübing was born in Berlin on 24 February 1907; from 1927 to 1937 he served in the Berlin Schutzpolizei [Metropolitan Police]. He transferred to the Gestapo on 1 February 1937 and was promoted Kriminalkommissar shortly thereafter. He joined the General SS in 1937 and the Nazi Party in 1940. He was promoted SS-Obersturmführer on 1 September 1942.[1]

124

the leaders of this spy organization and where were their most important agents? The captured messages provided one clue: the names "Choro" and "Arwid" were continually recurring.

Strübing reached for the message of 10 October 1941 in which Moscow had told Kent, its chief agent in Brussels, to visit the three leading members of the Berlin circuit, Lieutenant Harro Schulze-Boysen, Dr. Arvid Harnack, the civil servant, and Dr. Adam Kuckhoff, the writer. Strübing compared the messages with the names of the three agents. Perhaps "Choro" was the Russian form of Harro, he thought, and therefore indicated Harro Schulze-Boysen; "Arwid" might mean Arvid Harnack.

A glance into the Gestapo files on Schulze-Boysen swept away Strübing's initial doubts. "Schulze-Boysen had been known to the Gestapo since 1933," one of Strübing's staff later recorded,[3] thereby confirming a statement of 1 April 1933 by the Berlin Criminal Police Office to the effect that an organization run by Schulze-Boysen had "extreme communist tendencies."[4] Strübing ordered Schulze-Boysen's telephone and those of the other two mentioned in the message to be tapped. The Gestapo's recorders registered the suspects' conversations and gradually there emerged an outline of the Berlin end of Rote Kapelle.

It became increasingly clear that Harro Schulze-Boysen was the driving force of the entire affair; he was a sort of charismatic leader who drove his team along, energetic, ruthless, reckless. He was of the ranks of the fanatical prophets with no time for moderate views. For one side he was an idealist, a romantic and a resistance hero, for the other a charlatan, a scatterbrain and a traitor. Günther Weisenborn, the playwright and one of his most faithful friends, says that he had a "fine, open face. In the eyes of his adherents he was the very picture of the young officer of the adventure novel, tall, blue-eyed, bold, and behind it all the power and drive of the politician of genius."[5] The anti-Nazi Rainer Hildebrandt says: "The cold fire which burned in his eyes, the pronounced bony chin in which the muscles sometimes worked, could belong only to a character ready to stake his all."[6] Heinrich Scheel, a meteorological inspector who worked with Schulze-Boysen, thought him "a man of fascinating intelligence and energy, a brilliant debater of astounding intellect and eloquence."[7] His defenders are still enthusiastic about him;

"Schulze-Boysen's manifold qualities, his liveliness and good humor made him the idol of his young supporters."[8]

His critics and his enemies saw him in a very different light. Alexander Krall, the judge who subsequently sentenced him, thought him an adventurer, "intelligent and ingenious . . . reckless and given to taking advantage of his friends, ambitious in the extreme."[9] David Dallin says that he was "unscrupulous in his selection of means . . . too emotional and unstable to become an obedient 'apparatchik.' "[10] A graphological institute in Hamburg which studied his handwriting said that it was that of "a fanatical disciple who would sacrifice everything to an idea."[11]

Many even of his fellow communists were horrified by his unthinking impetuosity. Kuckoff confided to his wife that Schulze-Boysen urgently needed some form of discipline;[12] Wilhelm Guddorf, an Old Guard communist, was so dismayed by Schulze-Boysen's violent ideas and complete disregard of all the conspiratorial rules that he kept him at arm's length.[13] In her death cell Cato Bontjes van Beek, a victim of Schulze-Boysen's imprudence, admitted: "Sch-B was in fact the ambitious adventurer which Heinz [Strelow] and I had thought him."[14]

Both friends and enemies, however, were agreed that one of his most characteristic traits was a tendency to irrationalism. The Swiss philosopher Adrien Turel, who was one of his friends, said that he was "handicapped by an education that was entirely romantic. As a result he developed a tendency to heroics."[15]

The East German historians still accuse him of having "temporarily succumbed to the crazy and contaminating romanticism of the so-called 'Young German Order' [Jungdeutsche Orden]" and of moving in "sectarian" right-wing circles.[16] This allows them to present Schulze-Boysen as an anti-fascist though not a communist.[17]

Even his associate Harnack, who was a strict Marxist, failed to wean Schulze-Boysen, the "scatterbrain," away from his political irrationalism; he seriously thought that he could be an agent of the Soviet Secret Service and remain a German nationalist.[18] He called himself a communist but even in September 1939 he still knew so little of the most elementary tenets of communism that he borrowed the works of Stalin and Trotsky from his friend Dr. Hugo Buschmann. Buschmann recalls: "At that time he knew nothing whatsoever about communism."[19]

Many a trait in his character showed that he was one of those leftovers of the German Youth Movement who had failed to achieve political maturity. Schulze-Boysen was representative of romantic revolutionary youth in revolt, a youth wishful to eliminate all class barriers and reorganize the bourgeois order of German society. They called themselves National Revolutionaries and, in the words of their sympathetic exponent Karl O. Paetel, felt that they had a "catchall platform" and that "with their disconcerting self-assurance they provided a forum for all the dropouts both from right and left"[20]—young sons of the bourgeoisie in revolt against the deadening creed of the property-owners, young workers in protest against the sterile arrogance of the proletariat, young aristocrats rebelling against the obsolete pride of birth.

They wanted to form a "Youth Front" to fight the ossified parties, both right and left; they wanted to form a Third Force to stand between the red-shirted and the brown-shirted marching columns already assembling for their final battle over the corpse of parliamentary democracy in Weimar Germany. These young men succumbed to the alluring illusion that they could reconcile these enemies and unite them under a new creed known as proletarian Nationalism or National Socialism.[21]

Though the brains of the "Youth Front" came from the bourgeoisie, emotionally its trend was to the Left. The National Revolutionaries could not conceive of a future other than in socialism, since only socialism could reconcile the opposing nationalist and proletarian forces and unite them in that "popular community" which was the prerequisite for the "genuine authoritarian state."[22] In 1932 Schulze-Boysen pronounced: "Our answer to the mechanical organizational concept of the state and to nationalism is the idea of the popular community. The notion of 'the people' will be our aim and it will acquire fresh reality; the purpose of the State we regard as to serve the perpetual rejuvenation of the community as a whole."[23]

The "Youth Front" prophets preached a doctrine of worldwide class warfare, showing thereby that their creed was an odd mixture of emotionally based socialism and the expansionism of the traditional nationalists. Germany should copy the Soviet Union's planned economy, they thought, and with Soviet help a "League of oppressed nations" should be formed to break the "fetters of Versailles."[24] Socialism as the conveyor belt for an imperialist policy—even that figured among the "Youth Front's" ideas.

These young men differed from their intellectual descendants of the Federal Republic, who saw their utopia in an uncontrolled society. Though they criticized the 1932 "establishment," their ideal was a strong state of world-power status. Schulze-Boysen said: "A state which is neither able nor willing to expand on an imperial scale or which is incapable of drawing the foreign policy conclusions from a genuine revolutionary ethos . . . is in practice condemned to impotence."[25]

The strong state, however, so ran the further thoughts of the National Revolutionaries, could only be brought about by socialistic methods; only a socialist state could cleanse Europe of "chaos and disorder," could guard the continent against the American "campaign of persecution" and "the divisive tendencies of capitalism or the liberal illusion of freedom of the individual."[26] But what did socialism want and what was it? Their answer was: total mobilization of the people. Schulze-Boysen explained: "Socialism does not mean irresponsibility, lack of leadership or renunciation of the spirit of enterprise. It means: a General Staff, production armies, planning, the community at work, the ultimate in selfless effort and responsibility—that is socialism."[27]

The language was reminiscent of the Nazi vocabulary; yet the National Revolutionaries abhorred the Nazi Party. For a short time they had, in fact, been impressed by the Hitler Movement. Fred Schmid, the Swiss aircraft manufacturer, who was both the "Youth Front's" high priest and its source of funds, admitted that he had thought the phrase "National Socialism" to be *the* solution;[28] Turel, his fellow-countryman, wanted to build "a sort of bridge to National Socialism"—until he was arrested by the Nazis.[29]

But the Nazi renunciation of their original anti-capitalist program and Hitler's swing toward big business and the German Nationals destroyed all the National Revolutionaries' illusions. For them Hitler was henceforth the embodiment of crude fascism relying solely on force. When the extreme left wing under Otto Strasser split with Hitler,[30] the petty bourgeois opportunist, crying "The Socialists are leaving the Party," the leaders of the "Youth Front" were clear: the Nazis were traitors to socialism.

In Harro Schulze-Boysen's scheme of things, however, socialism was top priority in spite of the fact that he came of a conservative family and was a great-nephew of Grand-Admiral von Tirpitz. His revolt against bourgeois lethargy brought him into sharp conflict with his parents, who were German Nationals.

For Harro, who was born in Kiel on 2 September 1909, his father and mother typified the combination of loyal officialdom and upper-middle-class snobbery which he soon learned to despise. Commander Erich Edgar Schulze, top of his class in 1898, Chief of Staff to the German Naval Commander in Belgium during the First World War and subsequently on the boards of various large industrial concerns,[31] was related to the Tirpitz family through his mother who was a sister of the Grand-Admiral;[32] Marie-Louise Schulze was a Boysen, a well-known lawyer family in Flensburg, and was a leader of the most exclusive Kiel "society."[33]

Though even in his school days Harro called himself Schulze-Boysen, the complacency and social aspirations of his parents and their friends from business and service circles had no message for him. Revolution and secret societies attracted him from an early age. In 1923, when still at secondary school in Duisburg, he took part in the clandestine struggle against the French occupation authorities in the Ruhr; as his personal papers later showed, he had spent a short period under arrest for "active work in the Ruhr struggle."[34]

After matriculation (with classification "good")[35] Harro joined Arthur Mahraun's "Jungdeutsche Orden" in 1928; he was now a law student at Freiburg University and the nationalist, republican and pan-European mystique of the Order fascinated him.[36] He campaigned enthusiastically for Franco-German understanding.[37] Throughout his subsequent political development he was always captivated by the idea of an Order; to unseat the old society, he thought, a minority represented by an Order was required, an *avant-garde* after the manner of the old mendicant friars, Huguenots, Puritans, Jacobins and Bolshevists.[38]

In 1930 he transferred to Berlin University and lost his taste for Mahraun's bourgeois conservative concepts.[39] He rented a room in Wedding, the working-class quarter, and contact with the Berlin proletariat pushed him further to the Left.[40] He remained leader of the "Jungdeutsche" unit in Wedding until 1931 but then drifted toward Otto Strasser's "revolutionary National Socialists" and other extreme right-wing groups.[41]

In the summer of 1932 he joined a circle of National Revolutionaries in Berlin who were against all the political authorities in the Republic, including the democratic parties; for the disciples of the "Order" any party was a despicable "manifestation of bourgeois society."[42] Schulze-Boysen felt the call and became editor of the National Revolutionary newssheet, the *Gegner* [Opponent].

A number of young nationalists of various shades of opinion had grouped themselves around Franz Jung, an Old-Guard communist from Silesia who had broken with the Communist Party.[43] They christened their group after the *Gegner,* which was a 64-page ocatvo-size periodical with a circulation of 3,000 copies;[44] it was the most valuable item in the assets of a concern which had gone bankrupt due to taxation and currency difficulties.

Jung ran a publishing firm, the "Deutsche Korrespondenz," one of the protagonists of a European trade-union movement known as the "Building Plants Movement"; its object was to form international building cooperatives in opposition to the capitalist building trade. By the end of the 1920s the German trade unionists were in partnership with their French opposite numbers and planning the construction of great housing estates in both countries.[45]

In addition to the trade unionists the spokesmen for this socialistic enterprise were Le Corbusier, the modernistic French architect, and the Paris periodical *Plan,* a section of which was edited by Le Corbusier.[46] The French urged the Germans to produce a similar newspaper and this was the genesis of *Gegner* in 1931.[47] The editors of *Plan* handled agreements between the French trade unions and the German building cooperative movement, they publicized Le Corbusier's ideas and sponsored the social-revolutionary program of a politically ambitious barrister, Philippe Lamour, who was head of *Plan.*[48]

Jung was *Gegner's* publisher and remained so even after the Franco-German building partnership had been strangled by the increasingly impenetrable jungle of the currency regulations.[49] The paper was heavily in debt and Jung would have closed it down, had not a number of young men been attracted by the originality of *Gegner*'s theories.

The paper soon became a rallying point for the discontented in Germany; its title became their program. They wanted to combine all the "antis" both from Right and Left into a Third Force—against the democrats, the totalitarians and the establishment, but above all against the Nazis, or to be more precise, against fascism, which they regarded as the greatest threat to the future of Germany and of Europe.[50]

Apart from their antipathy to Nazism, however, the "Gegnerites" found it almost impossible to agree upon a common aim. Basically their program was an absence of program; they disliked concrete pronouncements and were quite happy merely to serve as a forum for German youth's protest against the "establishment" maintained by parties which no longer carried conviction.

Jung needed someone who could be both a leader in discussion and a mouthpiece, someone also who was familiar with the maximum number of the groups represented in the *Gegner* circle. He chose Schulze-Boysen,[51] who had the reputation of being in touch with practically every opposition youth group. Whenever parties of student extremists in Berlin University disagreed, Schulze-Boysen (who was reading politics, international law and journalism) was called upon to mediate.[52]

Schulze-Boysen was initiated by Jung into the editorial trade and on Jung's retirement became editor of the *Gegner*.[53] With every issue his warnings against the Nazi danger became more strident and the applause of nonconformists more enthusiastic. Schulze-Boysen even organized so-called "Gegner evenings" in Berlin cafes, when young people discussed articles appearing in the *Gegner;* he invited respresentatives of the political parties to discuss the future of German politics.[54] Even the skeptical Jung later had to admit: "At first the meetings were held in small rooms, but they were soon so crowded out that we had to hold overflow meetings. The atmosphere was extraordinarily disciplined; there was a remarkable comradeship between Left and Right. Young people, who would have beaten each other up at once if they had met on the street, listened to argument; they were all at one in their dislike of the swaggering doctrinaire Party bosses and the unbending superman."[55]

No concrete program was likely to emerge from these discussions, however; Paetel says: "There was an almost panic fear of being committed."[56] Schulze-Boysen and his closest associates were the only people to start formulation of a national-bolshevist platform. His general line of thought was as follows: The future of Europe lay in alliance between the elite of the youth movement, the proletariat and the Soviet Union, whence "a new Adam" would be bred.[57] He still found it scandalous that a German party (the Communist Party) should be dependent on directives from the Soviets;[58] yet he looked to Russia for salvation. The "basic phenomenon" of the age was the revolt of German youth against the immobility of the West; Russia was, and would remain, the prototype of the new mankind; Germany must never be found in opposition to the Soviet Union, for across the Rhine began the "foreign influence" of America; Western Europe was already "Pan-America."[59]

Without a qualm the *Gegner* acclaimed the brotherhood of the German and Soviet peoples. Jung says: "I am giving away no secret when I say that the Soviet Embassy made a regular financial contribution to the running of the *Gegner*."[60] Even after the victory of Hitler, the anti-bolshevist, Russia was still the *Gegner*'s Mecca. The last issue of *Gegner* in spring 1933 told its readers that the "new man" would arise in Russia; Germany was in convulsion; the West would become increasingly foreign to Germany, whereas the German people's affinity lay with the East.[61]

After 30 January 1933 Germany's new Nazi masters struck pitilessly at their pro-Soviet opponents. The *Gegner* was banned in April 1933.[62] A flying squad from No. 6 SS Standarte broke into the editorial offices at No. 1 Schellingstrasse, laid them waste and confiscated all copies of the paper.[63] Schulze-Boysen, the editor, and his two friends, Turel and Henry Erlanger, were carted off to one of the "wildcat concentration camps" on the outskirts of Berlin,[64] where the Nazi thugs used to "deal with" their opponents, as the term was.

According to Turel the three were thrown into "a diminutive cellar, rigged up like a police post. There was straw on the bare floor with large republican flags serving as bedclothes. We had to lie down there with the lights full on."[65] Being Swiss, Turel was soon released, but the other two were the victims of unrestrained sadism.[66]

In the courtyard Schulze-Boysen and Erlanger had to run the gauntlet of two ranks of armed SS men who drove their prisoners forward with shouts and blows from lead-weighted whips. Three times (the regulation sentence) Schulze-Boysen fought his way through the hail of blows, naked, gasping, bleeding, desperate. Suddenly he rushed back uninvited and ran through the ranks of his torturers for the fourth time. Though half-fainting he clicked his heels together and shouted: "Reporting for duty! Order carried out plus one for luck." Some of the SS men were so impressed that they called: "Good Lord, man, you belong to us!"[67]

Schulze-Boysen survived this dance of death but Erlanger, the sensitive intellectual, did not.[68] Schulze-Boysen never recovered from the murder of his friend. Erlanger's death, more than all his own sufferings and wounds, determined him never to have dealings with a regime which included such sadists.

Harro would probably never have emerged from the SS torture camp had not his mother, always more forceful than her retired sea-captain husband, taken immediate action. Hearing from her brother-in-law Werner Schulze, who was a barrister [Kammergerichtsrat], that her son had disappeared, Marie-Louise Schulze journeyed to Berlin.[69] Werner Schulze told her that the application for his nephew's arrest had been made by Standartenführer Hans Henze, whose unit was acting as an "Auxiliary Police Commando."[70]

Frau Schulze made use of the fact that she was President of the Women's Section of the "German Colonial Association" which had Nazi affiliations; she therefore considered herself entitled to preferential treatment in the new Germany. She put up a Party badge, rallied a number of her husband's ex-shipmates (including von Stosch, later a Captain) and drove to Henze's headquarters at 29 Potsdamer Strasse, where were also the offices of the "Reich Association of German Naval Officers."[71]

In face of Frau Schulze's broadside Henze gave way. He had no wish to be responsible for keeping a member of the Tirpitz family in prison; moreover, as a good Party comrade, Frau Schulze promised that her son would immediately cease any "anti-State activity" and would leave Berlin by the most rapid means. The torturers gave up their prisoner.[72]

Frau Schulze recalls: "But what a sight he was! White as a sheet with deep black shadows under his eyes; his hair had been cut with garden shears and there was not a single button on his suit. He told me how they had beaten Erlanger, the half-Jew, to death in the most bestial fashion."[73] As the daughter of a lawyer, however, Frau Schulze had not yet grasped what the word "law" meant in Adolf Hitler's Reich—she filed a complaint with the police against No. 6 SS Standarte for the murder of Erlanger.[74]

The SS retaliated. On 30 April they seized Schulze-Boysen once more; again he disappeared behind bars. Indignantly his mother intervened with Admiral (retired) Magnus von Levetzov, the Berlin Police President. His deputy produced Schulze-Boysen, handcuffed; with some bitterness he said: "Mama, you've got me in here; now get me out again," to which Frau Schulze replied: "You'll be a free man tomorrow or I'll be in prison too."[75]

"Tomorrow" turned into a fortnight; Harro was released in mid-May.[76] On 19 May 1933 Sturmbannführer Kolow of SS Abschnitt [Sector] III sent a registered letter to "Herr Schulze-Boysen, 203 Düsseldorfer Strasse, Duisburg" as follows: "After discussion with the Criminal Police the keys of the rooms rented by you at No. 1 Schellingstrasse are enclosed; at the same time you are informed that these rooms are at your disposal."[77] But Schulze-Boysen had no further need of the offices of the *Gegner;* he knew other ways of fighting the Nazis.

Ever since his release all Schulze-Boysen's thoughts had been concentrated on methods of bringing down the Nazi tyranny. At the end of 1933 Ernst von Salomon, who had also written for the *Gegner,* met him in the street and "barely recognized him. His face was very changed. Half an ear was missing and his face was scored with scarlet, semi-healed wounds. He said: 'I have put my revenge into cold storage.' "[78]

Schulze-Boysen's first concern was to find some safe position in the jungle of the neo-German hierarchy. He had already told von Salomon that his future lay with the Reichswehr;[79] the military profession offered the best protection against the regime's watchdogs; many of the Nazis' enemies had taken refuge in the faceless field-gray mass.

Schulze-Boysen wanted to join Hermann Göring's air

force. As the son of a naval officer he had for some time been of two minds whether he should join the Navy or not; in 1929 he had attended a course in Neustadt on the Baltic run by the "Hansa High Seas Defense Sports Association,"[80] and had had a passion for sailing ever since. But the Navy seemed too reactionary to him; so he compromised and became a naval airman.

In mid-1933 he joined a twelve-month observers' course at the "German Airline Pilots School" in Warnemünde,[81] one of the civilianized camouflage institutions for German air rearmament. His time in Warnemünde was a sore trial, for he found it "immensely difficult to live among people whose ideas were quite different, in an (intellectually) foreign environment."[82] The others on the course sensed his refusal to participate in the boisterous enthusiasm of the "national revolution" and treated him as an outsider. "Recent months have indeed been difficult," he wrote to his parents on 3 September 1933; "My special 'friends' here have thought up all kinds of vexations for me and at first I hardly knew how I could stand it all."[83] He stood it fairy well. On 1 January 1934 he was appointed to Naval Air Headquarters W (Warnemünde)[84] and earned the good will of his superiors so rapidly that they soon came to regard him as their best man; with some soldiers and SS officers he was allowed to go on an educational trip to the League of Nations headquarters in Geneva,[85] where, being much-traveled, he could make use of his language qualifications.

His knowledge of languages was remarkable—he could speak French, English, Swedish, Norwegian, Danish and Dutch.[86] He was accordingly tempted to leave the somewhat monotonous duties of naval observer and visualized a brilliant career at the center of German power. He learned Russian and applied to the Luftwaffe for a post as interpreter.[87] He had to wait a long time, however, before his services were required.

Schulze-Boysen's progress was next assisted by an attractive blonde, a Nazi enthusiast and ex-Labor Service leader. He had made her acquaintance while sailing on the Wannsee in the summer of 1935. She was called Libertas ("Libs") Haas-Heye and was a granddaughter of Prince Philipp zu Eulenburg und Hertefeld (1847–1921), a favorite of the music-loving Wilhelm II; her ambition was to

become a film actress or a journalist and she had poetic
leanings:

Weisst Du noch damals—bei Kerzenflimmern	Didst thou know at the time, as the candlelight played
Roter Rosen duftigem Schimmern	On the sheen of red roses while music we made,
Bei Singen und Klingen ohne Ende	Voices and instruments tireless and sweet,
—legte ich mein Herz in Deine Hände . . .	That my heart I then laid at thy feet—
Mir klang es so süss: In Deine Hände—[88]	How lovely it seemed—at thy feet.

By a series of odd coincidences "Libs" was in high favor
with the dignitaries of the Third Reich. Her father, Professor Wilhelm Haas-Heye, had run an art school at No. 8
Prinz-Albrecht-Strasse, Berlin,[89] where Göring had established the Gestapo's headquarters of terror; her mother,
Thora Countess zu Eulenberg (as she called herself after
her divorce from the Professor) lived on the family estate
at Liebenberg near Berlin where she was a neighbor of
Göring, who liked to come over from the ostentatious
Karinhall and listen to the Countess playing the old
Prince's sentimental songs.[90]

"Libs" fell in love with Schulze-Boysen, the yachtsman,
and on 26 July 1936 they married.[91] Göring, who was a witness at the wedding, gave the young bridegroom a job in the
Reich Ministry of Aviation. Marie-Louise Schulze did not
approve of her daughter-in-law, saying that she was a
"naïvely optimistic girl who liked to gossip and was very
easily influenced"—according to the landlord of the first
apartment rented by the young couple.[92] In fact she did
not like the marriage at all; it was not "respectable"
enough for her; Libs was not sufficiently domesticated, she
said, and too immature to keep the unruly Harro steady
—moreover, her friends remembered only too well scandalous stories about Prince Philipp's homosexual orgies.[93]

Harro thought otherwise. Both he and his wife were
greedily in love with life and, moreover, the Haas-Heye
connections enabled him to penetrate into the regime's
centers of power. In 1936 the Ministry of Aviation offered
him a private contract and he became a member of the
Ministry's press office.[94]

The job was a small one but capable of expansion. The

Press Office (known as "Genst. Pr."—General Staff, Press) under Major Werner Bartz[95] formed part of Section 5 of the Luftwaffe General Staff, "Genst. 5" in the local jargon. "Genst. 5" was the "Foreign States" section charged with keeping a watch on foreign air forces; in the General Staff hierarchy only the "Mapping Group" and the "Strategy Section" came between it and the Chief of Staff of the Luftwaffe. Schulze-Boysen was therefore on the fringe of the Ministry's nerve center.[96]

Schulze-Boysen began to expand his little empire. He did not confine himself to reading foreign newspapers, sticking in cuttings and reporting on what he had read. Back in his bed-sitter on the Hohenzollerndamm he read politico-military books to enable him to show some military knowledge;[97] he volunteered for reservist training (he had been appointed Sergeant-Major in July 1937 and was carried on the books of the Air Force Replacement Unit in Schleswig)[98] and was promoted Lieutenant. "He was very studious," his ex-landlord says, "always wanting to know more."[99]

Schulze-Boysen made his mark in the Ministry primarily by his industry. The energetic young desk officer soon came to the notice of his superiors. Captain Hans Eichelbaum of the Press Desk in the Central Office of the State Secretary of the Ministry of Aviation (the Ministry's real press department)[100] frequently made use of him when he wanted someone to write an article for the *German Luftwaffe Year Book,* a regular publication which Eichelbaum was responsible for editing.

Schulze-Boysen was always ready with his pen. In the 1939 Year Book, for instance, he voiced anxiety about the "politico-military plans of bolshevism" which, he said, was pursuing its dangerous course of rearmament "using methods which were definitely not invariably above reproach legally."[101] He commented with satisfaction on his Führer's blackmail policy during the Sudeten crisis: "After the Munich decisions the reduced depth of the Czech–Slovak–Carpathian–Ukrainian defense area can no longer represent a threat to the Greater German Reich. The enemies of National Socialism will now have to desert the 'aircraft-carrier' of which they have talked so much and which they have now torpedoed."[102]

Thus camouflaged, he penetrated ever further into the secret departments of the Ministry; he made new acquaintances; he forged new contacts. The secret information on which his official journalistic activities were based left him entirely convinced that Adolf Hitler was heading for war. As early as 15 September 1933 he had written to his parents: "I have the vague but definite feeling that, in the long run, we are heading for a European catastrophe of gigantic proportions."[103] Now report after report, authentic and indisputable, proved to him that the dictator's policy was one of unscrupulous adventurism and was bound to end in another world war. On 11 October 1938 he wrote to his parents: "I now say that in 1940/41 at the latest, but probably even next spring, there will be world war in Europe with class warfare as its sequel. I state unequivocally that Austria and Czechoslovakia were the first 'battles' in this new war."[104]

But what good could this knowledge do him? How to prevent the catastrophe? Schulze-Boysen took counsel with six friends who had been meeting regularly for a long time; they were the germ of the organization later known as the Schulze-Boysen group.

It had all started with a chance encounter on the street a few months after Schulze-Boysen had been released from the SS torture camp. He had met Kurt Schumacher, a sculptor from Stuttgart with whom he had worked on the *Gegner*. Schumacher was a Swabian, son of a trade-union official, and had been in Berlin since 1920; he was one of the new regime's outlaws since, as a graduate of the Berlin School of Fine Arts, he was an exponent of abstract art and therefore, with the triumph of "healthy" popular sentiment as imposed by the Nazi art censors, had been banned from all exhibitions.[105] He had been able to keep body and soul together only by occasional work and the earnings of his wife Elizabeth Hohenemser, a half-Jewess, daughter of an engineer; she was a poster artist and later trained as a photographer.[106] Schumacher consequently had plenty of time to think about the authorities who had ruined his career. He began to analyze the Nazi system of tyranny.

Both communist and Nazi legend later turned the two Schumachers into faithful Communist Party members, ready to obey any call from the Party.[107] Everything goes to show, however, that they never belonged to the Party; they were simply part of an artistic elite which revolted against any restriction of liberty either by the State or bourgeois society. Kurt Schumacher was "too intelligent and too sensitive not to strive" for that in which he believed all his life—"a peaceful community of peoples who, by the work of their own hands, could create an existence worthy of humanity."[108]

Any lack of analytical capacity or ideological enthusiasm shown by Schumacher, however, was more than made good by a communist who had broken with the Party. This was Walter Küchenmeister, a wartime volunteer for the imperial Navy, then a member of the KPD and until 1926 editor of the communist *Ruhr Echo*.[109] The Party had later expelled him; whatever the reason may have been, for an orthodox communist ex-comrade Küchenmeister was a traitor.*

On losing his editorship Küchenmeister joined an advertising firm. On the Nazi seizure of power he was carted off to a concentration camp by the SA and then incarcerated in Sonnenburg prison. After nine months under arrest he was provisionally released as a very sick man (he suffered from stomach ulcers and tuberculosis of the lungs).[111] He was now unfit for work but he was helped by a devoted and selfless admirer, Dr. Elfriede Paul, also a communist; she had been head of the municipal orphanage in Hamburg and had been practicing as a doctor in Berlin since 1936; she had been friendly with Schumacher since 1923 and through him came to know Küchenmeister. She went and lived with the invalid.[112]

In 1936–7 this circle was joined by two activists who were not prepared merely to sit in private meetings and moan about Hitler's tyranny. The first was an Ambassador's daughter, Gisela von Poellnitz, a passionate Young Communist, but a sick woman;† she had been on the staff of the American "United Press" agency in Berlin[114] and clamored for something decisive to be done. Second was Günther Weisenborn who had returned after several years' exile in America; he was a pacifist and a left-wing democrat sociological critic (his writings included *U-Boat S 47* and *Barbarians*) and he too wished to see some action taken against the regime.[115]

These six were drawn to Schulze-Boysen almost automatically; they trusted him as they did no one else. Kü-

---

* According to Kraell, President of the Court at the Rote Kapelle trial, Küchenmeister had been expelled for embezzling Party funds.[110]
† She died of tuberculosis in Switzerland in 1939.[113]

chenmeister and Schumacher had known him since 1930, Weisenborn since 1932; Gisela von Poellnitz was a distant relative.[116] He was the group's only hope. He wore the uniform of the regime. He was on terms with senior Nazi functionaries. He had a finger, admittedly only a small one, on the levers of power.

The discussion evenings in his friends' apartments had hardened Schulze-Boysen's decision to do something spectacular against the regime. He had felt frustrated for years; he found the double game he was playing in the Ministry of Aviation almost intolerable; some action against the regime would lift a weight from his mind. Moreover, Libertas, his wife, who had long since turned anti-fascist, at least superficially, was ready to support any coup by the "crazy" Harro.

"If you are anti, must you not acutally do something against it?" Schumacher asked one day at one of their meetings. Weisenborn nodded, Schulze-Boysen agreed, and soon a plan was concocted to hit the regime on a sensitive spot.[117]

The Spanish Civil War, which had now been raging for months, offered an opportunity; for ideological purists the bloody struggle beyond the Pyrenees was no less than an invitation to embark on an anti-fascist crusade. Without stopping to think of its peculiarly Spanish background or of the implications of a civil war which had nothing to do with Europe, thousands of German communists, socialists and democrats hastened to the aid of the hard-pressed Republic; one of Schulze-Boysen's friends, Paul Scholz, son of a building contractor, was one of them.[118] To the conspirators grouped around Schulze-Boysen Spain looked like the first testing-ground in a war in which what they called anti-fascism would prove its worth. Lieutenant Schulze-Boysen knew a method of dealing the fascists a blow.

The Reich Ministry of Aviation had formed a "Special Staff W" under General Helmuth Wilberg to direct German assistance to General Franco.[119] Responsibility for the transport of volunteers, arms and munitions to Spain lay with this Ministry.[120] From the Ministry of Aviation ran all the secret links to Franco's partisans fighting against the left-wing republic—and Moscow had declared support of that republic to be the most urgent task for the anti-fascist Peoples Front.

Schulze-Boysen assembled all the information he could about the "Special Staff W"—details of German transports to Spain, officers and men employed, and the German Abwehr's operations behind the republican front. All this was incorporated into letters which Gisela von Poellnitz pushed through the letter box of the Soviet Trade Delegation at No. 11 Lietzenburgen Strasse, Berlin.[121]

The Gestapo subsequently stated that Schulze-Boysen had betrayed "secret Abwehr business" to the Soviets;[122] Heinrich Scheel recalls a Gestapo official saying: "During the Spanish Civil War we sent some of our own people as spies into the International Brigade. Schulze-Boysen knew their names and passed them to the Reds. Our people were thereupon put up against the wall."[123]

But the Gestapo were soon on the trail of Schulze-Boysen's conspirators. In 1937 Gisela von Poellnitz was arrested and the plotters thought that they had been discovered.[124] Küchenmeister departed for Köln, to be near the Dutch frontier;[125] Schulze-Boysen and Weisenborn were preparing to take refuge in Luxemburg,[126] when Gisela von Poellnitz was suddenly released again.[127] She had given away nothing. Schulze-Boysen escaped with a warning from the Gestapo.[128]

Schulze-Boysen was not to be discouraged; for him espionage was still only a passing phase of his resistance activity against the Nazi tyranny. The incident had shown, however, the lengths to which he was prepared to go. But this did not imply that he had as yet definitely entered the service of Soviet secret intelligence. Weisenborn says: "There was as yet no political commitment; one could not at that time detect any political trend in favor of specific foreign powers."[129]

At this point Schulze-Boysen still felt political enlightenment to be the aspect of underground work holding out the greatest prospect for the future. Werner Krauss, one of his later associates, says that his purpose was to contribute "to the enlightenment of the widest professional circles" by means of pamphlets, oral propaganda and posters and so initiate the "formation of an intellectual elite."[130] During secret meetings at home Schulze-Boysen drafted a newssheet, *Der Vortrupp* [Advance Guard]; Schumacher and Küchenmeister wrote anti-fascist proclamations and others scattered them in the streets of Berlin

during the night.[131] Weisenborn says: "The leaflets were
left in bus shelters, telephone kiosks, etc. Another more
systematic method of distribution was to send them in
franked envelopes. Addresses were typewritten and usually
taken, by professions, from the telephone directory. Leaflets were produced on a duplicator."[132] The leaflets were
typed in a room in No. 2 Waitzstrasse rented through Dr.
Herbert Engelsing, an anti-Nazi lawyer; propaganda material was stored in Schumacher's cellar.[133]

Gradually Schulze-Boysen's circuit began to expand; an
increasing number of anti-Nazis were attracted by his discussion evenings and secret propaganda campaign. Anti-
Nazis of varying degrees of determination joined the seven
founder-members of Schulze-Boysen's enterprise. They included gentle beings such as Oda Schottmüller, the dancer
and sculptress, who was a friend of Schumacher and was
soon on terms of close personal friendship with Schulze-
Boysen; she was ready for anything.[134] Others were Dr.
Hugo Buschmann, a cement merchant and a far more
cautious operator,[135] also Scholz, the building contractor.[136]

A shadow was soon cast over this political resistance
activity, however; Gisela von Poellnitz's letters had meanwhile aroused the curiosity of the Soviet Secret Service.
The man now entered Schulze-Boysen's life who was to
prove the undoing of many an anti-fascist—the Soviet
agent-recruiting officer, Alexander Erdberg.

His real name was as obscure as the world in which he
moved. As a member of the staff of the Soviet Trade
Delegation in Berlin he called himself Erdberg; in the
Berlin communist underground he was known as Karl
Kaufmann, to Razvedupr he was Colonel Alexksandrov.[137]
Today Schulze-Boysen's friends are convinced that he was
really Vassily Berger, born in Moscow in 1905, reader for
the Moscow publishing firm "Geograski" in 1929 and a
Soviet agent from 1930.[138]

What is certain, however, is that Erdberg had been
working in the Soviet Trade Delegation in Berlin since
1935 and that his job was to form an espionage circuit in
Germany.[139] He had inherited an embryonic organization
from Sergei Bessonov, the Embassy Counselor, who had
vanished from Berlin in February 1937 under somewhat
mysterious circumstances and had ended in the toils of

the Stalin purge.*[140] Bessonov had linked the Trade Delegation with an informer network reaching into the Reich Ministry of Economics. The principal informer carried a famous name: Doctor (Law and Philosophy) Arvid Harnack was the son of the historian Otto Harnack and nephew of the great theologian Adolf von Harnack; he himself was one of the best brains in the German bureaucracy.[141] Retiring, intelligent, not without humor and a taste for violent argument, with a touch of asceticism, apparently the prototype of the senior German ministerial official, he had been serving his Soviet masters unquestioningly for years. He had the severity and conviction of the doctrinaire, but lacked the drive and impulsiveness of his later partner, Schulze-Boysen.

Harnack was born in Darmstadt on 24 May 1901. He had soon become preoccupied with Marxist economic theory and had turned into a convinced communist.[142] He was an adherent of the so-called "Giessen School" directed by Professor Friedrich Lenz, which thought that the German national economy should adopt (in his own words) "the principle of total planning in an economy free from exploitation."[143]

This principle Lenz considered was exemplified in the Soviet Five-Year Plan; for a time he was in touch with the national-bolshevist "resistance" circle led by the ex-Social Democrat Ernst Niekisch.[144] In Lenz's view, however, it was questionable whether the Soviet planned economy could form a pattern for that of Germany which was half-way between capitalism and communism. He was opposed to slavish acceptance of the Russian planned economy; his basic theme was "a Germany independent both of East and West" and this postulated "a positive showdown with eastern imperialism as revived by bolshevism" in order eventually to find an economic structure for Germany "suited to the peculiarities of our situation."[145]

Lenz's disciple, Harnack, however, did not stop there. For him nothing could be more equivocal than a German policy vacillating between East and West. Germany's future lay in the East, he said; Germany could only assure

---

* At the Lüneburg trial Roeder stated (Vol. VIII, p. 25) that in 1941 German agents had received their payments from Bessonov, but this is incorrect since Bessonov had been sentenced to 15 years' imprisonment at the Bukharin-Rykov trial in 1938 (Dallin: op. cit., p. 237).

her own national existence through partnership with communist Russia.[146]

For him this was not a question of power politics but of ideology and the structure of the society. As early as the summer of 1931 he had been telling his friend, the historian Egmont Zechlin, during their nightly walks in Marburg that the time for political sail-trimming was over, that every German must now decide whether he wished to side with the workers or the capitalists and that the national problem had become a social one.[147]

His conviction stemmed from a two-and-a-half-year Rockefeller fellowship at the University of Madison, Wisconsin.[148] He had gone to America in 1926 with the upbringing of a "national" family background, but work on his thesis, "The Pre-Marxist Labor Movement in the United States," had brought him increasingly into contact with socialism.[149] America's uncontrolled capitalism, leading straight to the catastrophe of Black Friday and the world depression, seemed to him to pave the way to Marxism.

Harnack was supported in his conviction that the American economic structure provided no answer to the contemporary crisis by an austere but captivating American woman, Mildred Fish, lecturer in literature at Madison University; she was caught up in the social reform protest movement common to American universities at the time. Both her erudition and her extremist democratic leanings appealed to Harnack, and in 1926 they married.[150] As a wife Mildred followed her husband's line; moreover, she was basically non-political. Literature remained her interest—even in her death-cell she was translating Goethe.[151]

As a student Arvid Harnack found that America had no message for him. Even in his thesis on the history of American trade unionism he prophesied that the United States would go the way which he had chosen for himself —towards Marxism.[152] Lenz's lectures increased his certainty that the future lay in communism.

Harnack first gained contact with Russia on completion of his economic studies at Giessen University in 1930.[153] Together with Lenz he formed a "Society for the Study of Soviet planned Economy" (known as "Arplan") in Berlin and was soon receiving active support from the Russian Trade Delegation and Embassy.[154] Most of the members of Arplan were by no means communists; they included scholars such as the Eastern experts Hötzsch and Mehnert who showed little predilection for communism when they spoke at the Society's annual meetings in the "Deutscher Kaiser" Hotel, Berlin.[155]

Slowly, however, Bessonov, the Counselor and one of the most plausible speakers and conversationalists of Berlin society at the time, won over to the Soviet Union those of the Arplan members who had Marxist leanings. Bessonov established contacts designed primarily to bind Harnack, the secretary of Arplan, ever more tightly to the Russians. In 1933 he arranged a trip to Russia for his friend Harnack and twenty-three other members of Arplan, where they were received by senior Soviet functionaries.[156] For Harnack his most memorable encounter was that with Osip Piatnitsky, the head of OMS and organizer of one of the most important circuits of communist agents. One of Harnack's friends believes that he entered Soviet service at this point.[157]

The Nazi seizure of power, however, compelled Lenz and Harnack to disband Arplan. Harnack had to leave Berlin for a time and complete his legal training in Jena.[158] Nevertheless, he clung to his vision of the future, an enlightened, specifically German, form of communism. He returned to Berlin in 1934, determined to prepare for his Reich, that of the fully planned economy.

Harnack now ranked as an assessor; he joined the Ministry of Economics as scientific assistant and was allotted the foreign currency desk.[159] He was promoted Government Counselor [Regierungsrat] and in 1942 Senior Government Counselor [Oberregierungsrat],[160] testimony to an efficiency which had earned him the good will of his most exalted masters. No one in the Ministry doubted that the Desk Officer for "America—Basic Questions" was an assidious servant of the Third Reich; he had meanwhile (on 8 July 1937) joined the Nazi Party as member No. 4,153,569; he gave proof of the requisite National Socialist zeal as a lecturer at Rosenberg's Foreign Policy School.[161] Hardly a soul knew, however, that his conventional civil servant exterior concealed the fanaticism of a Marxist doctrinaire, determined to follow his course unswervingly to the end—in the closest touch with his Russian friends.

There is no knowing when Harnack received his first assignments from the Soviet Secret Service. When Margarethe (Greta) Lorke, the economist and a convinced Marxist like Harnack, who had studied with him, regained contact in Berlin in 1933, he was already an informer on the books of the Soviet delegation. Greta Lorke says that Harnack was then drafting economic reports for Moscow and had been ordered by his Russian masters to keep strictly aloof from the German Communist Party.[162]

In contrast to Harnack, Greta Lorke was a Party member and fully *au fait* with the underground maneuvers of the communist machine. They had known each other at Madison University but had then lost touch.[163] In 1930 Greta had gone to Zurich, officially as assistant to a lawyer, but actually on behalf of the Party; her job was to watch Party interests in the "League for Intellectual Professions," a group of left-wing intellectuals, in Greta Lorke's words "organized as a cover organization, but in fact under communist direction."[164]

The Party did not summon Greta back to Hitler Germany until three years later and there she found her new associate—Harnack. She became a teacher of American commercial law and in addition worked for the Nazi Racio-political Office; she translated into English Goebbels' speeches and sometimes also parts of Hitler's *Mein Kampf*.[165] In her spare time, however, she copied out the secret reports which Harnack smuggled out of the Ministry of Economics; she noted down any verbal information given by Harnack and then passed on the reports to the couriers.[166]

The nearest "post-box" was in Neukölln, the contact being Johannes ("John") Sieg, a German-American from Detroit. He had been a member of the German Communist Party since 1929 and since 1931 had worked for *Red Flag*, the main communist newspaper, under the name "Siegfried Nebel." He was the contact man to the communist underground.[167] He had led an adventurous up-and-down life, being in turn teacher at a teachers' training college, stevedore, casual laborer, motor mechanic and journalist;[168] this had taught him to be both wily and adaptable, qualities which he found only too necessary in underground warfare against the Nazis. He was in touch with an underground communist group in Leipzig which passed on his and Harnack's reports to Russia.[169]

Sieg had a number of other informers in Berlin. In addition to certain comrades in Berlin industrial concerns they included a large man with whom Greta Lorke was destined to form a liaison—the writer Dr. Adam Kuckhoff. He was a Rhinelander, son of an industrial family in Aachen; Sieg had come to know him while working on the youth newspaper *Die Tat,* of which Kuckhoff had been editor until 1930.[170] Kuckhoff was a romantic nationalist; for a time he had sympathized with the Nazis but had become a violent anti-Nazi at the time of the "Gleich-schaltung" terror in 1933. Via Sieg he was brought into contact with the communist underground.[171]

Henceforth Kuckhoff called himself a communist. He was continually in trouble over money, however, and had some difficulty in reconciling his more highly patriotic poems such as "The German of Bayercourt" and "A Life for Ireland" with work in the communist underground. Greta Lorke helped him out of his ideological difficulties; she taught the somewhat slow-witted Kuckhoff the ABC of conspiratorial work; in 1937 she married him.[172]

"We held instructional evenings," Greta Kuckhoff says, "and discussed academic problems such as American litera-ture and intellectual matters; finally we turned to Marxist questions and the theory of National Socialism so as to be well-informed about it and so be able to oppose it."[173] Regular attendants at these meetings were the two Har-nacks, John Sieg and some of his friends including Schlösinger, the communist, his wife Rose, and Karl Behrens, an engineer in AEG.[174]

From 1937 one of the well-known figures of the Weimar Republic was among their number, Prussia's last Social-Democrat Minister of Culture, Dr. Adolf Grimme.[175] He and Kuckhoff had known each other at Halle University, had fallen out but had come together again after 1933;[176] Grimme had been a teacher and had won the Goethe Medal. Kuckhoff brought him along. Even his aversion to the Nazi system, however, could not persuade Grimme to become an active member of the Harnack-Kuckhoff circle; he remained a background listener.[177]

Frau Kuckhoff frequently had to mediate between the different varieties of anti-fascism; in particular the argu-ments between Kuckhoff, eking out a living as reader for the Deutsche Verlag publishing firm, and Harnack, the prosperous civil servant, were a frequent source of irrita-tion to the others. Frau Kuckhoff says: "Harnack's posi-tion in our circle was a difficult one."[178] She had not told her husband all the truth about Harnack. No one was to know of his espionage activities—such was the order from Russia.[179]

Kuckhoff thought Harnack an unprincipled careerist and a petty bourgeois who would leave the revolutionary party in the lurch. He once became so furious that he turned Harnack out on to the street and hit him in the face. Frau Kuckhoff says: "From Harnack's reaction I could see that he understood perfectly and was quite unperturbed."[180]

The garrulous Kuckhoff also did not know who had been backseat driving the Harnack group for some time—Alexander Erdberg. The Razvedupr recruiter was, of course, located in the Soviet Trade Delegation but Greta Kuckhoff says: "Harnack got his orders from the Embassy."[181] Erdberg now became increasingly prominent, for Major-General W. I. Tupikov, the Soviet Military Attaché in Berlin and Erdberg's superior, had received fresh orders from Moscow.

Harnack's information was primarily economic; important though this was to Moscow, the approach of World War II now necessitated intelligence on every aspect of the German war machine. What the Soviet Secret Service now wanted were details and still more details about Hitler's Wehrmacht. Gisela von Poellnitz's letters showed where Razvedupr should put its oar in. Schulze-Boysen was the man to provide military information. Erdberg formed a plan to combine the Schulze-Boysen and Harnack groups.

The first step was taken by Greta Kuckhoff, who established contact with the Schulze-Boysens. In the summer of 1939 Engelsing, the lawyer and also a producer for the "Tobis" film concern, brought the Kuckhoffs and Schulze-Boysens together in his house in the Grunewald.[182] The pretext was their common interest in the film business; Kuckhoff was hoping for a job as film director; Libs Schulze-Boysen, who had meanwhile become a scriptwriter for the Propaganda Ministry's Film Center, was friendly with a number of film producers, such as Wolfgang Liebeneiner.*

Shortly thereafter the circle was joined by Harnack who introduced his master Erdberg. Before the invasion of Poland, Arvid Harnack and Harro Schulze-Boysen were

---

* Libertas later obtained for Kuckhoff the job of directing the documentary *Posen—Stadt im Aufbau* [Posnan—a City Reconstructed].[183]

working together; only the hangman of Plötzensee brought their teamwork to an end.

Harnack did not, in fact, view with much enthusiasm the boyish, unruly Lieutenant, who immediately attempted to assume leadership of both groups.[184] Harnack was typical of the unsentimental Marxist who insisted on decency and good order both in his public and private life; the romantic national-revolutionary Schulze-Boysen with his super-gay sailing- and bottle-parties seemed to him more like an immature nihilist than a man to whom should be entrusted so dangerous a task as the leadership of a resistance and intelligence organization. Greta Kuckhoff says that her husband recognized at once that "Schu-Boy needs some discipline"[185]—a reference to Schulze-Boysen's exotic private life and the lightheartedness with which he and Libertas, both trying to escape from a marriage which was rapidly breaking up, embarked on a colorful series of new love affairs. These the two Kuckhoffs regarded, not as a breach of bourgeois morals, but as a crime against Moscow's rules of conspiracy. Other communists from Harnack's circuit also thought that Schulze-Boysen was playing fast and loose with the rules; many of them recoiled from working with this "drawing-room communist," particularly since they knew that the Party disapproved of Schulze-Boysen's association with Küchenmeister, whom the Party had expelled.[186]

At this point, however, both Schulze-Boysen and Harnack were compelled to take account of the view of the official German Communist Party leadership since, alongside the two groups, appeared a band of professional communist revolutionaries, more fanatical and strict than anything to which the German anti-Nazis had been accustomed. These orthodox communists were following the orders of Comintern headquarters which had decreed reconstruction of the German Communist Party so largely destroyed by the Gestapo; Party policy and the intelligence requirements of the Soviet State were therefore going hand in hand.

Shortly after the signature of the Russo-German Non-Agression Pact in August 1939, communist leaders in Moscow had given way to the remarkable illusion that the alliance between the two dictators would enable the German Communist Party to resume legal existence inside the Third Reich. Just as the Japanese war had forced Marshal

Chiang Kai-Shek, the anti-communist dictator of China, to tolerate his communist enemies, they argued, so war against "western imperialism" would compel Hitler to tolerate the German communists.[187]

The view of the German communist leaders in exile in the Soviet Union was that everything should be done to assist Hitler in this attitude of toleration. Walter Ulbricht admonished his comrades that they should not jeopardize the "legal possibilities" for future KPD work by "crude anti-fascism";[188] Fürnberg, a Comintern functionary, even went as far as to say that "many prejudices must be jettisoned"; if socialism could be achieved via the Russo-German pact, then the Party must accept even concentration camps and Jewish pogroms as necessary evils.[189]

In addition, in the view of the Soviet experts on Germany, Red Russia was now so popular in the Reich that the Nazis would not dare to oppose the communists or the Soviets. Samoilovicha, a female Soviet functionary, had a marvelous tale to tell about a journey through Poland: German soldiers on the demarcation line were eager collectors of Soviet stars; a complete Red Army platoon had had to parade and tear all the buttons and stars off their uniforms to present them to the German troops.[190]

The notion that Russo-German friendship would lead to some relaxation on the part of the Hitler regime induced the Comintern to take spectacular action. In January 1940 the two most senior officers of the Comintern, Georgi Dimitrov, the Secretary-General, and Dimitri Manuilsky, the Second Secretary, invited the members of the Central Committee of the German Communist Party to Moscow and subjected them to a Party inquest. With no thought for the feelings of their German friends they accused the KPD leaders of total failure in the fight against fascism.[191] Manuilsky thundered that there were no communists in Germany any more. Dimitrov grumbled that the KPD had ceased to exist as an independent party in Germany; nothing had been heard of it since the Spanish Civil War. Wilhelm Pieck, the Chairman of the KPD, rejected such generalizations. The internecine quarrel waxed fiercer.[192]

Finally, Dimitrov brought argument to an end and came to the point. The object, he declared, was to form new communist cells in Germany and then combine them into a Party which would act as a body. A secretariat of reliable comrades should be formed in Stockholm; it should establish contact with cells still existing in Germany, form new ones and then itself move to Berlin as the headquarters of the new KPD; local Party headquarters should be manned by "legal" comrades, who, however, must be supervised by men of the illegal organization; the secretariat would also remain illegal until it could be legitimized as a "Reich Directorate."[193]

As head of this organization the Comintern nominated a member of the Central Committee, Herbert Wehner (cover name Kurt Funk), a man of strong will and generally regarded as an expert in conspiratorial Party work.[194] He had been in the German underground until 1935, had fought in the Saar against union with Germany and, after many arguments with the "politruks" of the Party leadership, had imposed his policy of intensified struggle against the Nazi regime.[195] He was not to intervene until Karl Mewis, the leader-designate for the Berlin area, and two other members of the Central Committee, Heinrich Wiatrek and Wilhelm Knöchel, had made all necessary preparations in Stockholm for the move into the Third Reich.[196]

Hardly had Mewis (alias Fritz Arndt) set to work, however, than Dimitrov showed that his interest was confined to mere Party work by despatching to Stockholm one of his closest collaborators.[197] "Richard," as he was known in the Party with some trepidation, appeared as the secretariat's watchdog and driving force. He was Arthur Illner, a carpenter from Königsberg, who had served his apprenticeship in the old M-Apparat, was a graduate of the Moscow M School and a Razvedupr agent whom the Comintern had subsequently taken over; during the Spanish Civil War, under the cover name "Richard Stahlmann," he had been deputy commander of the eleventh battalion of the International Brigade, in which capacity he had been responsible for a number of murders of left-wing and right-wing deviationists.[198]

Illner's orders were to form an intelligence apparat in Germany. The KPD's new plans envisaged an M organization entirely divorced from the Party; its members were to carry out espionage and sabotage missions.[199] Illner shipped the first men of his apparat to Germany via a courier system working through Swedish ships plying in the Baltic.[200]

Wehner, who was despatched to Stockholm in February

1941, also made use of his international contacts.[201] Via Swedish seamen he maintained a secret postal traffic with the Comintern's West European intelligence network, the Dutch end of which was the Rote Kapelle agent Winterinck. "The Fat Man" (Winterinck's cover name) was in touch with Knöchel of the Central Committee, who now began to infiltrate his "instructors" into western Germany from Holland.[202]

The coded reports from the comrades working in Germany began to pile up in Wehner's secret headquarters at No. 63 Blekingegatan, Stockholm.[203] Wehner himself prepared agents to operate in Germany. As one of his principal "trusties" he despatched the communist Charlotte Bischoff, having first taken the precaution of cutting her hair short and dressing her up as a man. She was shipped to Bremen with 700 marks and some equipment from Wehner.[204]

But Dimitrov's master plan did not work out. Only a few of the communists infiltrated from abroad succeeded in working in Germany; the majority fell into the hands of the Gestapo. Dengel, an exalted functionary living in the security of Moscow, exhorted his comrades, saying that anyone working in Berlin need now have no fear of being beheaded, since Stalin would insure that Hitler's terror was kept within bounds[205]—yet many Party members were unwilling to embark on so deadly a venture.

Even the leaders of the Stockholm secretariat did not venture into Germany. Illner found that he had urgent duties in Sweden, Wiatrek simply refused to go, giving no excuse, Mewis refused to commit himself and Wehner took cover behind a notice placed in the *Berliner Lokal-Anzeiger* by Charlotte Bischoff warning against travel to Berlin.[206] Only Knöchel later contrived to force his way through.[207]

The communists inside Germany were thus cut off from their self-appointed leaders abroad and so they formed themselves into new action groups. They, of course, knew nothing of the complex tactical considerations which weighed with the Moscow headquarters; they would in any case have understood them as little as they did many of the proclamations from the Party leaders who had taken refuge abroad. The German Communist Party was split by the invisible line dividing the emigrés from those who had remained at home. What could the German communists be expected to understand from "creation of the anti-fascist peoples front against the anti-Soviet war plans of imperialist forces" or "recruitment of Social-Democrat workers and the National Socialist labor force for the common struggle" which figured in the KPD's "political platform" of December 1939?[208] The comrades at home, who were anyway confused by the Hitler–Stalin Pact, could not read more into this than: reconstruction of the KPD and continuation of the struggle against Hitler. And this they were prepared to do.

They were helped by an act of clemency on the part of the Nazi regime. During 1939 the medium-level functionaries of the old KPD were released from the prisons and concentration camps—against a promise to take no further part in political activities. They immediately set about forming new resistance groups.[209]

A beginning had been made some months before by Robert Uhrig, a metal worker and a Communist Party functionary, who had also been released from a concentration camp. He formed a resistance organization in Berlin which maintained cells in various works and included Social-Democrats as well as communists.[210] At the same time the Köln communists formed themselves into groups of five under a central headquarters and in Mannheim Georg Lechleiter, ex-communist deputy in the provincial parliament, created a similar organization.[211] In Hamburg, Saxony and Thuringia the old comrades collected together once more under the most varied forms of cover.[212]

Berlin was the center of activity. There a number of communist journalists recently released from detention met one day in the house of their old friend John Sieg. They were all old acquaintances from the time when they had worked together on *Red Flag*—Walter Husemann, the toolmaker and youth leader,[213] Martin Weise, employee in a publishing firm,[214] Herbert Grasse the printer,[215] and Guddorf the bookseller.[216] They decided to stick together and work against the regime in their various Berlin employments.

As their leader they elected the cleverest and best educated of them all, Wilhelm Guddorf. He came of a learned family; he himself was both a linguist and an economist; he had passed through the Soviet Party schools and had then become editor of *Red Flag*. In 1934 he was sentenced to three years' imprisonment for planning treason; since his release from a concentration camp he had been employed in the Berlin bookshop, Gsellius.[217]

He assembled people of his own way of thinking from firms and offices and soon had an organization going. Its members were primarily hard-line communists such as Eugen Neutert, an electrician,[218] Wolfgang Thiess, an ex-Hitler Youth leader,[219] Jutta and Viktor Dukinski.[220]

Guddorf was indefatigable in his calls for action; he had no intention of waiting for the "instructors" from Moscow announced by the Stockholm secretariat. He appointed himself a member of the still non-existent Directorate[221] and contacted other communist groups in Germany. He was particularly anxious to work with Bernhard Bästlein, Franz Jacob and Robert Abshagen, the Party functionaries in Hamburg, who had collected a number of resistance fighters in the old KPD waterfront sector.[222]

Eventually Sieg introduced Guddorf to the Schulze-Boysen/Harnack group which was already doing exactly what Guddorf dreamed of. Schulze-Boysen and Harnack accepted him with alacrity since his cells in the Berlin factories could give the organization the solid foundation which it still lacked. But Guddorf was hesitant to join the two "drawing-room communists"; as an Old-Guard communist he found Schulze-Boysen's histrionics disturbing.[223]

The Moscow headquarters had to issue a direct order before Guddorf declared himself ready to work with Schulze-Boysen and Harnack. In 1941 he joined the circuit as the official KPD representative.[224] Erdberg also had a hand in cementing the alliance. He was continually urging cooperation and pressing for an expansion of the organization. With the discreet assistance of the Russian, Schulze-Boysen was now able to sweep up into his organization the last survivors of the Comintern's German apparat.

These included Klara Schabbel, an Old-Guard communist who had fought in the Spartacist movement and had then been secretary of the Soviet Trade Delegation; she was the mistress of Henry Robinson, the Comintern representative now working for Rote Kapelle in Paris.*

---

* Klara Schabbel had come to know Robinson in Berlin in 1921 and had moved to Moscow with him in the same year. In 1922 she returned to Berlin where her son Leo was born. She kept in touch with Robinson later when he was employed in the West and for a time, from 1934 to 1936, lived with his father in Paris.[225]

Another was Kurt Schulze, a Soviet-trained radio operator, who had left the KPD in 1927 on orders from the Party and transferred to the Soviet intelligence organization.[226] Finally came the oddest of all the Comintern's secret products—the Hübner/Wesolek family of agents.

Emil Hübner was a baker who had joined the KPD in 1919 and had been working for the Soviet Secret Service since the end of the 1920s.[227] After 1933 one of his sons emigrated to the Soviet Union;[228] the other, Max Hübner, who had equally been a member of the Communist Party since 1919, helped his father in the business of passing on newly arrived Soviet agents.[229] The Russian Secret Service set the Hübners up in Berlin in a radio and photographic business, the back rooms of which contained a passport-forging workshop. By the outbreak of war Hübner's shop was the principal "safe house" in Berlin for Soviet secret agents[230] and the more frequent the arrivals from Moscow, the more members of her family did Opa Hübner make available—starting with her daughter Frieda and the daughter's husband Stanislaus Wesolek and ending with her grandchildren Johannes and Walter Wesolek.[231]

In addition to the Comintern survivors another group of communist anti-Hitlerites joined Schulze-Boysen's and Harnack's organization. Here again chance took a hand. Shortly after the outbreak of war Lotte Schleif, a librarian, asked friends of Schulze-Boysen for help; she was in constant terror lest the Gestapo get on her trail at any moment, since she was hiding a friend in her apartment, the socialist Rudolf Bergtel. He had escaped from a labor camp a few days before, having been sentenced to eight years' imprisonment for plotting treason. Lotte's only thought was to get him away.[232] In desperation she turned to an acquaintance, a communist named Ilse Schaeffer, whose husband, the municipal librarian Dr. Philip Schaeffer, was also languishing in prison for political reasons.[233] Lotte Schleif knew that Ilse was in contact with resistance circles capable of smuggling hunted anti-fascists abroad. Frau Schaeffer was willing to help. She introduced Lotte Schleif to her friend Elfriede Paul, Küchenmeister's mistress, and she in turn passed Lotte on to Elizabeth Schumacher. Bergtel was soon in safety; Kurt Schumacher got him across the frontier into Switzerland.[234]

Henceforth Lotte Schleif, who was librarian at Prenzlauer Berg, was one of the Schulze-Boysen circuit and she opened new contacts with other anti-Nazis. She knew Heinrich Scheel, for instance, a student of philosophy and a member of a students' circle of predominantly Young Communist leanings.[235] New names appeared: Hans Coppi, ice vendor and metal worker, Rote Kapelle's future radio operator, who had been sentenced to a year's imprisonment for distributing cigarette cards with anti-fascist inscriptions;[236] Hans Lautenschläger, a shopkeeper's assistant, in the army since 1938 and a future distributor of leaflets for Schulze-Boysen's group.[237] Scheel, Coppi and Lautenschläger had all attended the same school, a training farm founded as an experimental institution, on Scharfenberg Island near Tegel on the outskirts of Berlin.[238]

In 1941 Schulze-Boysen came in contact with a second, even larger, group of students. Their spokesman was Dr. John Rittmeister, the nerve specialist; he was the eldest son of a Hamburg businessman of Dutch-Huguenot extraction and was described by his friend Professor (of psychology) Kemp as "highly gifted and sensitive, a weak man with a delicate, almost ingratiating, exterior."[239] He was a disciple of Freud, yearned for a "new humanism" and so had his doubts about the bourgeois system; eventually he turned to radical socialism in which he saw man's hope of liberation from all constraints. He consequently became so immersed in Marxism that in 1937, when working at the cantonal sanatorium in Münsingen, the Swiss authorities expelled him as a communist propagandist.[240] In fact he had no connection with the communist party; he was a skeptic, a philosopher and an aesthete and nothing would have been further from his thoughts than to act as minion for the crude interests of the Party. All his life he was a brooding skeptic, befuddled by his yearning to recapture that compatibility with his environment which he had lost since childhood; he longed to "put a full-stop to the depressions" which ruled his life; he grieved over a childless marriage, the "emptiness of his profession" and the brutality of the times.

The joylessness of his existence produced in John Rittmeister "perturbation and depression of mind" (his own words) which "contributed to my inclination to join Sch-B, quite apart from the intolerable material situation created by Hitler's war and the system as a whole."[241] His "attraction to SB" seemed temporarily to release him from his inhibitions; Schulze-Boysen's influence intensified his aversion to the regime. But revolutionary action was not in the brooding Rittmeister's makeup. In his diary he says: "People are apparently unwilling to believe that I am not basically disposed to action."[242] He regarded resistance to Hitler's system not so much as a practical struggle to put an end to a depraved dictatorship, but as an exercise in morals. When he took over as senior practitioner of the psychotherapy clinic of the Berlin "Institute for Psychological Research and Psychotherapy,"[243] Rittmeister collected around him a circle of young men who thought that the population could be won over to a fundamental change in the politics of the country by means of intensive discussions and evening reading rather than the more spectacular method of plastering posters on walls.

Many of Rittmeister's disciples were pupils at Dr. Heilscher's night school in Berlin, which was also frequented by Eva Knieper, later an actress.[244] She came of an impoverished German-nationalist bourgeois family; Rittmeister made her acquaintance in February 1938 and introduced her into his "social welfare" world.[245] In July 1939 they married.[246] Frau Rittmeister kept in touch with her ex-fellow-pupils of the night school and won a number of them over to her husband's ideas; they included Ursula Goetze, the daughter of a hotel-keeper,[247] Otto Gollnow, the Hitler Youth leader,[248] Fritz Rehmer, a foreman fitter,[249] and his girlfriend Liane Berkowitz,[250] Fritz Thiel, a metal worker,[251] and his newly married wife Hannelore, *née* Hoffmann.[252]

Subsequently other anti-Nazis joined Rittmeister's circle. One of them was Dr. Werner Krauss, a friend of Rittmeister's student days and now Professor of Roman Studies at Marburg University; he was posted to Berlin as an army interpreter and rented a room from Ursula Goetze.[253] Another was Hans Helmuth Himpel, a dentist whom the regime's anti-Semitic laws had driven into opposition—he was forbidden to marry his fiancée Rosemarie Terwiel, daughter of a local government official [Regierungsvize-präsident].[254] Yet another was Cato Bontjes van Beek, an art dealer from Bremen; she joined the resistance because she had witnessed the kidnapping of two of her flat-mates who were Jews;[255] she brought with her her boy friend Heinz Strelow, son of a Hamburg businessman and formerly a member of the communist youth movement.[256]

Such were the people who formed Harro Schulze-Boysen's shadowy army. Month by month his contacts widened; more and more Red anti-fascists flowed into Schulze-Boysen's and Harnack's camp. But before they could fully complete their organization the day of decision was upon them. Adolf Hitler's Panzer Armies were assembling for the invasion of the Soviet Union.

Erdberg gave the signal for action. The Soviet Secret Service chiefs in Moscow, who had seen the German attack coming earlier and more clearly than Stalin and his diplomats, radioed their final instructions to Erdberg—not a moment more to lose: all agents on the alert.[257]

On 14 June 1941 Erdberg summoned his senior German agents to separate meetings—for Adam and Greta Kuckhoff at a station on the underground, for Harro Schulze-Boysen and Arvid Harnack at a tram-stop. Hans Coppi, the future radio operator, was also given an assignation with the Soviet representative.[258]

Erdberg had obtained one or two radio sets, each concealed in a suitcase. With an ordinary ticket he traveled to the agreed station. There the suitcase changed hands. Silently the Germans took over their sets and silently they went away. Distribution of sets was followed by a final ideological exhortation. Erdberg admonished his German friends not to leave the Soviet Union in the lurch in its hour of greatest need; every military detail, every scrap of information about the Wehrmacht would help the Red Army to fight the fascist aggressor.

Each member of the Berlin spy-ring was given a cover-name by which he was known to the Moscow headquarters. Harnack (cover name "Arwid") was given a codebook,[259] Coppi (cover name "Strahlmann") a radio traffic schedule.[260] A packet of banknotes was produced for the recruitment of new agents; Erdberg paid out 11,500 marks, distributed by Harnack as follows: 3,500 to the Kuckhoffs, 5,000 to Behrens, 1,000 to Rose Schlösinger and 3,000 to Leo Skrzypezinski, a manufacturer whom Harnack hoped to recruit.[261] The remainder Harnack retained.

The organization was divided into two parts, the encoding group "Arwid" under Harnack and the informer group "Choro" (Schulze-Boysen's cover name) under Schulze-Boysen; the latter was also to assume overall leadership of the organization.[262] On the withdrawal of Soviet representation from Berlin, Schulze-Boysen was to maintain contact with Moscow via the radio sets already distributed and the Rote Kapelle groups operating in Western Europe.

The start was inauspicious. On the return journey from her meeting on the underground station Greta Kuckhoff dropped the suitcase containing the radio set and when she and her husband tried to test it at home, no sound emerged.[263] The two were panic-stricken. They hid the useless but dangerous instrument in the house, but even this did not seem safe enough. Adam Kuckhoff took the set out and buried it in a neighbor's garden.[264]

Coppi was no more fortunate with his set. He was an inexperienced operator anyway and the set given him by Erdberg was an obsolete battery machine of inadequate range and frequency. Coppi could not make head or tail of it and Schulze-Boysen had to ask Erdberg for a better one.[265]

The Soviets provided better equipment. The Russians repaired the Kuckhoffs' set[266] and Coppi was handed a new suitcase on Deutschlandhalle Station; it was an up-to-date transmitter and receiver using alternating current.[267] Now at last the spy-ring could start to work. Even before Hitler's columns moved into Russia the German spies' radio sets were ticking away.

Report after report came from Schulze-Boysen to the Soviet General Staff; many of his messages told the Red Army where the main weight of the German attacks was to come. Greta Kuckhoff says: "Harro was immeasurably valuable. The first news of war preparations came from Harro and it included even the cities which were to be the first objectives."[268] Harnack too provided first-class information; when Erdberg left for the Balkans he took with him a memorandum on the strengths and weaknesses of the German armaments industry.[269]

Had they any doubts, any scruples about betraying their country's secrets to the enemy? Any resistance movement based on patriotic or liberal motives sets itself certain limits, but most of the members of this particular spy-ring were not afraid to cross them. The principle that state secrets should not be betrayed to the enemy if this would jeopardize the interests of one's own country, or the lives of one's own soldiers, had no validity in the eyes of these Red agents. Such ideas were foreign to many of Schulze-

Boysen's adherents. The spy-ring included among its more active members orthodox communists who, even under the Weimar Republic, had been taught that, in the event of a Russo-German war, it was their duty to come to the assistance of Moscow, no matter where blame for the war might lie—and in 1941 the blame lay unequivocally at Germany's door.

With Schulze-Boysen himself nationalism did not weigh in the struggle against Hitler. In 1932, as editor of the *Gegner,* he had proclaimed that "all revolutionary minorities" must rally to the defense of the Soviet Union, and among these minorities he had included German youth; Germany, he had said, must never be found in opposition to Russia.[270]

At that time he had admittedly accused the German communists of over-dependence on Moscow; he had thought that the Soviet Union was pursuing its own selfish power policy which could never be consistent with German interests. Now, however, for better or for worse, he was prepared to support Stalin's change of heart; the Soviets seemed to him to be "sober intelligent planners who would not be so stupid as to squander the moral advantage they had gained as the first uncompromising enemies of fascism."[271] With equal insouciance he had been prepared to draw up government lists for the future German Soviet Republic and to plan for a Russo-German war.[272] One day he had described to his friends with almost masochistic pleasure how Russian troops would invade and put an end to the brown-shirted horror. At a birthday party in September 1939, when the honeymoon of the Hitler-Stalin Pact was at its zenith, he had forecast: "When the time comes the Russians will strike and emerge as victors."[273]

Many anti-fascists acquiesced in such political fanaticism either not at all or only with reluctance. In his plea to the Court, Harnack himself later attempted to show that he had only spied for the Soviet Union in wartime because of his personal pledge to Erdberg;[274] even Greta Kuckhoff said in her peculiar brand of obscure language that the decision to work as an intelligence agent for "foreign agencies" had been a "weighty step" for many of them.[275]

Some flatly refused. Leo Schabbel, Henry Robinson's son, upbraided his mother for sheltering Soviet parachute agents.[276] Kurt Schumacher's mother demanded the removal of a radio set stored in her cellar.[277] The majority of members of Rittmeister's resistance group proved to be so unforthcoming that Schulze-Boysen found it advisable not to divulge to them too many of the secrets of his espionage activities. Even certain KPD functionaries such as Heinz Verleih and Heinrich Schrader,[278] who had been in a concentration camp with Guddorf, shared the view of Herbert Wehner; when subsequently arrested in Stockholm, he said that he had refused all espionage missions from Moscow—"though implacably opposed to the Hitler government, my basic conception of my relationship to the German people prevents me carrying out an activity which could be characterized as espionage."[279]

Even some of Schulze-Boysen's closest associates had scruples at times. Horst Heilmann, who was a sort of secretary to Schulze-Boysen, said to his friend Rainer Hildebrandt that one might pass information to the enemy but it must not lead to the death of German soldiers.[280] Desperately he mulled over the question whether a man was justified in committing treason and could find no answer. He told Hildebrandt that it was "an offense, not only against one's own conscience or even only against one's country; it was an offense against world order and mankind. If one reaches the point when one is even visualizing the idea of treason, one must realize that it carries with it an almost incalculable measure of guilt."[281]

What plea could they offer in mitigation of this guilt? Indignation at the crimes of a regime which had brought Germany and Europe to catastrophe; disgust with a political system which, with its concentration camps, Jewish pogroms, thought control and steam-roller machinery, had made the German Reich a byword for barbarity and injustice.

But for the scruple-merchants this was insufficient motivation for high treason. The evil deeds of the Nazi dictatorship could not excuse selling one's soul to the service of a foreign espionage organization or working exclusively for a country which, with its system of terror, its millions of murdered citizens and its grisly fake trials, was as shocking to democrats as the injustices of Nazism.

So the scruple-merchants discovered an additional motive never before adduced as justification for treason—the nationalist motive. Adam `Kuckhoff wanted to construct a

Soviet Germany "on a national basis";[282] Schulze-Boysen's
object in serving the Russians was to earn for the future
Reich a modest existence of its own by Moscow's side;[283]
Wilhelm Guddorf proposed the "creation of a Soviet Germany to end Germany's enslavement [by the Allied victors]
and prevent the dismemberment of Germany."[284] Arvid
Harnack even visualized a conventional German state allied to Russia but completely independent. He explained
to the conservative anti-Nazis how he saw the future:
Germany together with Russia and China would form a
bloc which would be "economically and militarily impregnable"; Stalin would not insist on the sovietization
of Germany; he would be content with a peace-loving
Reich.[285]

Such nationalist pretexts for treason, however, could
not hold water for long; they savored too much of illusion. The question remained how men who had once
figured on the Soviet Secret Service's payroll could later
become free agents *vis-à-vis* Moscow if they were the
leaders of a Soviet Germany.

Harnack's concept was based on the notion that there
would be no conflict of interest between Germany and
Russia. If there were, however, what would happen then?
Harnack, as a statesman, would be fair game for any form
of Soviet blackmail; he would have been no better off than
Rudolf von Scheliha, the timorous German Foreign Service officer—to allay his suddenly aroused scruples the
Soviet Secret Service sent him photostat copies of the
accounts recording payments made to him for espionage
services.[286]

Even this did not solve the crisis of conscience, however.
It raged throughout Rote Kappelle's existence—and it is
still raging today. After the end of the war came another
attempt to explain and justify. Schulze-Boysen's friend
Weisenborn was the protagonist in his books. According
to him the Schulze-Boysen/Harnack circuit should be respected as a resistance organization; espionage was a secondary activity; there was an "inner circle" of resisters
concerned only with internal politics and an "outer circle"
of anti-fascist spies.[287]

This theory does not stand up to closer examination.
Members of an "inner circle" could only have been
Schulze-Boysen's closest associates and they were in fact
the people who did the spying. There were five com-

ponents to Schulze-Boysen's organization: his own group, the Harnack group, the Guddorf group, the Scharfenberg-Schüler group and the Rittmeister group; with a few exceptions the members of the first four groups can all be proved to have been concerned in espionage. The fifth group, that of John Rittmeister, did form an "outer circle"; only in this case is the term justified. The Rittmeister group was only loosely connected with Schulze-Boysen's organization; its members hardly knew of the others' espionage activities.

The fate of the first four groups themselves, moreover, shows the artificiality of Weisenborn's differentiation. Intelligence and resistance activities were inseparable. Chance was frequently the deciding factor.

Weisenborn himself could testify to this. He was a westernized democrat and did not therefore feel that he could spy for the Soviet Union. In 1941, however, he became an editor in the news department of the German Radio and there he was able to check whether encoded messages for Moscow were included in the news broadcasts. He came to the conclusion that they were not—and so he concluded that the editor responsible for the final drafting of the news summaries was not trustworthy! The plan to use the news summaries was a failure—but Günther Weisenborn was at heart a resister.[288] The incident shows that Schulze-Boysen was able to persuade almost any antifascist in his circle to undertake some sort of espionage. Initially even he had hoped that he could work for Moscow's Secret Service with the help of only a few close associates. At heart he did not like espionage—working in forbidden territory and collecting scraps of information. He would have preferred to work in the open, to satisfy his own ambitions, self-destructive though they might be.

Moreover in his eyes active resistance to the Nazi system was the most important task of the anti-fascists. His bent was toward bold propaganda action; he saw himself at the head of columns of billstickers creeping around in the night. Even he had his second thoughts and he could only stifle them by offensive action against the regime. Recklessly he attacked the system without thought for his friends; many of his associates began to wonder whether they had not cast in their lot with an unscrupulous adventurer.

There were many doubters. His friend Hugo Buschmann

once said to him: "Don't go gossiping with young people; you only put them in danger,"[289] and he advised against propaganda activity. But Schulze-Boysen merely replied: "We have got to do it. If the Russians come to Germany (and they will come) and if they are to play some role in Germany, we must be able to show that there was a meaningful resistance group in Germany. Otherwise the Russians will be able to do what they want with us."[290]

He was firmly convinced that it was his historic mission to bring down the Nazi system by revolutionary methods. He set no store by an attempt to assassinate Hitler; his gospel was that only a social revolution could bring about the decisive change in German government and society.[291] And he saw himself as the guiding spirit of this revolution; he regarded himself as the Lenin of the new upheaval.

Schulze-Boysen was a restless spirit, yearning for relaxation and human sympathy. He saw himself as a man with a mission who could achieve the impossible. Hildebrandt, with whom he discussed at length, says: "He wanted to cover Germany with a network of resistance groups . . . and so to direct each cell and each group . . . that the discovery of one would not lead to that of others or of the central directing agency. By means of a system of real and fictitious contact-men the members of individual groups were to be kept in the dark as to who their true master was."[292] Schulze-Boysen believed that, by revolutionary methods, he could bring about the "rapid collapse" of Hitler Germany—"like an avalanche"; he thought that this might happen in 1943.[293] By that time his propagandists would have changed the political outlook of the regimented Germans; even the foreign workers in the Reich could be made ripe for revolution.

The central feature of the plan was what Werner Krauss calls "the enlightenment of the various professions." By means of leaflets, posters and clandestine newssheets the population was to be "made aware of their vital interests and compelled by concrete proofs to direct their thoughts to the future and to draw their conclusions from the hopelessness of the military situation."[294] The spearheads of this propaganda offensive, however, were the pedestrian Communist Party scribes directed by Guddorf; their material was the secret information provided by Schulze-Boysen and Harnack.

In a summer-house belonging to Max Grabowski, a KPD comrade living in Berlin-Rudow, Guddorf and Sieg set up a printing press producing handbills and leaflets. By the end of 1941 *Die Innere Front* [The Home Front] edited by Sieg was appearing twice monthly.[295] Schulze-Boysen and Harnack provided data and also their own contributions; nevertheless, *Die Innere Front* was a Communist Party organ and followed every twist and turn of Soviet propaganda.[296]

"It is not Mr. Churchill who is pledged to the second front," the newssheet said; "the protagonists and guarantors of the second front are the worker masses of all countries; they are determined to put an end to Hitler's regime of cannibal incendiaries." In 1942 it proclaimed: "Stalin's inspired strategy, the Red Army's heroism and the resistance of the Soviet Union's workers have broken the back of Hitler's army."[297] How such empty phrases were supposed to rouse the Germans to resist the regime when Hitler's military success was at its height was a secret known only to the Communist Party editors.

In a room in No. 2 Waitzstrasse were to be found Corporal Heinz Strelow and his girlfriend Cato Bontjes van Beek, duplicating newssheets; Strelow was a careful soul and always worked in gloves.[298] The two were joined by Eva-Maria Buch, the bookseller, Guddorf's mistress; she translated the resistance news into French.[299]

Schulze-Boysen and Rittmeister generally decided on the contents of the newssheets when they met in Schulze-Boysen's new apartment at No. 19 Altenburger Allee.[300] At Rittmeister's suggestion they were signed "Agis" after Agis IV, King of Sparta in the third century BC, who had tried to free the people of the burden of debt and divide the land up among his citizens.[301] Schulze-Boysen frequently contributed secret information from his office including "unknown data such as production capacity of the United States aircraft industry and penetrating expositions on Russian strategy."[302]

A flood of anti-fascist literature descended on Berlin. Every headline told the Germans what they must get into their heads: that the war was lost and that Hitler must be brought down in time, before the Reich was ruined. Articles appeared entitled "A call to all professions and organizations to resist the government" or "A revealing memorandum by north German industry on the events leading to war"; the resisters philosophized about "Freedom and Force"; they issued an appeal "to those who work with brain or muscle not to fight against Russia."[303] Schulze-Boysen himself took to his pen and wrote "The Life of Napoleon." Buschmann said: "He was very proud of it. I thought it twaddle."[304]

But Schulze-Boysen was not satisfied with drafting resistance literature; he wanted revolutionary action and the activists, it seemed to him, were to be found among the foreign forced laborers in the Third Reich; the Nazi system, he thought, could be brought down by Hitler's foreign slaves.

He formed a fantastic plan: The foreign workers were to be formed into "legions" and raised against their German masters.[305] He was continually visiting the "Bärenschenke" bar in the Friedrichstrasse, Berlin, where foreign workers forgathered; there, he thought, the revolution would take shape.[306] But he was doomed to disappointment; the West European workers did not understand what he was talking about. Krauss says: "The psychological difficulties were very great; readiness to collaborate or at any rate political apathy were widespread, particularly among the French workers."[307]

Once more Schulze-Boysen searched for some means of triggering off his revolution. He could find nothing and was reduced to propaganda. His most dramatic enterprise was at the same time the oddest ever undertaken by the head of an espionage organization. Krauss says that he wanted "to give the people the impression that we were still there and that internal resistance forces were ready for action."[308]

The occasion was the Nazi propaganda spectacle in the Berlin Lustgarten, "Soviet Paradise"; Moscow had ordered some spectacular action against it. During the night 17/18 May 1942, a small communist resistance group under Herbert Baum was ordered to set fire to the "Inflammatory anti-Soviet Exhibition."[309] Baum's comrades set forth armed with a bomb and some incendiary material.[310]

Baum contacted Schulze-Boysen, who declared himself ready to cooperate as soon as he heard of the operation. He had handbills printed which his people were to stick over the official posters, so that they then read: "Permanent Exhibition: The Nazi Paradise—War—Starvation—Falsehood—Gestapo. How long?"[311] On the night in question, dressed in full uniform, Schulze-Boysen went out with his billstickers. Hardly one of them thought the operation advisable (Krauss says: "The moment could not have been worse chosen") but Schulze-Boysen would brook no opposition.[312] So determined was he, that he drove his friends ahead of him with his revolver and many of them were afraid that it might actually go off. The subsequent Gestapo report says: "As an indication of his fanaticism—when some of his men wanted to stop, he threatened them with a loaded service revolver."[313]

Schulze-Boysen's friends were only too right to be displeased. A few days after the exhibition had been set on fire[314] Baum's entire group was arrested by the Gestapo and its members condemned to death by the Peoples Court;[315] subsequently many of Schulze-Boysen's friends who had had nothing to do with resistance were condemned to death simply because they had taken part in the operation of 18 May.

Schulze-Boysen's semi-religious ardor gradually began to seem somewhat sinister to many of the anti-Nazis. A few months earlier Cato Bontjes van Beek and Strelow had broken off contact with him because they feared that the gambler would drive them into the arms of the Gestapo.[316] Guddorf severed all relations with Schulze-Boysen because he found so dilettante a conspirator dangerous.[317] Rittmeister began to doubt whether Schulze-Boysen was suited to be leader of a resistance group.* Buschmann said: "Because of his imprudence we had to be extremely careful. When he was in full voice, one would have thought that he was a Gestapo spy, he was so indiscreet."[319]

The more his ability as leader was questioned, however, the more pertinaciously did Schulze-Boysen devote himself to espionage. Moscow's orders in any case compelled him to concentrate more and more on expanding his intelligence network. The war was going badly for the Soviets and so their demands for total commitment by their friends in the enemy's camp became shriller.

Schulze-Boysen had meanwhile extended his circuit of informers considerably. He had started with only four

---

* Typical of the relationship between Rittmeister and Schulze-Boysen was the fact that the latter never told Rittmeister beforehand of the 18 May operation "because one knew that he would be against from the outset."[318]

couples—himself and his wife, the Kuckhoffs, the Coppis and the Harnacks. They all knew exactly what Moscow expected of them and they would meet regularly on the Wannsee in the 25-meter yawl *Duschinka,* owned jointly by the Schulze-Boysens and the Weisenborns, to discuss their individual plan.[320] Each knew his or her place and each collected information from the sphere in which they worked. Greta Kuckhoff was in the Nazi Racio-Political Office and could observe internal Nazi Party matters; as an author Kuckhoff was in contact with literary and artistic circles; Harnack drew his information from the Reich Ministry of Economics; his wife Mildred was a teacher of languages in the Faculty of Foreign Scholarship at Berlin University and so could survey the academic world; Libertas Schulze-Boysen made use of her connections with the Reich Ministry of Propaganda (as a member of the Cultural Film Center she had access to the Ministry's secret papers) and with the film world; Hilde and Hans Coppi were the radio operators.

Schulze-Boysen himself, however, had created the most productive channels of information. Since January 1941 he had become a member of the First Echelon of the Operational Staff of the Luftwaffe, housed in a hutted camp at Wildpark Werder near Potsdam.[321] In this camp were located all the most secret sections of the German Luftwaffe; Wildpark Werden was the "Reich Marshal's [Göring's] Headquarters"; it was the command post of the Head of the Luftwaffe Signals Service and the "Air Intelligence Regiment Ob.d.L [Oberbefehlshaber der Luftwaffe —Commander-in-Chief of the Luftwaffe]; it was the emergency location for the Reich Ministry of Aviation.[322]

Schulze-Boysen had meanwhile left Major Bartz's Press Group and had been transferred to the Attaché Group. This meant that he was now an intelligence officer, a member of the General Staff section in fact, dealing with enemy intelligence—of decisive importance, of course, for his secret work. The Group formed part of Section 5 under Colonel Beppo Schmidt.[323]

This section was the collecting point for all diplomatic and military reports originating from the Air Attachés in German embassies and legations.[324] Schulze-Boysen had only to copy or photograph these secret reports and he knew exactly what the Axis Powers were thinking about the war situation. There was no difficulty about smuggling the reports out for, as far as their own officers were concerned, the Wildpark security guards were extremely lax; it was necessary only to show a pay-book at the exit; pockets were never searched.[325]

Schulze-Boysen's actual job gave him considerable insight into the secrets of the Hitler coalition. His duty was to keep in touch with the Air Attachés of the Third Reich's allies and the neutrals. He therefore learned much about the worries and problems of the Axis air forces; he noted down the current gossip among the foreign military.

In addition he tried to be on the best of terms with his section head since, in addition to the coffin of Frederick the Great stored in a concrete bunker, Colonel Beppo Schmidt was the guardian of a prize of far greater interest to a spy—the target maps for the bomber force.[326] Colonel Schmidt appreciated his Lieutenant's devotion to duty. The two were soon on such good terms that Schulze-Boysen was regarded in the headquarters as Schmidt's right-hand man. No one found this surprising since, despite being somewhat jumpy, Schulze-Boysen was generally looked upon as "extraordinarily likable, versatile and gay."[327]

Even these achievements did not satisfy Schulze-Boysen, however. He became friendly with another Colonel to whom he could speak his mind much more openly than to Schmidt, who was a favorite of Göring. This was Colonel Erwin Gehrts, head of Group III in the "Regulations and Instructional Appliances" Section of the Training Department. To him Schulze-Boysen could acknowledge that he was an anti-Nazi, though Gehrts, a devout Christian, would have had no sympathy for espionage in favor of the enemy.[328]

Gehrts was also anti-Nazi. He and Schulze-Boysen had known each other since the end of the 1920s when both were in journalism. They had met again in Berlin in 1932 when Schulze-Boysen was editing the *Gegner* and Gehrts the *Tägliche Rundschau* which had supported the left-wing democrat experiment of the Chancellor, General Kurt von Schleicher.[329] The Nazi seizure of power had driven Gehrts, who had been in the air force in World War I, into military service like Schulze-Boysen. He rose to a senior position in the Reich Ministry of Aviation, but he was a melancholy being, feared for his incalculable outbursts of rage; although a convinced Christian, he was an astrologist; he no longer took much pleasure in life.[330]

Schulze-Boysen wormed his way into Gehrts' good graces by doing him many little good turns and in almost every case they had something to do with Anna Kraus. She ran a profitable business as a fortune-teller in the Stahnsdorf quarter of Berlin. Gehrts, who often consulted Nostradamus, found that she was just the sort of person he liked to talk to.[331]

Gehrts had confided his anxieties to Schulze-Boysen, who had effected the introduction to Anna Kraus. She comforted Gehrts over his marital troubles; she advised him over his erotic problems in the office and she even influenced his official decisions.[332] Perhaps it was some question of promotion, or new regulations for the Luftwaffe, or disciplinary problems—Gehrts always had one or two secret files with him in order to show them to Anna Kraus in the semi-darkness of her consulting room.

Gehrts did not know that Anna Kraus was one of Schulze-Boysen's informers. She was a widow and passed on any information from Gehrts to her old friend Toni Graudenz.[333] Toni's husband, Johannes ("John") Graudenz, from Danzig, was one of the most important members of Schulze-Boysen's spy circuit. He was a bon viveur who hardly seemed to fit into this circle of idealists and fanatics; many thought him a pure opportunist, intent only on insuring himself a secure future.[334]

He had led a varied life, showing that at least he had enterprise; he had been in turn a waiter in Western Europe, a tourist guide in Berlin, on the staff of "United Press" in Moscow, correspondent of the *New York Times,* proprietor of a photographic business and at this time was an industrial salesman;[335] he represented the Wuppertal firm of Blumhard which made undercarriages for aircraft and so often had business in the Reich Ministry of Aviation.[336] There he made the acquaintance of Schulze-Boysen, whose aversion to Nazism he shared, particularly since Anna Kraus had warned him to be prepared for a Soviet invasion of Berlin.

Anna Kraus gave many proofs of her powers of second sight and exerted considerable influence on the spy organization. As early as 1940 she had foretold war with Russia and a Soviet occupation of Germany. Unfortunately her gifts deserted her on a fatal occasion in the summer of 1942 when she said that Schulze-Boysen was traveling on duty whereas he had in fact long since been languishing in the Gestapo prison.[337] Nevertheless Frau Graudenz still maintains today: "I am convinced that this woman really had the gift of clairvoyance."[338]

Fortified by Frau Kraus' warning about the future, Graudenz joined the ranks of Schulze-Boysen's informers. He had no difficulty in establishing contact with the engineers in the "Master-General of Air Ordnance" department in the Ministry of Aviation. It was soon common knowledge that he occupied a position of special confidence in the Ministry.[339] He was on good terms with senior officers who frequently lent him secret books on production statistics. Many of his unconscious informers were people who would never have dreamed of opposing the Nazi regime—Hans Henninger, a government Construction Inspector, for instance, and a desk officer in the planning section,[340] Martin Becker, an engineer colonel and head of the construction section.[341] Graudenz industriously entered in a notebook everything he read or heard; being fond of his food, his own private code was based on a number of varieties of sausage; "2,500 grams of shooting sausage,"* for instance, meant 2,500 fighter aircraft.[342]

Schulze-Boysen was also in contact with the headquarters of the other services. He hoped to infiltrate Werner Krauss, who was in the Foreign Censorship Agency of the Abwehr, into Army headquarters [OKH—Oberkommando des Heeres] and so gain some insight into the Army's occupation policy in Russia.[343] His primary object was to counter any attempt by moderate army officers such as Colonel Graf Stauffenberg gradually to give occupied Russia some measure of political autonomy and so win the Russian population over as allies against Stalin.

Here was another instance of the divergence between Schulze-Boysen's organization and the plans of the 20 July conspirators. Schulze-Boysen had no sympathy for the nationalist motives of the men who engineered the attempt on Hitler's life. He wished simply to re-establish the tyranny of the Soviets in the zone now occupied by the Germans; Stauffenberg and his associates, on the other hand, visualized a system as different from Stalin's methods of oppression as it was from Hitler's "sub-humans" policy. Schulze-Boysen, however, simply refused to recognize that the

* The German word "Jagd" (hunting or shooting) means "fighter" when applied to aircraft ("Jagdflugzeug" = fighter aircraft. [Translator.]

Stalinist terror had existed; he took it for granted that in the East the rule of Stalin should be restored.

Kraus, the interpreter, however, was too prudent to accede to Schulze-Boysen's plan for OKH. He thought that he had enough to do with "the rewarding task of subverting the troops" and proposed his friend Martin Hellweg for the OKH job. Hellweg was already in the East and already doing exactly what Schulze-Boysen proposed;[344] Krauss says: "He was employed as a radio operator and was working on the same lines as us, both in his job and through his continuous contacts with the pro-Soviet elements of the population, some of whom he infiltrated into the German military administration."[345]

The man who went to OKH was Horst Heilmann, a radio operator and interpreter, in whom Schulze-Boysen placed great hopes. As a student Heilmann had been an enthusiastic Nazi. Schulze-Boysen had made his acquaintance at the Foreign Scholarship Institute of Berlin University, which he (Schulze-Boysen) had joined as a seminar leader.[346] Heilmann had graduated when only 17; he had joined the Luftwaffe Intelligence Service where he was regarded as a first-class brain.[347] He was posted to the Interpreter Unit in Meissen where, being a high-class mathematician, he passed an examination in codes and ciphers with distinction; he accordingly ended in the "Decoding Section East" of WNV/Fu III, the office which was to become responsible for decoding the Soviet spies' radio messages.[348] He was a shy youth of lower-middle-class background and he became the devoted admirer of the worldly-wise Schulze-Boysen; moreover, he had turned against Nazism and discovered that, both intellectually and materially, the only prospect for the future lay in Marxism.

Heilmann became Schulze-Boysen's closest technical adviser, his mentor and his amanuensis. He wrote fundamental theses for his master and worked out for the organization what might be called a blueprint for a Germany based on the Soviet system.[349] Moreover, clever though he was, he was an unhappy man and he was captivated by the unpredictable feminine ways of Libertas Schulze-Boysen; the two became very close friends.

Heilmann also became a recruiter for Schulze-Boysen's circuit of informers. He tapped new sources in OKH, though admittedly they did not know whom they were serving. Alfred Traxl, for instance, who worked in the same office as Heilmann and had been a 2nd Lieutenant in the Czechoslovak army, was quite unsuspecting; he was now a warrant officer in Section 4 of OKH Intelligence and head of "Decoding Section West"; he recounted his section's achievements in decoding Soviet radio messages simply because he loved to tell a good story.[350]

One of Schulze-Boysen's best informers was equally unsuspecting. This was Lieutenant Herbert Gollnow, a naïve young officer working in Section II of the Abwehr dealing with sabotage. He became Mildred Harnack's lover[351] and never perceived that, while in bed with her, he was being systematically interrogated. Mildred Harnack, who was a highly sensitive and intelligent being, was admittedly by no means promiscuous, as were many of the leaders of the Schulze-Boysen/Harnack group. Their liaisons formed a curiously checkered pattern. It was an open secret that Schulze-Boysen had three mistresses, Oda Schottmüller and two secretaries in the Ministry of Aviation;[352] Libertas Schulze-Boysen cohabited with Kurt Schumacher,[353] and Hans Coppi with Gräfin [Countess] Erika von Brockdorff. She was a lady of easy virtue, daughter of a postman in Kolberg; her friendship with Elizabeth Schumacher (the two had worked in the Reich Agency for Industrial Safety) had brought her into the Schulze-Boysen group. Any member of Rote Kapelle who was interested had a standing invitation to her bed.[354]

Some of the more squeamish of the anti-fascists later protested that even the mention of these love affairs was tantamount to slander of the dead, while after the war ex-Nazi functionaries took pleasure in recounting spicy stories of the sex orgies supposed to have taken place in Schulze-Boysen's apartment. The majority of such tales are figments of the imagination. Buschmann says: "I was present on one occasion. If that was an orgy, then young people today who drink Coca-Cola and dress in beatnik rags, are also engaged in an orgy. Of course people were merry; they were, after all, living dangerously and probably wanted some outlet. But it was certainly no orgy."[355]

Schulze-Boysen's more sensitive champions, moreover, clearly overlook the fact that their case is based on a bourgeois puritanism entirely foreign to the main figures on the stage at the time. Love affairs were accepted; even in 1932 Schulze-Boysen had inveighed against the "bourgeois mar-

riage prison" and had said: "We intend to deny ourselves
nothing of life, youth or pleasure."[356] Schulze-Boysen's
uncle, Dr. Jan Tönnies, confirms that "both the Schulze-
Boysens had relations with other partners with full recipro-
cal knowledge and understanding on both sides" and that
"unfaithfulness did not imply lack of trust."[357]

Mildred Harnack, however, was a reserved academic
without the others' lust for living; she was respected by all
who knew her as a "noble spirit."[358] There is no knowing
what attracted her to Gollnow. She may have been in love
with the gauche, impetuous officer who could forget the
disappointments of his life when at her side; alternatively
she may simply have been obeying an order from her husband. The only statement she herself made indicated the
latter possibility; under interrogation by the Gestapo she
gave as the reason for her action: "Because I had to obey
my husband."[359]

In fact Arvid Harnack was very interested in Gollnow.
He had entered the Harnacks' lives through a newspaper
advertisement. He came of a Berlin family and was an
ambitious officer, in civil life a member of the Consular
Section of the Foreign Ministry; he wanted to enter the
diplomatic service.[360] He had reached his present position
by studying on his own and was looking for a private tutor
to teach him foreign languages.[361] The private tutor turned
out to be Mildred Harnack; she took the young man under
her wing.

Arvid Harnack was all for these meetings since Gollnow
was in an important position in Admiral Canaris' office;
he was desk officer for "Air-transported and Parachute
troops" in the Sabotage Section of the Abwehr; he therefore
knew all about the secret operations of German agents behind the Soviet front.[362] Harnack would start talking to
Gollnow and, by sceptical references to the war situation,
lure him into giving away official secrets; the more pessimistic Harnack's remarks, the more eager did Gollnow become to quote figures, names and details of operations to
prove how good the German commanders were and how
satisfactory the situation was. He was, after all, a young
Hitler disciple and any disbelief in ultimate victory seemed
to him mere folly.[363] While Mildred Harnack and her pupil
were alone together she extracted further revelations from
him. Meanwhile another visitor, also an intelligence officer,

appeared—2nd Lieutenant Wolfgang Havemann, an assistant judge in civil life, who was on a course in Berlin; he was a relative, a nephew of Harnack; his mother was Harnack's sister.[364]

Havemann was also in a post of interest to Soviet spies. He was assistant to the Head of Section III of Naval Intelligence and undoubtedly knew many of Naval Headquarters' secrets.[365] Had he been willing to play his uncle's game, Rote Kapelle would have had a foot in the door of the Naval High Command. Once or twice he had prattled away and had blabbed out a number of secrets; Moscow headquarters had even given him a cover-name and had ordered Kent to check Havemann's aptitude for espionage work.[366] As soon as he realized what they were doing, however, Havemann refused to be further persuaded by his uncle and aunt. Harnack argued vehemently but in vain; the nephew insisted that what his uncle was doing amounted to betrayal of his country.[367] He repeatedly warned Harnack, but was unwilling to denounce his uncle.

Even without Havemann, however, Harnack and Schulze-Boysen now had an intelligence system which could tell them all the more important secrets of German strategy. Every night, as soon as the Berlin spies' radio sets were on the air, the Soviet General Staff learned what its enemy was thinking and planning, what had gone wrong and what he was afraid of.

Schulze-Boysen's intelligence service reported to Moscow, for instance, that on searching the Soviet Consulate in the Finnish town of Petsamo, German soldiers had found a codebook;[368] it found out that, since the capture of certain British codebooks, the Abwehr now knew of allied convoys between Iceland and the north Russian ports before they had even sailed;[369] it knew the points at which German U-boats lay in wait outside Murmansk in order to intercept the convoys.[370] Schulze-Boysen and his men had a sight of many German orders and construction plans—orders for the employment of Russian anti-communist volunteer formations on the Eastern Front, drawings of new Luftwaffe equipment, tables of arms production.[371] One of his messages read: "New Messerschmidt fighter has two cannon and two machine-guns mounted side by side in the wings. Can reach a speed of 375 m.p.h."[372]

Schulze-Boysen's informers produced reports of so-called "iconoscopic" bombs;[373] they knew about new Luftwaffe direction-finding gear;[374] they reported on hydrogen peroxide fuels for missiles.[375] They inquired into homing torpedoes; they knew about the "Luftengel-Bodenengel" ground-to-air weapon; they spirited drawings out of the safes in the super-secret underground factory at Orainenburg.[376] In addition they provided Moscow with strategic intelligence.

On 9 December 1941 Schulze-Boysen's agents reported: "The fresh assault on Moscow is not the outcome of some strategic decision; it is indicative of the dissatisfaction prevailing in the German army over the fact that, ever since 22 June, new objectives are always being set and never reached. As a result of Soviet resistance Plan I (Urals), Plan II (Archangel-Astrakhan) and Plan III (Caucasus) have all had to be abandoned."[377] Three days later they radioed: "German army proposes to settle down for the winter early in November on the line Rostov-Smolensk-Vyasma-Leningrad. Germans are throwing everything they have in the way of material against Moscow and the Crimea."[378]

The spies had partial knowledge of the offensive plans prepared for the summer of 1942 by the German Army Group B in the Voronezh area;[379] they reported to Moscow the objectives for the German Caucasus offensive.[380] Schulze-Boysen's radio tapped out: "Source: Choro. Plan III with objective Caucasus comes into force in spring 1942. Concentration to be completed by 1 May. From 1 February all supply geared to this objective. Concentration area for Caucasus offensive; Losovaya-Balakleya-Chuguyev-Belgorod-Aktirka-Kransnograd."[381]

Schulze-Boysen's agents gathered up every scrap of information which might show the Russians what the German General Staff was thinking. A message dated 22 September 1941 read: "OKW regards all intelligence about a special Russian winter army as false. OKW convinced that Russians have thrown everything into present offensive and have no further reserves."[382] A month later the spies reported: "Senior generals in OKW now reckon on a further thirty months of war, after which compromise peace possible."[383] By 12 August 1942 the picture had changed: "Serious differences of opinion in OKW regarding operations in southern sector of Eastern Front. Prevailing view is that attack in direction Stalingrad now useless and success of Caucasus operation questionable. Hitler demands Stalingrad offensive and is supported in this by Göring."[384]

Moscow was continually demanding further details of German strategy and Schulze-Boysen was indefatigable in his efforts to answer the Director's questions. One message read: "The Hermann Göring Division is not a panzer division but merely a motorized division";[385] and another: "1. Strength of German Luftwaffe now 22,000 first- and second-line aircraft with in addition 6,000–6,500 Junkers 52 transport aircraft. 2. At present 10–12 dive-bombers are being produced in Germany per day. 3. Luftwaffe ground-attack formations hitherto located in Crete are being transferred to the Eastern Front, part to Crimea and the remainder distributed across the front. 4. German air losses on Eastern Front from 22 June to end September have averaged 45 per day."[386]

Again and again the reports from Berlin revealed the intentions and plans of the German leaders—the attack on Maikop,[387] series production of German aircraft in the occupied territories,[388] the fuel position in Germany,[389] location of chemical warfare materials in the Reich.[390] Queries were continually coming from Moscow; on 25 August 1942, for instance: "Establish and report forthwith existence and movement of Infantry Divisions 73, 337, 709 and SS Division 'Reich.' There are indications that Divisions 337 and 709 have moved from West to East and 73 and 'Reich' from East to West. Where are they at present?"[391]

The Soviet spies proved to be particularly well informed on German commando operations behind the Soviet lines. They listened in to the plans and orders of "Walli II," the Abwehr's forward observation post and the control post for mobile detachments which blew up bridges and railway lines in the Soviet rear areas, attacked Red Army soldiers and occupied strategic points.[392] The Soviets had foreknowledge of twelve of the Abwehr's sabotage operations; ten German commando detachments were met by the machine-gun fire of Russian ambushes.[393]

Razvedupr gained considerable insight into the operations of the German Secret Service. The Director in Moscow, for instance, knew of the plan to occupy the oil town of Baku with German parachute troops.[394] He learned of German preparations to sabotage United States transoceanic aircraft.[395] He knew that the Abwehr was planning to infiltrate agents into Britain from Norway.[396]

To the leaders of the beaten Soviet armies Rote Kapelle's radio reports must have sounded like messages of salvation. The General Staff in Moscow, of course, could not tell whether they came from some highly organized system embracing all aspects of German strategy, or were the chance products of industrious, but disorganized and amateurish, espionage. The Soviet Generals, however, demanded more and more information. Every report gave them fresh hope; every message over the air revealed weaknesses in the German war machine, opening up the possibility for the Russians that, despite all their defeats and discouragements, one day they would gain the upper hand and drive the invader back.

But the Berlin circuit suffered from a fatal weakness: its communication system was continually failing. In matters of short-wave radio Coppi was a dilettante who had received some exiguous training from Husemann, an Old-Guard communist. He did his best to operate his set—but his best was not very good. Moreover, Coppi was the only operator available to Schulze-Boysen's organization. The Soviets had handed out three sets in good working order, one each to Harnack, Kuckhoff and Coppi—but there were no operators to go with them. Hans Coppi was expected to work them all.[397]

Then, in the words of Coppi's son, "it happened"—"My father put the plug of the set into an alternating current socket. But the set was constructed only for direct current. Result: the fuses were blown and other parts of the set damaged. Replacements for all the parts had to be obtained. All this produced many difficulties."[398] Helmut Marquardt, a seventeen-year-old amateur, repaired the set.[399]

Then another difficulty arose: Coppi misinterpreted Moscow's traffic schedule. He could not understand when he was supposed to send and when to receive; he was always mixing up the times and frequencies laid down by Razvedupr. As a result the Berlin set was often not receiving when Moscow's orders came through and Berlin was on the air when the Moscow station was not on watch.[400]

The more urgently and the more often did the Soviets ask their Berlin spies for information, the more unpredictable did Coppi become. The three sets were housed by the Kuckhoffs, the Harnacks and the Schumachers, who lived some distance apart from each other; as a precaution against the German direction-finders each set had to be used at irregular intervals. Coppi therefore had to chase from one to the other;[401] one or other of the sets was continually going "dis." All in all Coppi threw the Moscow headquarters into considerable confusion; Director Peresypkin lost his temper and threw caution to the winds.

By this time Moscow had broken practically every rule of conspiracy. As its chief organizer it was using a man who had been known to the Gestapo as an opponent of the regime ever since 1933 and was prepared to tramp about the streets at night, dressed in full uniform, sticking up anti-fascist posters. It relied entirely on amateurs who had had no form of secret service training. It had failed to provide the circuit with a trained radio operator. It allowed a veritable cat's-cradle of crossed lines to develop, so that soon everybody knew everybody—a glaring breach of the golden rule that no more than three members of any one circuit should know each other. And now Moscow abandoned all discretion. On 10 October 1941 headquarters sent Kent, the head agent in Brussels, the famous message giving the precise addresses of the leading agents in Berlin; he was asked to find out "why radio contact was continually failing." As a postscript there followed "Remember 'Eulenspiegel,' " the title of a play written by Adam Kuckhoff.[402] Even he, amateur though he was, realized that Moscow's message, if deciphered by the Gestapo, was tantamount to a death sentence. Agitatedly he said to his wife: "Something extremely stupid has happened. They've sent a radio message from which I could easily be identified."[403]

Kent hurried to Berlin, soothed his colleagues' ruffled feelings and re-established radio contact. A few days later, however, communications between Berlin and Moscow broke down again; the German Signals Security direction-finders had worked their way close to the transmitter and Schulze-Boysen had had to order immediate wireless silence.

Moscow thereupon reorganized the Berlin circuit. Information was now to be sent to Brussels by courier and thence radioed to headquarters; at the same time Coppi and his sets moved to new hideouts. One set was installed in the bedroom of his mistress, Erika von Brockdorff, and another in the studio of Schulze-Boysen's mistress, Oda Schottmüller.[404]

In addition headquarters brought into play a group hitherto entirely separate from Rote Kapelle but more qualified to observe Soviet Secret Service professional standards. The leader of this group was a woman journalist, Ilse Stöbe (cover-name "Alta"), working in the Public Relations Section of the Foreign Ministry.[405] She had joined the Soviet Secret Service through her lover Rudolf Herrnstadt, later an East German official. The two had known each other in the offices of the *Berliner Tageblatt* when Herrnstadt was preparing himself to go off as East European correspondent and Ilse Stöbe was working as private secretary to the editor, Theodor Wolff.[406] They had met again in 1936 when Herrnstadt was correspondent of the German-language *Prager Presse* and Ilse was representing certain Swiss newspapers in Warsaw, at the same time acting as cultural adviser to the local Nazi organization. At this point Herrnstadt revealed to her his true function: he was working for the German Section of Soviet espionage headquarters.[407]

The two discovered a No. 3 who became both their ally and their victim. This was Rudolf von Scheliha, Counselor [Gesandtschaftsrat] at the German Embassy in Warsaw, a member of the Silesian aristocracy and a bon viveur. By involving him in shady currency deals, Herrnstadt contrived to inveigle von Scheliha further and further into the Soviet espionage network.[408] By 1937, if not before, "Arier" (von Scheliha's cover-name) was firmly in Soviet pay and was passing on to Moscow all he knew of Foreign Ministry business.[409] He was well paid for his services; in all the Soviets paid 50,000 marks into his account with the Julius Bär & Co. bank in Zurich.[410]

On the outbreak of war von Scheliha was recalled to the Foreign Ministry in Berlin; Ilse Stöbe was still on hand, however, to maintain contact between him and the Moscow headquarters. Her master in Moscow was Captain Petrov of Razvedupr and "Alta" passed on his requests to von Scheliha.[411] Though becoming visibly more hesitant as the months went by, von Scheliha disgorged the information—the Third Reich's secret diplomatic negotiations, the Reich government's foreign policy plans, secrets about the Axis leaders.[412]

The "Arier" circuit also included Kurt Schulze, a Post

Office driver but also a communist espionage professional and a Moscow-trained radio operator.[413] Moscow now ordered him to join Rote Kapelle and really teach Coppi the technique of radio operation. Contact between the two was established by Husemann, the communist functionary who had tried to teach Coppi and was now at his wit's end.[414] Schulze started his lessons in November 1941.[415]

Radio traffic between Berlin and Moscow now began to flow more smoothly. The Moscow headquarters rubbed its hands. Then contact suddenly ceased once more. Schulze's set, which he had had since before 1939, went "dis" and proved beyond repair; Captain Petrov was now entirely out of touch with the "Arier" circuit.[416] Coppi too had to restrict his time on the air, since the German Signals Security had resumed their search for the Berlin transmitters.

Faced with this situation Moscow resorted to a last desperate step, particularly risky in a country where police surveillance had been brought to so fine an art that the system was practically impenetrable. The Soviet Secret Service decided to despatch agents to Germany by parachute; they were to take with them new radio sets and impart some impulsion into the leadership of the Berlin circuits.[417]

Immediately after the outbreak of the Russo-German war, Razvedupr officers had assembled certain exiled German communists who had volunteered to serve as agents in Germany, in two training camps near Ufa and Pushkino.[418] Since the Third Reich's frontiers were hermetically sealed and completely impassable for agents, Razvedupr could think of only one way of despatching them—by air. The agents were to be dropped into Germany by night from Soviet aircraft.

The German communist volunteers in the two camps were accordingly trained both as parachutists and radio operators. Political indoctrination was in the hands of KPD leaders such as Ulbricht, Pieck and Weinert; Soviet Secret Service officers undertook the training in intelligence-gathering, codes and radio operation.[419] There followed a one-week course with a Soviet parachute unit. Finally came ideological instruction in a special camp near Moscow.[420]

The agents were then given false identities. In most cases pay-books were used taken from German prisoners of war or German dead; to increase the parachutists' security against suspicious Germans they were given freshly printed food and clothing cards (mostly inaccurate copies).[421] SS Headquarters later reported: "The agents were frequently provided with the papers of dead German officers and dressed in the corresponding uniform on the assumption that this would enable them to move freely about Germany. Even cases of misuse of the Knight's Cross have been reported."[422]

The first agents were ready to be dropped early in 1942.[423] Razvedupr, however, considered that the prospects of a direct drop into Germany were poor and wished initially to infiltrate their agents from the West. The first teams therefore had to start from England; they were flown to Manchester via Murmansk and thence passed on to the Soviet Embassy in London where they were provided with British radio sets; finally they were flown to the continent from an air base south of London in an aircraft of 138 Squadron RAF.[424] The Russians soon found this procedure too cumbersome, however, and, since there was still no radio contact with Berlin, ordered the next agents to be dropped directly into Germany.

By mid-May two pairs of agents were ready to jump. Erwin Panndorf (cover-name Erwin Stepanow), an ex-Communist Party Youth leader, was provided with papers in the name of Rudolf Scheffel[425] and was to make his way to Berlin with Anton Börner[426] (cover name Anton Belski) of the Saxony Communist Party as his radio operator; Wilhelm Fellendorf,[427] another Communist Party functionary, traveled with Erna Eifler,[428] a representative of the Comintern, and was to contact Bästlein's group in Hamburg.

The four agents were dropped over East Prussia during the night 16/17 May 1942.[429] They buried their equipment near their dropping zone and on 27 May they went their separate ways.[430] Börner and Panndorf traveled via Konitz and Berlin to Thuringia; Fellendorf and Eifler set off for Hamburg.[431] They were followed later by two further agents parachuted from the Soviet Union, Albert Hössler who had fought in Spain,[432] and Robert Barth, an ex-*Red Flag* journalist.[433]

Many of Schulze-Boysen's friends who had hitherto confined themselves to internal political resistance found themselves dragged into spying for the Russians as a result of this large-scale employment of Soviet parachute agents and radio operators. Guddorf's group, for instance, which had so far been used for agitation only, now had to work for Soviet espionage; even the most unsuspecting idealists in Schulze-Boysen's organization found themselves suddenly confronted with the necessity of carrying out menial tasks for the Russians. Erika von Brockdorff housed Hössler;[434] the Schumachers provided transit accommodation for other parachute agents;[435] Scheel, the meteorological inspector, concealed the uniform and revolver of one of the parachutists;[436] Schaeffer, the librarian, provided a safe house for one agent;[437] Hans Lautenschläger kitted out another of Moscow's emissaries.[438]

Between the resistance organization and the newly arrived Soviet spies there were therefore manifold links, only too easily discoverable by the Gestapo sleuths. The whole futility of Moscow's use of its agents was revealed. The parachutists were trying to worm their way through the minefield of the Gestapo's surveillance system and they led the hunters of the RSHA straight into the enemy camp.

Only three days after the first agents had jumped into East Prussia the RSHA learned that spies were being dropped by parachute and the chase began.[439] On 22 May the Gestapo issued a teleprint circular to the effect that "on 19.5.42 three ex-KPD functionaries dropped by parachute from a Soviet aircraft near Insterburg."[440] On 30 May SS-Gruppenführer Martin, Police President of Nuremberg, called for "the most intensive search measures" and issued "Personal descriptions" such as the following: "Börner, 34 years of age, about 5′ 8″ tall, black hair, brown eyes."[441]

Nothing escaped the Gestapo. One circular read: "Panndorf's sister Frau Elli Ortel, now in the Municipal Hospital at Gera, was approached about 7:15 a.m. on 26 May 1942 by a woman unknown to her. The woman handed over a piece of paper from Erwin Panndorf requesting Frau Ortel to give her brother lodging. He was said to have bad or injured feet and to be in urgent need of rest. Probably he sprained or injured his feet when landing by parachute."[442] By 9 June the RSHA knew that the agents they were hunting "were in possession of false passports, employment books, identity cards, police entry and exit forms, large quantities of coupons for meat, butter and bread and considerable financial resources in German and American currency, including Reich Savings Certificates."[443]

The parachute agents were not likely to escape so highly organized a police machine for long. On 8 July the Gestapo tracked down Börner in Vienna; he confessed everything and led his captors to the East Prussian hideout where both pairs of agents had concealed their radio sets.[444] At the same time the Gestapo were able to arrest Panndorf.[445] The confessions of these two prisoners put the Gestapo on the trail of the other parachute agents. The guardians of the regime were getting closer to the Red spy-ring.

But Schulze-Boysen and his friends were still lulling themselves into a sense of false security. Only one member of the organization sensed the danger and attempted to warn them—Horst Heilmann. He, after all, was working with Signals Security's chief cryptanalyst, Lieutenant (Dr.) Wilhelm Vauck, and for weeks Vauck had been deciphering one Soviet radio message after another. His friend Traxl told Corporal Heilmann proudly how well Vauck was getting on.[446]

By the end of August 1942 Heilmann knew for certain what danger his friend Schulze-Boysen was in. So far he had not known that the mysterious "Choro," whom the Gestapo and Abwehr were hunting, was none other than Harro Schulze-Boysen.[447] Then Traxl showed him the decoded message which gave away everything—Moscow's order of 10 October 1941 with the three addresses of the Kuckhoffs, the Schulze-Boysens and the Harnacks. Horst Heilmann rushed off to warn his friends.

5

Treachery in the
Prinz-Albrecht-Strasse

HORST HEILMANN WAS determined to warn his friends. He was only a corporal occupying a lowly position in Signals Security's decoding section, but chance had now given him the knowledge that a mortal threat was hanging over Harro Schulze-Boysen's espionage organization. The Gestapo might strike at any moment.

Heilmann had long sensed danger. On the street he always felt that he was being followed; he thought that he was shadowed by the Gestapo even in his Berlin apartment.[1] He discussed with his friend Rainer Hildebrandt what he could do if, one day, the Gestapo struck. Hildebrandt's advice was to escape across the Swiss frontier, but that seemed to Heilmann like betrayal of his friend Schulze-Boysen. "I can't do that," he said. "I should be depriving Harro of any chance to get out of this, if indeed he has one."[2]

From this time onward he was determined either to save Schulze-Boysen or die with him. And now the moment had arrived when this oath of friendship must be acted upon, now on this 29 August 1942 when the garrulous Traxl had just passed him the decoded radio message from Moscow giving the addresses of the three leading agents in Berlin. Heilmann read the message of 10 October 1941 over and over again. It seemed like an invitation to the Gestapo to give Stalin's spies the *coup de grâce;* they were being offered to the Gestapo on a plate —unless he, Horst Heilmann, could warn the victims at the last moment.

He called Schulze-Boysen at his private apartment but could not contact him. He gave Schulze-Boysen's maid his office telephone number and asked that Schulze-Boysen call him back at once[3]—a risky proceeding since it was a punishable military offense to give the telephone number of a secret agency.

When he had still heard nothing from Schulze-Boysen by midday on the 30th, he hurried along to the Altenburger Allee, where he found Libertas Schulze-Boysen. He handed her the decoded message and she grasped the implications at once.[4] She seized the telephone and called the Ministry of Aviation. Harro must be warned before it was too late.

But instead of the well-known tones of her husband, on the other end of the line was a cold-voiced Major, whose name Libertas Schulze-Boysen had never heard before. Major Seliger told her that Lieutenant Schulze-Boysen had had to leave a few hours previously on an official journey which would keep him away from Berlin for some days; Frau Schulze-Boysen was not to worry if he did not appear for a time.[5] The two in the Altenburger Allee were not taken in by this; what the Major had said could only mean one thing: the Gestapo had arrested Schulze-Boysen.

Anna Kraus, the fortune-teller, pronounced oracularly that Schulze-Boysen was in fact on a highly secret official journey,[6] but Heilmann and Libertas Schulze-Boysen sounded the alarm notwithstanding. In great agitation they cleared all Schulze-Boysen's political papers out of their hiding places and tumbled them all into a suitcase—illegal pamphlets, notes, drafts, including one in Schulze-Boysen's own handwriting entitled "Origin and Causes of the First and Second World Wars."[7]

But what to do with the suitcase? Heilmann had an idea; he took it to Reva Holsey, an actress with whom he was friendly; she had an apartment in No. 8 Hölderlinstrasse, where Heilmann also lived with his parents.[8] The actress was only willing to keep the dangerous thing for a month and then it was to go to Arnold Bauer, a journalist and school-friend of Schulze-Boysen.[9] Frau Holsey's nerves gave way after a mere few days, however; agitatedly she despatched Ingenohl, the theater director, to see Günther Weisenborn, the playwright.[10]

Weisenborn casually opened the suitcase and, as he says, "went cold with terror."[11] He immediately joined in Heilmann's round of warnings and alerted other friends. The tidings of doom went from house to house; everyone warned the next down the line; all Schulze-Boysen's associates cleared their houses of incriminating material. Hans Coppi's mother and wife together carted a radio set out of their house;[12] Hannelore Thiel took another set in her perambulator and dumped it in the River Spree.[13] Johann Graudenz too took steps to rid himself of his radio set; he placed it in a large suitcase bound with wire, which he proposed to leave with the dentist, Hans Helmuth Himpel.[14]

As a close associate of Schulze-Boysen, however, Himpel was forced to contemplate arrest by the Gestapo at any moment. He knew a better hiding place—the house of Helmut Roloff, the pianist; he was in touch with Rittmeister's group of resisters and was prepared to conceal the suitcase.[15] When he saw the ungainly package, "his immediate thought was that the object must be to get the set to safety." Roloff took the suitcase into his house and hid it behind a music press. As Himpel left he said: "We know one thing: if that's found, off with our heads," to which Himpel replied: "That's why it must not be found."[16]

Though everyone was visualizing the possibility of arrest, many still hoped that the Gestapo would pass them by. Anna Kraus was indefatigable in her prophecies that "nothing would happen to any of the men";[17] Countess Brockdorff, as carefree and optimistic as ever, comforted the wife of one agent, saying: "Even if it goes a long way, it won't get further than Coppi."[18]

On 5 September 1942 the Gestapo claimed their first victim—Heilmann; Gestapo officials arrested him in the Hölderlinstrasse in the presence of his brother Hans (the parents were on holiday) and carted him away to the RSHA prison in the Prinz-Albrecht-Strasse.[19] Frau Holsey rushed off in tears to Heilmann's friend Bauer, crying: "They have taken away my Horst."[20]

Heilmann never knew that it was his dramatic attempt to save his friend which had forced the Gestapo to arrest him in a hurry. The fact that, on reading the decoded

message from Moscow with the three addresses, he had at
once tried to telephone Schulze-Boysen, had horrified the
RSHA.[21]

During the night 29/30 August Lieutenant (Dr.) Wilhelm Vauck, Signals Security's chief decoder, had been
working late. He heard a telephone in the next-door room
ringing and ringing. The room was Heilmann's but he had
already gone home. Finally Vauck answered it. On the
other end of the line was Harro Schulze-Boysen; it was
the call for which Heilmann had waited in vain. Vauck
could hardly believe his ears when he heard the voice of
the man who, more than any other one person, had kept
Signals Security and the Gestapo on tenterhooks for weeks.
All he could think of to say was: "Do you spell your
name with a 'Y'?" Schulze-Boysen said he did. The conversation was over in a matter of moments.[22]

In consternation Vauck put down the receiver. How
could it be that Corporal Heilmann was in contact with
the officer whom the initiated knew to be the head of the
communist espionage organization? But he did not hesitate
for an instant; he called the RSHA forthwith and reported.[23] The potentates in the RSHA shared Vauck's
panic. If Heilmann, a member of Signals Security,
they ruminated, was in league with Schulze-Boysen, the
enemy knew how far their investigations had gone and
might be able to evade the Gestapo. Therefore—they must
strike before Schulze-Boysen could bring his agents and
equipment into safety.

Gestapo headquarters in fact sent out their arrest squads
most reluctantly, for Heilmann's attempted rescue operation cut across the tactics planned by the RSHA ever since
the Gestapo had become solely responsible for the "Berlin
Rote Kapelle" case. SS-Gruppenführer Heinrich Müller,
the Head of the Gestapo, had originally intended to observe the spy-ring patiently, establish who all its members
were and then sweep them all up in one operation.[24]

In charge of the observation phase was Kriminalrat and
SS-Sturmbannführer Horst Kopkow, head of Desk IV A 2
(counter-sabotage) in Gestapo Headquarters; he was regarded as one of the sternest of the regime's guardians.[25]
He had started as an apprentice in the "Rathaus" drugstore in Allenstein, had been a Nazi since 1931 and had
been "in the front rank" for Adolf Hitler in numerous
meeting-hall battles; he had repeatedly received specia

commendation from Himmler and had been awarded the German Cross in Silver "for particular services in dealing with agents dropped by parachute." He was continually impressing on his men that in the battle against Rote Kapelle the Reichsführer-SS expected from them unsparing devotion to duty and assured success.*

Kopkow placed his cleverest detective in charge of the investigations. This was Kriminalkommissar and SS-Untersturmführer Johann Strübing, a typical regulation policeman, always ready for duty, with no political sense and prepared to serve any regime.[27] Born in 1907, Strübing had grown up in the Weimar Republic's Regular Police force, the Schutzpolizei; he had been a member of the Gestapo and of the General SS since 1937. Later he even found his way into the security forces of the Federal Republic, until in 1963 revelations by Werner Pätsch, another member of the force, about telephone conversations he had overheard, led to Strübing's expulsion from his familiar job of counter-espionage.[28] In Kopkow's office Strübing dealt with "Action against enemy parachute agents and radio operators."[29] Moreover, he was a natural selection for the Rote Kapelle job, since he had long been studying Soviet espionage methods. Strübing set to work.

What was the best way of making a clean sweep of Rote Kapelle in Berlin? The decoded messages passed over by Fu III at the end of July gave a lead into the center of the organization but they gave details only of a few leading members of the spy-ring, not the entire network of informers. Yet this must remain the object: to discover and destroy the whole organization with all its agents, informers and channels of communication.

The Gestapo knew only the names of the three leading agents, Schulze-Boysen, Harnack and Kuckhoff; they had seen only a fraction of the messages radioed to Moscow. That was the sum total of their knowledge. They had to find out much more before taking action. Strübing ordered the telephones of the three Rote Kapelle leaders to be

---

* Horst Kopkow was born in Ortelsburg, East Prussia, on 29 November 1910. He matriculated in 1928 and was apprenticed to a chemist, working in the "Rathaus" drugstore in Allenstein until 1934. He joined the Nazi Party in 1931 (membership number 607,161) and the SS a year later. His Gestapo career began in Allenstein in September 1934 and he was seconded to Gestapo headqquarters in 1938, becoming head of the "counter-sabotage" desk. He was promoted Kriminalrat in 1941 and Kriminaldirektor in 1944.[26]

tapped and every visitor to their houses to be checked
unobtrusively. Very soon his list of persons to be kept under surveillance was growing longer. The extent of the
enemy's network became ever clearer to him.

Strübing had only just submitted the first report on his
investigations to Kopkow, when Heilmann's action apparently drove a coach and four through the Gestapo's plan.
Kopkow and Strübing feared that, coming from Signals
Security headquarters, Heilmann's information would enable their opponents to escape the Gestapo altogether.[30]
Agitatedly they launched into hectic action, as if the spies
were on the point of dissolving into wraiths.

Early on the morning of 30 August the RSHA decided
to strike at once. A few hours later the black Gestapo
cars were roaring through the streets of Berlin and one
after another the members of Rote Kapelle were arrested.
The first arrest was that of Schulze-Boysen; Kopkow did
it himself.[31] About midday on 30 August he presented
himself to Colonel Bokelberg, Headquarters Commandant
of the Reich Ministry of Aviation, and told him the story.
Since the Gestapo was not allowed to make arrests on
military premises,[32] Bokelberg summoned Lieutenant
Schulze-Boysen, declared him under arrest and handed
him over to Kopkow.[33] The remaining arrests passed off
equally smoothly, though less ceremoniously.

On 3 September Strübing arrested Libertas Schulze-
Boysen at the Anhalter Station when she was already in a
train en route to friends on the Moselle—she had meanwhile been hiding in the house of her friend Alexander
Spoerl.[34] On 7 September a Gestapo detachment searched
the Fischerdorf pension on the Kurische Nehrung, East
Prussia, and by breakfast-time had found their quarry—
the Harnacks on holiday. Mildred Harnack put her hands
to her face and moaned: "The disgrace of it, oh, the disgrace of it!"[35]

One after another the Gestapo swooped on them, silent-
ly and unobtrusively. In the second week of September
came the turn of Adam Kuckhoff, Graudenz, Coppi, Sieg,
Kurt Schumacher and Ilse Stöbe;[36] they were followed by
Küchenmeister, Scheel, Schulze and Weissensteiner on 16
September,[37] Himpel and Roloff on 17 September,[38] and
Weisenborn and Rittmeister on the 26th.[39]

The robot-like precision with which their detachments

struck, however, could not conceal the fact that, from the Gestapo's point of view, the arrests were a second-best solution. Strübing was still working in the dark; he hardly knew how he was to convict his prisoners or those suspected of high treason. The fact that in the first ten days following 30 August only five people were arrested[40] is in itself sufficient proof of the inadequacy of the Gestapo's knowledge of Rote Kapelle. Strübing therefore had to try to make the arrested agents talk. The staff of Desk IV A 2 was too small, however, and so he had to ask for reinforcements.

Within the RSHA the "Rote Kapelle Special Commission" was formed; it included the best interrogators in Gestapo headquarters.[41] Of its twenty-five members the majority (thirteen) came from A 2 and the remainder from A 1 ("Communism, Marxism"), A 3 ("Reaction, Opposition") and A 4 ("Security Precautions, Special Cases").[42] The head of the organization was Friedrich Panzinger,* a senior official [Oberregierungsrat], of the same age as Gestapo Müller and, like him, a Bavarian, who headed Group A; the actual work was done by Kopkow.

For ten years these men had been trained in an interrogation technique which employed every wile and knew no compunction. The RSHA inquisitors set to work on their victims. At first, however, the prisoners refused to say anything; hardly one was willing to talk. Schulze-Boysen admitted nothing which could not be proved to him in black and white. Strübing recalls: "Initially he denied any connection with foreign agents and naturally also any treasonable activity, citing his background as proof."[44] Even when shown photostat copies of the decoded radio messages from Moscow, he refused to confess. He stuck to his story: He and his friends had met for private purposes; occasionally they had discussed politics, but he knew nothing of any treasonable activities.[45]

Strübing dropped the subject. He inveigled Schulze-

---

* Friedrich Panzinger was born in Munich on 1 February 1903. He joined the police in 1919 and worked alongside Müller as a medium-level official from 1927 to 1929; he was employed in Section VI of Munich police headquarters. He was promoted to the higher ranks in 1934, joined the Gestapo Office in Berlin in 1937 and in 1939 was seconded to the RSHA, Branch IV (Gestapo), becoming head of Group IV A shortly thereafter.[43]

Boysen, who was initially allowed to wear his uniform, into deep discussions on literature and the natural sciences, taking care that no word the prisoner said was recorded. He would stroll with him for hours through the garden of the RSHA in almost friendly conversation,[46] but Schulze-Boysen still said nothing.

Reinhold Ortmann, another of the interrogators, had a similar experience with his prisoner, Johann Graudenz. He says: "I interrogated Graudenz on several occasions without any success at all. All he would tell me was that he was a close friend of Schulze-Boysen and that they had spent a summer holiday together."[47] Ortmann thought the case so hopeless that he returned the Graudenz files to Kopkow.[48]

Similarly negative reports streamed into Kopkow's office from the other interrogators. Adam Kuckhoff was as obstinate as Arvid Harnack in his refusal to admit anything or to help the Gestapo by saying anything of substance.[49] For a short time it seemed as if all Schulze-Boysen's associates now under arrest formed a common front, impervious even to the most sophisticated ruses of the interrogator.

But the picture of a conspiracy of silence was deceptive; cracks began to appear in the façade, revealing inner conflicts and tensions current among Schulze-Boysen's friends even before their arrest. After a few days began a process which, even today, is barely explicable: the self-surrender of the communist agents, termed by David Dallin "Treason en Gros."[50]

First to break silence was Libertas Schulze-Boysen. In her the fact of imprisonment had destroyed a world of illusions. For a long time she had not believed that her husband's conspiratorial activities were serious business; what to him was a destiny and a calling was to her a mere game. She had only come to believe in the final months, but by then the two had become so estranged that their life together was intolerable and Libertas had been wanting a divorce; only an urgent appeal from Schulze-Boysen not to leave "the cause" in the lurch had kept the naïve, artistic but inconsequential girl at his side.

She managed to convince herself that all would not turn out so badly as she sometimes feared. Her arrest showed her that that was wrong, however. The old illusions now gave way to a new one: that belief that, as granddaughter of a Prince, the Gestapo would let her go, provided that she turned King's Evidence against her friends at the forthcoming trial. She was encouraged in this hope by a woman to whom Libertas turned in her predicament. This was Gertrud Breiter, shown in the Gestapo list as employed in the typing pool of Desk IV E 6.[51] She had been allotted as shorthand-typist to Alfred Göpfert, a criminal police official [Kriminalobersekretär] who was interrogating Libertas Schulze-Boysen.[52] The two women had come to know each other in Göpfert's office. When Göpfert left the room on one occasion, they began to talk. It was late one afternoon and Gertrud Breiter felt drawn to what she later called "just a conversation between ourselves." Frau Schulze-Boysen began: "Well now, how do you come to be here?" Gertrud Breiter shrugged her shoulders and mumbled: "One doesn't have to be in one-hundred-percent agreement with what goes on to be here. After all it's wartime."

Frau Schulze-Boysen began to gain confidence in the typist. After some ten minutes of cautious probing, she blurted out: "I have only one favor to ask you; I can't tell you the address, but will you warn Hans Coppi." As a good National Socialist Gertrud Breiter knew what to do.

"I was all excited," she recalls. "I was merely afraid that Göpfert would stay away too long and that I should forget the name again. When Göpfert came back, I signaled to him and said: 'Excuse me, but I must go out for a moment.'" She dashed up to the third floor of the RSHA building into Kopkow's office and told him what she had heard. At first Kopkow was put out by this irregular interference on the part of a secretary and told her that such reports should be made in writing and through the official channels. Only when Gertrud Breiter lost her temper, did he take her information seriously. Coppi was arrested that night.[53]

As a result of this success Kopkow was inspired to use Gertrud Breiter for further "conversations between ourselves." Twenty-five times the two women met, twenty-five times they embraced and twenty-five times Libertas Schulze-Boysen blabbed out secrets of Rote Kapelle. "She was very intelligent," Gertrud Breiter says today, "but very, very unstable. I could well have been the same sort."[54] Hugo Buschmann ruminated: "Why did she betray us? Well, she was a nice young girl and simply wanted to go on living. Libertas was a charming person who loved life and basically understood very little of Harro's activities."[55]

Libertas produced names which the RSHA interrogators had never heard of—Jan Bontjes van Beek, his daughter Cato, Havemann, Harnack's nephew, Countess von Brockdorff, Buschmann, Rosemarie Terwiel and others. Willi Weber, Schulze-Boysen's young assistant, says: "She gave away her husband's entire group";[56] even Schulze-Boysen's mother lamented: "Very many people went to the gallows as a result. Very sad."[57]

But Libertas Schulze-Boysen's revelations were no isolated instance. Harnack too began to talk, disowning his partner Schulze-Boysen; the latter also produced names of many of his associates and friends.[58] After a month of brainwashing Strübing asked Schulze-Boysen who his accomplices had been and the prisoner jeered: "Yes, if you knew all that! They include some very senior gentlemen who are still in office today"[59]—and he reeled off the names of Colonel Gehrts, Lieutenant Gollnow, Kraus the fortune-teller and Mildred Harnack.[60]

Adam Kuckhoff's tongue also suddenly became loose and he betrayed his partners, Sieg and Grimme.[61] As Werner Kraus, one of the prisoners, noted in the case of Fritz Thiel, the anti-fascist, many of them "suffered a moral collapse as a result of their interrogation. He tried to save his own life and that of his wife by presenting himself as the misguided victim of an intellectual conspiracy; in particular he was virulent in his accusations against Ursula Goetze."[62] Cato Bontjes van Beek wrote to her mother: "As far as I can see, Sch-B. and many of the other leaders have behaved shamefully and have brought an enormous number of people to their death."[63] Even Greta Kuckhoff was horrified by what her husband had said: "Finally they [Harnack and Adam Kuckhoff] told everything and gave away all the names in the belief that people had made themselves scarce. I was speechless when I heard that Adam had confessed; even his death sentence did not shake me so much as this news. I quarrelled with Adam."[64]

The most menacing from the point of view of the othe[r] prisoners was the readiness of the two Schumachers t[o] betray their friends. The wife of Philipp Schaeffer, th[e] resister, was held responsible for assisting a prisoner to escape solely on the basis of a statement by Elizabeth Schumacher;[65] for nights on end while in prison Weisenborn tapped signals on the wall: "You . . . must . . . retract . . . your . . . statement." In the neighboring cell No. 8 in the Gestapo prison was Kurt Schumacher, who had so incriminated Weisenborn that he was preparing himself for a death sentence. Schumacher did in fact retract his statement.[66]

Ortmann, who first interrogated Schumacher, could never forget a scene which took place in his office in mid-September. "One day," he says, "I wanted to eat my breakfast. Since I wished to do this in peace, I had to find something for Schumacher to do; he was sitting alongside me at my desk. I accordingly took up the 'Register of fugitive communists' and handed it to Schumacher asking him to look at the photographs and tell me which of the people depicted threin he knew."[67] Ortmann insisted later that he had "no particular purpose" in asking this; he merely wanted to be left to eat in peace. Suddenly he was interrupted by an exclamation from Schumacher: "That's him!" Ortmann goes on: "I was naturally astounded, looked at once at the number of the photograph and was immediately able to establish the name of the person represented by reference to a second register." The man thus revealed was Albert Hössler, one of the parachute agents despatched to Germany by Moscow in the summer of 1942. According to Ortmann's notes Schumacher then stated that Hössler had appeared at his house, as announced by Moscow, and had asked to be passed on to Schulze-Boysen; he had stayed two days and had also visited Coppi, to whom he had handed a radio set.

"The parachutist," so Schumacher said, "was intent on establishing whether he could get Moscow on his short-wave radio set. We plugged the set into the light and the parachutist tried to establish contact with Moscow—which he did at once. We had placed the headset of the radio on the table in our living room. We had to break off communication with Moscow at once, since the transmission was coming through so loud that I was afraid the neighbors might hear."[68]

However Schumacher's confession may have been obtained, his statements and those of the other prisoners about the arrival of Soviet parachute agents led the Gestapo to undertake a more intensive hunt for them and to use their sets for a cunning radio "playback" game with Moscow.

Radio "playbacks" were among the favorite methods of German counter-espionage. Regulations laid down that any secret enemy transmitter which might be captured, together with its operating personnel, was at once to be "turned round" and used against its original masters, the enemy espionage headquarters. The object of this was twofold: to gain better insight into enemy espionage activities in one's camp and to confuse the other side by passing false information.

On the capture of Rote Kapelle's Berlin sets Kriminal-kommissar Thomas Ampletzer, IV A 2's radio "playback" expert, at once set about preparing a radio "counter-game" for Moscow.[69] In this he was assisted by a renegade Soviet agent, Johann Wenzel, the head radio operator of Rote Kapelle in Western Europe, arrested in June 1942. He had already given the Gestapo much good service, having played a major part both in the hunt for the "Grand Chef's" agents in Belgium and in the decoding of the Soviet radio messages by Fu III.[70] Now he assisted Ampletzer to set up two channels of communication to the man who, for the Gestapo's counter-espionage sleuths, was the most mysterious being imaginable—the Director, the Head of the Russian Secret Service. Wenzel wrote down for his new masters the key to the Russian codes and Ampletzer was soon in contact with the headquarters of the Soviet Secret Service.[71] The object of his maneuver was to lure into Germany further parachute agents, from whom the Gestapo hoped to discover Rote Kapelle addresses which they did not yet know.

The Gestapo's plan came off. About 16 September Ampletzer's Soviet opposite number informed him that a newly arrived parachute agent would meet an important informer at 4:41 p.m. on 17 September at the Potsdamer Station, Berlin.[72] As identification the agent would be carrying half a playing card, the other half being in the possession of the informer.[73]

Gestapo officials were duly present when the two men met. The informer proved to be Dr. Hans Heinrich Kummerow, a telecommunications engineer and a money-grubbing lone operator, who had worked for various West European secret services during the 1920s but had been in the sole service of Moscow since 1932; manufacturing secrets of the German arms industry were his speciality.[74]

Kummerow had passed to Moscow drawings of a proposed remote-controlled bomb, manufacturing plans for the ground-to-air missile "Luftengel-Bodenengel" and drawings of new direction-finding gear. He had also offered the Russians some inventions of his own, such as a system of remote-controlled beacons to be mounted on the roofs of German arms factories to assist Soviet bombing attacks.[75] Among the papers which Kummerow had handed to the courier on the Potsdamer Station were the drawings of the remote-controlled bomb and when these were presented to Strübing, he inquired of OKW whether in fact work was being done on such a bomb. The arms experts were horrified; Strübing recalls: "Because of the very high secrecy classification involved, I had personally to take charge of the investigation and had to certify in writing that under no circumstances would I say a word to anyone about the proposed bomb, not even to my colleagues."[76]

Strübing drove down to Nauen, the base of the experimental establishment concerned. People there were "astounded that the existence of or plans for the bomb could have come to Kummerow's ears; they therefore suspected that he must have some go-between who was in touch with the Nauen establishment. No such go-between was discovered at the time, however."[77] Strübing could only find one person who was working with Kummerow, his wife Ingeborg; she had typed her husband's technical memoranda for Moscow on a specially prepared typewriter which produced a curious blurred effect; one of Kummerow's dissertations dealt with a plan to blow up Goebbels, the Propaganda Minister.[78] Subsequent investigations showed that Kummerow was not a member of the Schulze-Boysen/Harnack group; he had only tried to get in touch with the parachute agent attached to Schulze-Boysen because he had no regular radio contact with Moscow.[79] But, of course, the Gestapo were extremely interested in these parachute agents and Kummerow's statements helped them on their way. Finally chance enabled the Gestapo to make the decisive breakthrough. Among the persons under surveillance was Klara Nemitz, a communist who was in touch with several Red resistance groups.[80] Early in October she received a telephone call from Wilhelm Guddorf, the KPD functionary who had split with Schulze-Boysen but was nevertheless working with the agents parachuted into Germany.[81] Guddorf told Klara Nemitz that there was to be a major meeting in Hamburg with Comrade Bästlein's agents.[82]

The Gestapo reacted at once. On 10 October they arrested Guddorf and his mistress Eva-Maria Buch; at the same time they cordoned off Bernhard Bästlein's organization in Hamburg.[83] In mid-October they swept up Bästlein and his agents and shortly thereafter laid hands on Fellendorf and Erna Eifler, both of whom had landed by parachute;[84] their two companions, Hössler and Barth, had already been arrested at the beginning of the month.[85]

From Hamburg fresh trails led back to Berlin—to the radio and photographic business run by the Hübners and Wesoleks; on instructions from Moscow they had provided the parachute agents with money and forged passports. Between 18 and 20 October the Gestapo minions led away the entire communist family group—Emil and Max Hübner, Frieda, Stanislaus, Johannes and Walter Wesolek.[86]

By mid-October Strübing could report to his master Kopkow that the whole of Rote Kapelle in Berlin had been swept up. The Gestapo had arrested a total of 116 persons,[87] now held either in the RSHA prison or in that of the Berlin Police Presidency. They were a heterogeneous collection; some had spied out of political conviction, some were resistance fighters, others were mere venal traitors and unconscious informers; all were now victims of the Nazi rulers' ideology of State security—and so began the legend that all friends of Schulze-Boysen were spies and traitors.

Strübing's success story was marred by one question mark: he still did not know who was the senior German Foreign Ministry official who had worked for the Soviets for years under the cover name "Arier." Strübing was reasonably sure, however, that once again the Soviet Secret Service would—involuntarily—solve the Gestapo's problem.

As in the case of Schulze-Boysen, Harnack and Kuckhoff the Gestapo had become aware of the small "Arier" circuit as a result of a Soviet radio message. On 28 August 1941 the short-wave intercept station had taken down a radio message from Moscow which Wenzel deciphered for

the Gestapo a year later. It told Kent, the head agent in
Brussels, to visit the Berlin agent Ilse Stöbe, alias "Alta,"
in her house at No. 37 Wielandstrasse.[88] As soon as the
message was deciphered Ilse Stöbe was shadowed; she had
meanwhile moved to No. 36 Saalestrasse where she was a
tenant of the Schulz family.[89] On 12 September she was
arrested.[90] But she refused to say who "Arier" was. Ilse
Stöbe's Soviet biographers describe the scene as follows:
"Her first interrogation lasted uninterruptedly for three
days and three nights. Ilse was allowed neither to sleep,
eat nor drink."[91] But Ilse Stöbe saw it through; for seven
weeks she refused to talk.[92]

Then Ampletzer came to the rescue of the inquisitors.
He radioed to his Soviet opposite number asking Moscow
to despatch a parachute agent at once since "Alta" was
in trouble, primarily due to lack of money. Captain Petrov,
Ilse Stöbe's directing officer, fell for the Gestapo ruse and
a parachutist was set going forthwith.[93] In Moscow Heinrich Koenen prepared himself for the assignment. He was
an emigré KPD Youth functionary, son by his first marriage of Wilhelm Koenen, a member of the Central Committee; after 1933 he had worked as an engineer at a
power station in Siberia and in 1941 had been trained by
the Red Army as a parachutist and radio operator.[94]

On 23 October he was dropped near Osterode in East
Prussia with false papers in the name of Koester and a
quantity of money. He made his way to Berlin.[95] About
5:00 p.m. on 28 October he called Ilse Stöbe in the
Saalestrasse; a female voice answered. Koenen said: "I
would very much like to speak to you." He arranged to
meet "Alta" at the Savignyplatz tram stop, asking her to
come at once.[96]

She came. The man took two tickets out of his pocket
and they both climbed on to a tram heading for the Tiergarten. On the way he tested the woman out, putting her
some catch questions. "I am to bring you greetings from
your husband," he said, "from Rudi." This referred to
Rudolf Herrnstadt, Ilse Stöbe's lover, who had recruited
her into the Soviet Secret Service. The woman corrected
Koenen: "Excuse me; he is not my husband; he is my
boy friend." Koenen asked her to buy him two shirts and
arranged that they should meet next day—midday at the
Wittenberg Underground Station, under the clock.[97]

But instead of going back to the Saalestrasse the woman hurried off to the Prinz-Albrecht-Strasse—in some trepidation, for up to the last moment Gertrud Breiter, the Gestapo secretary, had been afraid that Koenen would realize that she was not Ilse Stöbe. She reported to Strübing. On 29 October Koenen was arrested.[98]

In his breast pocket the Gestapo found, in addition to banknotes, what they were looking for—clues to "Arier's" identity. Moscow had included a photostat copy of the first pay slip for 5,000 francs in favor of the Zurich bank Julius Bär & Co. and this proved that Counselor First Class Rudolf von Scheliha had been in Soviet pay as an agent ever since February 1938.[99] Koenen even knew what the money banked in Switzerland was used for. Strübing says: "He explained to me that his masters in Moscow had told him that Scheliha used the money in Switzerland for the maintenance of a mistress he kept there."[100]

But when Gestapo officials went to the Foreign Ministry to arrest the diplomat, they found that the bird had flown. Scheliha had gone to Switzerland.[101] In some alarm Panzinger, the head of the Special Commission, traveled to Basle with a Criminal Police official, hardly hoping ever to see Scheliha again. But Panzinger was wrong. On the night 29/30 October Scheliha appeared at the Badische Station in Basle and climbed into a train for Germany. No sooner were they on German territory than Panzinger arrested him.[102]

So both the members of Rote Kapelle and Moscow's lone operators in Berlin had been unmasked primarily as a result of imprudence and treachery within their own ranks. There was hardly one who had not come to grief through the statement of his or her friends: Schulze-Boysen, Harnack and Kuckhoff had been thoughtlessly exposed by Soviet Secret Service headquarters, John Sieg through the statements of his or her friends: Schulze-Boysen, Ursula Goetze incriminated by the Thiels, the Schaeffer family let down by the Schumachers, Coppi, Cato Bontjes van Beek and Buschmann delivered up by Libertas Schulze-Boysen.

Admittedly not all the prisoners yielded to the Gestapo's pressure. The KPD functionaries in particular had been trained for underground warfare and prepared for the most severe trials; they withstood the pressures; with them the Gestapo interrogators failed. When facing death Walter Husemann wrote: "It is easy to call oneself a communist so long as one does not have to shed one's blood for it. Whether one is really a communist, however, is shown when the hour of trial comes. Stay firm, father. Firm! Never give way! In any hour of weakness remember this last challenge."[103] Wilhelm Thews had no doubts: "I am satisfied with my life. It was a struggle for freedom, truth and justice and I can put an end to it without regrets."[104]

Walter and Martha Husemann, the Hübners and Wesoleks, John Sieg, Herbert Grasse, Eugen Neutert, Ilse Stöbe, Wilhelm Thews—all these preferred to risk ill-treatment and torture rather than tell the Gestapo anything. Many of the young idealists of John Rittmeister's circle also held their tongues; Ursula Goetze incriminated herself in order to save others;[105] Eva-Maria Buch seemed to the prison chaplain "like a saint."[106] But the more important men and women closest to Schulze-Boysen capitulated.

How can such self-surrender be explained? The champions and survivors of Rote Kapelle accept only one reason —Gestapo brutality. Only by means of "the severest interrogations and tortures,"[107] they say, was the Gestapo able to compel the prisoners to give away their associates; Greta Kuckhoff tries to lay responsibility for the downfall of her friends at the door of a secret torture chamber known as the "Stalin room."[108]

The Gestapo officials did in fact mete out severe treatment to the arrested members of Rote Kapelle; many a Gestapo man worked off on his prisoners the spite of his petty-bourgeois national instincts. Heinrich Scheel says that one official "struck him in the face and half-throttled him by twisting his tie";[109] Weissensteiner was "immediately beaten up" by Kriminalsekretär Habecker because, according to Weissensteiner's widow, "he said, quite truthfully, that certain figures written on a piece of paper referred to radio valves and were not telephone numbers, as Habecker thought they were."[110] Isolde Urban, who had worked with the KPD functionary Schürmann-Horster, had a similar experience; she was beaten up by Habecker at her first interrogation.[111] Frieda Wesolek was also beaten[112] and all his life Captain Harry Piepe will never forget the change in Johann Wenzel after his interrogation by the Gestapo.[113]

In the cells of the RSHA in the Prinz-Albrecht-Strasse and the police prison on the Alexanderplatz, everything was done to give "the Reds" the feeling that they were helpless pariahs in the Nazi community with no chance of survival. Even in their cells they were handcuffed; the majority were forbidden to write letters or receive visitors. Many of the female prisoners (they were almost all housed in the Alexanderplatz prison) were kept in unlighted cells; all books and photographs, even of their closest relatives, were removed.[114] Gestapo headquarters issued the strictest instructions to the interrogators to show no mercy. Gestapo Müller insisted on rigid compliance with his order that any prisoner was to be handcuffed when moved, even over the shortest distance; should a prisoner escape, the order continued, the official responsible would be arrested immediately.[115] Weisenborn said that at every mealtime each prisoner could hear from the neighboring cell "a distinctive click—the handcuffs snapping to."[116]

Though "wearing handcuffs," as he recorded, Kurt Schumacher managed to write: "Can any man conceive of the depths of pain, affliction, distress, misery and despair which these unfortunates had to endure simply because they believed in a peaceful community of peoples?"[117] According to one report from Werner Kraus the prisoners were "subjected to ultraviolet rays; they lay about for weeks with badly swollen eyes."[118] The Gestapo's methods of interrogation were more than John Sieg could stand and he committed suicide;[119] his partner Herbert Grasse also abandoned the struggle and threw himself from the fifth floor of the Berlin Police Presidency.[120] Mildred Harnack was only prevented from committing suicide with the greatest difficulty.[121] Kummerow later killed himself on hearing his sentence.[122] The interrogators were continually using threats of the most brutal tortures. Hans Henze, a criminal police officer, told Greta Kuckhoff: "Since your husband and Arvid Harnack have contributed nothing toward clearing up this case, we have now employed the necessary methods to loosen their tongues." Frau Kuckhoff asked: "Are they still alive?" to which Henze replied: "Yes, but it will depend on you whether they get through next time."[123]

Certain prisoners were in fact tortured—with the soulless, pedantic application of bureaucratic method which the Gestapo considered to be proof of propriety. Application had to be made in writing to the Chief of the Security Police for an "intensified interrogation," the euphemism for torture; provided he agreed, an official authorized to apply torture would appear with an SS medical officer and administer to the prisoner a prescribed number of strokes. The doctor had to testify to the effect of the torture on the prisoner's state of health. A record was then drawn up, for in Heinrich Himmler's world even sadism had to be reduced to paper in proper form.*

Torture was kept within limits, however. When Schulze-Boysen at first refused to say anything, he was given twelve blows with a pick-helve.[125] Harnack, Graudenz and Kuckhoff were all beaten by Gestapo officials;[126] Alexander Kraell, the judge, recalls that they were given "a certain number of blows on the buttocks with a rubber truncheon."[127] There is no proof of any instances of torture apart from these four. In most cases nothing worse than threats and psychological ruses were used; the vast majority of prisoners would agree with Alexander Spoerl who said: "These interrogations were conducted quite properly, though they were sophisticated; they were exhausting, but I was never tortured."[128]

The inquisitors employed every known trick. In several cases Gestapo stool pigeons masquerading as prisoners were introduced into the cells;[129] Krauss, the university professor, for instance, found himself talking to an Engineer Schulze-Boysen who pretended to be a cousin of Harro but of whom none of the family had ever heard.[130] One Gestapo man said to Schumacher: "Now be sensible, Schumacher, and tell the truth. You are physically incapable of withstanding what has been done to Schulze-Boysen and Coppi."[131] In fact Coppi had not been maltreated. The Gestapo interrogators took pleasure in spreading tales of horrifying interrogations which the prisoners equally took pleasure in repeating. All too many confessions were extracted that way.

Such "innocent" practices were unnerving enough for men who found themselves in the headquarters of bureaucratized terror and who had no reason to doubt that the Gestapo functionaries were perfectly prepared to make good their cold-blooded threats at any moment. Undoubted-

---

* An office minute still exists recording the torture of a member of the Rotholz resistance group which was allied to that of Schulze-Boysen.[124]

ly, had their prisoners proved more reticent, the Gestapo
would have resorted to worse tortures.

But can these actual or threatened tortures provide sufficient explanation for the self-surrender of Schulze-Boysen's
friends while under arrest? What brought them to heel in
front of the Gestapo's arc-lights seems to have been, in the
words of David Dallin, a "sudden moral weakness and loss
of fighting spirit which was the psychological prelude to
surrender."[132] The anti-fascist legend-writers subsequently
presented the attitude of the prisoners as one of heroism
and martyrdom. In fact the Prinz-Albrecht-Strasse cells
were silent witnesses to a moral collapse on the part of
human beings which must surely be unparalleled in the
history of espionage.

With its members in solitary confinement, cut off from
the outside world and maltreated by the sophisticated interrogators of the totalitarian police machine, the anti-
fascist front cracked because it was composed of disparate
elements incapable of withstanding the ultimate and most
brutal test; there were idealists and adventurers, spies and
resistance fighters, anti-Nazis and opportunists, hired assas-
sins and chance adherents. What, for instance, was there in
common between Herbert Gollnow, the faithful member
of the Hitler Youth, and Schulze-Boysen, the uncompromising champion of Stalin; between Gehrts, the devout
Christian, and Harnack, the doctrinaire Marxist; between
Rittmeister, the left-wing social theorist, and Kummerow,
the opportunist; between Anna Kraus, the fortune-teller,
and Koenen, the Russo-German parachutist? Even the
logical Harnack admitted, whatever his reasons, that as a
German he ought not to have acted as he did in time of
war.[133] Cato Bontjes van Beek wrote to her mother:
"Mama, there is no particular glory attached to involvement in this business."[134]

In any case, what could they still believe in when they
heard that the Rote Kapelle organization in Western
Europe had been broken up and, worse still, that its Soviet
leaders had gone over to Himmler's Gestapo? The arrested
Soviet officers, after all, were doing their best to help their
new German masters to convert the last remaining Rote
Kapelle agents. The word had already gone round that
Kent, the leading agent, was to be found in the basement
of the Prinz-Albrecht-Strasse, writing voluminous memo-

randa for the Gestapo about his work with Schulze-Boysen and Harnack.[135]

The war news offered them no hope either. Hitler and his allies were approaching the zenith of their power: in the Caucasus the Red Army seemed on the point of defeat, in North Africa Rommel was driving the British troops in front of him, in the Far East the British Empire and America's Asiatic possessions were collapsing before the Japanese attacks.

Only Schulze-Boysen refused to give the game up for lost; irrationalism remained his rule of life. While in prison he thought up a plan by which he believed that he could save his friends. Toward the end of September he hinted that he had smuggled secret German official documents to Sweden and that, should they be published, they would implicate the leaders of the Third Reich in a highly embarrassing manner. Kopkow and Panzinger were so impressed that they immediately summoned Schulze-Boysen's father (he had meanwhile rejoined the Navy and was serving as Chief of Staff of the German Naval Commander in Holland) and asked for his help.[136] The essentials of the story about papers in Sweden were given by Captain Erich Edgar Schulze as follows: "Should he [Schulze-Boysen] or his friends be condemned to death, the documents would be handed to the British or Soviet governments and published by them. Should his plans remain undiscovered, Germany lose the war and the Hitler government fall, the documents would be proof that he and his associates were qualified to be leaders of a new German government."[137]

Panzinger offered Captain Schulze a deal: if he could persuade his son to get the papers back to Germany, the charge of high treason would be dropped when Schulze-Boysen came for trial and he would be accused only of traitorous activities. The Captain went dutifully to work, but Schulze-Boysen waved his father away.[138]

Early in October he seemed to change his mind and himself proposed a deal: he would hand over the papers in Sweden against a promise from the Gestapo not to carry out the anticipated death sentences on him and his friends earlier than Christmas 1943—by which time he thought that the war would be ended.[139]

Cold-bloodedly Kopkow agreed to the deal; he knew, after all, that the authorities responsible for executing death sentences would not bother their heads about some promise from the Gestapo. Once more Captain Schulze had to make the pilgrimage to Berlin; on 12 October he met his son again. This time, however, Schulze-Boysen admitted that there was no such thing as the Swedish papers; he had merely invented the story in order to help his friends.[140] Schulze inquired anxiously whether the Gestapo would nevertheless abide by their promise. Strübing recalls: "Kopkow gave some sort of reply to the effect that he was not authorized to give such a promise."[141] Schulze-Boysen understood. He had lost the game completely.

Doubt now began to grow in the minds of many of the prisoners whether they had acted rightly; they did not all share Horst Heilmann's burning desire to die at the side of his chief. Even Schulze-Boysen began to give signs of resignation. It became increasingly obvious that the animal desire to survive outweighed the old ideals; the instinct of self-preservation bore down principles once thought to be impregnable. Determination to survive led many to serve the regime they hated—and none more willingly than Schulze-Boysen who, in a curious mood half of mockery, half of cynicism, helped to track down his former friends of the Ministry of Aviation. Libertas Schulze-Boysen hoped to play the role of King's Evidence for the Gestapo; before committing suicide Kummerow offered to design new weapons for the Wehrmacht;[142] Koenen helped the Gestapo play their radio game with Moscow.[143] Even Greta Kuckhoff began to compose verses in honor of Adolf Hitler.[144]

Such a moral collapse was only too well calculated to confirm Rote Kapelle's enemies in their petty-bourgeois instincts and anti-communist illusions. This was how they had always pictured the "bolshevist world enemy"—without moral backbone, ready to betray their own country at any time, contemptuous of national norms and bourgeois morals.

From the Nazi regime's point of view there was no object in trying to distinguish between the various motives actuating the individual friends and associates of Schulze-Boysen; it was better to brand them all collectively as traitors. The regime's minions were therefore relieved of the burden of reflecting on their prisoners' motivations. With remorseless monotony the thinking of the Nazi functionaries ran as follows: here were enemies of the state, traitors, venal agents and in many cases adulterers—so off with their heads.

As early as mid-October Gestapo Müller considered the case closed and proposed to Himmler that the members of Rote Kapelle should be brought before a Peoples Court forthwith.[145] Himmler hastened to carry the proposition to the Führer's headquarters. Hitler was in full agreement; his aide, Karl Jesko von Puttkamer, noted that the Führer was "highly indignant" and ordered "the bolshevists within our own ranks" to be exterminated at once and without mercy.[146]

If, however, Himmler had hoped that Hitler would place him in charge of the proceedings, he was disappointed. The task was allotted to Himmler's rival, Hermann Göring; he was to preside over the legal liquidation of the Schulze-Boysen/Harnack group.[147] We can only guess why this was done. Göring was the Number Two of the Nazi regime; some of the more important prisoners (Schulze-Boysen, Gehrts, Gollnow and Heilmann) belonged to the Luftwaffe. This may have been the reason why the "Reich Marshal" was put in charge.

Göring set to work to carry out Hitler's order. The final Act in the drama of "Red Orchestra" in Berlin had begun.

6

The Road to Plötzensee

ON THE AFTERNOON of 17 October 1942 Hermann Göring, Commander-in-Chief of the Luftwaffe, summoned to the command car of his special train near the Ukrainian town of Vinnitsa Dr. Manfred Roeder, the Judge Advocate-General and presiding military legal officer of Air Region III. The subject of the interview, the Reich Marshal said, was a "Top Secret" matter of the utmost urgency.

Roeder was further enlightened when Major Berndt von Brauchitsch, Göring's aide, handed him a Gestapo investigation report. It dealt with the Schulze-Boysen/Harnack spying. Would the Judge Advocate please read the document and report again to Göring late that evening. When Roeder once more presented himself to his master, he was given further details.[1]

"It was explained to me," Roeder recalls, "that summary proceedings against the 117 Rote Kapelle prisoners were to be taken immediately and under conditions of the strictest secrecy. The Führer had approved the Gestapo's proposal that the trial should be conducted before the Peoples Court; Göring was to supervise the proceedings as convening officer, but Hitler had reserved to himself confirmation of the more important sentences."[2]

Roeder had misgivings about a summary trial before the Peoples Court. The prisoners' liability to punishment under criminal law, he explained to Göring, was not yet established in all cases; the degree of guilt seemed to him to differ so widely that he had serious doubts about a summary trial. In addition the Peoples Court could hardly be the correct forum; this was a case of military espionage and in accordance with Paragraph 2, Section 4 of the special wartime legal code the sole competent authority was the Reich Court Martial [Reichskriegsgericht—RKG], the highest military tribunal in the Third Reich.[8]

Göring was appalled. He could not possibly propose that to the Führer, he said; the Führer had an extreme aversion to this institution; had Roeder forgotten Hitler's Reichstag speech of April 1942 with its outbursts against lawyers[4]—they had clearly been directed against the gentlemen of the Reich Court Martial.

The dictator had borne a grudge against the RKG ever since it had refused to comply with his wish to proceed against generals who had disobeyed orders and withdrawn their formations from positions in front of Moscow during the winter 1941–2.[5] Here was an illustration of the paradoxical fact that, of all the courts in Germany, the one with the least autonomy still preserved some remnant of those legal norms which had long been arbitrarily expunged from the rest of the legal system by the Nazi minions. The Reich Court Martial had originally been only a court of appeal intended to insure that the law was uniformly applied within a certain sector, in this case throughout the Wehrmacht's legal system. In 1938, however, the regime had removed from the Wehrmacht all authority in so-called cases of war crimes and, as a result, the RKG had ceased to be a court of appeal; it remained merely a court of first instance for cases of treason, treasonable activities, espionage and willful damage to military equipment.[6] The clearest illustration of the RKG's lack of autonomy was the fact that its decisions did not become law after the lapse of a specific interval, as was the case with other courts, but required confirmation by a senior military commander, in special cases by Hitler himself.[7] Even this, however, does not give a complete picture of the RKG's state of subordination.

The Reich Court Martial was an organ of OKW [Oberkommando der Wehrmacht—High Command of the Armed Forces], whose instructions it was bound to follow; the head of OKW's legal department invariably checked both the validity and expediency of RKG decisions before submitting them for confirmation. The President of the RKG

was not an independent judge; he was a military officer,
bound by his instructions.[8] Professional judges did act as
presidents of the four chambers of the RKG, but for every
trial the court was so constituted as to insure the predom-
inance of officers bound by instructions—three officers of
General's or Admiral's rank to two professional judges.[9]
Whenever the military and the lawyers disagreed, the latter
invariably had to give way, since they had neither power
nor independence. Naturally, whenever the interests of the
professional lawyers in preserving their autonomy coincided
with those of the military in defending the principles of
the Prussian-German military tradition, the RKG mani-
fested an independence, whose effect in the Third Reich
was well-nigh sensational. In the struggle against the undermining of the Wehrmacht by Nazi ideology the military
were only too ready to let the lawyers take the lead, particularly seeing that the RKG bench included conservative
jurists whose debating skill was frequently able to convince
the more slow-witted officers.

Prominent among the RKG lawyers was Dr. Alexander
Kraell, President of the Second Chamber of the Reich
Court Martial and ex-Public Prosecutor of Darmstadt.*
He used his military cover to maintain the legal norms—
in face of resistance from the Nazi judiciary, the Gestapo
and the Party. President of the RKG was Admiral Max
Bastian, an unimaginative military-minded man, ex-Captain
of the battleship *Schlesien;*[11] Kraell's convincing arguments
frequently succeeded in persuading Bastian to walk the
tightrope between the law and open disobedience to the
regime—always provided, of course, that he could prove
that it was in the Wehrmacht's interests to do so.

Dr. Rudolf Lehmann, the Judge Advocate-General [Ge-
neraloberstabsrichter] who was head of the OKW Legal
Department, generally supported RKG's decisions and was

---

* Alexander Kraell was born at Kirch-Beerfurth in the Odenwald
on 19 May 1894. He studied law at the universities of Giessen, Berlin, Heidelberg and Marburg and was called to the bar in 1922. A
year later he was appointed to the Public Prosecutor's office in Darmstadt, becoming District Court Attorney [Landgerichtsrat] in 1930,
member of NSDAP and Senior Public Prosecutor [Oberstaatsanwalt]
in 1933. In 1938 he joined the Wehrmacht Legal Service and became
an attorney of the Reich Court Martial; he was appointed President
of a Chamber in 1942, promoted Judge Advocate [Oberreichskriegs-
anwalt] in 1943, and Judge Advocate-General [Generaloberstabs-
richter] in 1944.[10]

occasionally able to enlist the help of Göring, since he sometimes liked to appear to the military as the level-headed traditionalist averse to the Nazi disdain for the law —always provided that he did not incur Hitler's wrath thereby.[12] The mistrustful dictator, however, was not deceived by the RKG's "flabby" maneuvers; he suspected that it was trying to keep the Wehrmacht legal system free of Nazi lawyers.

This was why Göring was so horrified when Roeder told him that the Reich Court Martial alone was competent to try the Rote Kapelle spies. Göring foresaw a conflict with his Führer and turned the proposal down flat. Finding that he could not gain his point, Roeder alerted two of his colleagues who happened to be in Göring's special train, Kraell, the President of one of the Chambers, and Christian von Hammerstein, head of the Luftwaffe Legal Service.[13]

Hammerstein mobilized Bastian and Lehmann and the five of them soon agreed to support Roeder's proposal; it could not be in the interest of the Wehrmacht, they felt, to allow officers and soldiers to be tried by the Peoples Court, which was open to all kinds of pressure from the Gestapo.[14] Lehrmann, Hammerstein and Roeder sought a further interview with Göring.

They argued at such length with Hitler's vacillating Number Two that he eventually gave way.[15] With some trepidation Göring appeared before his Führer at the end of October and recommended that the Rote Kapelle trial take place before the Reich Court Martial. To avert the anticipated explosion of wrath he proposed that Roeder be entrusted with the case for the prosecution. Hitler agreed, seeing that Roeder was regarded as one of the sternest and most loyal officers in the Military Legal Service.[16]

A few days later Roeder with two secretaries, Adelheid Eidenbenz and Erika Strey, moved into the office in the Reich Ministry of Aviation previously occupied by Colonel-General Jeschonnek, Chief of Staff of the Luftwaffe.[17] He was subsequently reinforced by another Judge Advocate [Kriegsgerichtsrat], Werner Falkenberg from the Court of Air Region III.[18]

Although on paper a "Special Representative of the Reich Marshal," Roeder was still a military Judge Advocate on the staff of RKG and he had to wait a whole fortnight before the RSHA made up its mind to hand over the

Gestapo's records of interrogation. Roeder says: "The first files, together with the Gestapo's final report, arrived early in November; the files were those of Schulze-Boysen, Harnack, Graudenz and Coppi. A few days later the Schumacher files arrived. The files on Kent, alias Vincente Sierra, which were essential for proper understanding of the entire affair, however, were still missing."[19]

Meanwhile, on 12 November, Kent, the ex-organizer, had been arrested in Marseilles and taken to Belgium, where the Gestapo interrogated him.[20] Kent's very first statements made it clear that he had been the channel for transmission to Moscow of much of the intelligence gathered by the Berlin agents; with Kent available, therefore, there was no difficulty in proving that Schulze-Boysen and his friends had been working for the Soviets. Roeder despatched an official to Brussels to fetch the Kent records; a few days later Kent himself was transferred to the Prinz-Albrecht-Strasse.[21]

By mid-November Roeder had all the Rote Kapelle files and could begin his ghastly work.[22] From this point the story of Rote Kapelle is largely his story, the record of its doom his record. "The bloody judge," as Greta Kuckhoff called him,[23] became the prisoners' nightmare.

Roeder's martial bearing was only too well calculated to make him appear as the villain of the piece. Even today the Rote Kapelle survivors retain so vivid an impression of his harsh boorish manner, tinged with cynicism, that to them he is the inhuman murderer incarnate.

Falk Harnack, Arvid's brother, considered him "one of the bloodiest and cruellest persecutors of German antifascists";[24] Greta Kuckhoff thought him a torturer actuated "by personal ambition and thirst for revenge";[25] to Heinz Strelow's mother he seemed "merely a Gestapo agent";[26] and Marie-Louise Schulze calls him "a beast of a man, of indescribable brutality."[27] Even Adolf Grimme thought that Roeder showed himself to be "one of the most inhuman, cynical and brutal Nazis it has ever been my misfortune to meet."[28]

The prisoners' hatred of their accuser reached such emotional heights that they attributed to Roeder an almost magical influence over generals, judges and Nazi leaders. Greta Kuckhoff, for instance, says: "He had a permanent room in the Prinz-Albrecht-Strasse; an aircraft was always standing ready so that he could report without delay to

Hitler or Göring."[29] His threats, she said, had made the Reich Court Martial "docile."[30] Jan Bontjes van Beek thinks that "he was in such a powerful position that he could have saved people, had he wished."[31] According to Falk Harnack "this well-known murderer" intervened on several occasions with Hitler to insure that "innumerable German and foreign anti-fascists could neither defend themselves nor obtain a remand."[32] Liane Berkowitz' mother believes that Roeder "conducted this fake trial simply to curry favor with the Reichsführer-SS, Himmler."[33]

These statements and opinions are merely reflections of the baseless rumors current in the prisoners' cells; they bear no relation to the truth. The waiting aircraft was a legend, as were Roeder's repeated visits to the Führer's headquarters—he never had an interview with Hitler. His devilish power over the Court was a fairytale, his room in the RSHA a misunderstanding, his familiarity with Himmler a figment of the imagination.

Nevertheless, when the West German lawyers examined his conduct after the war, Roeder could not clear himself of all the charges against him. Significantly, he was the only man whom the Rote Kapelle survivors blamed, not one of the RKG judges who had pronounced sentences of death or severe terms of imprisonment. It cannot be disputed that Roeder is one of the most controversial figures ever thrown up by the German military Legal Service.

Many of his fellows and superiors had no great liking for the ambitious publicity-hunting prosecutor. Many would agree with Judge Eugen Schmitt, who asked "why Roeder had earned the hatred of so many men" and answered the question as follows: "My general opinion of Roeder is that there was something lacking in his temperament; he did not possess the normal man's sympathy for the sufferings of others, so that he did not mind witnessing an execution or undertaking unpleasant tasks."[34]

After service in the First World War Manfred Roeder had had a varied career*—student, legal adviser to a firm,

---

* Manfred Roeder was born in Kiel on 20 August 1900, son of a county court clerk [Landgerichtsdirektor]. He attended preparatory school in Recklinghausen and high school in Berlin. In late 1917 he volunteered for service as a cadet in Field Artillery Regiment 83; in 1919 he was attached to the Guards Cavalry Rifle Division and in 1920 to the West Russian Volunteer Army in the Baltic States; shortly thereafter he retired with the rank of Lieutenant. In 1921–2 he studied law, qualifying as Doctor of Law; until 1931 he worked

farm manager and student once more, before entering the legal profession in 1934; he was hardly one of the more notable figures in German law. He passed his preliminary law examination with no better qualification than "Fully satisfactory" and as regards his finals there was merely a note on the file. Many regarded him as a very moderate lawyer.[36]

Kraell's opinion was that "he was too insensitive and biased for any good judge."[37] Roeder's methods were continually giving rise to complaints; he left behind him a broad trail of personal altercations, official protests and disciplinary proceedings. Many officers were revolted by his boorish ways; the Commander of the "Brandenburg" Division even boxed his ears because he considered that his troops had been insulted by Roeder.[38]

The less Roeder felt himself respected as a lawyer, however, the more aggressively did he play the blustering loud-mouthed soldier—which he was not. He was one of the few military legal officers who did not measure up to Göring's requirements that every Luftwaffe Judge Advocate must be at least a reserve officer; in the Luftwaffe messes it was even said that in the early days of German rearmament when Roeder, the ex-World War I Lieutenant, had applied, the Luftwaffe had refused him.[39]

However this may be, Roeder's attitude to officers was one of suspicion which those concerned often felt amounted to hatred.[40] Yet he was beloved by his subordinates, for whom he showed an almost touching solicitude; he would invariably protect his staff. If required to investigate charges of corruption or high-handedness on the part of senior officers, however, there was no more courageous apostle of truth than Manfred Roeder.[41]

With his appointment as senior Judge Advocate of Air Region III, Roeder finally became one of the leading figures among military lawyers.[42] Air Region III included

in industry and agriculture. He passed the preliminary law examination on 4 May 1931 and the State finals on 17 August 1934. Three months later he applied for a post in the Reich Ministry of Aviation and on 1 April 1935 entered the Luftwaffe Legal Service, being initially attached to Artillery Commander I in Königsberg. In late 1935 he was appointed Judge Advocate [Kriegsgerichtsrat] of Air Region I and in 1937 Senior Judge Advocate of Air Region III. He was promoted Judge Advocate-General [Oberstkriegsgerichtsrat] in 1941 and in 1942 Judge [Generalrichter] and Chief Legal Officer, Air Fleet IV.[35]

Berlin with its ministries and senior headquarters and so all Luftwaffe cases of major importance or political significance automatically became Roeder's business. His great chance came with the suicide of Ernst Udet, head of Luftwaffe Equipment, in November 1941. Consternation throughout the military hierarchy was such that Göring was compelled to order a thorough investigation of the mystery, particularly seeing that many suspected the General's suicide to be a face-saver for the Luftwaffe's technical failures, for which Udet could be held responsible.[43] As Head of the Ministry of Aviation's Legal Section, Hammerstein was commissioned to assemble a Commission of Inquiry composed of judges from the Reich Court Martial; he picked Kraell, Ernst and Grell, with Kraell in the chair. Roeder was subsequently seconded as assistant to the Commission and he proved a resourceful investigator.[44] His detective ability had much to do with the Commission's conclusion that (in Hammerstein's words) "Udet had neglected his duties in most culpable fashion and, when this came to light, had shot himself."[45]

The Udet investigation established Roeder's reputation as an astute, pertinacious lawyer with a nose for crime. Once on a trail, nobody and nothing could stop him pursuing his quarry to the end and nailing it down. Lehmann of OKW said sarcastically: "We must keep Roeder out of this case; he is quite capable of arresting the Pope and bringing him in front of us."[46]

More important from the point of view of Roeder's career, however, was the fact that the Udet affair had brought him into close personal touch with Göring. Roeder's manner suited Göring; his glib tongue and innuendoes about the military hierarchy touched some answering chord in his Commander-in-Chief. Hammerstein, always somewhat jealous of his more successful rival, says: "He could put a case over very suavely and he knew what Göring liked to hear. In passing he would tell a number of little tales and so became a great favorite."[47] Göring was in fact so impressed by Roeder that he appointed him his special representative with the Reich Court Martial, while retaining him in his previous post.[48] Roeder was therefore the obvious candidate for the star role of prosecutor when Göring was placed in charge of the Rote Kapelle trial.

The conservative gentlemen of the Reich Court Martial were less enthusiastic about their new colleague. Kraell, the

President of the Chamber, said: "Roeder is no great lawyer; his theoretical knowledge is no more than average"; moreover, he found Roeder's manner "that of a policeman" and his arguments "not up to the standard of the Reich Court Martial."[49] Schmitt, the other member of Kraell's bench, also had his doubts, saying: "He was typical of the prosecutor ill-suited to his bench. For me he bragged far too much about his success as an investigator. I and my colleagues, therefore, frequently did not take him seriously."[50] Roeder attempted to make good his shortcomings as a lawyer by zealous devotion to Nazism. He became the terror of the accused; anyone could quote examples of his Nazi conformist megalomania—including the Rote Kapelle prisoners and their relatives.

To Falk Harnack, who had submitted a request, he countered with: "That might suit you very well! We do not propose to produce martyrs. Anyway how loyal are you to the National Socialist state?"[51] There were frequent violent scenes with the accused. When Schulze-Boysen's mother asked what her son was being charged with, he replied indignantly: "Treason and treasonable activities on the largest scale. Your son will have to pay for it." Frau Schulze leaped from her chair and screamed: "That's not true." Roeder drew himself up and shouted: "I would draw your attention to the fact that you are speaking to a representative of the highest German court and that you will have to suffer the consequences of this insult."[52]

Many others had "major altercations with Dr. Roeder"; Elsa Boysen, for instance, Schulze-Boysen's aunt, "will never as long as I live forget his frigidity and brutality."[53] Ursula Goetze's father was haunted by the sight of Roeder "leaning back haughtily in his chair, chain-smoking and taking no notice of me whatsoever."[54]

His manners were in fact dictated not so much by Nazi fanaticism as by his ambition and personal vanity; his bluster accorded with the picture he had made of himself as the prosecutor feared by all. When no longer the prosecutor, however, but himself presiding over a court martial, he usually showed himself "very lenient," in the words of Graf Westarp, one of his co-Presidents, who was an anti-Nazi and later a Public Prosecutor.[55] Loyal Nazi though he was, as a lawyer Roeder was averse to the Nazi circumventions of the law as practiced by men like Freisler. He refused to accept any participation by the Gestapo in a court's preliminary investigations and was opposed to the RSHA practice of introducing Gestapo stool pigeons into the cells of prisoners under detention.[56] Whenever a prisoner was brought to him handcuffed, he immediately had the handcuffs removed.[57] He insisted on proper legal aid for prisoners.

In the case of women he often found it specially hard to play his role of pitiless prosecutor. When Mildred Harnack was first sentenced to imprisonment, he said: "Let's let her go";[58] Eva Rittmeister, one of the accused and an actress by profession, thought that he had behaved with such impartiality during the trial that she rewarded him by reciting one of the Gretchen monologues from "Faust" in his office; she even presented him with a photograph with the inscription: "In gratitude for your loyal behavior, your Eva Rittmeister."[59]

On several occasions he persuaded Göring to commute death sentences on women to terms of imprisonment. When he subsequently presided over the court martials on the members of Rote Kapelle in France and Belgium, he let off many of the accused with remarkably light sentences.[60] Even after the war Frau Henniger, wife of one of the accused, maintained that her husband had been very fairly treated and said that Roeder was "not simply 'inhuman' but was quite capable of being humane and sympathetic."[61]

Such incidents confirm that the standard concept of the "Nazi judge" is not strictly applicable to Roeder. He had been a member of the Stahlhelm* and (until 1935) of the SA, but he was not a member of the Nazi Party; during the de-nazification period he was able to cite many proofs of virtue—that he had stood aloof from the Party, that he had furthered the cause of Christianity in the irreligious Luftwaffe, that he had disapproved of the Nazi regime's "excesses."[62]

In fact Dr. Manfred Roeder was more typical of the authoritarian reactionary lawyer; he belonged to the conservative wing of National Socialism which saw in Adolf Hitler's state a continuation of the Kaiser's empire. He was not blinded by National Socialist ideology; the limit of his horizon was the all-embracing concept of the State, worshipped with semi-religious fervor.

Like many of his class and generation Roeder believed

---

* A conservative Ex-Servicemens Association. [Translator.]

in the bourgeois conservative concept of the State leading a curious form of separate existence behind the monolithic Nazi façade of the Third Reich; it might be misused or distorted by the Nazi upstarts, but, whenever the authority of "the State" had to be enforced, it was always there. What authority? That of the State as such—in the eyes of the legal practitioners "the State" was an absolute concept, independent of any political or social structure.

To this was added the glorification of the military virtues peculiar to Roeder's generation. He had been wounded in World War I and had also been a gas casualty; he wore the Iron Cross Second Class and the War Wounded Badge; to him nothing could be more monstrous than to throw doubt on the virtues of the soldier and the patriot.[63] In wartime he could not conceive that any German could do other than offer himself unquestioning to the military machine, no matter whether the flag of the State was the swastika or the national colors. For this very reason Roeder's thinking and his behavior are typical of the category of German leader which has managed to find a place in the Federal Republic and which still exerts a decisive influence on the German view of Rote Kapelle. His was a totalitarian concept of patriotism and it therefore ignored the true nature of the Hitler regime; there was no place in it for communists or pacifist resisters. Such widely differing personalities as Roeder, the fire-eater, Kraell, the aristocratic President of a Chamber, and Harry Piepe, the conservative pursuer of Rote Kapelle, all had one thing in common—the belief that the State, even though founded on concentration camps and coercion, had a valid claim to the loyalty of its citizens. Resistance to the State, particularly in wartime and with the help of the Soviets to boot, was in their eyes a crime to be mercilessly punished.

Even today these men still vehemently refuse to admit that, however questionable an activity espionage by men like Schulze-Boysen may have been, it was partly motivated by a spirit of internal German resistance. When questioned on the subject, ex-Captain Harry Piepe merely rumbled: "Nothing but a lot of traitors—nothing to do with resistance."[64] With obvious indignation Kraell declared after the war that he was "opposed to any attempt to label Rote Kapelle as primarily an internal political resistance movement."[65] The language shows that in his views on the state and the political structure of society

Kraell, the protagonist of the state founded on the rule of law, is barely distinguishable from Roeder, the prosecutor. Kraell was not to be moved; Schulze-Boysen's and Harnack's spy-ring, he insisted, "was primarily and basically an espionage organization working for Soviet Russia. The anti-government activities were a side-issue and the means to the end. From the moment when the Soviet Union, the protagonist of communism, appeared as Germany's military opponent, any support of communism was tantamount to support of the enemy in the field."[66]

The argument is, of course, historically inaccurate and politically questionable. In practice it means that any resistance to the regime by the extreme Left was furtherance of communism and therefore support of the Soviet enemy; consequently high treason [Hochverrat], meaning internal political activities aimed at bringing down the leadership of the State, and treasonable activity [Landesverrat], meaning cooperation with and espionage for the enemy, were the same thing.

The implication of this line of argument, however, was that under no circumstances could it be admitted that the members of Rote Kapelle had acted for internal political reasons. Anyone who unconditionally accepted the Third Reich as *the* German State, while at the same time overlooking its specifically Nazi characteristics, could not admit that men might exist prepared to resist this Nazi State out of revulsion at certain of its manifestations.

This was the point which distinguished the Rote Kapelle case in the Third Reich from similar cases of treason, whether against the government or the country, in other states. In Allied countries the law prescribed severe punishment for giving aid and comfort to the enemy (though generally excluding the death sentence); their courts, however, distinguished more sharply between treason against the government and treason against the country. If a man had the good of his country at heart, they did not simply brand him as a traitor.

Roeder cannot be blamed for bringing the communist spies to justice. He was a Public Prosecutor, bound by his instructions; he could only act within the framework of the current law. Moreover, at no time did he infringe even a paragraph of either the civil or military code. The only case which can be brought against him by history or humanity is that in some cases he may have been over-zealous in demanding the death sentence for men who had never participated in Schulze-Boysen's espionage activities, even for individuals who disapproved of them and had become estranged from the head of the organization.

Even this Roeder did not do for the sheer pleasure of doing so. He was acting on the instructions of his masters, though admittedly he did so with the ghastly zeal with which the natural subordinate carries out the orders of his superiors, particularly when he can satisfy his own ambitions thereby. He continually succumbed to the temptation to impute dishonorable motives to Schulze-Boysen's friends and associates.

Manfred Roeder was determined to prove that these people were actuated by many motives—with the single exception of the all-important one without which the story of Rote Kapelle makes no sense: that of political resistance. To Roeder any statement to the effect that "Rote Kapelle was formed as an anti-Hitler resistance organization" was, and still is, "an historical falsehood."[67] In his eyes it was "a clandestine enemy, working from his lair with novel but insidious methods while at the same time paying lip-service to the ideas of freedom, humanity and patriotism."[68]

After a fortnight's intensive study of the files Roeder had built up a picture of a colossal conspiracy by denizens of the underworld.[69] There they were pursuing their nefarious activities—"gamblers by trade, communist fanatics, disoriented introverts and drug addicts, disillusioned bourgeois, anarchists on principle, people whose sole motive was a passionate desire to live it up, communist outlaws acting as couriers, agents and saboteurs, deserters and émigrés."[70]

Had they political motives beyond those normally to be found in an orthodox communist? For Roeder the answer to this question had to be "No." Nevertheless, his bourgeois nationalist dreamworld permitted him to attribute idealistic motives to communistic functionaries and members of the Communist Party, for one of the more remarkable articles in the authoritarian anti-bolshevist creed was that communists were invariably fanatical and obdurate, always ready to sacrifice themselves for Moscow to the extent of self-destruction if need be.

In the case of Wilhelm Guddorf, who was a member of the KPD, Kraell was always prepared to "testify that he had acted as an idealist and solely from political conviction";[71] in this he was undoubtedly at one with Roeder. Roeder himself bore witness to his respect for Heinrich Koenen, the parachutist.[72] Other apparatchiks of the world communist movement were given astonishingly good marks; the prosecution hardly seemed able to speak well enough of them—seeking to prove thereby that Rote Kapelle had been acting, not against the Nazi State, but against Germany as such.

Those who did not belong to the official communist organization but were communists nevertheless, could not claim the perilous advantage of Roeder's good will. In his anti-bolshevist world there was no place for men "of good family" who accepted communism. Since he could not admit internal political reasons or anti-Nazi resistance as motives, he found more jejune explanations—opportunism and ambition. Harnack, the doctrinaire ascetic, turned into a man "of split personality" because he had allegedly wished to become Minister of Economics in a German Soviet Republic;[73] Schulze-Boysen's ambition to be Minister of War was chalked up against him;[74] Adam Kuckhoff was described as an opportunist who had failed as an author;[75] Graudenz's reason for entering Soviet service was said to be purely his acquisitive instinct.[76]

But all this was not enough for Roeder. Schulze-Boysen had to be built up into the central figure actuated by the basest motives, as the great seducer leading young men to their ruin. But what were his weapons? Roeder could only think of two—money and women.

Roeder soon coined a phrase which seemed to him to explain everything—"wages of treachery." He became obsessed with the discovery of Soviet remuneration for espionage as the background to every action by Schulze-Boysen and his closest friends. Everything was bought with the "wages of treachery"—Schulze-Boysen's yacht,[77] a plot of ground in Teupitz,[78] leather goods during a trip to Holland.[79] Roeder was indefatigable in the discovery of fresh clues involving money. In Frau Grimme's wardrobe had been found 2,000 marks given by Kuckhoff to his friend Grimme for safe keeping—"wages of treachery" of course.[80] Countess Brockdorff had "bought" her husband with money from a suspect source;[81] Hübner, the long-standing communist and allegedly "Rote Kapelle's banker," had supported the organization with 230,000 gold marks in specie.[82]

In short—"Everybody in the service of Moscow was paid by the Soviets for their activities which cost the lives of innumerable German soldiers, women and children."[83]

Wherever no proof could be found for the "wages of treachery" Roeder, the strict bourgeois moralist, spied the dissolute practices of sexual perverts and adulterers. Even now, twenty-five years later, he can still remember in detail who was associating with whom. According to him Schulze-Boysen was "intimate with Oda Schottmüller, Gräfin Brockdorff, Frau Schumacher and two shorthand-typists in the Reich Ministry of Aviation";[84] Libertas Schulze-Boysen was a lesbian who also had relations with other men.[85] Marie-Louise Schulze remembers Roeder asking her indignantly whether "I knew that my daughter-in-law had had relations with three or four men, not even all of her own class."[86] Any story of eroticism, however trivial, seemed to Roeder to have criminal implications. The Gestapo had discovered some photographs, taken by Schumacher, of Libertas Schulze-Boysen in the nude; Roeder never tired of showing them to Schulze-Boysen's relatives, though the majority of them found the photographs not particularly exciting.[87] In Roeder's eyes, however, they were proof positive of the alleged orgies which he was sure had taken place in Schulze-Boysen's flat. Roeder's tireless imagination constructed "a succession of wild parties" at which "the female guests might wear no more than 15 clothing coupons would buy—and that was very little indeed."[88] Gräfin Brockdorff had apparently achieved the feat of "having intimate relations with four Soviet agents in a single night";[89] Kuckhoff had become "the pliant tool of Moscow" because of "his passionate attachment to Libertas Schulze-Boysen";[90] Ilse Stöbe seduced her victims "with passion, when argument failed."[91] Roeder even discovered traces of eroticism among the most innocent and unsuspecting of Schulze-Boysen's accomplices. The young members of Rittmeister's group became a "wanton sex-obsessed society";[92] Cato Bontjes van Beek had "drifted into the business because of her sexual connections with her circle of friends with whom she wished to curry favor."[93]

The introduction of the erotic motive into the Rote Kapelle case had a very definite purpose. By dramatizing the manners and customs of Schulze-Boysen's friends (and they were undoubtedly uninhibited) Roeder hoped to create the impression that anarchism and license had been the main ties between Schulze-Boysen and his agents, the majority of whom were young.

Another of Roeder's favorite words was "enslavement." Eva-Maria Buch, the bookseller, had been "totally enslaved" by Guddorf;[94] Krauss, the professor of Roman studies, had found his way into Schulze-Boysen's circle as a result of "his experience with Ursula Goetze."[95] Roeder discovered instances of psychic domination in the case of men too—Schulze-Boysen was said to have "enticed Heilmann into his house" and transformed him into "a willing tool."[96]

All this relieved Roeder of the necessity of investigating and accepting any political motives on the part of the prisoners. Eroticism, anarchism, avarice, communist fanaticism—any motive was good enough for him provided it allowed him to overlook the overriding internal political reasons which would have exposed the regime.

So Roeder soon had his case ready. On 16 November 1942 he began to draft the case for the prosecution at top speed; in a month he and his assistant Falkenberg had put together 800 pages of text.[97] They dictated uninterruptedly to their two secretaries, sleeping for at most three hours a night on camp beds in their office. Hitler and the Gestapo were pressing them; the dictator insisted that the main trial must be finished by Christmas; Gestapo Müller was grumbling that he could not understand this "useless waste of time in so clear a case."[98]

With a case conducted on these lines there could be no doubt regarding either the substance of the case for the prosecution or the outcome of the trial. Schulze-Boysen and his immediate friends had carried on espionage on behalf of the enemy and in the Third Reich (as indeed in other belligerent states) the punishment for this was death. The only point at issue was how those of Schulze-Boysen's political adherents who had not been involved in espionage, and his unconscious military accomplices, would be dealt with. There was little hope for these people either, however, since the regime had prescribed the severest punishments for any form of political opposition or military indiscipline, characterizing both as "aid and comfort to the enemy."

Paragraph 91b of the Reich Criminal Code laid down that "anyone who, in wartime, furnishes assistance to an enemy power or acts to the detriment of the Reich's war effort" was guilty of providing "aid and comfort" worthy of death. Worse still, according to Paragraph 5 of the Special Wartime Criminal Code "anyone who publicly urges or incites any member of the German Wehrmacht to refuse to fulfill his duty" or "anyone who induces a soldier to disobey orders" was guilty of "undermining the war effort," which also carried the death penalty.

Schulze-Boysen's military accomplices were vulnerable on two counts. The paragraph in the Reich Criminal Code dealing with state secrets laid down that: "Anyone who betrays a state secret will be punished with death"; paragraph 92, dealing with indiscipline, said in Section 1: "Anyone who disobeys an official order and thereby, either deliberately or through negligence, endangers the security of the Reich or the efficiency or the training of the troops will be punished by close arrest for not less than one week or by imprisonment or by fortress arrest up to ten years"; and Section 2: "If the crime is committed in the field or if the case is particularly serious, the death sentence or life imprisonment or a term of hard labor may be imposed."[99]

These paragraphs gave Roeder full legal backing to demand the death sentence for practically all Schulze-Boysen's and Harnack's more important friends and associates. Even the distribution of a leaflet he presented as sabotage and detriment to the war effort; transport or repair of a Soviet radio set was in his eyes execrable spying.

Adolf Hitler had every reason to be satisfied with his inquisitor. Of the 117 persons arrested 76 remained to stand trial; for procedural reasons Roeder divided them into a number of groups, but otherwise no distinction of any importance was made between them. Twelve separate trials were prepared at which Schulze-Boysen and his friends were to be condemned as common traitors.[100]

The procedure prescribed by military justice was as crude as the case for the prosecution. At the end of November 1942 the President of the Reich Court Martial approved Roeder's submission and proposed arrangements for the trials and decided that they should take place before the Second Chamber of the RKG.[101] No sooner had he done so than the prisoners were given eloquent proof of what passed for military justice in the Great German Reich.

A few days before the opening of the main trial the doors of the cells beneath the RSHA and Police Presidency buildings were swung open and an official appeared to inform the prisoners curtly when their cases would be taken. Heinrich Scheel says: "It must have been shortly before midnight when the door of Kurt Schumacher's cell was unlocked; he was lying handcuffed on the plank bed. Schumacher was about to get up when the official, accompanied by the warder on duty, entered the cell with the words: 'Stay where you are. You are Kurt Schumacher? You will appear tomorrow before the Second Chamber of the Reich Court Martial. You are accused of the following crimes . . . (here followed a recital of the paragraphs concerned). Have you understood it all? Good.' The entire process lasted barely a minute."[102]

None of the prisoners knew precisely what the case against them was; only a few, such as Weisenborn, were permitted even a cursory glance at anything on paper. Weisenborn says that the visitor to his cell "held a piece of paper in front of me which he covered with his hand, so that I could only take a hurried glance at a few lines."[103] Adolf Grimme says: "I was never given a copy of the case against me. Until called upon to give evidence, therefore, I was forced to rely upon pure conjecture concerning the accusations made against me."[104]

Initially defense counsel also found themselves working under great difficulties. Since the trials were held in secret, only lawyers accredited to the Reich Court Martial were permitted to act—four defense counsel for 76 defendants![105] They too were told of the opening of the main trial only at the very last moment, Dr. Kurt Valentin, for instance, Grimme's defense counsel, only the day before the trial began.[106] Grimme was introduced to his defense counsel only minutes before his trial when Valentin "entered the room in which we were waiting for proceedings to begin. He came up to me and told me that he . . . had not yet had an opportunity of studying the papers."[107] For defense counsel "it was extraordinarily difficult to distinguish between individual cases when the proceedings opened."[108] They hardly even knew what the indictments were; these were in fact distributed beforehand, but defense counsel nevertheless had to undertake not to show them to their clients, to return them as soon as sentence had been pronounced and thereafter to preserve "total silence and secrecy."[109]

The trial would have been a complete legal farce, had not the RKG judges insisted on a minimum of juridical propriety. The court was composed of two professional judges and three officers* and they were ultimately responsible for safeguarding the rights of the accused; defense counsel were permitted to peruse the papers in full and the prisoners were allowed complete freedom of speech.

Moreover, the Second Chamber was generally considered to be the most broad-minded of the Reich Court Martial. This was due primarily to its Chairman, Kraell, who frequently defended the accused against the cruder of Roeder's outbursts. Though at heart his view of the misdeeds of the accused was probably as severe as that of the prosecutor, he kept an ever-watchful eye lest, via Roeder, the evil of Nazism seep into the sanctum of the Reich Court Martial.

Werner Krauss says that the Reich Court Martial "was at pains throughout to preserve proper legal decorum," whereas Roeder "with his coarse Party language put himself quite outside the pale."[111] Even so severe a critic as Greta Kuckhoff later called Kraell "a man of high moral principle and sense of responsibility."[112] Werner Müller-Hoff, Kummerow's defense counsel, thought Kraell "a military judge of transparently honest character"—an opinion which has never been disputed.[113]

Roeder brought his first accused to trial at 9:15 a.m. on 14 December 1942 in the main courtroom of the Reich Court Martial at No. 4–10 Witzlebenstrasse, Berlin-Charlottenburg. They were Rudolf von Scheliha, the Foreign Service Counselor, and his assistant, the agent Ilse Stöbe.[114]

The trial lasted only a few hours; judgment was pronounced the same day. Rudolf Behse, von Scheliha's defense counsel, says: "The case was completely hopeless from the start, as von Scheliha admitted to me."[115] Evidence for the prosecution was completely watertight. Roeder was able to produce decoded Soviet radio messages and the photostat copies of von Scheliha's payslips found on Koenen, the parachutist. They proved indisputably that the accused had been working for the Soviet Secret Service for years.[116]

---

* In addition to Kraell the Second Chamber included two professional judges, Ranft and Schmitt, together with Generals Mushoff and Bertram and Vice-Admiral Arps.[110]

Rudolf von Scheliha made a full confession (as did Ilse Stöbe); he pretended, however, that he did not know which country he was spying for.[117] Ilse Stöbe's communist pride, on the other hand, did not permit her to use this excuse; she testified that from the beginning they had worked for Moscow.[118] The sentence came shortly thereafter: "On a count of treason the defendants, von Scheliha and Stöbe, are condemned to death and permanent loss of civil rights."[119]

The evidence for the prosecution was equally convincing when, on 16 December, Roeder produced the second and most important group of defendants: Harro Schulze-Boysen and Dr. Arvid Harnack, their wives, Kurt Schulze and Hans Coppi, the radio operators, the two Schumachers, Countess Erika von Brockdorff, assistant radio operator, Horst Heilmann, Schulze-Boysen's secretary, John Graudenz, the intelligence agent, Edwin Gehrts and Herbert Gollnow, military informers.[120]

The trial lasted four days but none of the defendants could dispute the prosecution's evidence. Schulze-Boysen's closest friends had made such full confessions during their interrogations that the judges had merely to preside over the formal closure of the proceedings.

Schulze-Boysen confided to his defense counsel that he had worked so hard against the Nazi state, and had had to admit so much to the police, that any defense was useless.[121] The leaders nevertheless held their heads high before the court and before history. Kraell recalls that "at the trial Schulze-Boysen admitted his deeds openly and with a certain pride";[122] Schmitt, his colleague, long remembered the "special impression" made on him by Arvid Harnack's final plea to the court, when he explained that "as the result of promise which he had given before the outbreak of the Russo-German war to Erdmann [he meant Erdberg], a Russian national with whom he was friendly, he had felt himself morally bound to assist the agents depatched to him."[123] Horst Heilmann emphasized that, as a convinced communist, he could not have acted otherwise.[124] Kurt Schumacher made so passionate a confession that his defense counsel considered him "one of the political fanatics in this trial."[125] One after another they proclaimed that what had brought them all together was their disgust and indignation with the regime they all hated.

Only one of the defendants refused to look the truth in the face—Libertas Schulze-Boysen. Up to the time of the trial she had lived on the illusion that, since she had told everything she knew, she would be released immediately afterward as having turned "King's Evidence." When she heard that she too was to be condemned to death, however, she broke down. Behse, her defense counsel, had to request a suspension of the session. It was a long time before Libertas really understood the scurvy game which the Gestapo had played with her.[126]

This did not stop the judges, however, doing what was expected of them. On 19 December 1942 Hitler's wishes were met and, as far as the law was concerned, the hard core of Rote Kapelle was liquidated: the principal defendants were condemned to death.* In four cases the court refused to take Roeder's line. Two of these concerned Schulze-Boysen's involuntary helpers who had provided military information without being involved in the work of the spy-ring; they had been victims and tools of Rote Kapelle rather than agents.

The first case was that of Colonel Erwin Gehrts, whom his defense counsel described as "psychologically a somewhat curious personality."[128] He had been a chatterbox of an officer and a believer in all sorts of occult powers; he had given Schulze-Boysen and Anna Kraus, the fortune-teller, many official secrets but had not considered this an act of resistance. His wife is prepared to swear that, though an anti-Nazi, "he was an officer and a German through and through, so that he could never have devoted himself to traitorous activities or espionage"; he had never once "actively participated in any traitorous plot" and, despite his aversion to National Socialism, had intended to continue to work even after the war "no matter what the color of the political leadership."[129]

Behse, Gehrts' defense counsel, however, proposed to exploit the peculiarities in the character of his client to save him from the death sentence. He applied to have the Colonel examined as a case of diminished responsibility. The court thereupon decided to take the Gehrts case separately from the main trial—everyone on the bench was in fact secretly hoping that Behse would succeed in

---

* They were: Harro and Libertas Schulze-Boysen, Kurt and Elizabeth Schumacher, Arvid Harnack, Horst Heilmann, Kurt Schulze, Hans Coppi and John Graudenz.[127]

saving his client from the executioner on the strength of Para. 51 of the Criminal Code.[130]

Lieutenant Herbert Gollnow of the Abwehr, Mildred Harnack's lover, had also given away official secrets without realizing that he was thereby collaborating with an enemy espionage organization. Gollnow was a National Socialist and had only been trying, by producing concrete information, to bring the sceptical Harnack to believe in an ultimate German victory. The court, and defense, and even Roeder himself, made no secret of their sympathy for "a young man who had drifted into this affair without evil intent."[131]

Nevertheless, the court considered it proved that Gollnow's information had contributed to the death of numerous German soldiers on the Eastern Front. He was accordingly condemned to death for military indiscipline, not for treason; the court, however, petitioned the Führer's headquarters to commute the sentence.[132]

Though the court's findings in the Gehrts and Gollnow cases were vexing enough to Roeder, its decisions in those of Mildred Harnack and Countess Brockdorff turned him into an enemy. In these two cases the court used against him his own arguments about the influence of eroticism. The court ruled that Countess Brockdorff had assisted communist radio operators solely to satisfy her own personal lusts and should therefore be judged merely as accessory to espionage. The judges accepted that "in the last analysis the motive for her actions was not a political one."[133] Kraell said: "All the young men who spent the night in her house for the reason alleged [to operate a radio], slept with her."[134] Result for the defendant Brockdorff: ten years' hard labor.[135]

Frau Harnack, on the other hand, was given only six years' hard labor, since the court considered (in the words of Ranft, one of the judges) that "she had acted more out of loyalty to her husband than of her own volition."[136] Here again the sentence was clearly influenced by sympathy for "a highly educated woman interested in all questions of public, and particularly social, affairs" (Kraell's words).[137] Kraell continued: "In view of the personal impression made by Frau Harnack, the court over which I was presiding was hesitant to impute to her any traitorous intent in the questions she put to Gollnow."[138] She was therefore sentenced only as an accessory to espionage, not for complicity.

Göring observed with consternation that the Reich Court Martial was once more going the right way to infuriate the dictator. When the two legal functionaries, Roeder and Lehmann, sought an interview with Göring shortly after the conclusion of the Schulze-Boysen trial, they were told that he was not prepared to compromise himself with Adolf Hitler in this way. Lehmann records: "Göring exploded at the word 'imprisonment.' He had been commissioned by the Führer," he said, "to 'cauterize this abscess.' The Führer would never agree to this."[139]

Göring proved to be right. OKW's Legal Department approved all the Second Chamber's sentences and forwarded them to Hitler in the normal way,[140] but Hitler refused to approve those on the two women; they were returned from the Führer's headquarters without comment[141]—and an unconfirmed sentence meant a fresh trial.

Kraell was forced to relinquish both cases to the next senior Chamber, the Third, and the President of this, Dr. Karl Schmauser, did not share the "pussyfoot" views of his colleague Kraell. Schmauser pledged himself at once to prove that there had been a miscarriage of justice in the Second Chamber.

Schmauser reproached his colleagues of the Second Chamber with having disregarded the principles of the Reich Court Martial which it had itself drawn up. These laid down that "in law any deliberate preparation for treason in favor of bolshevism or communism undertaken after the outbreak of the Russian campaign was tantamount to the crime of 'furnishing aid and comfort' and therefore, in accordance with Para. 73 of the Criminal Code should be punished under Para. 91b, Section 1." This paragraph prescribed hard labor for life or the death sentence.[142]

To Schmauser, however, a more decisive argument was that "their own ideology and their own political views had led the defendants Harnack and von Brockdorff to approve and participate in the efforts of the Schulze-Boysen/Harnack circle in favor of Russia." Consequently "instead of being mere accessories to preparations for treason as accepted by the Second Chamber (always assuming that such a crime is recognizable under criminal law), it must be accepted that the defendants are guilty of preparation for treason in complicity with the other accused."[143]

Schmauser also based his case on the fact that, after Gollnow had been sentenced, fresh evidence of his betrayal of secrets, and therewith also of the part played by Mildred Harnack, had come to light.[144] Gollnow had told Frau Harnack about twelve planned Abwehr sabotage operations behind the Soviet lines; she had passed the information to her husband and Harnack had in turn passed it to Moscow. The Abwehr saboteurs had immediately run into Soviet machine-gun fire.[145] Schmauser's conclusion: "The information passed by the defendant Harnack to her husband therefore resulted in the death, not only of Gollnow, but also of approximately two to three dozen German soldiers."[146]

The Third Chamber considered it proved that during her intimate sessions with Gollnow Mildred Harnack had systematically questioned him. The court therefore thought similarly to Strübing, the Criminal Police Inspector, who subsequently stated in the inimitable language of the Gestapo functionary that "it was incomprehensible to him how a woman in bed with her lover could put to him questions bearing no actual relationship to what was happening at the moment, unless she did so with treasonable intent."[147]

On 12 January 1943 Schmauser's Chamber condemned both Mildred Harnack and Countess von Brockdorff;[148] in the latter case, too, fresh evidence had been produced. In addition the Rote Kapelle prostitute had annoyed the court by her "somewhat outrageous behavior" (as even her easygoing defense counsel put it).[149] She kept interrupting the proceedings by interjections and laughter, so that the President eventually admonished her: "To me this case is too serious for laughter; you too will have the smile taken off your face in the end." To which Erika von Brockdorff yelled: "And even on the scaffold I'll laugh in your face."[150]

Roeder's campaign could now proceed. Shortly thereafter even the Second Chamber condemned Colonel Gehrts to death since, as Kraell put it, "the anticipated evidence in his favor did not materialize."[151] The medical report pronounced him fully responsible and he was thereupon sentenced to death for betrayal of secrets and damage to the war effort.[152] The court was not prepared to consider

as a mitigating circumstance the fact that Gehrts had
known nothing of Schulze-Boysen's espionage activities;
it was sufficient for them that the Colonel had handed to
a Soviet agent secret material which it was his duty to
keep under lock and key.

Roeder now applied for his next death sentence. This
time, on 14 January 1943, he produced defendants who
had had nothing whatsoever to do with espionage and in
some cases had even disowned Schulze-Boysen in so far
as his internal politics were concerned. Fritz Rehmer, the
foreman fitter, and his fiancée Liane Berkowitz, the two
Thiels, Heinz Strelow, the NCO, Cato Bontjes van Beek,
the art dealer, Professor Werner Krauss and his friend
Ursula Goetze, Otto Gollnow, the war service soldier[153]—
all had resisted the regime in some way; they had printed
leaflets, distributed anti-fascist handbills and in discussion
had made no secret of their longing for a change in Germany. But espionage and treason?—not at all.

The prosecution did contrive to show that Hannelore
Thiel, who was only 18, had hidden a Soviet radio set
from the Gestapo;[154] they managed to throw suspicion on
Fritz Thiel of having known about the intelligence activities of Schulze-Boysen's inner circle.[155] The other defendants, however, were entirely divorced from the Moscow spy-ring.

August Ohm, the prison chaplain, called Cato Bontjes
van Beek "a transparently honest person actuated by the
highest motives";[156] even after the war Kraell "made it
abundantly clear that Cato Bontjes had not been involved
in any particular espionage activity."[157] Heinz Strelow's
mother confirmed to his Gestapo interrogator that as early
as January/February 1942 her son (together with Cato
Bontjes van Beek) had split with Schulze-Boysen on account of political differences of opinion.[158] Even the Gestapo thought the two Thiels so insignificant that they
never even mentioned them in the Final Report on the
Rote Kapelle case.[159] According to Kraell "no proof of
intelligence activity could be brought" against Otto Gollnow;[160] as far as Bergmann, the defense counsel, can remember "Ursula Goetze, and probably Professor Krauss
too, had had nothing to do with radio operation."[161]

Of course the majority of them were communists; whatever the Nazis might say, they would cling to Russia. But
their resistance to the Third Reich was limited to a moral

protest. Fritz Rehmer, the soldier, said while in hospital: "Anyone who has seen what we have done in Russia must think it an eternal disgrace to be called a German."[162] Almost all of the prisoners thought that way.

Their consciences were so clear that no thought of a demand for the death sentence ever entered their heads. Heinz Strelow smuggled out a note to Cato Bontjes van Beek's father saying that he expected two years' imprisonment for Cato and four years' hard labor for himself.[163] Cato herself later said bitterly: "With what high hopes did I go to my trial!"[164]

But Roeder hammered away pitilessly at the youthful defendants; in his eyes each one of them deserved death. As the basis of his submission he maintained that what was already known about the defendants justified the death sentence, quite apart from all their other crimes still undiscovered.[165] All were guilty of "furnishing aid and comfort" and possibly also of treason—and the penalty for either was death.

Despite the inadequacy of proof the Second Chamber was unwilling to exclude the possibility that the accused had rendered some auxiliary service to the spy-ring and on 18 January 1943 condemned them all to death for "furnishing aid and comfort,"[166] with the exception of the two youngsters Otto Gollnow and Hannelore Thiel, who received prison sentences.* Almost every one of the prisoners found the court's decision incomprehensible. Cato Bontjes van Beek lamented: "It all seeems so unreal that I continue to hope—it just can't be true. Everyone was astounded, the police, the lawyers and ourselves."[168]

After the war the surviving members of the Reich Court Martial had considerable difficulty in explaining why these purely political resisters had been sent to their death. In most cases the judges simply had a lapse of memory. One of them, Franz Ernst, said cryptically: "My general impression today—and at the time too—is that, in so far as there was any question of treason, this case was concerned with fringe figures only."[169] Kraell, on the other hand, tried to justify himself by saying that the court could do no other than condemn the defendants in the Rehmer trial to death; he admitted that "not all those guilty of treason-

---

* The length of Otto Gollnow's sentence is not known; Hannelore Thiel was condemned to six years' imprisonment.[167]

able activities had been harnessed to the service of espionage"; treasonable activities against the government, however, were tantamount to treason against the country in the sense of "furnishing aid and comfort" under Para. 91b of the Criminal Code, "because the object of these activities was to damage the war effort."[170]

In saying this, however, Kraell overlooked the fact that even the savage provisions of the Criminal Code left the Court considerable elbowroom for the exercise of its own judgment; Section 1 laid down that "anyone who . . . furnishes assistance to an enemy power or acts to the detriment of the Reich's war effort" was to be "punished with death of hard labor for life"; Section 2 even prescribed "hard labor for not less than two years, if the act results in only insignificant damage to the Reich . . . and only insignificant advantage to the enemy." In other words Kraell's Chamber could well have sentenced the accused to hard labor for life or even shorter terms of imprisonment—for who could seriously believe that these little resisters with their leaflets could have "significantly advantaged" the Soviet enemy? The subsequent actions of the RKG judges showed that they did not believe it themselves.

No sooner had sentence been pronounced than Neuroth, President of one of the Chambers and the RKG's legal expert, developed doubts about onward transmission of the case with his approval; at least, he thought, a recommendation for mercy ought to be submitted to Hitler in the case of Cato Bontjes van Beek.[171] He discussed the matter with Kraell, who agreed at once, and very soon all the members of the Second Chamber were recommending mercy in the case of almost all the defendants.[172] Kraell went to Göring and won even him over to the idea of a plea for mercy. As was to be expected, however, it was turned down by Hitler.[173] (The only one of the accused whom Kraell was subsequently able to save from execution was Krauss.[174])

The RKG judges repented too late; the damage had already been done. There could now no longer be any doubt: German military justice was quite prepared to apply the elastic paragraphs of the legal code dealing with "aid and comfort" to anti-fascists who had nothing whatsoever to do with espionage. The sentences pronounced at the Rehmer trial laid the basis for a sinister development in which pure resistance activity was equated with activity as an agent of Moscow—and the latter, though born of resistance, had long since become an end in itself.

Roeder now saw his way clear. Step by step he laid bare the links between extreme left-wing resistance and the so-called traitors to their country until even the most altruistic anti-Nazi could find himself ensnared in the deadly mesh of the laws against treason. On 18 January the Court had condemned Rehmer and his companions, all of whom were resisters pure and simple. On 19 January Roeder arraigned Hilde Coppi, Karl Behrens and Rose Schlösinger, all of whom had merely rendered some small service to the spies; all were condemned to death.[175] On 26 January Oda Schottmüller, Schulze-Boysen's friend, appeared and was duly told that her agreement to allow a radio set to be worked from the Schottmüller house meant the death sentence for her.[176] On 27 January the Court condemned to death Hans Helmuth Himpel and Marie Terwiel, who had run some espionage errands.[177] On 28 January the prosecutor presented a clever combination of agents and resisters, Paul Scholz, Richard Weissensteiner, Klara Schabbel and Else Imme, achieving three death sentences and one term of hard labor.[178] With the inexorability of a hailstorm Roeder's submissions and the Court's sentences descended on the accused. Adam Kuckhoff,[179] Wilhelm Guddorf,[180] Walter Küchenmeister,[181] Philipp Schaeffer[182] the Hübners and Wesoleks,[183] John Rittmeister and his closest friends[184]—all received the death sentence.

Roeder's speeches became more savage; the prosecutor attacked his victims ever more mercilessly. His rodomontades echoed through the courtroom; he interrupted the statements of the defendants; he denigrated the motives of the resisters. Lotte Schleif says: "The entire proceedings were a farce because Roeder . . . gave me no opportunity at all to defend myself against his accusations and insults."[185]

The youth of a criminal, Roeder shouted at Eva-Maria Buch, Guddorf's girlfriend, was often considered a reason for leniency by sentimentally-minded judges; the bottomless infamy, however, given expression in the statements of the accused (she had read an anti-regime article which she had drafted), showed that youth, particularly the female element, was rotten to the core.[186] When Professor Krauss denied that the distribution of leaflets had any political significance, Roeder bounded from his seat and bellowed: "That is an impertinence."[187] During the same trial he declared that the State could hardly be expected to go on pampering such criminals in its prisons.[188]

Roeder's immoderate language eventually got on the nerves even of the judges. Kraell, the President, was disturbed by the "lack of substance" in Roeder's speeches; "its place was frequently taken by mere rhetoric," he said; "it made no impression on the court but may well have been considered improper by the defendants."[189] His colleague Schmitt disliked "the manner in which he [Roeder] went more or less straight to his plea for a death sentence without going into the evidence or considering legal points. I can well imagine that this procedure had a crushing effect on the defendants, particularly seeing that he invariably stressed the negative aspects of a case and made these the basis of his plea."[190]

The accused soon noticed that they were often protected from the prosecutor by the judges themselves. Dr. Valentin, one of the defense counsel, says: "In view of the extremely humane attitude of the court it was not too difficult for the defense to counter Dr. Roeder's arguments, which quite overshot the mark."[191]

Lotte Schleif was dissatisfied with her defense counsel and the court allowed her to conduct her defense herself. She says: "I pointed out that there were errors in the case for the prosecution and explained that all my friends and relatives were in great misery under National Socialism. I cannot remember what reason the President gave for refusing the death sentence. I do know, however, that the court listened to my statements most attentively."[192] Paul Scholz recalls: "I had the impression that Roeder was vexed because one of the judges, a Colonel I think, put questions to me which I thought were intended to evoke exonerating statements."[193]

In face of such difficulties even the Führer's prosecutor wearied. His speeches became more careless, his pleas for punishment more threadbare; to many it seemed that Roeder was losing interest in the Rote Kapelle case. One of the judges whispered to his colleague Ernst: "Roeder's speeches are getting thinner and thinner, like soup cubes; ultimately there'll be nothing there at all."[194]

The more moderate of the RKG judges seized the opportunity to snatch many of Roeder's victims from him.

After sentence had been pronounced on the main Schulze-Boysen/Harnack group Hitler had passed the prerogative of confirmation, first to Göring and then to the President of the Reich Court Martial. Admiral Bastian was accordingly able to intervene on several occasions: he ordered a fresh trial for Krauss who had been condemned to death, with the result that he received five years' hard labor;[195] he allowed Henniger to exchange a term of imprisonment for a probationary period at the front;[196] he refused to confirm the death sentence in Greta Kuckhoff's case.[197]

Kraell had advised Bastian to refuse confirmation in the case of Greta Kuckhoff and had instituted inquiries which would permit a fresh trial. Nevertheless, Frau Kuckhoff was unwilling to believe that the outcome would be any better. Then she received encouragement from the most unexpected quarter—the deputy prosecutor. For the prosecutor was no longer Roeder; another military Judge Advocate had taken his place. During a pause in the proceedings he came up to the defendant, put his hand on her shoulder and said: "Frau Kuckhoff, don't be so spiritless and apathetic. You must help me. This time we must succeed in getting you off."[198] The two of them did succeed. In October 1943 Greta Kuckhoff was sentenced to five years' hard labor, the prosecutor having "explicitly stated" (Frau Kuckhoff's words) that he was only asking for imprisonment "with reluctance," since he knew "that I had not been guilty of any dishonorable act."[199]

Nevertheless, in the vast majority of cases Roeder had achieved what his Führer expected of him. Out of 76 accused he had obtained 46 death sentences, 15 sentences of hard labor and 13 of imprisonment. Only in six cases had his plea for the death sentence been refused.* Manfred Roeder could happily leave the final touches to others.

The first death sentences were carried out before the end of 1942, though even this almost exceeded the time limit imposed by the dictator. Speaking on Hitler's behalf, Göring had demanded from his military lawyers that by Christmas 1942 Schulze-Boysen and his immediate associates be "extinguished." German bureaucracy, however, bade fair to prevent this.

Sentence in the main Rote Kapelle trial had been pro-

---

* Those of Otto Gollnow, Paul Scholz, Dr. Adolf Grimme, Dr. Eltriede Paul, Günther Weisenborn and Lotte Schleif.

nounced on 19 December 1942; the 24th, however, was
the beginning of the period during which, by tradition, no
executions might take place and this lasted until 6 January.[200] The executioners had not much time, for,
despite Hitler's orders, the official channels had to be observed—how could it be otherwise in Germany! First the
sentences of the Reich Court Martial had to be forwarded
to the Legal Department of OKW, whence they were passed
to the Führer's aides and from them to Hitler; then came
confirmation and finally return to the Prosecutor's office
of the Reich Court Martial.

The sentences, confirmed by Hitler, did not reach the
Reich Court Martial until the morning of 21 December.[201]
A few hours later the Public Prosecutor's Office of the
Berlin Provincial Court was informed, since execution of
persons deprived of the "right to bear arms" was the business of the civilian authorities. The Berlin Public Prosecutor
was ordered to arrange forthwith for the execution of
eleven extremely important criminals at the Berlin-Plöt-
zensee prison.[202]

In addition, in the case of the male prisoners, Hitler
had decreed the most degrading form of death, death by
hanging. Hitherto, however, only decapitations had taken
place at Plötzensee. In the utmost haste workmen constructed a large gallows with eight meathooks in one of
the prison sheds.[203] Now, however, it was found that the
Chief Public Prosecutor of the Reich Court Martial was
sick, and without his signature the executions could not
take place. Eichler, the responsible official, hastened to
his master's sickbed and returned with the vital signature.[204]

The condemned knew that they had only a little time
left. On the evening of 21 December they were transferred
to Plötzensee; all of them—Schulze-Boysen and his flock,
Scheliha and Ilse Stöbe—wrote their farewell letters.[205]
Schulze-Boysen wrote to his parents: "This death suits
me. Somehow I always knew that it would come. All
that I have done springs from my mind, my heart and my
convictions."[206] Arvid Harnack said to his relatives: "You
must celebrate Christmas properly. That is my last wish.
Also sing: 'I pray to the Power of Love.' "[207] They were
all quite composed; only Libertas Schulze-Boysen was still
wrestling with herself and against her fate. To her mother
she wrote: "I had to drink the bitter cup of finding that I
(and you) had been betrayed by a person in whom I had

placed complete confidence, Gertrud Breiter. But now it is a case of 'eat the fruits of your labors; anyone guilty of treachery will themselves be betrayed.' Out of egoism I have betrayed my friends; I wanted to be free and come back to you. But, believe me, I would have suffered terribly for the wrong I had done. Now they have all forgiven me and we go to our end with a sense of fellowship only possible when facing death."[208]

They trod the last road on the evening of 22 December 1942.[209] Silently they marched along the corridors of the prison. In his cell in the RSHA prison Harro Schulze-Boysen had hidden a final message to posterity:

Die letzten Argumente	By noose and guillotine
sind Strang und Fallbeil nicht,	shall the last word not be
und unsere heut'gen Richter	spoken;
sind	our judges of today
noch nicht das Weltgericht.	World Court do not betoken.[210]

Eichler, the court official, records: "The executions took place in a single room but in separate compartments divided by curtains. The hangman stood on a stool. The prisoner was lifted up, handcuffed, and the hangman placed the noose round his neck. The prisoner was then lowered. As far as I could see, complete unconsciousness came at the very instant when the noose tightened."[211]

The three women were executed by guillotine, the eight men hanged. Schulze-Boysen and Harnack died calmly; Scheliha struggled until the very last moment. Harnack shouted: "I regret nothing. I die as a convinced communist."[212] Libertas Schulze-Boysen screamed: "Let me keep my young life."[213]

The first executions were soon followed by others. Next came the turn of the two military men, Gehrts and Gollnow, together with Mildred Harnack. Gehrts was hanged in Plötzensee on 19 February[214] and two days later Herbert Gollnow was shot—the only "favor" granted to him by his Führer.[215] Four days later his lover was summoned; her hair had turned gray and she was terribly emaciated. The last words of the American Mildred Harnack before her execution were: "And I have loved Germany so much!"[216]

On 13 May another group went to their death, again in Plötzensee—Behrens, Countess von Brockdorff, Guddorf,

Himpel, Husemann, Küchenmeister, Rehmer, Schaeffer, Rittmeister, Strelow, Thiel, Thomfor.[217] Husemann wrote in his farewell letter: "My dear father, be strong. I die as I have lived—a soldier of class-warfare."[218] Erika von Brockdorff too remained true to her character. When Ohm, the prison chaplain, tried to speak words of comfort to her, she waved him away. The chaplain says: "Even at the very door of the place of execution she said to me that she did not care if her body was to be turned into a cake of soap in a few hours' time."[219]

The executions of the largest group of Schulze-Boysen's adherents took place three months later, on 5 August 1943. Apart from two men, Emil Hübner and Adam Kuckhoff, all were women—Liane Berkowitz, Cato Bontjes van Beek, Eva-Maria Buch, Hilde Coppi, Ursula Goetze, Else Imme, Anna Kraus, Ingeborg Kummerow, Klara Schabbel, Rose Schlösinger, Oda Schottmüller and Marie Terweil.[220] Their parting words lacked the pathos which the men apparently felt was indicated. Oda Schottmüller wrote to her mother: "That all should now be over is entirely according to plan for me. I have never wanted to grow old—there is nothing nice about getting slowly stiffer and stiffer."[221] Cato Bontjes van Beek was resigned: "It is only sad that I do not know why I have to die. Mama, there is no great glory attached to involvement in this business."[222] They went to their death composedly.

But their prosecutor was not there to hear the last words of his victims. In mid-February Judge Advocate-General Roeder had been called to Brussels and Paris.[223] His mission was to liquidate the last remnants of Rote Kapelle in Western Europe, the wreckage of the "Grand Chef's" organization.

7

The Game Is Up

LEOPOLD TREPPER PICKED his way uneasily through the ruins of his espionage empire, ready for the next blow from his German opponent to fall at any moment. The "Grand Chef's" leading agents had gone to ground; the emergency hideouts stood ready; part of the informer circuit in France had been put in cold storage. He was determined to leave no trace to help his German pursuers.

The "Grand Chef" felt a mortal threat hanging over his organization. Soviet espionage in Western Europe had lost all impetus since 30 July 1942, when the Germans had captured Rote Kapelle's chief radio operator, Johann Wenzel, together with his set in Brussels. With the disappearance of Wenzel and his radio set the Belgian circuit had lost its central figure and the organization as a whole its technical radio mastermind.

In other areas too Rote Kapelle's German pursuers had been destroying one strongpoint after another. The Gestapo had bagged the entire Berlin group, the "Grand Chef's" best source of information; even before that, with the arrest of the Sokols, the husband-and-wife radio operator combination, the Germans had made serious inroads into Trepper's French circuit. Even more vexatious from the "Grand Chef's" point of view was the fact that, with the loss of Wenzel, he now had no radio communication with Moscow. Admittedly there were still two sets in France in the hands of Robinson and Kent, but these two had been so unnerved by the German counter-espionage successes that they refused to place their sets at the "Grand Chef's" disposal.

But Trepper was not yet prepared to admit defeat. He knew that the Belgian circuit was still operating and had sets ready for work; most of the agents of Konstantin Yefremov's Brussels organization were still at large. Better still, the Dutch circuit under Anton Winterinck was indefatigably transmitting to Moscow all the information which came its way.

The more eager the Soviet General Staff became to learn of the possibilities of an Anglo-American Second Front in Western Europe, the more important became the part played by the groups of agents still operating in Belgium and Holland. Even before the capture of Wenzel the Director had instructed the "Grand Chef" to concentrate all available radio sets in the West in order to give Razvedupr a picture of all important invasion areas in the event of a landing by British and American troops. Trepper had to report to Moscow every two days.[1]

The reconnaissance missions allotted by the Director to the groups in Brussels and Amsterdam were sufficient proof of Moscow's interest in the Second Front. On 13 April 1942, for instance, the Director wanted to know the strength of German formations in Belgium, their present locations and any movements in progress.[2] On 31 May Yefremov was asked to state where Field Marshal von Rundstedt and his three subordinate Army Corps in France were located.[3] On 27 June 1942 came a further request: the strength and composition of German infantry divisions in Normandy, Brittany and Holland.[4]

"Bordo" (Yefremov's codename) had dutifully radioed back to Moscow. On 28 April he sent a report on German troop concentrations in the Cambrai area,[5] on 4 May a report on requisitioning of private cars and horses from the Belgians by the occupying forces and increased movement of German units from Belgium into France,[6] and on 12 May information on the strength of the German garrison in Brussels.[7]

"Tino" (Winterinck's codename) was also the recipient of an increasing number of requests from the Director. On 1 May he was instructed to find out the state of morale of German troops in the Netherlands and in addition to establish what German air force formations were located in Holland and where.[8] On 15 June the Director wished to know where were the headquarters of German troops in the Netherlands and whether it was true that the German Military Administration was located in the town hall at Hilversum.[9]

After the capture of Wenzel's set the Netherlands group of agents moved into the forefront of Moscow's battle for enemy intelligence. It was now ordered to obtain information from Germany and step up its radio traffic with Moscow.[10] Finally it made available an ancient battery-operated radio set, through which the "Grand Chef" was able to re-establish direct communication with the Director.[11]

But how long would it be before the Germans were on the trail of "Hilda" also? Trepper could not rid himself of a feeling of disquiet. He could not forget that in Wenzel the Germans had laid hands on a man who knew practically every secret of Rote Kapelle in Western Europe—and so far the Germans had contrived to loosen the tongue of almost every prisoner they had caught. Treachery was a long-standing fellow-traveler for those in communist espionage organizations.

Trepper's instinct was not at fault. Wenzel gave away courier lines, cipher systems and coding techniques. But Trepper had overlooked another traitor. The Germans succeeded in rolling up the last groups of Rote Kapelle agents with the active assistance of a spy whom the "Grand Chef" trusted completely.

The very first successful operation against Rote Kapelle, the coup of the Rue des Atrébates in Brussels in December 1941, had set the Abwehr on the tracks of the Polish forger Abraham ("Adash") Raichman. From the statements of arrested agents the Abwehr soon gained the impression that Raichman must be one of the key figures in Rote Kapelle; wherever he made his appearance, whether in Belgium or in France, his forged passports and his beautifully copied rubber stamps formed the very basis of existence for the communist spies. "The Manufacturer," as Raichman was known in the Rote Kapelle jargon, seemed to the Abwehr so important an agent that they decided to place him and his contacts under surveillance in order thereby to learn more about the scope of the organization as a whole.[12] Had they arrested him, they would have cut all the threads. Instead, therefore, he was shadowed by the Abwehr.

In the spring of 1942 the Abwehr office in the Rue de la Loi, Brussels, managed to arrange for Raichman to make the acquaintance of Mathieu, a Belgian Criminal Police Inspector, who had secret contacts to certain resistance groups.[13] What his friends in the underground did not, of course, suspect was that "Carlos" (Mathieu's codename) was among the most important informers for Lieutenant Bödiker of the counter-espionage desk in the Abwehr office, Brussels.[14]

Raichman cultivated Mathieu since, for the forger, an Inspector of the Brussels Criminal police was an almost indispensable assistant—he could produce genuine passes. The two were soon on such good terms that in May 1942 Raichman asked his new friend (presumably without Trepper's knowledge) to take over a suitcase which had become "too hot" for him. The suitcase contained one of the reserve radio sets intended, according to Trepper's plans, to come into action at a later date. Mathieu agreed and hid the set in his garage.[15]

The next day Mathieu informed his master Bödiker and shortly thereafter the Abwehr despatched experts who carefully photographed every part of the radio set. Bödiker notified Captain Harry Piepe and his partner, Gestapo Commissar Karl Giering, who were in charge of the Rote Kapelle case. The three compared the photographs of the Raichman set with that captured in the Rue des Atrébates; there could be no doubt—both sets clearly originated from the same source.[16]

Piepe and Giering thereupon placed "the Manufacturer" under even stricter surveillance, but at first without result. Raichman seemed to be leading a comparatively dull existence with his mistress Malvina Gruber. Not until July did he bestir himself again. Once more it was Mathieu who gave the Germans the information. "Carlos" reported to Bödiker that Raichman had asked him to obtain a police identity card for a friend. Bödiker inquired who the friend was, but Mathieu did not know. Bödiker then instructed Mathieu to promise the card to "the Manufacturer" but first to demand a passport photograph of Raichman's friend, using the argument that he could even get the card stamped by the relevant authorities if he had a passport photograph.[17] Raichman handed over the photograph and a sensational piece of news with it—his friend was head of a group of communist agents with whom he too was working.[18]

Piepe and Giering gazed at the photograph through their magnifying glass, but in vain; it showed a young fair-haired man who was a total stranger to them both.[19] For some reason, however, they both felt that he belonged in some way to the "Grand Chef's" organization. They decided to play for a grand slam and quite simply to arrest him.

"Carlos" persuaded Raichman to send his friend to him, Mathieu, in order to fetch the card. The meeting was agreed for midday on 30 July at the bridge in the Botanical Gardens, Brussels.* Just behind the bridge Piepe was waiting with some men of the Field Security Police. No sooner had Mathieu handed the card to the stranger than the police were upon him.[21]

The man now standing in front of Piepe and Giering had papers showing that he was a Finnish student, Eric Jernstroem, from Vasa. He denied vehemently that he was working for Soviet espionage; he was studying chemistry at Brussels University, he said, and was moreover well known to the Finnish Consulate-General.[22] The Finnish representative in Brussels in fact confirmed Jernstroem's statements. A house search yielded no suspicious clues; nothing was found except one or two postcards from America showing that Jernstroem had lived in the United States and was in receipt of regular remittances of money from that quarter.[23]

His cover would have been perfect, had the alleged Finn been able to speak better Finnish. He could barely produce a single fluent sentence.[24] In addition he began to involve himself in little inconsistencies, admittedly only noticeable to trained ears. Giering and Piepe were at their wit's end.

In their embarrassment the two interrogators took refuge in a desperate subterfuge. They arranged an apparently fortuitous meeting between Jernstroem and Wenzel, who had also been arrested on 30 July. If the Finn belonged to Rote Kapelle, Wenzel was bound to know him. The two prisoners fell into each other's arms. Wenzel was unable to regain his composure quickly enough; that was

---

* Perrault (op. cit., p. 155) gives this information as coming from Piepe. Piepe is wrong, however, in giving the date of Yefremov's arrest as 30 June 1942. Dallin gives the correct date (30 July).[20]

"Bordo," he admitted; that was his leader, the Soviet Military Engineer Third Class, Konstantin Yefremov.[25]

Piepe and Giering could now initiate the final stage of their pursuit. Wenzel's statements left Yefremov no alternative but to play the German game; faced with the choice of being shot forthwith or staying alive if he collaborated, the Ukrainian opted for the latter.[26] For a few days he tried to temper his statements with caution and set the Germans off on false trails; a week later, however, he had completely gone over to the German side. Perhaps some curious change had taken place in him, as had happened in the case of other arrested spies; perhaps his professional interest was aroused and he succumbed to the fascination of the chase.

Soon he saw himself in the role of adviser, showing the clumsy Germans the right way to do things. "You are wrong," he would say, "you must do it another way."[27] And Piepe and Giering listened, almost enthralled by their new assistant as he led them ever deeper into the Soviet espionage network.

The next blow delivered to the Belgian espionage circuit could therefore be laid at Yefremov's door. One after another he betrayed his agents to the Germans. Germaine Schneider ("Schmetterling"—"Butterfly"), the group's courier and Wenzel's girlfriend, was arrested by the Abwehr, though admittedly she was released again.[28] In Ostend the Germans captured Augustin Sesée, the reserve radio operator, together with his set.*

In mid-August Yefremov gave his new masters an opening into the Dutch circuit. Piepe and Giering had been particularly neglectful of Holland, although Signals Security and the Ordnungspolizei had known that a communist radio group was working in the Netherlands ever since early 1941.† In addition, at the beginning of July Kruyt, a parachutist who had landed in Belgium only a few days before, was captured; he was a Dutch ex-priest and communist party functionary, was equipped with a radio set

---

* Piepe's statement quoted by Perrault. Piepe's assumption that no radio set was discovered with Sesée is incorrect. The Gestapo Final Report says (p. 3): "We were able to capture another sending and receiving set in Sesée's house."[29]

† Piepe's memory is at fault when he says (Perrault, op. cit., p. 158) that the Abwehr "had no notion of the existence of a Dutch group"; the opposite is the case.[30]

and was intended to support the Belgian circuit; another man had jumped with him who was to work in the area of The Hague.[31] This led the Abwehr to suspect that the same espionage organization covered both Belgium and Holland.

But where was the connecting link between the spies in the two countries? How did the two groups collaborate? Here too Yefremov promised to help. Twice in the week, he told his interrogators, he had had to meet a courier who brought him information from Holland; he was the liaison officer between the Belgian and Dutch groups.[32]

The Germans were now so confident in Yefremov that they took the bold step of allowing him to go to the habitual meeting point—shadowed from a distance by Field Security Police. But both Yefremov and the Germans waited in vain; the courier did not arrive. A few days later they tried once more. This time two couriers appeared simultaneously at the agreed spot. They were immediately arrested.[33]

Yefremov explained to the Germans whom they had arrested. The first was Maurice Peper (codename "Wassermann") who was the contact to Winterinck's circuit in Amsterdam;[34] the second was called Hermann Isbutsky (codename "Lunette") and proved to be an ex-KPD functionary who had previously belonged to the Kent circuit.[35] Isbutzsky refused to have anything to do with fascists, but Peper declared himself ready to lead the Germans into the Dutch lair.*[36]

Captain Piepe, accompanied by Peper, left for Amsterdam to administer the *coup de grâce* to "Hilda." Once more he had to rely on the communist agents destroying each other. Peper was only too eager to conduct the German sleuths to the Amsterdam café where he habitually met Winterinck, the chief Dutch agent. He was there on 17 August, hoping to contact Winterinck; Piepe posted his policemen, but "Tino" did not appear.[37]

Piepe was disconcerted but allowed his prisoner to go to a "post-box" address, the house of Jacob and Hendrika Rillboling where Peper always left messages for Winter-

---

* Here again Piepe's memory is at fault. In Perrault (op. cit., p. 158) he is recorded as saying that he went to Amsterdam with the Belgian-Dutch courier "Lunette" (Isbutzsky). In fact Isbutzsky never acted as a courier, but Maurice Peper did, as is shown by the Gestapo Final Report (p. 3).

inck. This time he found a missive from "Tino": he would come to the café the next day.[38]

Once more Piepe's men lay in wait; once more Piepe kept watch for his victim. He was about to give up when a massive man appeared whose girth explained why he was known in the communist party as "The Fat Man." Winterinck looked round for Peper; at once Piepe's officials fell upon him and dragged him out of the café.[39]

Piepe says: "There was quite a row inside. The occupants of the café took the prisoner's side and threatened my Field Security policemen. They had to force their way to the door with drawn revolvers. Finally we managed to fight our way through."[40] The old story was then repeated; at first the prisoner refused to say anything; he would not even give his name. Later, however, he too collaborated.[41]

Piepe now knew enough anyway to tear the "Grand Chef's" Dutch network to pieces. The two Rillbolings were arrested; Winterinck's apartment was searched and the radio set hidden there confiscated.[42] The remaining members of the Dutch circuit, however, succeeded in escaping with two radio sets; they were Johannes Lüteraan, Winterinck's deputy, Wilhelm Voegler the reserve radio operator, Daniel Goulooze the Comintern functionary, and Hendrika Smith.[43] Nevertheless the "Hilda" group was now dead.

Piepe returned to Brussels to try to discover further connections between the Belgian circuit and neighboring countries. He was in a hurry since at any moment his opponent might discover that Yefremov was a traitor and Raichman might realize what part his friend Mathieu was really playing. To delude the "Grand Chef" Piepe even permitted Yefremov to be released from arrest for a few days and live in his apartment ostensibly as a free man.[44]

However much Yefremov cudgeled his brains, however, in order to tell Piepe of further foreign links maintained by the Belgian circuit, he had no new ideas. All he could think of was that Germaine Schneider, Wenzel's girlfriend, had frequently traveled to France and Switzerland on behalf of the "Grand Chef." But the Abwehr had let "The Butterfly" go, convinced that she was Wenzel's mistress and nothing more.[45]

The Germans accordingly concluded that no one knew more about the "Grand Chef's" overall organization than Germaine Schneider. No matter how, they had to lay hands on the woman again. Piepe had an idea: Yefremov should use his old underground contacts to get in touch with the elusive agent. In fact Yefremov did have a talk with Germaine Schneider. What he proposed to her we do not know; probably he advised her to collaborate with the Germans in view of the collapse of Trepper's empire.[46]

But Germaine Schneider remained faithful to the "Grand Chef" and alerted him, whereupon she was ordered to withdraw to the Lyon circuit, which was still untouched.[47] Nevertheless, she very nearly fell into the German trap, for she had no pass into unoccupied France—and what was more natural than to ask Raichman to obtain the necessary papers?

Once more Raichman had to contact Mathieu and so the Germans learned of the matter. Piepe proposed to play the old trick by which he had caught Yefremov. A meeting was arranged between Mathieu and "The Butterfly" but she did not come.[48] Instead Raichman appeared on her behalf.[49]

The Abwehr was not slow to grasp the significance; the other side had seen through their game; for the Germans, therefore, Yefremov, Raichman and Mathieu had lost their value as voluntary or involuntary baits for agents. Yefremov was carted off to prison once more; on 2 September Piepe had Raichman and his girlfriend, Malvina Gruber, arrested and taken to the Gestapo prison at Breendonck near Brussels.[50] The Pole at once declared himself ready to collaborate, but when his statements did not satisfy his interrogators, Giering's two principal assistants Kriminal-obersekretär Wilhelm Berg and Kriminaloberassistent Richard Voss, they fell upon the prisoner in a rage.[51]

Piepe maintains that he once arrived unannounced at one of these torture sessions and immediately stopped the mal-treatment of Raichman. "Don't misunderstand me," he said, "but that is an official crime."[52] The unhappy man's appear-ance apparently distressed him so much that he "went out and got Raichman a bagful of grapes to calm him down." Piepe agreed with Giering that Raichman should hence-forth only be interrogated in his (Piepe's) presence.[53]

Piepe was undoubtedly a humane man, but he neverthe-less had a special reason for treating Raichman well. A last despairing effort of memory on the part of Yefremov had turned the telltale Raichman once more into an im-portant contact man.

Yefremov reported that, while he was acting as head of the "Bordo" radio group, there had been a somewhat mysterious firm in Brussels which must have been in some form of business contact with the "Grand Chef" in France; he himself had been forbidden to have any contact with this firm.[54] All Yefremov knew about it was that the firm was called "Simexco" and that its offices were at 192 Rue Royale, Brussels. Piepe could hardly believe his ears since he too lived at 192 Rue Royale under the not particularly ingenious cover name of Riepe.*

Piepe was so dumbfounded by this discovery that even today he still seriously thinks that he must often have passed the "Grand Chef" and his principal agents on the staircase of No. 192. He says: "We had always raised our hats politely to each other. If you read that sort of thing in a novel, you would say that the author had laid it on too thick."[56] However this may be, Yefremov's disclosures caused Piepe to initiate inquiries about Simexco.

The researches of the Abwehr revealed that Simexco's shareholders were perfectly innocent Belgian businessmen, unlikely to be carrying on espionage.[57] The only remaining possibility, therefore, was that communist spies were making use of the firm in order to maintain courier lines and smuggle money for illegal purposes under cover of normal business activities. This theory was supported by the fact that one member of the board, Señor Vincente Sierra, seemed to be permanently abroad.

The Abwehr had long known that Sierra was identical with the organizer Kent, who had fled to France in December 1941 after Piepe's coup in the Rue des Atrébates. Moreover, Malvina Gruber recalled that Margarete Barcza, Kent's mistress, had told her at the time that they were going to Marseille;[58] finally a watch kept on Simexco's telephones disclosed lively traffic with Paris.[59] Piepe and Giering accordingly decided that France was the place in which to search for the "Grand Chef" and his last faithfuls.

As pathfinder they proposed to use Abraham Raichman, who had offered to lead them to the "Grand Chef." In October Piepe, Giering and twenty Gestapo officials moved to Paris, where they formed the core of the "Special Rote

* In Perrault (op. cit., p. 172) Piepe gives his cover-name as "Riepert." André Moyen, on the other hand, the Belgian ex-Abwehr officer who interrogated Piepe after the war, says that Piepe told him that the name he used was "Riepe."[55]

Kapelle Squad" organized a few weeks later on the pattern of (and subordinate to) the RSHA "Special Commission."[60] They occupied offices on the fourth floor of No. 11 Rue de Saussaies, the past and future location of the French Security Police headquarters.[61]

Giering and Piepe had soon put out their first decoys. They let Raichman loose in Paris and he went round all the known "post-boxes" of the Trepper organization, leaving the same message in each case: he must speak to the "Grand Chef" at once.[62] But ever since the "Butterfly" affair Trepper was suspicious. He did not come.

Every morning a morose Piepe met Raichman for breakfast at the Café "Viel" in the Boulevard des Italiens and listened to his stool pigeon's tale of failure.[63] Once more Raichman attempted to get into conversation with the "Grand Chef." He used every contact offering him any prospect of gaining touch with Trepper. But the "Grand Chef" remained undiscoverable. Piepe and Giering were forced to recognize that Raichman's Paris contacts were inadequate.

They now had no alternative but to hunt for the "Grand Chef" themselves. They only had one small clue from which to start—the remarkable frequency of the telephone conversations between Simexco in Brussels and a Paris firm of similar name, Simex. The conversations tapped and recorded showed that the main subject of discussion was building contracts for the Wehrmacht, and on this point

* At this point it should be noted that almost all the technical details of the organization of the "Special Rote Kapelle Squad" given in the various books on the subject are wrong. The "Special Squad" was not an SD organization as Jacques Delarue says in *The Gestapo* (p. 219 et seq.), nor was it an agency formed of members of all German counter-espionage organizations, as Dallin thinks (op. cit., p. 167). Perrault too (op. cit., p. 126 et seq.) maintains that the "Special Squad" was formed early in 1942, allegedly on an order from Hitler, as a combined agency of the Abwehr, the Gestapo and the SD. The facts are as follows: early in 1942, after Piepe's first successes in Belgium, a number of RSHA officials were sent to Brussels to support him. After the arrest of Schulze-Boysen and his friends in September 1942 the RSHA formed the "Rote Kapelle Special Commission" which was initially concerned exclusively with the Schulze-Boysen/Harnack group. The RSHA officials despatched to the West only formed the "Special Rote Kapelle Squad" after the "Grand Chef's" West European organization had been broken up. Both these special organizations were agencies of the RSHA; the Abwehr had no part in either of them.

no one could be better informed than the Todt Organization.*

Giering and Piepe presented themselves at the headquarters of the Todt Organization in Paris and interviewed Nikolai, the liaison officer responsible for contacting and supervising French firms working on Wehrmacht installations.[64] He was bound to know Simex. He did. Giering and Piepe were told that Simex was a reliable firm with which the Todt Organization worked most satisfactorily.[65]

When Piepe showed Nikolai the photograph of Trepper found in the Rue des Atrébates, the OT man nodded: Yes, that was Monsieur Jean Gilbert, managing director of Simex who lived on the third floor of No. 8 Boulevard Haussman. The two visitors then divulged to Nikolai who Gilbert really was.[66] The three decided to lay a trap for the "Grand Chef": Trepper's pass for unoccupied France was due to run out in the next few days and he was to be arrested in OT headquarters when he came to renew it.[67]

This plan was frustrated by over-enthusiasm on the part of Nikolai. He wrote to the manager of Simex asking him to call since his pass was due for renewal. Piepe and Giering could hardly conceal their fury with the presumptuous official, since the letter would undoubtedly have alerted the "Grand Chef" prematurely.[68] A new plan was prepared: Piepe and Giering proposed to appear in the guise of German merchants trying to buy industrial diamonds from Simex and insist on dealing solely with Monsieur Gilbert. They thought up a story to the effect that they had come from Mainz in order to buy industrial diamonds in Paris.[69] Piepe was convinced that this would work: "Diamonds for one-and-a-half million marks—that must attract anybody."[70]

But how to get in contact with Simex? Nikolai knew how: working in the OT was the widow of a White Russian officer Maria Likhonine, *née* Kalinina; she had good connections with Simex and had already acted as intermediary between the Todt Organization and the firm on many business matters.[71]

Maria showed extreme interest in the diamond deal proposed to her by Piepe.[72] It seemed quite natural to her, apparently, that the alleged merchant from Mainz should

---

* The official German military construction agency, so named after its first Director, Dr. Todt—abbreviated OT.

insist on doing business only with Gilbert. She hurried off to find him. The Germans did not, of course, realize that she went to warn him: The Germans are after you.[73]

Week after week the Russian postponed the meeting between Gilbert and the merchant from Mainz. At one time Monsieur Gilbert had gone into a sanatorium, at another his business prevented him coming.[74] Finally a meeting was arranged for the Brussels South Railway Station, after which the diamond deal was to be signed at once. But the "Grand Chef" did not appear. Piepe says: "He had a good nose."[75]

Gradually Piepe and Giering realized that it was not going to be quite so simple to catch the "Grand Chef." He could only be outmaneuvered by blocking all his escape lines and breaking up his circuit at several points simultaneously. Southern France was still totally untouched; the "Grand Chef" still had the possibility of getting his best agents to safety in North Africa that way.

In fact Trepper had long been planning gradually to run down his French circuit and set himself up in North Africa. As a first step he had despatched to Lyon and Marseille all his agents on the run—Germaine Schneider, Kent, Schumacher, Isidor Springer and the rest; he himself and his two closest associates, Katz and Grossvogel, were to go to ground in southern France in emergency.[76] As early as mid-June Jules Jaspar had been commissioned to find a new headquarters in Algiers.[77]

On 8 November 1942, however, American and British troops landed in North Africa and three days later Hitler ordered the occupation of southern France. Trepper's escape plans were checkmated. Worse still: Gestapo and Abwehr were now free to hunt communist agents in Unoccupied France. One of Piepe's and Giering's squads set forth, led by Raichman, avid for fresh laurels.[78]

Piepe recalls: "He betrayed very many things to us, very many things; most important of all, he could give us Lyon."[79] Raichman may not have shown himself over-knowledgeable in Paris, but in southern France he was only too quick to discover the trail of his old friends of the Brussels days. He scoured one "post-box" after another, pumped mutual friends and unearthed the hideouts of those who had gone to ground. The German spy-hunters began to get the measure of the Marseille and Lyon circuits.[80]

On 12 November five French policemen, acting on behalf of the Abwehr, forced their way into an apartment in
the Rue de l'Abbé-de-l'Epée in Marseille and arrested its
illustrious tenants, the ex-"Petit Chef" Kent and his mistress Margarete Barcza.[81] They were handed over next day
to a Gestapo squad which took them to Paris. Piepe and
Giering ordered Kent to be taken on to Brussels, the scene
of his previous activities. Perhaps they thought that, since
the story of Rote Kapelle had begun in Brussels, that was
where it should end.[82]

Moreover, for Piepe and Giering, it was still possible
that Kent might know some members of his old Belgian
circuit still working underground. Meanwhile they themselves returned to Brussels and interrogated Kent for several days on end before despatching him to Berlin as King's
Evidence for the forthcoming Rote Kapelle trial there.
After some initial hesitation Kent declared himself ready
to tell all.[83]

Kent's statements gave Giering and Piepe for the first
time a concrete picture of Rote Kapelle's scope, personnel
and methods. He was not, of course, *au fait* with the
"Grand Chef's" immediate plans, but the information he
gave was sufficient to enable Giering and Piepe to mount a
final synchronized onslaught on the remnants of the espionage organization.

Meanwhile the Abwehr and Gestapo investigation squads
in southern France had ringed their enemy round so closely
that they could take action at any moment. The offices of
Simexco, the organization's last retreat in Brussels, were
under observation and in Paris Simex could be raided at
once if necessary. Piepe and Giering accordingly decided
to institute a major synchronized manhunt in Brussels,
Paris, Lyon and Marseille. It was agreed that the flying
squads would go into action in all four cities on 24 November 1942.[84]

But the two leaders had not taken into their calculations
the burning zeal of Kriminalobersekretär Erich Jung, who
had taken over command of the Paris office in the Rue de
Saussaies on the departure of his master Giering for Brussels. He yearned to bring the "Grand Chef" to book single-
handed.

On 19 November, without informing Giering in Brussels,
Jung struck in Paris.[85] He lured Alfred Corbin, the director

of Simex, and Vladimir Keller, its interpreter, into the Todt Organization headquarters and there had them arrested; meanwhile Gestapo officials and French police searched the twelve-room offices of Trepper's firm, confiscated all the files and carted off to prison all the staff present.[86]

If Jung had hoped, however, to find some clue leading him to Trepper, he was doomed to disappointment. In vain he fell upon the prisoner Keller, who he thought must have intimate knowledge of all Simex's secrets. When Keller did not produce the required information, Jung belabored his prisoner like a madman. After each blow he yelled: "Where is Gilbert?" Keller shrugged his shoulders. Further blows, further silence.[87] Such was the limit of Erich Jung's sagacity.

In a fury Giering hurried back to Paris on 23 November to call his unruly minion to order.[88] Jung tried to excuse his precipitancy, saying that he had feared the birds might fly, but Giering brushed this aside.[89] He demanded to see the record of interrogation but could make nothing of it. Giering himself carried out a further interrogation—nothing, no trace of the "Grand Chef."

Then suddenly, about 11 a.m. on 24 November, Madame Corbin, the wife of the director of Simex, remembered a tiny detail which she was quite prepared to tell the Germans: Monsieur Gilbert had recently complained of toothache and her husband had recommended him a dentist.[90] Giering and Jung pricked up their ears. What was the dentist's address? Dr. Maleplate, 14 Rue de Rivoli, Paris.[91] Giering at once notified Piepe who had also just returned to Paris, and an hour later the two were in Dr. Maleplate's waiting room. He was not at home—during the mornings he worked as resident dentist at Laennec Hospital; the door was opened by his dental mechanic. He was ordered to call Maleplate forthwith. The dentist arrived.[92]

Giering and Piepe demanded to see Maleplate's list of appointments and asked him to read out every entry, without at first telling whom they were looking for. Maleplate read—line by line. At last the Germans heard the name for which they were waiting—"Gilbert," booked for 3:00 p.m. on 27 November.[93] Piepe and Giering moved not a muscle, not even when the dentist suddenly remembered that Gilbert's appointment had been advanced. "He is coming today at 2:00," Maleplate said.[94] The two visitors nodded, murmured a word of thanks and left.

In a café below the dentist's rooms Giering and Piepe held a short council of war. They had little time left before 2:00 p.m. and so they ordered up from the nearest German headquarters two NCOs and an armored car.[95] At 1:45 they presented themselves once more to the dentist and let him into the secret: "We intend to arrest Gilbert."[96] Maleplate was ordered to send his assistant out; he was to deal with Gilbert alone, while Piepe, Giering and another Gestapo official hid in the apartment.[97]

Alone in his consulting room with his patient, however, the dentist was anxiously awaiting the arrival of the Germans, for in all the excitement Giering and Piepe had overlooked the fact that Gilbert had already entered the building by a back door. Only when they heard voices in the consulting room did they burst in. Trepper found himself looking down the barrels of two revolvers.[98]

Trepper put up his hands and said quite calmly: "I'm not armed." Even subsequently Piepe remained astounded by the "Grand Chef's" relaxed reaction: "Trepper was the calmest of us all. He never batted an eyelid." When Giering put the handcuffs on him, the Chief of Rote Kapelle chuckled and said: "Bravo, you've done your work well."[99]

With the arrest of Leopold Trepper the end had come for Rote Kapelle. One after another Piepe's and Giering's flying squads captured the last bastions of the spy organization. On 25 November the Field Security Police occupied the Simexco offices in Brussels and arrested everyone found working there; on the same day the Gestapo carried off the remaining members of Kent's group in Marseille—Jules Jaspar, his wife and Marguerite Marivet, his secretary; in Lyon another search squad captured Isidor Springer and Otto Schumacher.[100]

A few of Rote Kapelle's leading agents were still missing, but their pursuers could be sure of catching them with the help of the prisoners, all of whom were only too willing to talk. Even the "Grand Chef" himself, whatever his motives may have been, helped in the Gestapo manhunt. He knew that he was playing with death, for the Germans might shoot him at any moment.

"I am an officer and ask to be treated as such," he had said to Giering when arrested in Dr. Maleplate's surgery. Giering had promised him this and Trepper had shaken his hand, saying: "Thank you very much. You have my word."[101] And he set out at once to gain the Germans' confidence, giving away name after name and leading them into the last hideouts.

Hillel Katz, Trepper's secretary, was the first victim of the master whom he regarded with almost religious veneration. Trepper sent Katz a short message telling him to meet the "Grand Chef" at the "Madeleine" station on the Metro.[102] Giering sent a couple of his men to the rendezvous and Katz was arrested. When Katz was eventually faced with Trepper, his whole world collapsed around him, but Trepper remained quite unmoved, saying: "Katz, we must work with these gentlemen. The game is up."[103]

Having been so thoroughly outwitted, Trepper now gave himself up for lost and even revealed his intelligence contacts with German headquarters and agencies in Paris. As a result of his information it was possible to arrest Baron Basil Maximovich on 12 December and shortly thereafter his sister Anna and his mistress Anna-Margaret Hoffmann-Scholtz. They in their turn betrayed other informers: Käthe Voelkner, secretary on the French staff of the Sauckel agency, her husband Johann Podsiadlo, Kuprian, the Military Administration official, and Ludwig Kainz, an engineer in the Todt Organization.[104]

Only two of the "Grand Chef's" star agents now remained at liberty, Leo Grossvogel, the financier, and Henry Robinson, the representative of the Comintern. Here too, however, Trepper could give his interrogators fresh clues. Admittedly he did not know where his old friend Grossvogel was at the moment, but at least he could give the Gestapo a tip—and the tip was called Simone Phelter. She was Grossvogel's mistress and worked as a secretary in the Belgian Chamber of Commerce in Paris; Grossvogel had frequently used her as a courier between Brussels and Paris.[105]

Simone Phelter was first placed under unobtrusive surveillance, but in mid-December the Gestapo struck. She was lured to a rendezvous at the "Café de le Paix" near the Opéra and arrested on the way there. Under interrogation she revealed that all employees of the Chamber of Commerce had already gone off on Christmas holiday and that she was on duty in the office alone.[106]

The Gestapo suspected that in the empty offices of the Chamber of Commerce Simone Phelter was awaiting a telephone call from Grossvogel. They occupied the Chamber and Simone was forced to continue to answer the telephone. On 16 December Grossvogel duly rang and arranged to meet the girl at a restaurant at 7:00 p.m. that evening.[107]

The restaurant was occupied. The police did not take Simone Phelter along since they had a recent photograph of Grossvogel and he was known to them anyway. Once more, however, the over-enthusiasm of Kriminalobersekretär Jung almost wrecked the plan. Jung suddenly appeared in the restaurant with Simone Phelter, who immediately began to scream in order to warn Grossvogel at the last moment. Fortunately for the Gestapo he had not yet appeared. Half an hour later he was arrested outside the restaurant.[108]

Trepper also assisted the Germans in the hunt for the last important member of Rote Kapelle, Henry Robinson. He gave Giering the address of Medardo Griotto, an Italian engraver whose house "Harry" (Robinson's cover name) frequently used as a rendezvous with other agents.[109] Katz, Trepper's amanuensis, persuaded Griotto to summon Robinson to a meeting at the last station on one of the Paris Metro lines where he was to collect an important message from the "Grand Chef."[110]

The meeting with Robinson took place on 21 December. Three days later the Gestapo reported: "After extensive inquiries and the employment of various informers it was possible to arrest 'Harry' in connection with a previously arranged meeting; 'Harry' was sighted some 150 yards from the agreed meeting point and taken into custody by a Berlin official."[111] The Gestapo carted off the unsuspecting Griotto as well.[112]

All that now remained for the Gestapo net to sweep up were the "Grand Chef's" second-level agents. To complete the tale of woe, the following were eventually arrested: Rauch, the Czech Secret Service man, Guillaume Hoorickx, the Belgian painter, Nazarin Drailly, a shareholder in Simexco and finally the important courier Germaine Schneider.[113] By mid-January 1943 Karl Giering and Harry Piepe could report to their masters in Berlin that their hunt was at an end. Moscow's greatest espionage organization in Hitler's empire had been eliminated.

The story of Rote Kapelle might have been brought to an end here, had not the Germans followed the bizarre ritual which the Second World War Secret Services turned into the normal sequel to the destruction of an enemy spy-ring: use of the arrested agents against their own masters. A new Rote Kapelle arose—that of the Gestapo. Soon there was a new version of the old cry used on the death of a king—"Rote Kapelle is dead, long live Rote Kapelle."

Counter-espionage became espionage in reverse. The first requirement, of course, was to sift the material seized with the Rote Kapelle agents and form a clear picture of the methods used by Soviet espionage in Western Europe. This was the duty primarily of the "Special Rote Kapelle Commission" in Berlin and its newly formed offshoot in Paris, the "Special Rote Kapelle Squad."[114]

The Paris "Special Squad" was taken over by a counter-espionage professional from the Gestapo, Kriminalkommissar and SS-Hauptsturmführer Heinrich Reiser; he had been summoned at the end of November (after the trouble with Jung) to re-establish some order in the Rue de Saussaies where the anti-Rote Kapelle team was temporarily without a master.[115] Reiser was on familiar ground; only a fortnight previously he had been transferred to Karlsruhe after two and a half years as head of Desk IV A (Suppression of Communism) in Security Police headquarters, France.[116]

Reiser became an even more important cog in the wheel in the spring of 1943 when Giering, who had meanwhile been promoted Kriminalrat, fell sick of an old tumor complaint and had to leave his post.[117] Reiser, a desiccated bureaucrat, was a "natural" for the work of evaluation; he was known as an excellent and indefatigable interrogator who would never rest until every sentence in a statement, however apparently trivial, had been thoroughly discussed, elucidated over and over again and finally set tidily down on paper.

The Special Squad experts took two months to acquire a concrete picture of Soviet espionage and its methods. They had enough material to beat the Russians at their own game. They now had to try to "convert" the captured spies and, with their assistance, initiate a "radio playback" game with Moscow designed to disconcert the enemy by a sophisticated mixture of genuine and false information.

Ever since modern methods of espionage have been developed, counter-espionage has used the "radio playback" game as a weapon; a "playback" game, using converted agents, has become the traditional final chapter in the story of the destruction of an enemy spy-ring.* During the Second World War alone German counter-espionage carried on no fewer than 160 radio games with Moscow.[119] The Russians were particularly vulnerable to such methods; their low-grade radio equipment and their excessive use of amateur spies made them obvious targets for sophisticated "playback" games.

Gilles Perrault suspects that the Gestapo's "playback" games concealed some high-level political horse-trading, that they were an attempt on the part of the Germans to enter into political discussions with their Soviet enemy. In fact Kriminalkommissar Thomas Ampletzer of the RSHA Counter-sabotage desk, who coordinated the radio offensive against Moscow, had a much more prosaic object in mind—to confuse the enemy and lure him into giving away his own secrets.

The question was who should be used for the "playback" game. The judicial liquidator of Rote Kapelle was already on his way; on 18 February 1943 Judge Advocate-General Dr. Manfred Roeder arrived in Brussels at the head of a special tribunal with the sonorous title "Special Field Court Martial of the Commanding General and Commander-in-Chief of Air Region III."[120] More simply put—Roeder had arrived to condemn the red spies in accordance with martial law.

In a fortnight Roeder had passed judgment on the members of the Belgian circuit.[121] The three Soviet officers, Yefremov, Danilov and Makarov, were condemned to death,[122] though Makarov's sentence was not carried out because Roeder had discovered that he was a nephew of Molotov, the Soviet Foreign Minister.†[123] The directors of Simexco were given terms of hard labor;[124] Isbutsky and Sesée, the radio operator, were condemned to death.[125]

On 8 March Roeder's court moved to a house opposite the Elysée Palace in Paris and opened a new series of trials.[126] One after another Roeder's sentences echoed

---

* Werner Best says that radio "playback" games were among the normal methods used by the Secret Police radio monitoring service.[118]

† Yefremov was also granted a stay of execution because he was required for a radio "playback" game; he managed to escape at the end of the war.

through the hall; Grossvogel, the two Maximoviches, Robinson and Käthe Voelkner all received the death sentence.[127] To the other defendants Roeder showed unexpected leniency. Anna-Margaret Hoffmann-Scholtz was sentenced to six years' hard labor for treason through negligence,[128] Kuprian to three years' imprisonment for military indiscipline,[129] Keller, the Simexco interpreter, received a similar sentence[130] and Germaine Schneider was sent to a concentration camp.[131]

"I know," Roeder recalled, "that there were no more than 20–25 sentences in all. Of these, as far as I remember, about one-third were death sentences."[132] When he reported to his master Göring early in April he even pleaded for a pardon in the cases of the women involved or at least for non-confirmation of the death sentences. Göring agreed.[133]

Of greater significance for the future work of the Gestapo, however, were the men upon whom Roeder had *not* sat in judgment. Almost the entire elite of Rote Kapelle in the West was spared confrontation with the terrible judge. Trepper, Kent, Katz, Raichman, Winterinck, Schumacher and their wives or mistresses of the time—the Gestapo had reserved them all for its radio game with Moscow. They began to lead a shadowy existence in which political and ideological loyalties no longer counted and the professional pride of the agent acquired a curious validity as an end in itself.

In the eyes of the moralists the fact that Trepper and his people worked for the Germans later came to be regarded as indicating "a morass of moral degradation and treachery . . . one of the most shocking chapters in the three-decade history of Soviet intelligence."[134] Such a verdict was supported by reference to theoretical textbooks setting out how a communist should behave when in prison. Rules of conduct issued in Prague in 1935 under the title "Our Struggle," for instance, laid down: "I never admit my guilt in any offense I am accused of. . . . As a matter of principle I do not divulge names, cover names, personal descriptions, addresses or places through which comrades could be contacted. . . . When I am told that others have already confessed, I do not believe it, and if others really have confessed, I will call them liars, always denying everything." The pedagogue even knew what (on paper) a man should do when under torture: "If I am tortured, beaten, I will let them kill me, torture me to death, rather than betray my organization, my comrades."[135]

One or two members of Rote Kapelle did work according to the book. Sophie Posnanska, for instance, preferred to commit suicide in her cell rather than give away her friends;[136] Isidor Springer threw himself out of a window of Lyons Prison before saying a word.[137] But they were the exceptions. For most of the men of Rote Kapelle the rules laid down in the espionage handbooks bore no relation to reality; they allowed themselves to be "converted."

Was all this mere treachery, capitulation to brute force? Certainly not. Even ex-Kommissar Reiser has testified: "The hard word 'treachery' is not applicable in this case."[138] The behavior of these men is in fact to be explained by a whole complex of motives, attempts at self-justification and excuses, difficult to disentangle; fatalism, the instinct of self-preservation, hope of escape in an unguarded moment and pure love of adventure all played their part, but above all there was the insatiable curiosity of the professional who longed to know how his adversary set about solving his problems.

Whatever may have driven the prisoners to work for the enemy, the most commonplace motive and the one most beloved of the storytellers hardly figured at all—destruction of will-power by torture. Of course the Gestapo used torture in individual cases; Keller was beaten, Hersch Sokol was clubbed to death[139] and his wife belabored with whips and truncheons.[140] The prisoners designated to participate in the Gestapo's radio game, however, were seldom if ever struck.

Even Gestapo minds had grasped the fact that brutality could not force an enemy agent to talk, still less cooperate. One of them, who had every reason to know, said: "I cannot extract the truth from a man by physical methods of pressure. He would answer leading questions but never give away his real secrets. . . . All the various combinations and possibilities are never so well known that circumstantial evidence alone is enough."[141]

If Rote Kapelle's ex-agents were really to be recruited for work against Moscow, they had at least to receive decent treatment. Reiser's "Special Squad" took care to insure that its staff-to-be was comfortably housed. Trepper and Katz were lodged in a feudal country house surrounded by a park in the Paris suburb of Neuilly. Later arrivals included Grossvogel, Otto Schumacher and Kent together with Margarete Barcza, so that the place eventually resembled a headquarters for the Gestapo's version of Rote Kapelle.[142]

The Gestapo forgot nothing which might make their selected prisoners' stay as pleasant as possible; each had his own room with a shelfful of books; good food was served by two maids; there were daily walks and occasional visits to the cinema in a small town on the western outskirts of Paris. The guards kept discreetly in the background. The prisoners found nothing unnatural in the fact that the doors of their rooms were locked behind them.[143]

The Gestapo's other involuntary assistants were kept in private houses in Paris and Brussels. Yefremov and Wenzel were lodged in a requisitioned house in the Rue l'Aurore, Brussels;[144] Winterinck also lived in Brussels[145] and Raichman with his Malvina was in Hillel Katz's old apartment in Paris.[146] They were more closely guarded than the Neuilly prisoners, but even so the Gestapo was at pains to keep them in a good mood—by providing supplementary rations, cigarettes and visits to the cinema.

The "Special Squad" soon thought its prisoners so willing to cooperate that the radio game could be started. On 22 December the "Special Rote Kapelle Commission" reported to Himmler: "In order to remain in touch with Moscow all opportunities for a radio game must be continuously exploited. Accordingly 'Bordo's' lines in Belgium and Winterinck's in Holland—the set was also located in Brussels—were taken into service. An attempt is being made to establish traffic over Kruyt's line."[147]

Immediately after the destruction of the spy-rings in Belgium and Holland, Ampletzer in Berlin had ordered radio "playback" games to be initiated with Moscow via the captured sets. Available sets were those taken from Wenzel, Raichman, Sesée, Kruyt and Winterinck. Kruyt's set proved to be useless,[148] but over each of the other four a game was started: Operation "Eiche" [Oak] with Sesée's set, Operation "Tanne" [Fir] with Winterinck's, Operation "Weide" [Willow] with Wenzel's and Operation "Buche-Pascal" [Beech] with Raichman's.[149]

When Trepper's organization in France was rounded up, two further sets became available[150] and two additional operations were initiated, "Eifel I" and "Eifel II." These two were later combined under the codename "Mars-

Eifel," "Mars" standing for Marseilles, since the Germans wished to maintain the fiction that Kent was still transmitting from that place.[151]

Ampletzer began conducting his phony radio orchestra in November 1942. Contact was quickly established with Moscow and soon traffic was flowing between Moscow and Western Europe as smoothly as if it had never been interrupted. The Moscow headquarters seemed to have no suspicions; the Gestapo had explained why the sets had not come on the air for some time (technical faults were given as the reason), and Moscow accepted the story.[152]

The Gestapo was, of course, far too wily to leave traffic with Moscow in the hands of Rote Kapelle's "converted" radio operators. Inevitably the Germans were afraid that at any moment their involuntary helpers might warn Soviet Secret Service headquarters by some previously agreed signal. A single wrong indicator group or call-sign would have been enough to bring to an end the laboriously prepared "playback" game.

Accordingly the Gestapo allowed none of the ex-agents to touch the actual keys of the sets; the "converted" operators were set down in front of training sets and tapped out their messages which were registered on records or tapes. By this means the Germans could learn, and thus imitate, the "handwriting" of each Rote Kapelle operator.[153] Every radio operator has his own individual quirks; one may leave longer and another shorter pauses between words and sentences; operators can be distinguished from each other by the rhythm and speed at which they transmit.

Having thus trained themselves in the "handwriting" of their ex-enemies, the Gestapo's operators then transmitted carefully prepared "playback" information to Moscow. Nevertheless, the "converted" operator had always to be present during the sending or receiving of messages; it could be that the Moscow master set would suddenly break into a transmission and demand passage of a previously agreed codeword; the German operator had always to be in a position to give it at once.[154]

What messages, however, could the "Special Squad" send to Moscow? Passage of exclusively false information would have been tantamount to suicide since it must be assumed that the Soviet Secret Service could check the intelligence provided; the only really false information which could be passed, therefore, was that not susceptible to checking by the other side. And that was very little. The Gestapo's "playback" material consequently had to consist largely of genuine intelligence.

This gave rise to a major dilemma. Moscow required primarily military information; to what extent, however, could this be given to the enemy without endangering the security of one's own troops? For the Gestapo this question was all the more agonizing in that they were dependent upon the good will of the senior Wehrmacht commanders, without whose approval no military intelligence might be passed on. OKW, which worked under the eye of Hitler and Himmler, might well be willing to cooperate, but in Western Europe the highest military authority was Commander-in-Chief West, Field Marshal Gerd von Rundstedt who was at daggers drawn with the Gestapo and also on principle mistrusted the secret service antics of counter-espionage.*

Ampletzer was forced to agree to a complicated procedure for obtaining approval. When the unsuspecting Director in Moscow asked his agents military questions, the "Special Squad" had to request the Abwehr's French Office, located in the "Lutetia" Hotel in Paris, to release the necessary information; the Abwehr in turn applied for approval to C-in-C West or his intelligence officer; if this was forthcoming, the Abwehr Office compiled the necessary material. Only after all this could the "Special Squad," together with the ex-agent concerned, draft the radio message for Moscow. The main work at this stage was done by Kent who encoded the messages. In the more difficult cases the "Special Squad" had to consult OKW's Signals Security office in the Boulevard Suchet and they checked the text once more. Finally the message was passed to the RSHA in Berlin and Ampletzer checked whether it fitted into the overall picture of the radio games with Moscow; he then submitted the text of the message (and all military queries from Moscow) to Section III (Counter-espionage) of OKW Foreign Intelligence.[156]

With so complex a procedure it is astonishing that Moscow could be deceived for so long. In spite of all the

---

* Commander-in-Chief West, with headquarters in Saint-Germain, commanded all German troops stationed in German-occupied Western Europe, including those under Army Groups and C-in-C Netherlands. Rundstedt was C-in-C West from 30 October 1940 to 10 June 1941 and again from 14 March 1942 to 2 July 1944.[155]

bureaucratic obstacles, however, Ampletzer and his experts in Paris contrived to give the Director prompt service. Traffic between Razvedupr and the Gestapo increased week by week; the questions asked by Soviet headquarters became even more interesting.

At the very beginning there occurred a vexatious mishap which might have entailed the failure of the whole of Ampletzer's radio offensive. Operation "Weide" had barely started when, in January 1943, the over-confidence of his guard enabled Johann Wenzel, the ex-operator, to escape.[157] The guard had left the key to the radio room on the outside of the door; Wenzel knocked him down, rushed to the door and locked it behind him. In a few moments he was swallowed up by the Brussels traffic.[158]

Wenzel went to ground first in Belgium and then in Holland. He avoided all contact with Soviet or communist agents, obviously fearing that his collaboration with the Germans was already known.[159] This was to the advantage of the Gestapo. They tried to carry on Operation "Weide" by themselves but in February 1943 were forced to abandon it.[160]

On the other lines Ampletzer's and Reiser's "playback" game was far more successful. Moscow's confidence in its agents in the West, still thought to be at large, never wavered for a moment. The Director's questions became increasingly urgent and precise.

On 1 February 1943 the Director radioed: "Try to establish: (a) Numerals of units being transported to the Spanish frontier; (b) types of guns and tanks."[161] On 21 February came an order: "Get the Manufacturer to observe transport and equipment of German troops, primarily those moving from France to Germany en route for our front but also movement back to France."[162] The next day the Director wished to know: "What German divisions are held in reserve in France and where? This question is of particular importance to us."[163] On 9 March 1943: "Inform us what German troops are located in Paris and Lyons. Numerals, arm of the service, ration strength and equipment."[164] On 18 March: "Check and inform us forthwith whether 462 Infantry Division is in Nancy, 465 Infantry Division in Epinal and 467 Infantry Division in France—we do not know its exact location."[165] Ten days later: "What divisions are located in Châlons-sur-Marne and Angoulême. We have information that 9 Infantry

Division is at Châlons-sur-Marne and 10 Panzer Division at Angoulême. Confirm truth of this intelligence."[166]

The Gestapo operators hastened to satisfy the Director. At the end of January, for instance, they reported to Moscow: "We are informed by a reliable source that in the closing weeks of December the Germans initiated extraordinarily extensive troop movements toward the Spanish frontier, particularly in the area Bordeaux-Angoulême-Hendaye. Between 10 and 20 December troop transport traffic was so dense that on many days up to eight troop trains were observed on the vital stretch of railway between Poitiers and Angoulême."[167]

On 16 March they reported "numerous troops from Antwerp and the vicinity moving in the direction of southern France" comprising "26 troop trains, 18 of more than 50 carriages and 8 of about 40—primarily infantry."[168] On 23 March the Director was told of "an increasing scale of troop transports and troop movements in Belgium and France,"[169] and five days later of "fresh Luftwaffe formations" in Brittany—"this seems to be a new combined formation of air-transported and parachute troops."[170] The Gestapo provided its customer in Moscow with the most minute details; on 2 April, for instance: "The new SS Division in Angoulême has neither numerals nor badges. The men wear field-gray uniform with black collar patches, tunic and SS badge. Equipment: an extraordinarily large number of motorized vehicles."[171] On 4 April further information was provided about this SS division: "Artillery: medium and heavy howitzers and heavy long-barreled guns, all motorized. In addition extraordinarily numerous anti-tank guns of modern type and numerous anti-aircraft guns. The division has a number of medium-heavy armored cars. Strength of the division about 16,000 men."[172]

The more detailed the Director's questions became, the more he was forced to reveal his network of informers still working in the West—and this was the Gestapo's object. The Gestapo was reasonably sure that the entire Soviet espionage organization in France, Belgium and Holland had been destroyed; there was still the Comintern network, however, and the underground circuit of the French Communist Party. They also were involved in spying for the Russians.

An even more important objective was Alexander Rado's Soviet espionage circuit in Switzerland; on the annihilation

of Schulze-Boysen's and Harnack's circuit this had assumed
the duty of providing Moscow with information from the
higher levels of the German Wehrmacht. Rado had abandoned any attempt to maintain his own agents within the
German sphere of influence; all he did was to tap the intelligence channels of the Swiss Army's secret service—
and the Swiss had some remarkably good links into the
Führer's headquarters.*

To track down Moscow's last remaining sources of information (the Comintern network, the French Communist
Party and the Rado circuit) there now appeared from
Paris a Gestapo man of a very different caliber from the
over-pedantic bureaucrat, Reiser, whom he ultimately succeeded as head of the "Special Squad." Kriminalrat Heinz
Pannwitz had been born in Berlin in 1911; he had been a
member of the Christian "Pathfinders" and even after becoming an SS-Hauptsturmführer had remained a member
of the Confessional Church. He had started in the Berlin
Criminal Police, where he had been in charge of the
"Serious House-breaking" desk, and had thence graduated
to the Gestapo. He had been Desk Officer for security in
the Gestapo office in Prague, where he had found membership of Reinhard Heydrich's immediate entourage a difficult assignment.[174] In the summer of 1942 he had been
placed in charge of the investigation into the background
to the murder of Heydrich and, during this process, he
had gradually become convinced that nothing could be
achieved by mere brutal persecution of anti-Nazi resisters.
In August of that year he expounded his views to Gestapo
Müller, arguing that the RSHA must "abandon pure persecution of espionage and resistance groups and play along
with them," as he puts it today.[175] Pannwitz gave his
reasoning as follows: the object should be to avoid sense-
less bloodshed; if a group were totally destroyed, a hundred
others would spring up after it—and that must be prevented.[176] Müller did not seem particularly impressed but

---

* The head of Intelligence Section I of the Swiss Secret Service, the
section responsible for Germany, was Captain Max Waibel; he had
been to the German Staff College and had kept up friendships with
German officers formed at that time; during the Second World War
these friends passed him information. This intelligence was summa-
rized and handed out to Allied secret services since, in view of the
permanent threat of a German invasion, the Swiss wished to retain
the good will of the Allies. Rado's circuit of informers had access to
this intelligence through these channels.[173]

when Reiser appeared to be making no further progress in tracking down new groups of agents in the West, his (Müller's) mind turned to Kriminalrat Pannwitz. He said: "Do what you proposed to me last year. Play for any stakes you like, otherwise with our few routine officials we shall never get the better of this situation."[177]

Heinz Pannwitz began to play. His object was to cause the Director in Moscow to reveal his last remaining agents in the West. The "Special Squad" had already scored one success while Giering was still there: via "Otto" (Trepper's codename) Soviet Secret Service headquarters had been persuaded to give the location of one of the French Communist Party's secret transmitters—and the Gestapo had seized it at once.[178]

Pannwitz continued what Giering had begun. One day Kent's set went "dis"; it could easily have been repaired by one of the "Special Squad's" technicians. The Gestapo in Paris, however, asked the Director to make available a reliable radio technician from the French Communist Party.[179] Moscow promptly nominated Comrade "Jojo," who built short-wave sets for the Party. Jojo was arrested; his statements uncovered a whole new chain of communist informers, all of whom fell into the hands of the Gestapo.[180]

With the information and equipment thus made available Pannwitz started a new ploy, this time directed against Rado's "Red Three." In the summer of 1943 the "Special Squad" despatched an emissary to Rado in Geneva, the Franco-German author, Yves Rameau; his real name was Zweig and the Gestapo had a hold over him because of his Jewish origin. Rameau presented himself as a member of Rote Kapelle, cited various mutual friends in Paris and asked for certain information.[181]

But the Gestapo had underestimated Rado. The Resident Director pretended not to understand Monsieur Rameau, saying that this must be a case of mistaken identity; actually the fact that the visit had not been announced by Moscow was a suspicious sign in the eyes of a veteran spy like Rado.[182]

Pannwitz had no greater success with a courier whom he despatched to Rado's head radio operator, Alexander Foote. Kent had worked out the following plan: in order to learn more about the Swiss network, an agent should be despatched as courier to fetch from Foote the money regularly paid to the French Communist Party underground. The agent duly made his way to Foote, but proved so garrulous that Foote became suspicious.[183] Kent was just able to persuade Moscow that the courier had been captured by the Germans and replaced by one of their agents. "A fortnight later," Foote recalls, "the Center informed me that my suspicions were correct and that the courier had been a German agent."[184]

Pannwitz was far more successful with another gambit which resulted in an entire communist espionage and resistance organization working for the Gestapo without knowing it.

In 1940 a Lithuanian Comintern functionary named Waldemar Ozols had formed a small espionage circuit on orders from the Soviet Air Attaché in Vichy. The Director, however, found its work unsatisfactory; its sole merit was that it maintained contact with other groups of agents. When two of its informers were arrested by the Gestapo in 1942, the Director decided to merge the remainder of the Ozols circuit into Rote Kapelle. In the summer of 1943 Kent was instructed to use Ozols' people for informer work within his organization.[185]

Via Kent, Pannwitz at once despatched the Ozols men to contact other communist groups, which thereupon came under control of the Gestapo. Most important of these was "Mithridate," a resistance organization under the French Captain Paul Legendre. Kent persuaded him to move to Paris and there enter the service of Moscow as "Agent 305." Up to the time of the German withdrawal from France in autumn 1944 neither Legendre nor Ozols knew that "Moscow" was in reality the Gestapo.[186]

With the support of these two groups Pannwitz was able to keep under surveillance wider and wider sectors of the French underground. Captain Karl von Wedel of Signals Security says that the reports of the Legendre-Ozols circuit "provided valuable pointers as to the weak points in our own security system and in some cases served to keep Moscow confident. In this way we succeeded in penetrating further into the organization of the French Communist Party and learning more about the kind of messages in which Moscow was most interested."[187]

Nevertheless, the "Special Squad" was finding it increasingly difficult to maintain the credibility of its "playback" game with Moscow. The Director was continually demanding detailed reports about the German Wehrmacht and C-in-C West was showing himself increasingly reluctant to release secret military information. Field Marshal von Rundstedt's aversion to the Gestapo's secret service operations reached its height on 31 May 1943, when the following message arrived through "Eifel I":

"Otto. Order The Manufacturer to discover whether the army of occupation is preparing to use poison gas. Is gas moved in its pure state (without adulteration)? Other secret consignments or movements will, of course, also be carefully camouflaged. Are there stocks of gas bombs on airfields and if so which? What is their quantity and size? What gas do they contain and what is the effect of this gas? Are experiments on the effects of the various poison gases being undertaken? Have you heard anything about a new gas named 'Gay-Hale'? The same questions are applicable to Gastronomy [codename for France]. Pass all intelligence about gases and poisons as quickly as possible. No. 38. Direktor."[188]

The "Special Squad" informed the Abwehr Office, France, and they thereupon applied to Rundstedt's headquarters for release of the information necessary to answer the Director's questions. But C-in-C West's Intelligence Officer would have none of it: "An answer to this inquiry is out of the question."[189]

On 21 June 1943 the Abwehr Office reported to Berlin: "The position of C-in-C West is that for some time the master station in Moscow has been putting such precise questions of a military nature that continuation of the 'playback' game is only possible if these precise questions can be answered with equal precision; otherwise the Moscow master station will see through the game. For military reasons, however, he finds it impossible to provide the material to answer the precise questions asked by Moscow, which continually include details of divisional and regimental numbers, numbers of commanders, etc. . . . . C-in-C West adheres to his opinion that in the present military situation in the West, no further interest attaches to deception of the Moscow master station."[190]

Ampletzer was not prepared to allow the military to rob him of his toy quite so easily. He gave the Abwehr and C-in-C West to understand that in the opinion of the RSHA "in order to obtain a complete picture of the organization, a certain amount of 'playback' material must

be provided if the radio game is to continue."[191] Thereupon
C-in-C West was even more explicit, saying that he saw
"no virtue in continuance of the radio game."[192] On 25 June
1943 the Abwehr Office, France, put an end to the correspondence: "The acquisition of misleading material from
C-in-C West has encountered difficulties in recent weeks
since C-in-C West is of the opinion that the enemy in
Moscow has already seen through the game. . . . For military reasons, therefore, C-in-C West is not in a position to
release the necessary material to answer these precise questions."[193]

In fact Pannwitz too had long been wondering whether
Moscow had not seen through the radio games of the
counterfeit Rote Kapelle. Reiser also confirms that in the
RSHA itself people had come to think that Rote Kapelle
in France and Belgium was now past history and so the
matter was brought to an abrupt end.[194] The deception
operation with the French underground continued but Rote
Kapelle's radio games gradually died away.

No one underlined the fact that Rote Kapelle was at an
end more clearly than the "Grand Chef" himself. On 13
September 1943 he asked his guard, Kriminalobersekretär
Berg, to drive him to a chemist's shop, Bailly near the Gare
St. Lazare in Paris, so that he could buy some medicine.
Berg remained in the car and gazed in boredom at Trepper
as he entered the door of the shop. He did not know that
it had a rear exit. Leopold Trepper ran through to the
street behind and disappeared. The Gestapo hunted him
furiously but unsuccessfully for months.[195]

From the underground the fugitive wrote Pannwitz one
or two sarcastic letters[196]—but until the end of the war
he remained undiscoverable. His escape brought the story
of the Rote Kapelle to an end. A few months later Winterinck also fled,[197] and even Yefremov managed to escape
death and reach South America.[198]

Only Kent and Raichman remained to the bitter end.[199]
The game was up.

8

Rote Kapelle: Fact and Fiction

THE "GRAND CHEF'S" circuits were dead, their members arrested and sentenced, their underground links severed. What remained, however, was a legend, the myth that Rote Kapelle had been the Soviet Secret Service's most successful organization, possibly exerting a decisive effect on the war.

Both friends and enemies of Rote Kopelle made an equal contribution to this legend. All wished to participate according to their lights in the panache of this unique communist spy-ring, the one side as allies and martyrs in an anti-fascist crusade, the other as the pursuers and eventual liquidators of a mighty organization of agents. Though poles apart in ideology and political morality, all were agreed on one thing: Rote Kapelle had been unique, incredibly successful and most remarkable.

The memoirs both of the hunters and the hunted produced a picture of a superlative intelligence organization, apparently capable of doing almost anything. Even so critical a historian as David Dallin says: "Seen in historical perspective the apparat . . . gave a performance that was remarkable and unique. . . . Never before had espionage played as prominent a role in wartime as it did for the Soviet Union in 1941–44."[1]

On what did Rote Kapelle exert this decisive influence?

273

Apparently everything—engagements, battles, offensives, perhaps even the war as a whole. As late as 1969 the American *Publishers Weekly* said that Rote Kapelle had been a circuit of agents "who worked so effectively in the very center of the German General Staff that the German battle plans for Stalingrad were in the hands of the Russians even before they had reached the German commanders at the front."[2]

Gilles Perráult says: "Think of it! Between 1940 and 1942—up to the time of Stalingrad—there were hundreds of radio messages telling the Moscow headquarters where the enemy would attack and where he was especially vulnerable; the entire German economic and defense potential was an open book; the Soviet General Staff could direct its operations in the light of the enemy's offensive plans as laid before it."[3]

Ex-members of the organization produced numerous details to support their theory that Rote Kapelle had played a historic key role. In an address in the Hebbel Theater, Berlin, in 1946, Günther Weisenborn said: "It is time that our country heard what happened. Our people should know who set fire to the anti-Soviet exhibition in the Lustgarten, who intervened decisively in the convoy battles north of Norway, who acted at Stalingrad . . . who initiated thousands upon thousands of operations inside the Third Reich and at the front."[4]

Willi Weber, one of Schulze-Boysen's associates, was even more precise. "From the beginning of the Russian campaign in 1941 Schulze-Boysen kept the Director informed of the German objectives in the areas of Leningrad, Smolensk, Orzha, Briansk, Kharkov, Voronezh, etc. He was responsible in 1941 for the stabilization of the front from Leningrad as far as Rzhev, Vyasma, Orel, Kursk, Rostov and Stalino. Had 'Rote Kapelle' not existed, it is possible that the German General Staff would have reached its 'Barbarossa' objectives."[5] Greta Kuckhoff too confirmed: "The first concrete intelligence about war preparations came from Harro; he even named the Russian cities first to be attacked."[6]

For these people no action was so vast, no task so delicate that it could not be ascribed to Rote Kapelle. They thought in all seriousness that it had caused Hitler's Wehrmacht hundreds of thousands of casualties. Weisenborn said: "Germans were being killed anyway. We had to decide between 100,000 casualties or two million. We opted for 100,000."[7]

The Third Reich's ex-functionaries also made their contribution to the picture of Rote Kapelle as a sinister ubiquitous organization. Their attempts at self-justification, their slanted memoirs and their crude ideas about a "bolshevist world enemy" endowed their dead opponent with a diabolical efficiency—and all this struck a chord in the heart of the simple German citizen, who anyway tended to lay the blame for the failure of the Nazi regime's warlike adventures at the door of traitors and occult forces.

One of those "in the know" said: "It was a deadly web which Rote Kapelle spun over Europe."[8] Manfred Roeder, the ex-prosecutor, declared: "This was a battle fought by the German soldier against an unseen enemy, who worked under cover using novel but insidious methods."[9] Ex-Captain Harry Piepe could "hardly think of a single city within our sphere of influence and certainly not in Germany" in which some Rote Kapelle group was not active;[10] in occupied France, he considered, the entire Wehrmacht had been infiltrated by the enemy: "Many senior officers were compromised by the two Maximoviches and were severely punished. That was quite a scene!"[11]

Having thus built Rote Kapelle up into something more than life-size, its ex-pursuers inevitably came to believe that it was still at work even after the war. In 1951 Roeder maintained that "a member of Rote Kapelle is to be found in some influential position in practically every major city in north Germany, down as far as Stuttgart";[12] even the cautious ex-Kommissar Heinrich Reiser says: "During the Second World War Rote Kapelle was far more than we ever thought it was—and it is still at work! Rote Kapelle exists now as much as it ever did."[13]

Such utterances are, of course, more indicative of the political opinions of their authors than of concrete fact. They bear no relation to the truth—which is that Rote Kapelle was of no decisive significance for the outcome of the war. Rote Kapelle made no contribution to the course of a single battle in the East; it was not the cause of the annihilation of any German division; it did not upset any of the Wehrmacht's campaigns. The course of the Second World War would have been no different had Trepper, Kent, Schulze-Boysen and Harnack never existed.

The tale of the decisive role played by Rote Kapelle was only believed because for years a stream of sensational literature suggested that the fate of nations depended primarily upon the unseen machinations of clever, highly trained agents and spies. The value of espionage was vastly overestimated. People seriously believed that the discoveries of a secret service could sway the policy of a government or the decisions of a General Staff.

In fact the history of the Second World War provides numerous instances when espionage exerted no effect at all, leading one to think that governments or General Staffs only take notice of and accept information provided by their Secret Service when this tallies with their own preconceived ideas; when it cuts across some course of action already decided or some preconceived opinion on the part of authority, it is generally ignored. Such was the experience of Colonel Sas, the Dutch Military Attaché in Berlin, who vainly warned his government in 1939–40 against a German invasion, of Göring's "Research Office," whose forecast that Britain would enter the war at the side of Poland went unheard, and of the U.S. Secret Service which fruitlessly issued warnings about a Japanese attack on Pearl Harbor.

Rote Kapelle warned of the German invasion of Russia, but no one in Moscow listened. W. M. Bereshkov, then First Secretary of the Soviet Embassy in Berlin, recalls that from the spring of 1941 they had "found ways and means of warning the Soviet Union against the threatened danger."[14] As early as February Major-General Tupikov, the Soviet Military Attaché and the direct contact for the Schulze-Boysen/Harnack circuit, had reported that three German Army Groups were being set up for the assault on the USSR and that they were directed on Leningrad, Moscow and Kiev respectively. Tupikov's message included: "Date of attack estimated as 20 May." On 14 March he passed on a statement by a German Major: "We are turning eastward, against the USSR. We shall take grain, coal and oil from the USSR. Then we shall be unconquerable." A few days later Tupikov reported that the German invasion must be expected "between 15 May and 15 June 1941."[15]

Not even General Golikov, head of Razvedupr at the time, was convinced. On 20 March he submitted an appreciation for senior commanders which included this:

"The rumors and documents purporting to show that war against the USSR this spring is inevitable must be regarded as false reports emanating from the British, and perhaps even the German, Intelligence Service." Similar reports from Captain (First Class) Vorontsov, the Soviet Naval Attaché, were no better received in Moscow.[16]

In desperation the diplomats and officers of the Soviet Embassy assembled early in May and checked once more all the reports received about German war preparations. Shortly thereafter they gave Moscow yet another warning in a special report: All Hitler's war preparations were concluded, they said, and the war might start at any moment. For the first time Razvedupr took the Berlin reports seriously; Stalin, however, clung to his view that Hitler did not want war and was only trying to blackmail Russia. He even remained unimpressed by a Secret Service report that 120 German divisions had moved up to the frontier. After all he had 149 divisions on his western frontier, the dictator said. Zhukov, the Chief of the General Staff, reminded him that a German division was twice as strong as a Russian, but Stalin retorted: "One can't believe everything the Secret Service says."[17]

Such disastrous misunderstandings illustrated the difficulties experienced by Soviet agents abroad in making themselves understood to their masters in the Kremlin. This applied particularly to Rote Kapelle. An insulating barrier of mistrust divided the Director in Moscow from his agents; moreover, Rote Kapelle frequently acted on its own initiative and the Director did not always know what his agents were doing. Many instances proved that the Soviet Secret Service by no means possessed the system and method ascribed to it by its Western admirers.

To all this must be added a practical difficulty to which any secret service is subject if it has agents working in the enemy's camp. The Soviet General Staff would not and could not discount the possibility that its agents had fallen victim to some deception maneuver on the part of the enemy or become party to some intelligence deal. This placed a limitation of principle on the credibility of information, however good, on enemy intentions; the Russians being prone to suspicion anyway, Rote Kapelle's reports can only have exerted a very limited influence on the Red Army's military decisions during the Russo-German war.

We do not, of course, know to what extent the Soviet General Staff's continuously changing estimate of the enemy situation relied on Rote Kapelle's reports. The comparable situation on the German side, however, can be used as a guide. The high-level picture of the enemy situation was built up from five sources: ground reconnaissance at the front, air reconnaissance, radio interception, study of the enemy and neutral press and secret service reports. In order of reliability agents' reports came last.[18]

Captain (Dr.) Will Grosse, formerly of the Abwehr, says: "Agents' reports were never used as the basis for overall direction of military operations. As a basis for operational decisions the general strategic appreciation of the situation played a far greater part than any views put forward by the Intelligence Service on enemy intentions, strength, disorganization or morale. On the German side account was generally taken of agents' reports only in so far as they fitted into the overall appreciation of the situation."[19]

Even supposing, however, that the Soviet General Staff did attribute some significance to agents' reports, the question remains whether Rote Kapelle's information was of such a quality as to justify greater account being taken of it in the formation of military decisions. Significantly the authors of the Rote Kapelle legend have so far evaded any detailed consideration of this problem.

Even those inexperienced in military matters must wonder what the Soviet army leaders in the East found so important in Trepper's and Kent's reports on the strength, equipment and location of German troops in the extreme West of Europe. Undoubtedly the agents employed in the West were industrious collectors of information; they reported to Moscow every detail seemingly of political or military significance; they watched the Germans wherever they could. But what was the good of their information to the Soviet armies fighting desperately for their existence? For the General Staff in Moscow it might be of some use to know what German troops located in the West were being moved to the East; it might be important to know how they were equipped and what their morale was like. But with the vast majority of reports from the West the Soviet leaders could do nothing; they included information about Dutch construction of high-tension pylons for Germany, about the distribution of sheet iron to Belgian shipyards,

about stocks in the fuel tanks at Ghent, about bottlenecks
in French locomotive production, about difficulties in the
supply to Belgian factories of special German valves for
the manufacture of tank wagons, about the situation in the
Amsterdam ship-repair yards, about the destination of Belgian steel products[20]—the list could be continued *ad in-
finitum.*

The Soviet General Staff learned practically everything
about the West except that which it required most urgently—information on the plans, thinking and objectives of
the German military. And the reason was simple: Trepper's informers had not managed to infiltrate into the
German military machine. The "Grand Chef" had good
relations with the Todt Organization and the Sauckel Office, but the German military staffs remained inaccessible
to him.

The Germans had four military headquarters in Western
Europe: the Commander-in-Chief of all fighting forma-
tions in France, Belgium and Holland (C-in-C West in
Saint-Germain), and three headquarters more or less
subordinate to him, C-in-C France in Paris, C-in-C Belgium
and Northern France in Brussels and the Wehrmacht C-in-
C Netherlands in The Hague. In none of them had the
"Grand Chef" been able to infiltrate his agents.

Rote Kapelle had had temporary entrée only to the so-
called Military Administration, a purely administrative
department under C-in-C France. In late summer 1940
Militärverwaltungsoberrat [lit: Senior Military Administrative Counselor—in effect a civil servant in uniform] Hans
Kuprian, a specialist working for the Representative for
Refugee Affairs attached to the Chief of Military Administration, had made the acquaintance of the refugee
Vasily Maximovich; his secretary, Anna-Margaret Hoffmann-Scholtz, had fallen in love with Maximovich and
introduced him to her friends. Maximovich thus had the
entrée to the Military Administration offices, though admittedly not for long—the Refugee Office was disbanded
at the end of 1940.[21]

But what about the "numerous senior officers" who, according to Piepe, were suborned by Rote Kapelle and
"severely punished?" What about the Generals who, according to Gilles Perrault, let Baron Maximovich into the
secrets of their anti-Nazi plans? None of them ever existed.
Perrault's "Colonel" Kuprian was merely the modest civil

servant in uniform, who in any case was serving as Head of Administration in faraway Bordeaux from April 1941;[22] his "General von Pfeffer" who collected a "group of officers" around him, turns out to be Regierungspräsident [Government Delegate] von Pfeffer who for a short time acted as Representative for Refugee Affairs attached to the Chief of Military Administration; he had left France before the Russian campaign was launched, in other words before Rote Kapelle had begun to function.[23]

Even the firebrand Roeder rated the espionage activities of Trepper's informers in Military Administration very low, as is shown by the sentences he meted out to them: Kuprian, three years' imprisonment for military indiscipline, Anna-Margaret Hoffmann-Scholtz six years' hard labor for treason due to negligence and three of her female friends from the clerical staff six weeks' close arrest for disclosing their Field Post numbers.[24]

The Berlin group under Harro Schulze-Boysen was militarily much better informed. Between 14 June 1941 and 30 August 1942 they had sent 500 radio messages to Moscow containing primarily military information;[25] they included Luftwaffe production statistics, Abwehr commando operations on the Eastern Front, details of new weapons, the political situation in occupied territories, the fuel position in Germany, tensions between the Führer's Headquarters and the Wehrmacht.

But what Colonel-General Peresypkin really wanted— troop information, operational dates and plans, details of conferences in the Führer's Headquarters—these Schulze-Boysen's agents could not provide, or only to a very limited extent. Schulze-Boysen's informants were seldom above the aide level; he could obviously only produce intelligence from offices in which he had his informers—and there were none in Greater Germany's strategic planning councils.

A glance at Schulze-Boysen's list of informers reveals both the strength and weakness of his intelligence network. He was well informed on Luftwaffe strategy through Colonel Gehrts, Henniger the Inspector of Construction and as a result of his own duties; he learned some of the Abwehr's secrets through Lieutenant Gollnow; he knew about Signals Security through Corporal Heilmann and Warrant Officer Traxl; but none of his informers had the entrée to the OKW Operations Staff, to the Army General

Staff or the Naval Staff. He was therefore reduced to passing on to Moscow what others had heard at third or fourth hand.

Moreover, if the Soviet leaders had based their decisions solely on the information received from Berlin, things would have gone very wrong at the front. Schulze-Boysen's intelligence was inaccurate, indeed in some cases actually false. This can be proved, as is shown by the following radio messages from Rote Kapelle in Berlin:

On 22 September 1941 the agents in Berlin reported to Moscow: "Early in August OKW decided to withdraw the Eastern Front to the line Riga–Odessa. This defense line is now being constructed by 900,000 men of the Todt Organization."[26] The facts were that on 12 August 1941 OKW issued a "Supplement to Directive 34" laying down that German formations should reach the Moscow area "before the coming of winter." No one in OKW, which was still drunk with victory, was even considering construction of a defensive line at the time.[27]

On 21 October 1941 the Soviet General Staff was told by Berlin: "Hitler's order is based on the capture of Leningrad by 15 September."[28] In fact Hitler decided on 5 September that Leningrad should become a "secondary theater of war" and that encirclement of the city was enough. In mid-September he halted any further advance against the city since he did not wish to risk his armored formations.[29]

On 22 October 1941 Berlin radioed to the Director: "Propaganda companies with armored vehicles are located in Briansk in readiness for the entry into Moscow, planned first for 14 and then for 20 October."[30] In fact it was not until 14 October that Hitler issued his order to Army Group Center that Moscow was to be captured before the onset of winter; the Germans did not succeed in breaking into the Moscow defenses until early November.[31] In any case there could have been no such concentration of armor as reported, since propaganda companies did not possess armored vehicles.

The Berlin agents were little better informed about other operational plans. Schulze-Boysen's messages contained mention of a sort of vast master plan worked out by the German General Staff; it consisted of three parts: "Plan I —Urals, Plan II—Archangel–Astrakhan, Plan III—Caucasus."[32] This threefold plan is nowhere to be found in the files of the OKW Operations Staff, though the German plan of operation did have three somewhat similar objectives: Moscow, Leningrad and the Caucasus. Schulze-Boysen was particularly interested in the German plans for the latter; on 12 November 1941 he reported to the Director that "Plan III with objective Caucasus" had been abandoned by the Wehrmacht and would only "come into force again in the spring of 1942."[33] Here again he was wrong.

Clearly the news had penetrated to Schulze-Boysen that on 3 November Field Marshal von Rundstedt, the Commander-in-Chief of Army Group South, had asked Army Headquarters to suspend the Caucasus operation; it was bogged down in mud and "the supply basis for the troops was inadequate." His informant, however, apparently did not know that this request had been turned down by Army Headquarters; on 13 November, at a commanders' conference in Orsha, Colonel-General Halder, the Chief of Staff of the Army, had said that "the onset of frost, shortly to be expected," would permit "a rapid resumption of offensive operations."[34]

Nevertheless, Schulze-Boysen reported the concentration area for the (new) German Caucasus offensive as: "Losovaya–Balakleya–Chuguyev–Belgorod–Akhtyrka–Krasnograd."[35] When the Caucasus offensive actually opened in the summer of 1942, however, the Germans moved forward on a front three times as broad as that reported by Schulze-Boysen. Moreover, the German summer offensive took the Russians completely by surprise. The Soviet High Command had expected the German attack almost anywhere except in the southwest toward the Caucasus.[36] Marshal Zhukov confirmed that "developments in May and June proved that the Headquarters had miscalculated."[37]

What is completely unfounded is the idea that the Soviet victory at Stalingrad and therefore the turn in the fortunes of war resulted from the work of Rote Kapelle. Gilles Perrault presents it thus: On 12 November 1941 Schulze-Boysen informed Moscow that the Germans would resume their Caucasus offensive in the spring of 1942 ("concentration is due to be complete by 1 May"). Perrault then says that "with the historic telegram of 12 November" Rote Kapelle had told the Red Army "where the decisive encounter on the far-off Volga would take place—at Stalingrad . . . Trepper and his men made the victory of Stalingrad possible."[38]

It is difficult to see why the announcement of a fresh Caucasus offensive should have led the Soviet General Staff to conclude that the decisive battle would take place at Stalingrad. Zhuvov's memoirs show that at this time the Russians were expecting a battle in the Moscow area[39] with a smaller German offensive in the south. In fact the Russian army leaders only saw their opportunity at Stalingrad in early spring 1942 when the German offensive flagged. But by that time Rote Kapelle in Berlin no longer existed.

Moreover, in November 1941 Schulze-Boysen could not possibly have prophesied the battle of Stalingrad since the German Generals themselves were not yet sure what their 1942 operations were to be. Hitler was in favor of the Caucasus offensive from the outset, but the Army General Staff wanted to adopt a tactical defensive until the German formations had recovered from their severe losses in manpower.[40] Hitler only began to insist on the Caucasus in February 1942 and the basic decision was not taken until March 1942 at the earliest.[41]

Anyone who still maintains today that, thanks to Rote Kapelle, the Soviet leaders knew of all the German plans beforehand, simply does not know what he is talking about. One of the striking features about the Soviet High Command up to the turning point of Stalingrad was that it was extremely badly informed about enemy intentions. The Soviet Secret Service underestimated the armored and motorized formations available to the German aggressor by 50 per cent;[42] Stalin prophesied that, under no circumstances, would the German attack on Moscow come in 1941;[43] it was all a tale of serious miscalculation on the Soviet side.

Nothing is more significant of the ineffectiveness of Rote Kapelle than the fate of the man who had once pulled its strings from behind. In September 1941 Major-General Tupikov, who had meanwhile become Chief of Staff of Army Group Southwest, was one of the victims of the greatest encirclement battle of the Second World War, that of the Kiev pocket. He had not perceived his enemy's intentions in time; no message from Rote Kapelle had told him that on 21 August Hitler had suddenly ordered the main weight of the German offensive hitherto directed on

Moscow to be diverted southwestward. So Tupikov remained ignorant of the fact that Guderian's Panzer Army had been detached from the formations destined for Moscow and was moving on Romny east of Kiev, where it was to join forces with Kleist's Armored Group moving up from the south. When Tupikov realized what was happening it was too late; the Soviet Army Group Southwest was already surrounded.[44]

In the later stages too Rote Kapelle did nothing to prevent the Russian military men misinterpreting German intentions. In the early summer of 1942 Soviet Headquarters was expecting the main German offensive in the Moscow area—something which never figured in the German plans.[45] The Soviet formations were distributed more or less evenly across the entire front, as if Moscow had never heard of a German plan for an offensive in the Southwest.[46] Moscow was planning a counter-offensive in the Orel area where no German attack was due to take place; it neglected the neighboring Kursk sector, where the German Caucasus offensive was bound to begin.[47] Lacking knowledge of the German plans, the Russians opened an offensive in the Kharkov area on 12 May 1942, thereby at once triggering off the German offensive planned for 18 May. The result was the destruction of an entire sector of the Soviet front, thus opening the way to the German advance on Stalingrad.[48]

In the light of Russian miscalculations and defeats of this magnitude Rote Kapelle can hardly be said to have cost the German Wehrmacht one hundred thousand men. After the war even Roeder was forced to admit (in an unobtrusive passage in his apologia *Die Rote Kapelle*) that "the military intelligence transmitted over the short-wave sets" of Schulze-Boysen and his friends was "somewhat more meager" than the other information provided.[49] If the casualties caused to Hitler's forces by Rote Kapelle be reduced to figures, the alleged losses of 100,000 shrink to some 36—the members of the twelve Abwehr sabotage groups betrayed by Gollnow, ten of which fell victims to Soviet ambushes.[50] Anything more than this is sheer imagination.

The Wehrmacht's counter-espionage experts never thought otherwise. Even during the war Colonel Joachim Rohleder, head of the "Counter-espionage" group in the Abwehr and therefore among the most knowledgeable on the subject of enemy espionage, wondered why Rote Kapelle, particularly the Berlin group, was being taken so seriously. He had read the decoded messages, he had perused the files on the investigation, he had himself interrogated Schulze-Boysen—and his opinion: "a lot of bloody amateurs!" He goes on: "Their espionage activity was conducted in a hopelessly dilettante fashion and does not seem to have caused any serious military damage." But what about the radio messages and the reports? Rohleder says: "We intercepted their radio traffic. As far as I remember this also produced no very shattering secret intelligence."[51]

If, therefore, militarily Rote Kapelle exerted no worthwhile influence on the course of the Second World War, its significance must lie on the political and moral planes. According to their lights, it may be maintained, its members belonged, like other Europeans, to that great resistance movement against the tyranny of the Third Reich which spread throughout the continent. This applies, of course, primarily to Schulze-Boysen's and Harnack's organization in Berlin.

Here too fact must be distinguished from fiction. Its former members stubbornly insist that the Schulze-Boysen/Harnack group was a major organization broadly representative of internal German resistance. According to Weisenborn it covered the whole range "from conservatives to communists";[52] Ernst von Salomon even discovered that it included "young men in good positions, ministerial civil servants and SS officers."[53] Falk Harnack, who is an indefatigable apologist for his late brother, says that Rote Kapelle had "firm and widespread cross-contacts with the '20 July' group and relationships with all major foreign powers."[54]

Such statements give to the Schulze-Boysen/Harnack group a political label which it never carried. It was a conglomeration of young communists, Marxists and left-wing pacifists; it drew its recruits from the working class and left-wing intellectual bohemians; though it had its sectarian undertones, it was determined to fight the Nazi dictatorship without compromise. But it can hardly be called representative of German non-conformism in the Third Reich. Rote Kapelle included no member of the social-democrat working class or of the Prussian aristocracy which on 20 July 1944 revolted against the ruination of the Reich by the Nazis. It did not provide a spiritual home for a single representative of the liberal bourgeoisie, a single professional officer, a single trade-unionist or more than a very few officials.

The apologists for Rote Kapelle who try to prove that it included conservatives in its ranks are driven back upon the subterfuge of including among its members all those for whose death it carries some share of responsibility. Men like Gollnow or Gehrts died for something of which they did not approve. By artificially including men such as this, the champions of Rote Kapelle attempt to make it appear as widely representative an organization as possible and divest it of its basic communist character. They were quite happy, for instance, to include bourgeois money-grubbers like Kummerow and Scheliha—until their real motives became known.*

Similarly, in the interest of historical accuracy, a clear distinction must be drawn between Schulze-Boysen's immediate associates and the resisters pure and simple, who had no wish to be involved in espionage and who devoted their lives to a struggle against the illegalities and injustices of the Nazi state. Schulze-Boysen was their idol and they knew nothing of his involvement in the intelligence machinations of the Soviet empire; it never crossed their minds that their friend would be prepared cold-bloodedly to sacrifice young lives on the altar of a crazy fanaticism. In their eyes there could be only one duty, only one code of morals: to oppose barbarism disguised as nationalist virtuosity and to fight for a better world more worthy of mankind.

Consequently it is these people, the uncontaminated resisters working with Schulze-Boysen, who are the truly tragic figures of this story. What could be more appalling than Cato Bontjes van Beek's last letter from her death cell: "Mama, there is no great glory attached to involvement in this business. . . . The only sad thing is that I do not know what I have to die for."[56] Both in her life and in her death she merits our special respect because to the very end she remained unsullied by that double-dealing morality which drove Schulze-Boysen and his friends to serve a foreign power.

---

* Lehmann, for instance, includes Kummerow and Scheliha among the members of Rote Kapelle.[55]

These others, however, the sworn conspirators grouped around Harro Schulze-Boysen and Arvid Harnack, deliberately accepted the fact that they were flying in the face of all convention and tradition; indeed this was the real basic background to their struggle against Hitlerism and the bourgeois world. They must still be regarded as what they were until they died—amateur agents acting from political conviction, industrious rather than efficient spies, the champions of a political protest movement which proved to posterity that, even in the age of conformism and the fellow traveler, men still exist who follow the dictates of their conscience alone.

Nevertheless, the particular method by which they chose to wage their warfare, espionage on behalf of a foreign power, means that Schulze-Boysen and his immediate associates cannot be included in the ranks of German resistance. The fact that they worked for the Soviet Secret Service has fixed a great gulf between them and the rest of German resistance, a gulf which will probably never be bridged; for the majority of German anti-Nazis Schulze-Boysen and his people were just traitors, clandestine minions of a power which would have suppressed liberty in Germany as effectively as National Socialism succeeded in doing.

This is not to say that, considered in connection with Adolf Hitler's Reich, there can be any such thing as treachery in the normal legal sense of the term. There cannot. The history of the German resistance movement shows instances of legitimate traitorous activity; as Eberhard Bethge, Dietrich Bonhoeffer's biographer, says, in time of emergency the patriot must do what would otherwise be the business of the common blackguard.[57] But this type of treachery can and must have a solely political purpose; it is possible to conceive of situations, for instance, in which one might contact and pass information to an enemy in order to induce him to act in a way which would facilitate the overthrow of an illegal regime in one's own country.

This and nothing else was the reason why in 1940 Colonel Hans Oster on three occasions divulged to the Western Powers the date of the German attack; he wished to induce the enemy to take counter-measures, thereby checking Hitler's warlike adventure in its infancy and conditioning the Generals to action against him.[58] The object of treachery in this case was unequivocally political; no thought of increasing the enemy's war potential or assisting him to victory ever entered Oster's head. In the eyes of a man like Oster that would have been the act of a common traitor worthy of the direst punishment.

Numerous attempts have been made to justify the traitorous activities of the Schulze-Boysen/Harnack group by citing the example of Oster, but they betray a grave misunderstanding of the case. Oster and his friends in the senior ranks of the German army were playing a perilous game; their object was to gain the backing of Germany's enemies for the liberation of Germany from the Hitler regime and to conclude a compromise peace with the Allies. Schulze-Boysen and his friends, however, who lacked any influence or power, simply turned themselves into cogs in the machine of a foreign espionage organization in the belief that their country could only be freed from Hitlerism through the victory of the Soviet Union over Germany.

Democratic opponents of Nazism can only regard this form of resistance as an unfortunate aberration. The work of the Schulze-Boysen/Harnack group on behalf of the Soviet Secret Service has therefore done more harm than good to the reputation of the German resistance movement. No country can allow its politically conscious citizens to become employees of a foreign espionage service.

Dramatis Personae

Arnould, Rita: Housekeeper. Courier for the Kent group in Brussels. Executed in 1943.

Barth, Robert: Journalist. Parachute agent. Liquidated in a concentration camp.

Beek, Cato Bontjes van: Dealer in ceramics. Member of Rittmeister's resistance group. Executed 5 August 1943.

Behrens, Karl: Engineer. Technical radio assistant to the Harnack group. Executed 13 May 1943.

Berg, Wilhelm: Criminal Police officer [Kriminalobersekretär]. On Giering's staff. Allegedly now in the service of the German Democratic Republic.

Berkowitz, Liane: Secretary. Member of Rittmeister's resistance group. Executed 5 August 1943.

Bessonov, Sergei: Counselor of Embassy. Recruiter for Razvedupr. Sentenced to 15 years' imprisonment in Moscow in 1938.

Böhme, Karl: Electrical mechanic. Constructed several sets for the Schulze-Boysen group. Executed 29 October 1943.

Breiter, Gertrud: Secretary employed in the Gestapo Head Office. Now lives in Lüneburg.

Brockdorff, Countess Erika von: Secretary. Assistant to Schulze-Boysen's radio group. Executed 13 May 1943.

Buch, Eva-Maria: Bookseller. Worked in Guddorf's resistance group. Executed 5 August 1943.

Buschmann, Dr. Hugo: Industrial manager. Friend of Schulze-Boysen. Lives in West Berlin.

Cointe, Suzanne: Secretary. Office manager of the Simex firm in Paris. Executed in 1943.

289

Coppi, Hans: Casual laborer. Radio operator of the Schulze-Boysen group. Executed 22 December 1942.

Corbin, Alfred: Businessman. Director of the Simex firm in Paris. Executed summer 1943.

Danilov, Anton: 2nd Lieutenant. Liaison officer for the Kent group in Brussels. Executed 1943.

Eifler, Erna: KPD functionary. Parachute agent. Executed.

Erdberg, Alexander: Secret service officer. Recruiter for Razvedupr in Berlin. Said to be living in East Berlin.

Fellendorf, Wilhelm: KPD functionary. Parachute agent. Executed.

Gehrts, Erwin: Colonel. Informer for Schulze-Boysen group. Executed 10 February 1943.

Giering, Karl: Criminal Police officer [Kriminalrat]. Head of Gestapo investigations into Rote Kapelle in Western Europe. Died in 1944.

Giraud, Pierre and Lucienne: Married couple. Assistant radio operators for the Gilbert group in Paris. Disappeared in 1946.

Goetze, Ursula: Student. Adherent of Rittmeister's resistance group. Executed 5 August 1943.

Gollnow, Herbert: Lieutenant. Informer for Harnack's group. Executed 12 February 1943.

Gollnow, Otto: Student. Adherent of Rittmeister's resistance group. Imprisoned and said to have emigrated to South America at the end of the war.

Grasse, Herbert: KPD functionary. Active in a number of communist resistance groups. Committed suicide while under detention on 24 October 1942.

Graudenz, Johann: Industrial representative. Informer for the Schulze-Boysen group. Executed 22 December 1942.

Grimme, Adolf: Ex-Minister of Culture. Member of the Harnack-Kuckhoff discussion group. Died in Degerndorf in 1963.

Griotto, Medardo: Engraver. Assistant to the Robinson group in Paris. Executed summer 1943.

Grossvogel, Leon: Businessman. Financial head of Rote Kapelle in France and Belgium. Executed 1944.

Guddorf, Wilhelm: KPD functionary. Leader in the Harnack group and decoder for Rote Kapelle, Berlin. Executed 13 May 1943.

Harnack, Dr. Arvid: Civil servant [Oberregierungsrat]. Head of the Harnack group and decoder for Rote Kapelle, Berlin. Executed 22 December 1942.

Harnack, Dr. Mildred: Lecturer. Assistant in her husband's group. Executed 16 February 1943.

Havemann, Dr. Wolfgang: Assistant judge. Harnack's nephew. Lives in East Berlin.

Heilmann, Horst: Corporal. Secretary and informer for the head of the Schulze-Boysen group. Executed 22 December 1942.

Henniger, Hans: Government Construction Inspector. Informer for the Schulze-Boysen group. Imprisoned. Killed on the Eastern Front in 1944.

Himpel, Dr. Hans Helmuth: Dentist. Member of the Schulze-Boysen group. Executed 13 May 1943.

Hössler, Albert: KPD functionary. Parachute agent. Executed.

Hoffmann-Scholtz, Anna-Margaret: Secretary. Informer for the Gilbert group in Paris. Lives in West Germany.

Hübner, Emil: Radio dealer. Contact man for the Soviet Secret Service. Executed 5 August 1943.

Husemann, Walter: KPD functionary. Member of a communist resistance group in Berlin. Executed 13 May 1943.

Isbutsky, Hermann: KPD functionary. Courier for the Kent group in Brussels. Executed 1943/4.

Jaspar, Jules: Businessman. Director of the "Foreign Excellent Trenchcoat" in Brussels. Lives in Belgium.

Katz, Hillel: Employee. Secretary to Trepper, the Resident Director. Executed 1944.

Kent, alias Victor Sukulov, alias Gurevich: Captain. Head of Brussels and Marseilles groups. Lives in Leningrad.

Koenen, Heinrich: KPD functionary. Parachute agent. Apparently disappeared at the end of the war.

Kopkow, Horst: Criminal Police officer [Kriminalrat]. In charge of Gestapo investigation into Rote Kapelle, Berlin. Lives in Gelsenkirchen.

Kraell, Dr. Alexander: President of a Chamber of the Reich Court Martial. In charge of the judicial proceedings against Rote Kapelle, Berlin. Died in West Germany during the 1950s.

Kraus, Anna: Fortune-teller. Informer for the Schulze-Boysen group. Executed 5 August 1943.

Krauss, Dr. Werner: University professor. Member of the Rittmeister resistance group. Lives in the German Democratic Republic.

Kruyt: Functionary of the Dutch Communist Party. Parachute agent. Executed 1943.

Küchenmeister, Walter: Journalist. Member of the Schulze-Boysen group. Executed 13 May 1943.

Kuckhoff, Dr. Adam: Author. Member of the Harnack group. Executed 5 August 1943.

Kuckhoff, Dr. Greta: KPD functionary. Member of the Harnack group. Lives in the German Democratic Republic.

Lautenschläger, Hans: Trade Union official. Member of the Schulze-Boysen group. Lives in the German Democratic Republic.

Makarov, Michail: Soviet Lieutenant. Radio operator for the Kent group in Brussels. Apparently disappeared at the end of the war.

Marquardt, Helmut: Technician. Assistant radio operator for

the Schulze-Boysen group. Lives in the German Peoples Republic.

Mathieu: Belgian police inspector. Informer for the German Abwehr in Brussels. Lives in Belgium.

Maximovich, Vassily and Anna: Brother and sister. Informers for the Gilbert group in Paris. Executed 1943.

Pannwitz, Heinz: Criminal police officer [Kriminalrat]. Directed the "radio playback" game with the help of converted Rote Kapelle agents. Lives in Ludwigsburg.

Panzinger, Friedrich: Civil servant [Regierungsdirektor]. Head of the Gestapo's "Rote Kapelle Special Commission." Committed suicide in 1959.

Paul, Dr. Elfriede: Doctor. Member of the Schulze-Boysen group. Lives in the German Democratic Republic.

Peper, Maurice: Employee. Courier for the Kent group in Brussels. Executed, probably in 1943.

Piepe, Harry: Captain. In charge of Abwehr investigations into Rote Kapelle in Western Europe. Lives in Hamburg.

Posnanska, Sophie: Secretary. Encoder for the Kent group in Brussels. Committed suicide while under detention in autumn 1942.

Raichman, Abraham: Engraver. Informer for the Kent group in Brussels. Sentenced to 25 years' hard labor by a Belgian court for collaboration with the Germans.

Rehmer, Fritz: Foreman fitter. Member of the Rittmeister resistance group. Executed 13 May 1943.

Rittmeister, Dr. John: Nerve specialist. Head of a resistance group in Berlin. Executed 13 May 1943.

Robinson, Henry: Comintern functionary. Head of a group of informers in France. Executed, probably 1943/4.

Roeder, Dr. Manfred: Judge Advocate-General. Prosecutor in the Rote Kapelle trials in Berlin, Brussels and Paris. Lives at Glashütten in the Taunus.

Schabbel, Klara: KPD functionary. Assistant to communist parachute agents. Executed 5 August 1943.

Schaeffer, Dr. Philip: Librarian. Member of the Schulze-Boysen group. Executed May 1943.

Scheel, Heinrich: Children's tutor. Member of the Schulze-Boysen group. Lives in East Berlin.

Schleif, Lotte: Librarian. Member of the Schulze-Boysen group. Lives in the German Democratic Republic.

Schlösinger, Rose: Employee. Assistant radio operator for the Harnack group. Executed 5 August 1943.

Schneider, Germaine: Secretary. Courier for the Kent group. Disappeared after the war.

Schottmüller, Oda: Dancer. Member of Schulze-Boysen's radio group. Executed 5 August 1943.

Schulze, Kurt: KPD functionary. Apprentice radio operator for the Schulze-Boysen group. Executed 22 December 1942.

Schulze-Boysen, Harro: Lieutenant. Head of the Schulze-Boysen/Harnack resistance and espionage organization. Executed 22 December 1942.

Schulze-Boysen, Libertas: Film scriptwriter. Member of her husband's organization. Executed 22 December 1942.

Schumacher, Kurt and Elizabeth: Married couple. Members of the Schulze-Boysen group. Executed 22 December 1942.

Schumacher, Otto: KPD functionary. Informer for the Gilbert group in France. Fate unknown.

Sieg, John: KPD functionary. Informer for the Harnack group. Committed suicide while under detention on 17 September 1942.

Sokol, Hersch and Myra: Married couple. Radio operators for the Gilbert group in Paris. Liquidated 1943.

Springer, Isidor: Businessman. Informer for the Kent group in Brussels. Committed suicide while under detention early in 1943.

Strelow, Heinz: Soldier. Worked with the Rittmeister and Schulze-Boysen groups. Executed 13 May 1943.

Terwiel, Rosemarie: Shorthand typist. Member of the Schulze-Boysen group. Executed 5 September 1943.

Thiel, Fritz: Foreman fitter. Member of the Rittmeister resistance group. Executed 13 May 1943.

Traxl, Alfred: Warrant officer. Informer for the Schulze-Boysen group. Imprisoned. Fate unknown.

Trepper, Leopold: Resident Director. Headed all Rote Kapelle groups in Western Europe. Lives in Warsaw.

Weisenborn, Günther: Author. Member of the Schulze-Boysen group. Died in Berlin-Charlottenburg in 1969.

Wenzel, Johann: Functionary. Technical radio head of all Rote Kapelle groups in Western Europe. Lives in the German Democratic Republic.

Wesolek, Stanislaus and Frieda: Married couple. Assistants to Soviet parachute agents in Berlin. Executed 5 August 1943.

Winterinck, Anton: Communist Party functionary. Head of the "Hilda" group in Amsterdam. Disappeared at the end of the war.

Yefremov, Konstantin: Military Engineer Third Class. Head of the "Bordo" group in Brussels. Escaped to South America at the end of the war.

Codenames and Cover Names

Alta	Ilse Stöbe
Arier	Rudolf von Scheliha
Arwid	Arvid Harnack
Bauer	Adam Kuckhoff
Bordo	Yefremov
Carlos	Mathieu
Choro	Harro Schulze-Boysen
Dora	Alexander Rado (and the Swiss circuit)
Gilbert	Trepper
Grand Chef	Trepper
Harry	Robinson
Hermann	Johann Wenzel
Herta	Yelena Stassover.
Hilda	The Dutch circuit
Juzefa	Sophie Posnanska
Lunette	Isbutsky
Manufacturer	Abraham Raichman
Otto	Trepper
Pakbo	Otto Pünter
Petit Chef	Kent (Sukulov—Gurevich)
Richard	Arthur Illner
Schmetterling	Germaine Schneider
Sierra (Vincente)	Kent
Strahlmann	Hans Coppi
Tino	Anton Winterinck
Verlinden (Anna)	Sophie Posnanska
Wassermann	Peper

Glossary

Abschnitt	A regional subdivision of the territorial organization of the SS.
Abwehr (full title Amt Ausland/Abwehr)	Military Intelligence. The Espionage, Counter-espionage and Sabotage Service of the German High Command.
AM	"Anti-militarist" apparat. A communist organization in Germany in the late 1920s, the primary object of which was to infiltrate the police, the army and opposition parties.
Ausland SD	The "external" branch of the SD (Sicherdienst) (q.v.).
BB	"Betriebsberichterstattung" — the "reports section" of the AM (q.v.). Later an independent apparat.
Brigadeführer	An SS rank equivalent to Major-General.
Cheka	Title of the Soviet Secret Police in the post-revolution period.
Chi—Chiffrierwesen	The German coding and cipher service. Part of WNV (q.v.).
Comintern	Communist International formed in 1919.
EKKI—Exekutiv-komite	The Executive Committee of the Comintern.
Fu—Funk	Radio.

295

Funkabteilung	Radio Section of WNV (q.v.).
Funkabwehr	Radio counter-espionage or Signals Security.
GBN—Generalbevollmächtigter für technishe Nachrichtenmittel	[lit: General Plenipotentiary for Technical Signals Resources]. An agency of WNV.
Generaloberstabsrichter } Generalrichter Generalstabsrichter	Ranks in the German Military Legal Service corresponding roughly to Judge Advocate or Judge Advocate-General.
Gesandschaftsrat	[lit: Legation Counselor]. A rank in the German Foreign Service.
Gestapa-Geheimes Staatspolizeiamt	Secret State Police Office. The Headquarters of the Gestapo.
Gestapo-Geheime Staatspolizei	The Secret State Police—later Branch IV of the RSHA (q.v.). Its head was Heinrich Müller ("Gestapo Müller").
GPU	"State Political Administration." Title of Russian Secret Police from 1922.
Gruppenführer	An SS rank equivalent to Lieutenant-General.
GUGB	"Supreme Administration for State Security." Title of Russian Secret Police from the time of the Stalin purges in 1934.
Hauptsturmführer	An SS rank equivalent to Captain.
Inland SD	The "internal" branch of the SD (Sicherdienst) (q.v.).
Inostranni	The foreign department of the GPU.
KPD—Kommunistische Partei Deutschlands	The German Communist Party.
Kriegsgerichtsrat	Legal officer of a Court Martial.
Kriminaldirektor Kriminalrat Kriminalinspektor Kriminalkommissar Kriminalobersekretär Kriminalsekretär Kriminaloberassistent Kriminalassistent	Ranks in the Security and Criminal Police given here in order of seniority. Officers down to Kriminalrat (incl.) ranked as "most senior," those down to Kriminalkommissar (incl.) as "senior" and those down to Kriminalsekretär as "medium-level."
Landgerichtsdirektor	Clerk of a County or District Court.
Landgerichtsrat	Attorney of a County or Provincial Court.

M (military) apparat	An activist communist organization in Germany in the 1920s.
Militärverwaltungs(ober)rat	An official of Military Administration in occupied territory.
MP (military-political) apparat	A subversive communist organization in Germany in the 1920s.
N (Nachrichten— intelligence) apparat	Communist organization in Germany in the 1920s.
NKVD	The Peoples Commissariat of the Interior in the Soviet Union.
Oberführer	An SS rank equivalent to Brigadier.
Obergruppenführer	An SS rank equivalent to General.
Oberregierungsrat	A rank in the civil service or the police equivalent to Kriminalrat or Lieutenant-Colonel.
Oberreichskriegsanwalt	A senior attorney in the Military Legal Service.
Oberstaatsanwalt	A Public Prosecutor of a civil court.
Obersturmbannführer	An SS rank equivalent to Lieutenant-Colonel.
OKH (Oberkommando des Heeres)	The High Command of the German Army.
Okhrana	Title of Russian Security Service in the late Czarist period.
OKW (Oberkommando der Wehrmacht)	The High Command of the German Armed Forces.
OMS	"International Liaison Department." The executive organ of the Comintern.
OO (Osobyi Otdjel)	A special division of the Russian GPU dealing with counter-espionage and intelligence.
Ordnungspolizei (Orpo)	The regular uniformed police in Germany.
OT—Organisation Todt	A semi-military German government agency established in 1933 for the construction of strategic highways and military installations.
OUN	Organization of Ukrainian Nationalists. A Russian émigré organization active before the war.
Razvedupr (Glavno Razvedyvatelno Upravlenie)	"Chief Intelligence Administration." The first title of the Russian Military Secret Service after the Revolution.

Regierungspräsident	The senior government official of a district in Germany.
Regierungsrat	Government Counselor. The most junior rank in the Higher Civil Service.
Reichsführer	Himmler's title as head of the SS.
Reichskriminaldirektor	The most senior rank in the Criminal Police—held by Müller as Head of the Gestapo.
RKG—Reichskriegsgericht	The Reich Court Martial. The most senior military court in Germany.
RO (Razvedky Otdjel)	A counter-espionage agency of the Red Army in the late 1930s.
RSHA—Reichssicher-heitshauptamt	Reich Central Security Department. Formed in 1939. Combined the Security Police (Gestapo and Criminal Police) and the SS Security Service (SD).
Schutzpolizei	The regular uniformed municipal and county constabulary.
SD (Sicherheitsdienst)	The Security Service of the SS formed in 1932.
Sicherheitspolizei (Sipo)	The Security Police comprising the Gestapo and the Criminal Police.
Standartenführer	An SS rank equivalent to Colonel.
Sturmbannführer	An SS rank equivalent to Major.
T (Terror) Apparat	A communist terrorist organization in Germany in the 1920s.
Untersturmführer	An SS rank equivalent to 2nd Lieutenant.
VVN—Vereinigung der Verfolgten des Nazi-regimes	"Association of Victims of the Nazi regime." An association formed in East Berlin after the war.
WEB—West European Bureau	A Comintern intelligence and operations agency in Berlin in the 1920s.
WNV—Wehrmachtnach-richtenverbindungen—Wehrmacht Intelligence Communications	The branch of the OKW Operations Staff responsible for all signals, radio and communications matters.
Z (Zersetzungs—subversion) apparat	A communist subversive organization in Germany in the 1920s.

Notes

Prologue

1. Otto Pünter: *Der Anschluss fand nicht statt*, pp. 141–2.
2. Winfried Martini: "Deutsche Spionage für Moskau 1939 bis 1945" in *Die Welt*, 20 October 1966.
3. David Dallin: *Soviet Espionage*, p. 4 et seq.
4. M. Azarov: "Peresypkin, Ivan Terenchevich" in *Porträts der UdSSR-Prominenz* [Sketches of Soviet Union Personalities] edited by the *Institut zur Erforschung der UdSSR* [Research Institute for the USSR], Munich, April 1960.
5. Collection of Soviet radio messages in the papers of Wilhelm F. Flicke (hereafter referred to as "Flicke collection"), p. 19; private collection, the owner of which wishes to remain anonymous.
6. Flicke Collection, p. 28.
7. Report by the Chief of the Security Police and SD, IV A 2-B dated 22 December 1942 (hereafter referred to as "Gestapo Final Report"), p. 7—copy in the archives of *Der Spiegel*.
8. Gilles Perrault: *L'Orchestre rouge*, p. 11.
9. Dallin: op. cit., p. 247 et seq.
10. Gestapo Final Report, pp. 5 and 2.
11. Dallin: op. cit., p. 167 et seq.
12. Ibid, p. 171 et seq.
13. Verbally from Harry Piepe, 14 March 1968.
14. Ibid.
15. Ibid; Dallin: op. cit., pp. 258–9.
16. Statement by Frau Marie-Louise Schulze on 5 December 1948 contained in the Final Report by the Public Prosecutor, Dr. Finck, on the case against the Luftwaffe Judge-Advocate Dr. Manfred

Roeder (hereafter referred to as "Roeder Final Report"), p. 555—in *Der Spiegel* archives.

17. Statement by Frau Schulze, Roeder Final Report, p. 556.

18. Statement on oath by Dr. Falk Harnack, 11 June 1948 —Roeder Final Report, p. 465.

19. From Piepe.

20. Text in letter dated 10 August 1941 from SS-Gruppenführer Heydrich to all Security Police and SD Commanders—files of the Personal Staff of the Reichsführer-SS and Chief of the German Police (hereafter referred to as RFSS), microfilm 72; Wilhelm von Schramm: *Verrat im Zweiten Weltkrieg*, p. 139.

21. From Piepe.

22. Verbal information from Heinrich Reiser, 4 March 1968.

23. Letter from SS-Gruppenführer Müller to Himmler 22 December 1942, RFSS microfilm 129.

24. "Die Katze im Kreml" in *Kristall*, No. 25 of 1950 to No. 8 of 1951.

25. Ibid.

26. "Das Geheimnis der Roten Kapelle," *Norddeutsche Rundschau*, 24 January to 20 February 1951.

27. "Rote Agenten mitten unter uns," *Stern*, 6 May to 1 July 1951.

28. "Frauen im roten Spiel," *Heidebote*, Lüneburg 1951.

29. "Eine Armee stirbt durch Verrat," *Der Hausfreund für Stadt und Land*, November–December 1953.

30. English translation: *The Secret War against Hitler*, Chap. 13.

31. Eugen Rentsch Verlag, Erlenbach-Zurich 1947.

32. Klaus Lehmann: Widerstandsgruppe Schulze-Boysen/Harnack, VVN-Verlag, East Berlin 1948.

33. Yale University Press, New Haven; Geoffrey Cumberledge, Oxford University Press, London.

34. Gilles Perrault: *L'Orchestre rouge*, Fayard, Paris 1967.

35. Deutsche Presse-Agentur, Information 1092, 5 September 1950.

36. *Die Reichszeitung*, 3 June 1951.

37. Ibid, 5 May 1951.

38. *Der Hausfreund für Stadt und Land*, 21 November 1953.

39. Richard Wilmer Rowan and Robert G. Deindorfer: *Secret Service*, p. 692.

40. Günther Weisenborn: "Im Widerstand" in *Adolf Grimme, Briefe*, p. 58.

41. *Die andere Zeitung*, 21 December 1961.

42. Letter from André Moyen, 8 July 1968.

43. *Der Journalist*, June 1952.

44. Gerald Reitlinger: *The SS*, p. 231.

45. Pechel: op. cit., p. 88.

46. Karl Balzer: *Der 20 Juli und der Landesverrat*, p. 246.

47. Information from Reiser.

48. Dallin: op. cit., pp. ix et seq., 139; see also the record of Roeder's interrogation by Robert M. W. Kempner on 30 June 1947 and Mr. Rodell on 9 July 1948—in Kempner's papers and *Der Spiegel* archives.

49. Information from Reiser.

50. Ibid.

51. Roeder Final Report, p. 76.

52. Grimme: op. cit., p. 162.

53. *Neues Deutschland*, 12 April 1947.

54. Roeder Final Report, pp. 76, 82.

55. Roeder Final Report, p. 78.

56. Ibid, pp. 89–90.

57. *Der Tagesspiegel*, 5 June 1948.

58. *Tägliche Rundschau*, 6 May 1951.

59. Letter from Professor Heilmann to Pastor Harald Pölchau, 22 June 1948—in Heilmann's private papers.

60. *Neues Deutschland*, 12 April 1947.

61. Roeder Final Report, pp. 2–3.

62. Ibid, pp. 82–3.

63. Letter from the Berlin Public Prosecutor to Professor Robert M. W. Kempner, 14 January 1948—in Kempner's private papers.

64. Letter from Secretary-General of the VVN to Professor Heilmann, 7 June 1948—in Heilmann's private papers.

65. Roeder Final Report, p. 618.

66. Letter from Professor Heilmann to the VVN, 7 June 1948—in Heilmann's private papers.

67. Roeder Final Report, p. 621.

68. Ibid, p. 622.

69. Ibid.

70. Ibid, p. 463.

71. Ibid.

72. Ibid.

73. Statement by Dr. Otto Krapp, Minister of Justice of Lower Saxony—*Frankfurter Allgemeine Zeitung*, 16 November 1951.

74. From a conversation with the Anglo-German writer Heinrich Fraenkel—verbal information from Fraenkel 15 June 1968.

75. Günther Weisenborn: *Der lautlose Aufstand*, p. 203 et seq.; see also Weisenborn: *Memorial*.

76. Letter mid-1951 from Grimme to his friend Hans Friedrich—see Grimme: op. cit., pp. 160–1.

77. *Der Mittag*, 12 February 1953.

78. Dallin: op. cit., pp. 143, 154.

79. Paul Leverkuehn: *Der geheime Nachrichtendienst der deutschen Wehrmacht im Kriege*, p. 149.

80. Flicke: *Agenten funken nach Moskau*, p. 24.

81. Dallin: op. cit., p. 287.

82. Schramm: op. cit., p. 152.

83. Philip W. Fabry: "War Verrat im Spiel?" German Radio, 2 July 1968 (script).

84. Dallin: op. cit., pp. 267, 152, 516.

85. Perrault: op. cit., p. 118.

86. Hans Rothfels: *Die deutsche Opposition gegen Hitler*, p. 18.

87. Helmut Heiber: *Hitlers Lagebesprechungen*, p. 150.

88. Egmont Zechlin: Arvid und Mildred Harnack zum Gedächtnis, pp. 4–5—in Zechlin's private papers.

89. Erich Kern: *Verrat an Deutschland*.

90. *Deutsche National-Zeitung*, 10 February 1967.

91. *Die Reichszeitung*, 5 May 1951.

92. Balzer: op. cit., p. 246.

93. Ibid, p. 261.

94. Paul Carell: *Scorched Earth*, p. 102 et seq.

95. *Der Hausfreund für Land und Stadt*, 21 November 1953.

96. Gestapo Final Report, p. 16.

97. Grimme: op. cit., p. 161; copy of sentence on Grimme on 4 May 1943—in Grimme's private papers.

98. Grimme: op. cit., p. 161.

99. Memorandum by the lawyer Dr. Noack in the case against Keller, 8 February 1952—in Wolfgang Müller's private papers.

100. Günther Weisenborn—address on the German resistance movement pubished in *Aufbau*, No. 6 of 1946, pp. 576–8.

101. Greta Kuckhoff: "Ein Abschnitt des deutschen Widerstandskampfes" in *Die Weltbühne*, No. 3/4 of 1948, pp. 61–2–3.

102. Günther Weisenborn: *Die Illegalen*, p. 59.

103. Ibid, p. 64.

104. Weisenborn's draft of a pamphlet on the Schulze-Boysen/Harnack group, used by Klaus Lehmann as the basis for his VVN article; Roeder Final Report, pp. 120, 128, 151.

105. Memorandum by Frau Kuckhoff for Weisenborn, originally intended for the poetess Ricarda Huch; Roeder Final Report, p. 249.

106. Greta Kuckhoff: op. cit., p. 61.

107. Roeder Final Report, p. 249.

108. Greta Kuckhoff: op. cit., p. 62.

109. *Neues Deutschland*, 10 October 1969.

110. Ibid.

111. Ibid, 22 December 1967.

112. *Junge Welt*, 22 December 1967.

113. *Für Dich*, 2 March 1968.

114. *Pravda*, 1–5 July 1967.

Chapter One

1. George F. Kennan: *Russia and the West under Lenin and Stalin*, p. 152; Ruth Fischer: *Stalin und der deutsche Kommunismus*, p. 65.

2. Kennan: op. cit., p. 207.

3. W. Nicolai: *Geheime Mächte*, p. 17.

4. See E. H. Cookridge: *Soviet Spy Net*, p. 9 et seq.; on the political and sociological standing of Section Three see Arthur von Brauer: *Im Dienste Bismarcks*, p. 72 et seq.; on the history of the Russian Secret Service as seen from the Nazi standpoint see Gestapo internal memorandum by Kriminalkommissar Wendzio, probably about 1937, entitled "Politische Polizei" in Files of the Personal Staff of the Reichsführer-SS and Chief of the German Police (henceforth referred to as RFSS), microfilm 432.

5. Nicolai: op. cit., p. 18.

6. Ibid, p. 31.

7. Ibid.

8. Ibid, p. 32.

9. David Kahn: *The Codebreakers*, p. 621.

10. Nicolai: op. cit., p. 33.

11. Ibid, p. 19.

12. Ibid, p. 88.

13. On the Russian civil war

see B. H. Liddell Hart: *The Soviet Army* (Weidenfeld & Nicolson 1956), pp. 33–44.

14. David J. Dallin: *Soviet Espionage*, p. 4.

15. See Adolf Ehrt: *Bewaffneter Aufstand*, p. 67; also Kyrill D. Kalinov: *Sowjetmarschälle haben das Wort*, p. 24.

16. *Junge Welt*, East Berlin, 23 December 1964.

17. Dallin: op. cit., pp. 4, 46.

18. Cookridge: op. cit., p. 45.

19. Dallin: op. cit., p. 4.

20. Unsigned memorandum on organization and duties of the Soviet intelligence service [Organization and Aufgabenbereich des sowjetischen Nachrichtendienstes], pp. 1–2—in archives of *Der Spiegel*.

21. Dallin: op. cit., p. 5.

22. Kahn: op. cit., p. 643.

23. Dallin: op. cit. p. 5.

24. Cookridge: op. cit., p. 114.

25. Ibid, p. 123.

26. Ibid.

27. Ibid, p. 114.

28. Extracts from and photographs of logbooks in Cookridge: op. cit., pp. 118–19 and following p. 128.

29. Ibid, p. 124.

30. Dallin: op. cit., p. 7 et seq.

31. Ibid, p. 9.

32. Ibid.

33. Ibid.

34. Ehrt: op. cit., p. 36.

35. Cookridge: op. cit., p. 122.

36. Dallin: op. cit., p. 43 et seq.

37. Cookridge: op. cit., p. 10.

38. Anonymous article "Die sowjetischen Sicherheitsorgane" in *Das Parlament*, 2 December 1959, p. 665.

39. Ibid, p. 667.

40. Study of Soviet counterespionage organization in "Politische Informationen" issued by RSHA Information Service 15 April 1944—15 January 1945, p. 2, RFSS microfilm 222.

41. Ibid.

42. Kahn: op. cit., p. 640.

43. Ibid, p. 641 (Note).

44. Dallin: op. cit., pp. 2–4.

45. Ibid.

46. Ibid, p. 4.

47. Ibid, p. 6.

48. Fischer: op. cit., p. 121.

49. Ibid.

50. Günther Nollau: *Die Internationale*, p. 104 et seq.

51. Ibid, p. 105.

52. Erich Wollenberg: *Der Apparat*, p. 9.

53. Principles and statutes of the Communist International, decision by the Second Congress of the Communist International in Moscow, 17 July–7 August 1920, p. 19.

54. Nollau: op. cit., pp. 128, 130.

55. Ibid, p. 130.

56. Ibid, p. 108; Fischer: op. cit., p. 440.

57. Ibid, p. 112.

58. Dallin: op. cit., p. 78; Fischer: op. cit., p. 388.

59. Nollau: op. cit., p. 108.

60. Ibid, p. 144.

61. Fischer: op. cit., p. 57.

62. Ibid, p. 250.

63. Ibid, p. 164.

64. Ibid.

65. Ibid.

66. Wollenberg: op. cit., p. 9.

67. Fischer: op. cit., p. 211.

68. Ibid, p. 69; Wollenberg: op. cit., p. 8.

69. Wollenberg: op. cit., p. 8.

70. Ibid, p. 9.

71. Ibid.

72. Ibid.

73. Cookridge: op. cit., p. 27.

74. Nollau: op. cit., p. 113.

75. Jan Valtin (alias Richard Krebs): *Tagebuch der Hölle*, p. 116.

76. Nollau: op. cit., p. 116.

77. A. M. Pankratova: "Der Ruhrkonflikt" in W. P. Potyomkin's *Geschichte der Diplomatie*, Vol. III, p. 294.

78. W. G. Krivitsky: *Agent de Staline*, p. 58.

79. Krivitsky: op. cit., p. 59.

80. Ibid.

81. Wollenberg: op. cit., p. 11.

82. Wilhelm Bauer: *Die Tätigkeit des BB-Apparates der KPD*, p. 3.

83. Section P of Prussian Ministry of State, files concerning the communist movement, Vol. 4 (situation as at 31 May 1935), No. 615—in Wilhelm Bauer's papers.

84. Dallin: op. cit., p. 88.

85. Walter Zeutschel (alias Adolf Burmeister): *Im Dienst der kommunistischen Terror-Organisation*, p. 20.

86. Krivitsky: op. cit., p. 59.

87. Fischer: op. cit., p. 212.

88. Fischer: op. cit., p. 396.

89. Wollenberg: op. cit., p. 10.

90. Ibid; Fischer: op. cit., p. 395.

91. Nollau: op. cit., p. 105.

92. Fischer: op. cit., p. 395.

93. See supplement to register of fugitive communists issued by the Gestapa on 10 June 1936 in Wilhelm Bauer's papers; also Wollenberg: op. cit., p. 10.

94. Zeutschel: op. cit., p. 13.

95. Ibid, p. 16 et seq.

96. Ibid, p. 24.

97. Ibid, p. 32.

98. Wollenberg: op. cit., p. 11; *Kölnische Zeitung*, 17 February 1925.

99. *Kölnische Zeitung*, 17 February 1925.

100. Wollenberg: op. cit., p. 11; Zeutschel: op. cit., p. 32 et seq.; *Kölnische Zeitung*, 17, 19, 24 February 1925.

101. Zeutschel: op. cit., 65; Fischer: op. cit., p. 395; *Kölnische Zeitung*, 23 February 1925.

102. Fischer: op. cit., p. 396; Zeutschel: op. cit., p. 65.

103. Zeutschel: op. cit., p. 66.

104. Ibid.

105. Ibid, p. 56 et seq.

106. Ibid, p. 67.

107. Ibid, p. 68.

108. Ibid, p. 133; Wollenberg: op. cit., p. 10.

109. Krivitsky: op. cit., p. 68.

110. Fischer: op. cit., p. 619.

111. Wollenberg: op. cit., p. 13.

112. Fischer: op. cit., p. 619; for the history of the Lenin School see Nollau: op. cit., p. 138.

113. Wollenberg: op. cit., p. 13.

114. Ibid, p. 14.

115. Ibid, p. 15.

116. Ibid, p. 46.

117. Ibid, p. 13.

118. Among them was Wilhelm Zaisser who was instrumental in instigating the communist revolt in Canton in 1927—Political Archives, OKP 009, August 1953. In 1929 Dr. Richard Sorge, Berzin's most illustrious pupil, followed Zaisser to Shanghai: he had first been in the M-Apparat, then the OMS and finally transferred to Razvedupr—*Neues*

Deutschland, 18 October 1964.

119. Dallin: op. cit., p. 76.

120. Zeutschel: op. cit., p. 89; *Kölnische Zeitung,* 5 May 1924; "Important Russian organizations and agencies in Germany," instructional pamphlet issued by the Police Institute Berlin–Charlottenburg for the 1933–4 course—in Lothar Heimbach's papers.

121. Dallin: op. cit., p. 78.

122. Ibid.

123. Ibid, p. 81.

124. Ibid, p. 78.

125. Ibid, p. 81.

126. Ibid, p. 79.

127. Ibid, p. 86; "Important Russian organizations and agencies in Germany."

128. "Important Russian organizations etc."

129. Fischer: op. cit., p. 624.

130. Dallin: op. cit., p. 92.

131. Ibid.

132. Ibid, p. 98.

133. Wollenberg: op. cit., p. 14.

134. Ibid; Bauer: op. cit., p. 2.

135. Bauer: op. cit., p. 2.

136. "Der BB Apparat"—report by the Gestapo, 22 March 1937, p. 11; in Bauer's papers.

137. Dallin: op. cit., pp. 83–4.

138. Ibid, p. 50 et seq.

139. Ibid, p. 51.

140. Ibid, p. 52.

141. Bauer: op. cit., p. 3.

142. Dallin: op. cit., p. 114.

143. Ibid, p. 113.

144. Ehrt: op. cit., p. 59.

145. Ibid, p. 148.

146. Wollenberg: op. cit., p. 14.

147. Dallin: op. cit., pp. 82–3.

148. Ibid, p. 83.

149. Ibid, p. 86.

150. Bauer: op. cit., p. 4.

151. Ibid.

152. Dallin: op. cit., p. 109.

153. Ehrt: op. cit., p. 64.

154. Dallin: op. cit., p. 107.

155. Valtin: op. cit., p. 164.

156. Wollenberg: op. cit., p. 14.

157. Fischer: op. cit., p. 620.

158. Bauer: op. cit., p. 2.

159. Ehrt: op. cit., p. 61.

160. Dallin: op. cit., p. 105.

161. Ibid.

162. Ibid, p. 130.

163. *Kölnische Zeitung,* 14 April 1931.

164. Ehrt: op cit., p. 61.

165. Ibid.

166. Ibid, p. 64.

167. Dallin: op. cit., p. 92.

168. Ibid, p. 29.

169. Valtin: op. cit., p. 165.

170. Dallin: op. cit., p. 110.

171. *Kölnische Zeitung,* 5 May 1924.

172. Zeutschel: op. cit., p. 88.

173. *Kölnische Zeitung,* 5 May 1924.

174. Zeutschel: op. cit., p. 89.

175. *Kölnische Zeitung,* 5 May 1924.

176. Ibid.

177. Ibid.

178. Hans Buchheim: *SS und Polizei im NS-Staat,* p. 32; Werner Best: *Die deutsche Abwehrpolizei bis 1945,* p. 24.

179. Ibid.

180. Gert Buchheit: *Der deutsche Geheimdienst,* p. 32.

181. Ibid, p. 33.

182. Ibid.

183. Ibid, p. 36.

184. Ibid.

185. Ibid.

186. Dallin: op. cit., p. 120.

187. Ibid, p. 103.

188. Nollau: op. cit., p. 116.

189. Valtin: op. cit., p. 199.

190. On the development of

the police in the Third Reich see Heinz Höhne: *The Order of the Death's Head*, p. 172 et seq.

191. Buchheim: op. cit., p. 32 et seq.

192. For the structure, expansion and staffing of the Gestapo see Shlomo Aronson: *Heydrich und die Anfänge des SD und der Gestapo (1931–1935)*, p. 288 et seq.

193. Höhne: op. cit., p. 183.

194. Ibid, p. 184.

195. Ibid, p. 185.

196. Ibid, p. 215.

197. Buchheim: op. cit., p. 34.

198. Ibid, p. 55.

199. Ibid, p. 65.

200. Buchheit: op. cit., p. 169; Best: op. cit., p. 27.

201. "Wesen der Geheimen Staatspolizei"—p. 1 of Gestapa memorandum of about 1937—RFSS microfilm 432.

202. Heinrich Himmler: *Die Schutzstaffel als antibolschewistische Kampforganisation*, p. 8.

203. Reinhard Heydrich: *Wandlungen unseres Kampfes*, p. 6.

204. Martin Broszat: "The Concentration Camps" in *Anatomy of the SS State*, p. 401.

205. Ibid, p. 403.

206. Ibid, p. 404.

207. Dallin: op. cit., p. 119.

208. Broszat: op. cit., p. 406.

209. Dallin: op. cit., p. 121.

210. Ibid.

211. Ibid, p. 120.

212. Speech by Himmler to the Prussian State Council—corrected manuscript of about 1936, p. 21, RFSS microfilm 89.

213. Lothar Heimbach: "Geheime Staatspolizei," monograph of January 1961, p. 21.

214. Ibid, p. 22.

215. "Der AM Apparat"—report by the Gestapa, 22 March 1937, p. 10.

216. Arthur Koestler: *Die Geheimschrift*, p. 12.

217. Dallin: op. cit., p. 119.

218. This also applied to the false papers Apparat—see Dallin: op. cit., p. 93.

219. "Lage und Tätigkeit des Marxismus," report by the Head of the SD for May/June 1934, p. 55, RFSS microfilm 415.

220. Wollenberg: op. cit., p. 16.

221. Case against Wilhelm Knöchel before the Peoples Court, p. 3—in Otto Schwardt's private papers.

222. Ibid, p. 4.

223. Ibid.

224. Ibid, p. 3.

225. Bauer: op. cit., p. 11.

226. Ibid, p. 6.

227. "Lage und Tätigkeit des Marxismus," p. 54.

228. Ibid, p. 55.

229. Letter from Heydrich to all Gestapo offices, 7 July 1938—RFSS microfilm 491.

230. Examples are to be found in the files on the communist movement maintained by section P of the Prussian State Ministry—in Wilhelm Bauer's papers.

231. Circular dated 16 August 1938 from Department III of the Gestapa entitled "Richtlinien für das abwehrpolizeiliche Fahndungswesen," p. 2 —RFSS microfilm 403.

232. Ibid.

233. Ibid.

234. Ibid, p. 6.

235. Ibid, p. 8.

236. Aronson: op. cit., pp. 129, 130, 305.

237. Höhne: op. cit., p. 177.

238. Aronson: op. cit., p. 130.

239. Ibid, p. 146.

240. Ibid, p. 306.

241. For biographical details of Panzinger see Chapter 5, p. 191 (footnote).

242. For biographical details of Giering see p. 109.

243. For biographical details of Kopkow see Chapter 5, p. 189 (footnote).

244. For biographical details of Strübing see Chapter 4, p. 124 (footnote).

245. Memorandum by Heydrich's staff of about summer 1939 entitled "Grundsätzliche Gedanken zur Neugliederung" (of Section II of the Gestapa), p. 8—RFSS microfilm 239.

246. Ibid.

247. Supplement to the register of fugitive communists issued by the Gestapa, 15 March 1937, p. 23.

248. Ibid, 7 September 1935, p. 8.

249. Ibid, 15 March 1937, p. 14.

250. Bauer: op. cit., p. 6.

251. Case against Knöchel, p. 4.

252. Bauer: op. cit., p. 6.

253. "Der BB Apparat"—report by the Gestapa 22 March 1937, p. 12.

254. Dallin: op. cit., p. 101.

255. "Die kommunistische Passfälscherorganisation"—report by the Gestapa, 22 March 1937, p. 8.

256. "Die Auswirkungen des VII-Weltkongresses" — report by the Gestapa, 22 March 1937, p. 4.

257. Ibid.

258. Dallin: op. cit., p. 123.

259. Case against Knöchel, p. 5.

260. Ibid.

261. Wollenberg: op. cit., p. 17.

262. Case against Knöchel, p. 9.

263. Ibid.

264. Dallin: op. cit., p. 122.

265. Ibid.

266. Ibid (Note).

267. Ibid, p. 123.

268. Nollau: op. cit., p. 116.

269. "Die kommunistische Passfälscherorganisation" (Note 255 above), p. 8.

270. Ibid; Dallin: op. cit., p. 124.

271. Anonymous: "Die sowjetischen Sicherheitsorgane," p. 668.

272. Ibid.

273. Leonard Shapiro: "Die grosse Säuberung" in Hart: op. cit., p. 74.

274. Nollau: op. cit., p. 150.

275. Dallin: op. cit., p. 137.

276. Nollau: op. cit., p. 152.

277. Ibid.

278. Shapiro: op. cit., p. 75.

279. *Murder International, Inc:* Hearings before the Subcommittee to investigate the administration of the Internal Security Act, 26 March 1965, p. 60.

280. Nollau: op. cit., p. 151.

281. Ibid.

282. Koestler: op. cit., p. 13.

283. Dallin: op. cit, p. 124.

284. Ibid.

285. *Murder International, Inc,* p. 61.

286. Ibid.

287. Ibid, p. vi.

288. Report by the Gestapa, 22 March 1937, p. 2.

Chapter Two

1. Stalin's speech to the 18th Congress of the Communist Party of the Soviet Union, 1939, in *The Soviet Army*, edited by B. H. Liddell-Hart, p. 265.

2. Alexander Orlov: *The Secret History of Stalin's Crimes*, p. 243.

3. Anonymous: "Die sowjetischen Sicherheitsorgane" in *Das Parlament*, 2 December 1959, p. 670; Boris Levitsky: *Vom Roten Terror zur sozialistischen Gesettzlichkeit*, p. 112.

4. Levitsky: op. cit., p. 115.

5. Ibid, p. 114.

6. Dallin: *Soviet Espionage*, pp. 137–8.

7. *Who's Who in the USSR*, 1961–2 edition, p. 584.

8. See *Porträts der UdSSR Prominenz* issued by Research Institute for the USSR, Munich, April 1960.

9. Counter-espionage section "Death to Spies" in Peoples Commissariat for Defense—see *Politische Informationen* issued by Information Service of the Reichssicherheitshauptamt [Reich Central Security Department], 15 December 1944–15 January 1945, p. 2—in files of the Personal Staff of the Reichsführer-SS and Chief of the German Police (henceforth referred to as RFSS), microfilm 222.

10. Ibid.

11. Dallin: op. cit., p. 14.

12. Report by Chief of the Security Police and SD to the Reichsführer-SS, 10 June 1941, in Walter Schellenberg: *Memoiren*, p. 380 (not in English translation).

13. David Kahn: *The Codebreakers*, p. 643.

14. Levitsky: op. cit., p. 129.

15. Kahn: op. cit., p. 643.

16. Levitsky: op. cit., p. 129.

17. Ibid.

18. Ibid.

19. Dallin: op. cit., p. 127.

20. Further details in Chapter 4 of this book.

21. *Neues Deutschland*, 18 October 1964.

22. See Chapter 4 of this book.

23. See Chapter 4 of this book.

24. John Nemo (pseudonym of a Gestapo official, name unknown): *Das rote Netz*, p. 7—in archives of *Der Spiegel*.

25. Dallin: op. cit., p. 138.

26. Nemo: op. cit., p. 7.

27. Günther Nollau: *Die Internationale*, p. 113.

28. W. F. Flicke: *Spionagegruppe Rote Kapelle*, p. 14.

29. Dallin: op. cit., p. 143.

30. Supplement to register of communist fugitives issued by the Gestapa, B-Nr. 5925/37g, 15 March 1937—in Wilhelm Bauer's papers.

31. Wenzel was allotted to the apparat of the West German BB representative, Hans Israel, who was sentenced to life imprisonment by the First Chamber of the Peoples Court on 7 September 1936; see Wilhelm Bauer: *Die Tätigkeit des BB-Apparates der KPD*, p. 6 —in Bauer's papers.

32. Report by Chief of the Security Police and SD, IV A 2-B, No 330/42 dated 22 December 1942 (henceforth re-

ferred to as "Gestapo Final Report"), p. 4.

33. Ibid.

34. Dallin: op. cit., p. 143.

35. Gestapo Final Report, p. 4.

36. Ibid, p. 3.

37. Dallin: op. cit., p. 143; Gilles Perrault: *L'Orchestre Rouge*, p. 154.

38. Dallin: op. cit., p. 143.

39. Nemo: op. cit., p. 10; Gestapo Final Report, p. 3.

40. Capitaine "Freddy" (André Moyen): "La Verité sur Rote Kapelle" in *Europe-Amérique*, 2 October 1947, p. 15; Dallin: op. cit., p. 142.

41. Perrault: op. cit., p. 132.

42. Capitaine "Freddy": op. cit., p. 15.

43. Nemo: op. cit., p. 10.

44. Ibid.

45. Dallin: op. cit., pp. 143–4.

46. Ibid, pp. 141–2.

47. Gestapo Final Report, p. 2.

48. Dallin: op. cit., p. 141.

49. Gestapo Final Report, p. 3.

50. Perrault: op. cit., pp. 44–5.

51. Telegram from SS-Obersturmbannführer Dr. Albath of Gestapo office Düsseldorf to Kriminalrat Kopkow in Berlin, 11 September 1942—in archives of *Der Spiegel*.

52. Ibid.

53. Perrault: op. cit., p. 108.

54. Ibid, pp. 44–5.

55. Nemo: op. cit., p. 12.

56. Telegram from Albath to Kopkow (see Note 51).

57. Perrault: op. cit., p. 44.

58. Dallin: op. cit., p. 141.

59. Perrault: op. cit., p. 43.

60. Ibid, p. 45.

61. Nemo: op. cit., p. 10; Dallin: op. cit., pp. 140–1.

62. Dallin: op. cit., p. 140.

63. Gestapo Final Report, p. 2.

64. Nemo: op. cit., p. 12.

65. Ibid., p. 9.

66. Ibid, p. 11.

67. Gestapo Final Report, p. 3.

68. Dallin: op. cit., pp. 139–40.

69. Perrault: op. cit., pp. 11–12.

70. Dallin: op. cit., p. 139.

71. Nemo: op. cit., p. 7.

72. Perrault: op. cit., p. 13.

73. Ibid, p. 14.

74. Note on Broide Sarah Maya in *Der Spiegel* archives; Perrault: op. cit., p. 18.

75. Dallin: op. cit., p. 143.

76. Nemo: op. cit., p. 9.

77. Dallin: op. cit., p. 55.

78. Nemo: op. cit., p. 9.

79. Dallin: op. cit., p. 54.

80. Ibid, p. 55.

81. Ibid.

82. Perrault: op. cit., p. 14.

83. Dallin: op. cit., p. 54.

84. Ibid, p. 56.

85. Perrault: op. cit., p. 16.

86. Dallin: op. cit., p. 56.

87. Ibid.

88. Perrault: op. cit., p. 17.

89. Ibid.

90. Nemo: op. cit., p. 7.

91. Dallin: op. cit., p. 56.

92. Perrault: op. cit., p. 17.

93. Dallin: op. cit., p. 56; Perrault: op. cit., p. 18.

94. Perrault: op. cit., p. 18.

95. Dallin: op. cit., pp. 139–40.

96. Nemo: op. cit., p. 9.

97. Ibid, p. 7.

98. Perrault: op. cit., p. 23.

99. Nemo: op. cit., p. 8.

100. Dallin: op. cit., p. 142.

101. Nemo: op. cit., p. 8.

102. Dallin: op. cit., p. 142.

103. Ibid.
104. Ibid.
105. Ibid.
106. Gestapo Final Report, p. 2.
107. Ibid; Nemo: op. cit., p. 9.
108. Nemo: op. cit., p. 8.
109. Perrault: op. cit., p. 23.
110. Ibid; Dallin: op. cit., p. 145.
111. Dallin: op. cit., p. 146.
112. Perrault: op. cit., p. 29.
113. Ibid, p. 59; Gestapo Final Report, p. 5; Nemo: op. cit., p. 9.
114. Ibid, p. 59; Gestapo Final Report, p. 5.
115. Ibid, p. 43.
116. Telegram from Albath to Kopkow, 11 September 1942; Dallin: op. cit., p. 142.
117. Nemo: op. cit., p. 5.
118. Dallin: op. cit., p. 143.
119. Nemo: op. cit., p. 10.
120. Gestapo Final Report, p. 3.
121. Dallin: op. cit., p. 142.
122. Nemo: op. cit., p. 15.
123. Gestapo Final Report, p. 4.
124. Capitaine "Freddy": op. cit., p. 15.
125. Gestapo Final Report, p. 3.
126. Perrault: op. cit., p. 44.
127. Gestapo Final Report, p. 4.
128. Nollau: op. cit., p. 113.
129. Gestapo Final Report, p. 4.
130. State Prosecutor's case for the prosecution against Wilhelm Knöchel before the Peoples Court in 1943—in Otto Schwardt's papers.
131. Ibid.
132. Dallin: op. cit., p. 144.
133. Ibid.
134. Gestapo Final Report, p. 4.
135. Ibid.
136. Ibid.
137. Ibid.
138. Ibid, p. 2.
139. Dallin: op. cit., p. 141.
140. Perrault: op. cit., p. 172.
141. Perrault: op. cit., p. 31.
142. Ibid, p. 44.
143. Ibid.
144. Ibid.
145. Ibid, p. 31.
146. Dallin: op. cit., p. 140.
147. Ibid, p. 144.
148. Perrault: op. cit., p. 35.
149. Gestapo Final Report, p. 2; verbal information from Harry Piepe, 14 March 1968 (henceforth referred to as "from Piepe"); Dallin: op. cit., p. 142.
150. Dallin: op. cit., p. 142; also from Piepe.
151. Perrault: op. cit., pp. 38–9.
152. Ibid, p. 38.
153. Ibid, pp. 45–6.
154. Nemo: op. cit., p. 10.
155. Perrault: op. cit., p. 42.
156. Ibid; note on Broide Sarah Maya in Der Spiegel archives.
157. Report by Chief of Security Police and SD to the Reichsführer-SS, 24 December 1942, p. 4, given in Wilhelm von Schramm: Verrat im Zweiten Weltkrieg, p. 369.
158. Dallin: op. cit., p. 145.
159. Ibid.
160. For further details on Klara and Leo Schabbel see Chapter 5 of this book.
161. Report to Reichsführer-SS (Note 157 above), p. 5.
162. Dallin: op. cit., pp. 158–9.
163. Ibid.

164. Ibid, p. 159.
165. Dallin: op. cit., p. 161.
166. Ibid, p. 160; Report to Reichsführer-SS, 24 December 1942, p. 5.
167. Report to Reichsführer-SS, p. 5.
168. Hans Umbreit: *Der Militärbefehlshaber in Frankreich 1940–1944*, p. 36; also Kuprian's personal history in archives of *Der Spiegel*.
169. Report to Reichsführer-SS, 24 December 1942, p. 6.
170. Dallin: op. cit., p. 160.
171. Nemo: op. cit., p. 14.
172. Ibid; Perrault: op. cit., p. 169 et seq.
173. Perrault: op. cit., p. 39.
174. Nemo: op. cit., p. 9.
175. Ibid; Perrault: op. cit., p. 172.
176. Nemo: op. cit., p. 9.
177. Perrault: op. cit., p. 39.
178. Dallin: op. cit., p. 146.
179. Perrault: op. cit., p. 169.
180. Ibid.
181. Ibid, p. 170.
182. Gestapo Final Report, p. 5.
183. Ibid, pp. 6 and 8.
184. Perrault: op. cit., p. 39.
185. Gestapo Final Report, p. 8.
186. Ibid.
187. Perrault: op. cit., p. 42.
188. Ibid, p. 39.
189. Ibid.
190. Ibid, p. 40.
191. Ibid, p. 92.
192. Dallin: op. cit., p. 147.
193. Ibid.
194. Ibid.
195. Ibid, p. 146; Gestapo Final Report, p. 5.
196. Perrault: op. cit., p. 177.
197. Gestapo Final Report, p. 5.
198. Perrault: op. cit., p. 174. In February 1942 the firm moved to 24 Boulevard Haussmann (Gestapo Final Report, p. 5.)
199. Dallin: op. cit., p. 147.
200. Perrault: op. cit., p. 180.
201. Dallin: op. cit., p. 147.
202. Perrault: op. cit., p. 182.
203. Ibid, p. 49.
204. Dallin: op. cit., p. 134.
205. Perrault: op. cit., p. 47.
206. Ibid, p. 48.
207. Ibid, p. 110.
208. Ibid.
209. Ibid.
210. Further details in Chapter 4 of this book.
211. Dallin: op. cit., p. 142.
212. Gestapo Final Report, p. 2.
213. Perrault: op. cit., p. 81.
214. Flicke: op. cit., p. 44.
215. Gestapo Final Report, p. 6.
216. Flicke: op. cit., p. 43.
217. Dallin: op. cit., p. 149.
218. Flicke: op. cit., p. 80.
219. Ibid.
220. Ibid, p. 62.
221. Ibid, p. 61.
222. Ibid, p. 62.
223. Perrault: op. cit., pp. 84–5.
224. Gestapo Final Report, p. 10.
225. Ibid.
226. Dallin: op. cit., p. 183.
227. Ibid, p. 187.
228. Ibid, p. 188 (note).
229. Collection of Soviet radio messages in the papers of Wilhelm F. Flicke (hereafter referred to as "Flicke collection").
230. Flicke collection, p. 2.
231. Ibid, p. 6.
232. Ibid.
233. Flicke: op. cit., p. 59.

234. Gestapo Final Report, p. 9.

235. Perrault: op. cit., p. 81.

236. Gestapo Final Report, p. 9.

237. Further details in Chapter 4 of this book.

Chapter Three

1. W. F. Flicke: *Spionage-gruppe Rote Kapelle*, p. 8.

2. Ibid, p. 9.

3. Ibid, p. 12.

4. Ibid, p. 17.

5. "Das Geheimnis der Roten Kapelle" in *Norddeutsche Rundschau*, 30 January 1951.

6. Oscar Reile: *Geheime Ostfront*, p. 184.

7. Gert Buchheit: *Der deutsche Geheimdienst*, p. 110.

8. Draft of a speech by Himmler to the Prussian State Council, probably in 1936, p. 30—Files of the Personal Staff of the Reichsführer-SS and Chief of the German Police (henceforth referred to as RFSS) microfilm 89.

9. Reile: op. cit., p. 226.

10. Ibid, p. 228.

11. Ibid, p. 174.

12. Ibid, p. 228.

13. Ibid, p. 227.

14. Alexander Dallin: *German Rule in Russia*, p. 114.

15. Reile: op. cit., p. 234.

16. Dallin: op. cit., p. 115.

17. Buchheit: op. cit., p. 254.

18. Filing plan of Section II of the Gestapa, approximately 1935–6, p. 5—RFSS microfilm 229.

19. "Basic ideas on reorganization of the Gestapa" dated 1939, probably drafted by Schellenberg, p. 16—RFSS microfilm 239.

20. Schedule of distribution of duties in the RSHA as at 1 March 1941—RFSS microfilm 232.

21. Schedule of distribution of duties in the RSHA as at 1 February 1940—RFSS microfilm 232; Shlomo Aronson: *Heydrich und die Anfänge des SD und der Gestapo*, p. 284.

22. RSHA distribution of duties schedule, 1 February 1940.

23. Walter Schellenberg: *Memoirs*, p. 46.

24. Ibid, p. 48; Walter Hagen (alias Dr. Wilhelm Höttl): *Die geheime Front*, p. 62.

25. Draft of an address on the duties of Section VI, completed on 23 January 1940, p. 13—in the private papers of an ex-SD official who wishes to remain anonymous.

26. Ibid, p. 14.

27. Draft of a speech by Himmler to the Prussian State Council, p. 24.

28. Special report on the Tukhachevsky affair issued in 1937 by IfA (SD headquarters information office), p. 7—RFSS microfilm 467.

29. Ibid.

30. Report by the Chief of the Security Police and SD to the Reichsführer-SS, 10 June 1941, given in Schellenberg: *Memoiren*, p. 380 (not in English translation).

31. Ibid, p. 387.

32. Schellenberg: *Memoirs*, p. 156.

33. Ibid.

34. Kyrill D. Kalinov: *Sowjetmarschälle haben das Wort*, p. 28; see also David Dallin: *Soviet Espionage*, pp. 134–5.

35. Dallin: op. cit., p. 13.

36. Buchheit: op. cit., p. 121.

37. David Kahn: *The Codebreakers,* p. 454.

38. Ibid; Buchheit: op. cit., p. 33.

39. Kahn: op. cit., p. 454.

40. Buchheit: op. cit., p. 113.

41. Kahn: op. cit., pp. 455, 459, 461, 465.

42. Buchheit: op. cit., p. 110.

43. Ernst de Barry: "Die Leistung der deutschen Funkabwehr" in Wilhelm von Schramm: *Verrat in Zweiten Weltkrieg,* p. 342. In a letter of 31 July 1943 to all Gestapo offices Gestapo Müller drew attention to the significance for police work of the law on "black transmitters"—RFSS microfilm 15.

44. Organization of Hauptamt Orpo—RFSS microfilm 229. On the position of the "Intelligence Communications Agency" in Ordnungspolizei headquarters see Hans-Joachim Neufeldt, Jürgen Huck and Georg Tessin: *Zur Geschichte der Ordnungspolizei,* p. 67.

45. de Barry: op. cit., p. 344.

46. Office minute by Schellenberg dated 8 September 1939, p. 1—RFSS microfilm 239.

47. IMT, Vol. XXXVIII, p. 21.

48. Schellenberg's office minute, p. 1 (see Note 46).

49. Letter dated 21 February 1968 from Dr. Wilhelm Höttl who at the time was deputy head of Section VI in the RSHA.

50. de Barry: op. cit., p. 342.

51. Ibid, p. 343.

52. Ibid.

53. Ibid.

54. Kopp's personal file in *Der Spiegel* archives.

55. de Barry: op. cit., p. 343.

56. Ibid; Buchheit: op. cit., p. 110.

57. This seems to be the deduction drawn from de Barry: op. cit., p. 343.

58. Robert J. O'Neill: *The German Army and the Nazi Party,* pp. 224–5; Albert Praun: *Soldat in der Telegraphen- und Nachrichtentruppe,* p. 225.

59. Kahn: op. cit., p. 455.

60. Praun: op. cit., p. 225.

61. Ibid. (Praun was Fellgiebel's successor.)

62. Ibid, p. 218.

63. Kahn: op. cit., p. 455.

64. Praun: op. cit., p. 225.

65. Ibid.

66. Ibid.

67. Ibid.

68. Ibid.

69. Ibid, p. 218.

70. de Barry, op. cit., p. 343.

71. Kahn: op. cit., p. 458.

72. de Barry: op. cit., p. 343.

73. Flicke: op. cit., p. 18.

74. As late as 1944 Göring was still trying to get Praun, Fellgiebel's successor, to make over the "Chi" section to him —Praun: op. cit., p. 228.

75. Flicke: op. cit., p. 18.

76. Ibid, p. 34.

77. Kahn: op. cit., p. 657.

78. Ibid.

79. Perrault: op. cit., p. 56.

80. Final report by Dr. Finck, the Public Prosecutor, in the case against Roeder, the ex-Nazi judge (henceforth referred to as "Roeder Final Report"), p. 58.

81. Roeder Final Report, p. 41.

82. Ibid.

83. *Stern*, 1 July 1951.

84. Roeder Final Report, p. 58.

85. Ibid, p. 41; "Das Geheimmis der Roten Kapelle" in *Norddeutsche Rundschau*, 31 January 1951.

86. Roeder Final Report, p. 41.

87. Ibid.

88. Ibid, p. 58.

89. Perrault: op. cit., p. 58.

90. Oscar Reile: *Geheime Westfront*, p. 482.

91. Ibid, p. 476.

92. Observator (pseudonym for Captain [Dr.] Will Grosse): "Wir wissen alles" in *Echo der Woche*, 5 May 1950.

93. Verbally from Harry Piepe on 14 March 1968 (hereafter referred to as "from Piepe").

94. Ibid.

95. Ibid.

96. David Dallin: op. cit., p. 152.

97. Ibid.

98. From Piepe.

99. Ibid.

100. Ibid.

101. Perrault: op. cit., p. 87.

102. Report by Chief of Security Police and SD, VI A 2-B, No. 330/42, dated 22 December 1942, p. 1 (henceforth referred to as "Gestapo Final Report").

103. From Piepe.

104. Ibid.

105. Perrault: op. cit., p. 89.

106. From Piepe.

107. Ibid.

108. Ibid.

109. Perrault: op. cit., p. 90.

110. Ibid.

111. From Piepe.

112. Perrault: op. cit., p. 90.

113. Ibid.

114. Dallin: op. cit., p. 153; Flicke: op. cit., p. 101; Perrault: op. cit., p. 91.

115. From Piepe.

116. Ibid.

117. Telegram dated 11 September 1942 from SS-Obersturmbannführer Albath of the Gestapo office Düsseldorf to Kriminalrat Kopkow—in *Der Spiegel* archives.

118. From Piepe.

119. Ibid.

120. Ibid.

121. Dallin: op. cit., p. 153.

122. Perrault: op. cit., p. 98.

123. B. S. Telpuchovski: *Die sowjetische Geschichte des Grossen Vaterländischen Krieges*, p. 92.

124. Perrault: op. cit., p. 111.

125. Ibid, p. 106.

126. Ibid, p. 107.

127. Ibid, p. 111.

128. Telpuchovski: op. cit., p. 101.

129. Ibid.

130. Perrault: op. cit., p. 111.

131. Ibid.

132. Ibid, p. 108.

133. Ibid. p. 111.

134. Ibid, p. 112.

135. Ibid.

136. David Dallin: op. cit., p. 145.

137. From Piepe.

138. Information from *Der Spiegel* archives.

139. Ibid.

140. From Piepe.

141. Perrault: op. cit., p. 127. This shows that, although well-informed about Rote Kapelle in Western Europe, Perrault appears to know less about the German Abwehr or police.

142. The text of the Gestapo/Abwehr agreement is to be found in Werner Best: *Die*

deutsche Abwehrpolizei bis 1945, p. 19.

143. Perrault: op. cit., p. 127.

144. From Piepe.

145. Perrault: op. cit., pp. 107–8.

146. Ibid, p. 117.

147. Perrault: op. cit., p. 96; Dallin: op. cit., p. 153.

148. RSHA telephone directory—RFSS microfilm 232.

149. Perrault: op. cit., p. 125; also from Piepe.

150. Ibid, p. 124.

151. Ibid, p. 123.

152. Telegram from Düsseldorf Gestapo to Kopkow, 3 September 1942.

153. Perrault: op. cit., p. 156.

154. Verbally from Heinrich Reiser on 4 March 1968 (hereafter referred to as "from Reiser").

155. Letter dated 8 January 1943 from Müller, the head of the Gestapo, to all Sipo and SD offices—RFSS microfilm 463.

156. Organization chart of Sipo and SD, April 1943—RFSS microfilm 232.

157. From Reiser.

158. Ibid.

159. Organization chart of Sipo and SD—see Note 156.

160. Kahn: op. cit., p. 650.

161. Ibid, p. 635.

162. Ibid, p. 656.

163. Ibid.

164. Ibid, p. 620.

165. Ibid.

166. Ibid, p. 636.

167. W. M. Vilter: *Die Geheimschriften*, p. 2.

168. Otto Pünter: *Der Anschluss fand nicht statt*, pp. 141–7.

169. Ibid.

170. *Der Spiegel* archives.

171. Ibid; also letter dated 12 June 1968 from H. J. Weber, one of Vauck's pupils.

172. Gestapo Final Report, p. 11.

173. Dallin: op. cit., p. 153.

174. Ibid.

175. Letter dated 31 March 1968 from Ernst de Barry.

176. From Piepe.

177. Dallin: op. cit., p. 154.

178. Perrault: op. cit., p. 141.

179. Roeder Final Report, p. 59.

180. Kahn: op. cit., p. 658.

181. Ibid.

182. Perrault: op. cit., p. 142.

183. From Reiser.

184. Ibid.

185. Ibid; Dallin: op. cit., p. 162.

186. Dallin: op. cit., p. 162.

187. From Reiser.

188. Dallin: op. cit., p. 162.

189. Perrault: op. cit., pp. 210–11.

190. Ibid.

191. Ibid.

192. Ibid.

193. Dallin: op. cit., p. 145.

194. Ibid, p. 154.

195. From Piepe.

196. Gestapo Final Report, p. 1; see also Perrault: op. cit., p. 145; Dallin: op. cit., p. 154.

197. From Piepe.

198. Ibid.

199. Perrault: op. cit., p. 147.

200. Ibid.

201. Letter dated 14 December 1966 from "Dr. H.B."

202. From Piepe.

203. Ibid.

204. Ibid.

205. Ibid.

206. Letter from "Dr. H.B." (see Note 201 above).

207. Roeder Final Report, p. 59.

208. Flicke: op. cit., p. 59.
209. Roeder Final Report, p. 59.
210. Ibid.
211. From Piepe.
212. Schellenberg: *Memoiren*, p. 251 (not in English translation).
213. Schellenberg: *Memoirs*, p. 325.

Chapter Four

1. *Der Spiegel* archives; also Final Report by Dr. Finck, the Public Prosecutor in the case against Dr. Manfred Roeder, the ex-Luftwaffe Judge Advocate (henceforth referred to as "Roeder Final Report"), pp. 59–60.
2. Report by Chief of Security Police and SD, IV A 2-B, No. 330/42 dated 22 December 1942 (henceforth referred to as "Gestapo Final Report"), p. 1.
3. Ibid, p. 14.
4. Otto Ernst Schüddekopf: *Linke Leute von rechts*, p. 509.
5. *Weltspiegel*, 22 February 1948.
6. Rainer Hildebrandt: *Wir sind die Letzten*, p. 138.
7. *Neues Deutschland*, 29 June 1968.
8. *Weltspiegel*, 22 February 1948.
9. David Dallin: *Soviet Espionage*, p. 241.
10. Ibid, pp. 240–1.
11. Graphological memorandum on Schulze-Boysen, undated—in Ritter von Schramm's private papers.
12. Statement by Greta Kuckhoff—in files of Public Prosecutor of Lüneburg Provincial Court on case against Dr. Manfred Roeder (henceforth referred to as "Lüneburg Trial"), Vol. VIII, folio 131.
13. Roeder Final Report, p. 169.
14. Letter from Cato Bontjes van Beek to her mother, 2 March 1943—in Bontjes van Beek's private papers.
15. Adrien Turel: *Ecce Superhomo*, Vol. i, p. 218.
16. Walter A. Schmidt: *Damit Deutschland lebe*, p. 321.
17. Institute for Marxism-Leninism (henceforth referred to as "IML") under the Central Committee of the East German Communist Party: *Geschichte der deutschen Arbeiterbewegung*, Vol. V, p. 280.
18. Roeder Final Report, p. 343.
19. Verbally from Dr. Hugo Buschmann on 26 June 1968 (henceforth referred to as—"from Buschmann").
20. Karl O. Paetel: *Versuchung oder Chance?*, p. 33.
21. Ibid, p. 32.
22. Ibid, p. 33.
23. Harro Schulze-Boysen: *Gegner von heute—Kampfgenossen von morgen*, p. 17.
24. Paetel: op. cit., p. 25.
25. Schulze-Boysen: op. cit., p. 28.
26. Ibid, p. 13.
27. Ibid, p. 23.
28. Schüddekopf: op. cit., p. 353.
29. Franz Jung: *Der Weg nach unten*, p. 386.
30. Alan Bullock: *Hitler, A Study in Tyranny*, p. 158; Paetel: op. cit., p. 32.
31. Verbally from Erich Edgar Schulze, 4 March 1968.

32. Olga Tirpitz married Georg Schulze, a Director of Studies—Gestapo Final Report, p. 10.

33. Statement by Marie-Louise Schulze, 14 February 1950; Lüneburg Trial, Vol. XII, folio 57.

34. Personal file on Schulze-Boysen in *Der Spiegel* archives.

35. Ibid.

36. Verbally from Marie-Louise Schulze, 4 March 1968.

37. Ibid.

38. Schüddekopf: op. cit., p. 353.

39. From Marie-Louise Schulze, 4 March 1968.

40. Elsa Boysen: *Harro Schulze-Boysen*, p. 8.

41. Personal file on Schulze-Boysen.

42. Boysen: op. cit., p. 9.

43. Paetel: op. cit., p. 198.

44. Jung: op. cit., p. 383.

45. Ibid, p. 343 et seq.

46. Ibid, pp. 371, 372.

47. Ibid, p. 371.

48. Ibid.

49. Ibid, p. 376 et seq.

50. Paetel: op. cit., p. 192.

51. Jung: op. cit., p. 381.

52. Arnold Bauer: *Erinnerungen an Harro Schulze-Boysen und Horst Heilmann*, p. 1.

53. Paetel: op. cit., p. 198.

54. Jung: op. cit., p. 384.

55. Ibid.

56. Paetel: op. cit., p. 195.

57. Schüddekopf: op. cit., p. 352.

58. Ibid, p. 354.

59. Ibid, pp. 352, 354.

60. Jung: op. cit., p. 386.

61. Schüddekopf: op. cit., p. 353.

62. Ibid.

63. Paetel: op. cit., p. 203.

64. Turel: op. cit., p. 219.

65. Ibid.

66. Ibid, p. 220.

67. Verbally from Marie-Louise Schulze, 4 March 1968.

68. Marie-Louise Schulze: *Warum ich im Jahre 1933 Parteigenossin geworden bin*, p. 3.

69. Schulze: op. cit., p. 1.

70. Ibid.

71. Ibid.

72. Ibid, p. 2.

73. Ibid, p. 3.

74. Ibid.

75. Ibid, p. 5.

76. Verbally from Marie-Louise Schulze, 4 March 1968.

77. Letter from Head of SS Region III, Henze Auxiliary Police Commando, 19 May 1933—in Willi Weber's private papers.

78. Ernst von Salomon: *Der Fragebogen*, p. 477.

79. Ibid.

80. Personal file on Schulze-Boysen.

81. Ibid.

82. Boysen: op. cit., p. 16.

83. Ibid, p. 15.

84. Personal file on Schulze-Boysen.

85. Ibid.

86. Ibid.

87. Ibid.

88. Verbally on 26 March 1968 from landlord (who wishes to remain anonymous) of the first apartment rented by the Schulze-Boysens; Thora zu Eulenburg: *Libertas*, p. 11.

89. Statement by Toni Gösch, 14 December 1966.

90. Winfried Martini: "Deutsche Spionage für Moskau" in *Die Welt*, 17 October 1966.

91. Boysen: op. cit., p. 16.

92. Verbally on 26 March 1968.

93. Statement by Marie-Louise Schulze, 14 February 1950—Lüneburg Trial, Vol. XII, folio 57.

94. Letter from Heysig, head of the editorial office, 19 November 1966.

95. Letter from Bartz's widow, Dr. Lydia Franke, 7 July 1968.

96. Duty list of Reich Ministry of Aviation, 1 December 1939, p. 3—in *Der Spiegel* archives.

97. Verbally from Schulze-Boysen's first landlord, 26 March 1968.

98. Personal file on Schulze-Boysen.

99. Verbally on 26 March 1968.

10. Letter from Heysig, 19 November 1966.

101. Harro Schulze-Boysen: "Wehrchronik (Luftwaffe) 1938" in *Jahrbuch der deutschen Luftwaffe 1939*, p. 40.

102. Ibid, p. 41.

103. Boysen: op. cit., p. 16.

104. Ibid, p. 17.

105. Statement by Schumacher's mother, Julie Schumacher, 20 October 1949—Lüneburg Trial, Vol. X, folio 13; Gestapo Final Report, p. 10.

106. Statement by Julie Schumacher; Gestapo Final Report, p. 11.

107. This is the view of Klaus Lehmann in *Widerstandsgruppe Schulze-Boysen/Harnack*, pp. 46–7, but see also the denial by Fritz Hohenemser, a brother of Frau Schumacher, in *Der Spiegel*, No. 29 of 1968.

108. Memorandum by Kurt Schumacher while under arrest, 2 November 1942—in *Der Spiegel* archives.

109. Gestapo Final Report, p. 12; Lehmann: op. cit., p. 69.

110. Roeder Final Report, p. 168.

111. Lehmann: op. cit., p. 69.

112. Statement by Dr. Elfriede Paul, 7 December 1949—Lüneburg Trial, Vol. X, folio 100; Gestapo Final Report, p. 12.

113. Statement by Günther Weisenborn, 6 March 1967—in Weisenborn's private papers.

114. Verbally from Gösta von Uexküll, 6 December 1968.

115. Statement by Günther Weisenborn, 29 July 1949—Lüneburg Trial, Vol. VIII, folio 63.

116. Roeder Final Report, pp. 243, 352, 379; also from Gösta von Uexküll, 6 December 1968.

117. Günther Weisenborn: *Memorial*, p. 3.

118. Statement by Paul Scholz, 30 November 1949—Lüneburg Trial, Vol. X, folio 80.

119. Manfred Merkes: *Die deutsche Politik gegenüber dem Spanischen Bürgerkrieg 1936–1939*, p. 28.

120. Ibid.

121. Gestapo Final Report, p. 20.

122. Ibid.

123. Lehmann: op. cit., p. 29.

124. Weisenborn: op. cit., p. 3.

125. "Rote Kapelle"—collective report on the survivors by Günther Weisenborn—Lüne-

burg Trial, Vol. VIII, folios 109–110.

126. Ibid.

127. Ibid, folio 64.

128. Weisenborn: op. cit., p. 3.

129. "Rote Kapelle" collective report, folio 64.

130. Roeder Final Report, p. 334; report by Werner Kraus, undated—Lüneburg Trial, Vol. X, folio 159.

131. Günther Weisenborn: *Der lautlose Aufstand*, pp. 206–7.

132. Ibid, p. 206.

133. Letter from Willi Weber, 8 May 1968; Roeder Final Report, p. 352.

134. Statement by Oda Schottmüller's mother, Dorothea Schottmüller, 2 December 1949—Lüneburg Trial, Vol. X, folio 84.

135. From Buschmann.

136. Statement by Paul Scholz, 30 November 1949—Lüneburg Trial, Vol. X, folio 80.

137. Statement by Greta Kuckhoff, undated—Lüneburg Trial, Vol. VIII, folio 131.

138. Letter from Willi Weber, May 1968.

139. Roeder Final Report, p. 37.

140. Dallin: op. cit., p. 237.

141. Ibid, p. 234 et seq.

142. Arvid Harnack's personal files—in Weisenborn's papers.

143. Weisenborn: *Der lautlose Aufstand*, p. 208.

144. Report by the Security Police to the Gestapa, 22 March 1937—RFSS microfilm 402.

145. Weisenborn: op. cit., p. 208.

146. Egmont Zechlin: *Arvid und Mildred Harnack zum Gedächtnis*, p. 4.

147. Ibid, p. 5.

148. Harnack's personal files.

149. Dallin: op. cit., p. 235.

150. Mildred Harnack's personal files—in Weisenborn's papers.

151. Lehmann: op. cit., pp. 36–7.

152. Dallin: op. cit., p. 235.

153. Lehmann: op. cit., p. 33.

154. Dallin: op. cit., p. 235.

155. Zechlin: op. cit., p. 4.

156. Arvid Harnack's personal files; Dallin: op. cit., p. 236.

157. Dallin: op. cit., p. 236.

158. Lehmann: op. cit., p. 33.

159. Gestapo Final Report, p. 10; Lehmann: op. cit., p. 34.

160. Lehmann: op. cit., p. 34.

161. Arvid Harnack's personal files; Gestapo Final Report, p. 10.

162. Statement by Greta Kuckhoff—Lüneburg trial, Vol. VIII, folio 131.

163. Ibid.

164. Ibid.

165. Greta Kuckhoff personal file in *Der Spiegel* archives; Gestapo Final Report, p. 10.

166. Statement by Greta Kuckhoff—Lüneburg Trial, Vol. VIII, folio 131.

167. Lehmann: op. cit., p. 55.

168. Gestapo Final Report, p. 12.

169. Statement by Greta Kuckhoff—Lüneburg Trial, Vol. VIII, folio 131.

170. Lehmann: op. cit., p. 52; Adam Kuckhoff's personal file in *Der Spiegel* archives.

171. Report by Alexander Kraell, 30 July 1946—Lüneburg Trial, Vol. III, folio 374.

172. Ibid; statement by Greta Kuckhoff, Vol. VIII, folio 132.

173. Ibid (statement by Greta Kuckhoff).

174. Roeder Final Report, p. 35.

175. Report by Alexander Kraell—Lüneburg Trial, Vol. III, folio 374.

176. Ibid.

177. Ibid.

178. Statement by Greta Kuckhoff—Lüneburg Trial, Vol. VIII, folio 131.

179. Ibid.

180. Ibid.

181. Ibid.

182. Ibid.

183. Letter from Alexander Spoerl, 27 June 1968.

184. Statement by Johannes Strübing, 18 January 1950—Lüneburg Trial, Vol. X, folio 198.

185. Statement by Greta Kuckhoff—Lüneburg Trial, Vol. VIII, folio 131.

186. Report by Alexander Kraell—Lüneburg Trial, Vol. III, folio 375.

187. Herbert Wehner: Notizen, p. 186.

188. Ibid, p. 184.

189. Ibid, p. 181.

190. Ibid, p. 184.

191. Ibid.

192. Ibid, pp. 185–6. ecutor's case against Wilhelm

192. Ibid, pp. 185–6.

193. Ibid, p. 186; Public Pros-Knöchel before the Peoples Court in 1943 (henceforth referred to as "case against Knöchel''), p. 6; Otto Schwardt's private papers.

194. Case against Knöchel, p. 7; Wehner acquired the name Kurt Funk at the Seventh Comintern Congress in Moscow in 1935—see statement by Wehner on an article in the Swedish newspaper Dagens Nyheter, 11 March 1957.

195. Further details in Wehner's Notizen.

196. Case against Knöchel, p. 7.

197. Case against Knöchel, p. 6.

198. Wehner: op. cit., p. 198; Dallin: op. cit., pp. 90–1; supplement on communist fugitives issued by the Gestapa, 5 May 1937, p. 32; Wilhelm Bauer's private papers.

199. Case against Knöchel, p. 6.

200. Dallin: op. cit., p. 91.

201. Wehner—statement on article in Dagens Nyheter, p. 2.

202. Ibid, p. 4; case against Knöchel, p. 13.

203. Ibid (Wehner), p. 5.

204. Report of investigations by Swedish police, 4 April 1942, reproduced in Rheinische Merkur, 22 March 1957.

205. Wehner: Notizen, p. 186.

206. Swedish police report, 4 April 1942.

207. Knöchel was in Berlin from January 1942 until his arrest in October of that year —case against Knöchel, p. 14 et seq.

208. IML (see Note 17), p. 252 et seq.

209. Ibid, p. 284.

210. Ibid, p. 278.

211. Ibid, p. 227.

212. Ibid.

213. Schmidt: op. cit., p. 325.

214. Ibid.

215. Roeder Final Report, p. 50.

216. Lehmann: op. cit., p. 56.

217. Ibid; Guddorf's personal file in Der Spiegel archives.

218. Schmidt: op. cit., p. 328.

219. Ibid, p. 329.
220. For details of the group centered on Neutert, Thiess, the Dubinskis and Wilhelm Schürmann-Horster (not mentioned here) see judgment of the Peoples Court 10 J 13/43 g dated 20/21 August 1943—Lüneburg Trial, Vol. X, folio 104 et seq.
221. *Zur Geschichte der deutschen antifaschitischen Widerstandsbewegung,* p. 188.
222. Ibid.
223. Roeder Final Report, p. 169.
224. IML, p. 281.
225. Statement by Klara Schabbel's sister, Margarete Almstedt, 28 November 1949—Lüneburg Trial, Vol. X, folio 71.
226. Gestapo Final Report, pp. 19–20.
227. Roeder Final Report, p. 215.
228. Statement by Alexander Kraell, 15 March 1950—Lüneburg Trial, Vol. XII, folio 109.
229. Ibid.
230. Ibid.
231. Statement by Johannes Strübing, 18 January 1950; ibid, Vol. X, folio 200.
232. Statement by Lotte Schleif, 29 November 1949; ibid, Vol. X, folio 73.
233. Ibid.
234. Ibid.
235. Statement by Heinrich Scheel, 26 November 1949; ibid, Vol. X, folio 65.
236. Statement by Coppi's mother, Frieda Coppi, 14 November 1949; ibid, Vol. X, folio 45.
237. Statement by Hans Lautenschläger, 30 November 1949, ibid, Vol. X, folio 60.
238. Ibid.
239. Professor Kemp: *John F. Rittmeister zum Gedächtnis,* p. 1.
240. Lehmann: op. cit., p. 58.
241. Entries in John Rittmeister's diary while in prison, September 1942–March 1943—Lüneburg Trial, Vol. X, folio 148.
242. Ibid, folios 153, 141.
243. Kemp: op. cit., p. 3.
244. Lehmann: op. cit., p. 58.
245. Ibid.
246. Kemp: op. cit., p. 3.
247. Roeder Final Report, p. 34.
248. Ibid.
249. Ibid.
250. Ibid.
251. Ibid.
252. Ibid.
253. Report by Werner Krauss—Lüneburg Trial, Vol. X, folio 158.
254. Statement by Ursula Terwiel, 20 October 1949—Lüneburg Trial, Vol. X, folio 16.
255. Evidence by Jan Bontjes van Beek before the restitution chamber of Stade Provincial Court, 12 February 1958—in Bontjes van Beek's papers.
256. Statement by Strelow's mother, Meta Strelow—Roeder Final Report, p. 366.
257. Dallin: op. cit., pp. 134–5.
258. Gestapo Final Report, p. 16; Statements by Alexander Kraell and Greta Kuckhoff—Lüneburg Trial, Vol. XIII, folio 96 and Vol. VIII, folio 131.
259. Report by Alexander Kraell, 30 July 1946—Lüneburg Trial, Vol. III, folio 370.

260. Roeder Final Report, p. 40.

261. Gestapo Final Report, p. 16.

262. Statement by Greta Kuckhoff and report by Alexander Kraell—Lüneburg Trial, Vol. VIII, folio 132 and Vol. XII, folio 106.

263. Statement by Alexander Kraell, 14 March 1950—Lüneburg trial, Vol. XII, folio 99.

264. Ibid.

265. Gestapo Final Report, p. 19.

266. Ibid, p. 16.

267. Ibid, p. 19.

268. Statement by Greta Kuckhoff—Lüneburg Trial, Vol. VIII, folio 132.

269. Report by Alexander Kraell, 6 August 1948, ibid, Vol, III, folio 382.

270. Schüddekopf: op. cit., p. 351.

271. Hildebrandt: op. cit., p. 151.

272. Report by Alexander Kraell, 6 August 1948—Lüneburg Trial, Vol. III, folio 387.

273. Dallin: op. cit., p. 242.

274. Statement by Eugen Schmidt, 25 July 1949—Lüneburg Trial, Vol. VIII, folio 61.

275. Statement by Greta Kuckhoff, 21 March 1947, ibid, Vol. VIII, folio 162.

276. Statement by Margarete Almstedt, 28 November 1949, ibid, Vol. X, folio 72.

277. Statement by Julie Schumacher, 20 October 1949, ibid, Vol. X, folio 13.

278. Statement by Alexander Kraell, ibid, Vol. XII, folio 106.

279. Wehner's final plea to the Stockholm court which condemned him to one year's imprisonment in 1942 for alleged espionage for the Soviet Union —Wehner: *Notizen*, p. 208.

280. Hildebrandt: op. cit., p. 156.

281. Ibid, p. 157.

282. Gestapo Final Report, p. 16.

283. From Buschmann.

284. Gestapo Final Report, p. 17.

285. Zechlin: op. cit., p. 5.

286. Statement by Alexander Kraell—Lüneburg Trial, Vol. XII, folio 104.

287. Weisenborn: *Der lautlose Aufstand*, p. 204.

288. Roeder Final Report, p. 383.

289. From Buschmann.

290. Ibid.

291. Ibid.

292. Hildebrandt: op. cit., p. 154.

293. Ibid, p. 155; also from Buschmann.

294. Report by Werner Krauss —Lüneburg Trial, Vol. X, folio 159.

295. Schmidt: op. cit., p. 323; IML, p. 309.

296. Ibid.

297. Schmidt: op. cit., p. 323.

298. Lehmann: op. cit., p. 83; Weisenborn: op. cit., p. 206.

299. Statement by Alexander Kraell—Lüneburg Trial, Vol. XII, folio 96.

300. "Rote Kapelle" collective report; statements by Alexander Kraell—Lüneburg Trial, Vol. VIII, folio 104 and Vol. XII, folio 103.

301. Statement by Rittmeister's widow, Eva Hildebrand, to the restitution chamber of the Stade Provincial Court, 12 February 1958—in Bontjes van Beek's papers.

302. Statement by Werner Krauss—Lüneburg Trial, Vol. X, folio 159.

303. Weisenborn: op. cit., p. 206.

304. From Buschmann.

305. Report by Werner Krauss —Lüneburg Trial, Vol. X, folio 159.

306. Ibid.

307. Ibid.

308. Ibid.

309. IML, p. 314.

310. Sentence of Peoples Court on Heinz Rotholz and others, December 1942 (henceforth referred to as "Rotholz sentence")—in Willi Weber's papers.

311. Report by Werner Krauss —Lüneburg Trial, Vol. X, folio 159; photostat copy of a handbill in IML, pp. 240–1.

312. Ibid (Werner Krauss).

313. Gestapo Final Report, p. 15.

314. Rotholz sentence, p. 2.

315. Ibid.

316. Letter from Cato Bontjes van Beek to her mother, 2 March 1943; statement by Meta Strelow; Roeder Final Report, p. 366.

317. Statement by Alexander Kraell—Lüneburg Trial, Vol. X, folio 110.

318. Report by Werner Krauss ibid, Vol. X, folio 160.

319. From Buschmann.

320. Letter from Alexander Spoerl, 27 June 1968.

321 *Der Spiegel* archives.

322. Letter from August Noiret to the author, 3 June 1968 (henceforth referred to as "from Noiret").

323. Verbally on 25 April 1968 from Urbanek, an engineer and ex-head of the Press Desk in the Reich Ministry of Aviation (henceforth referred to as "from Urbanek").

324. Ibid.

325. From Noiret, 3 July 1968.

326. From Urbanek, 25 April 1968.

327. Ibid.

328. Gestapo Final Report, p. 11.

329. Lehmann: op. cit., pp. 76–7.

330. Statement by Johannes Strübing, 18 January 1950— Lüneburg Trial, Vol. X, folio 196.

331. Roeder Final Report, pp. 131, 134, 239.

332. Statement by Johannes Strübing, 18 January 1950— Lüneburg Trial, Vol. X, folio 196.

333. Statement by Toni Graudenz, 15 November 1949— Lüneburg Trial, Vol. X, folio 48.

334. Statement by Alexander Kraell—Lüneburg Trial, Vol. XII, folio 98.

335. Lehmann: op. cit., p. 67; Gestapo Final Report, p. 10.

336. Statement by Toni Graudenz (Note 333 above).

337. Ibid.

338. Ibid.

339. Report by Alexander Kraell, 30 July 1946—Lüneburg Trial, Vol. III, folio 371.

340. Ibid.

341. Letter from Willi Weber, June 1968.

342. Statement by Reinhold Ortmann, 16 February 1950— Lüneburg Trial, Vol. XII, folio 65.

343. Report by Werner Krauss —Lüneburg Trial, Vol. X, folio 160.

344. Ibid.

345. Ibid.

346. Lehmann: op. cit., p. 70; Gestapo Final Report, p. 11.

347. Hildebrandt: op. cit., p. 141.

348. Ibid; statement by Gerhard Ranft, 7 March 1950—Lüneburg Trial, Vol. XII, folio 88.

349. Hildebrandt: op. cit., p. 141.

350. Gestapo Final Report, p. 11.

351. Statement by Alexander Kraell, 14 March 1950—Lüneburg Trial, Vol. XII, folio 98.

352. Statement by Manfred Roeder, 1 July 1949—Lüneburg Trial, Vol. VIII, folio 25.

353. Statement by Alexander Kraell, 14 March 1950—Lüneburg Trial, Vol. XII, folio 107.

354. Statement by Johannes Strübing, 18 January 1950—Lüneburg Trial, Vol. X, folio 195.

355. From Buschmann.

356. Schulze-Boysen: op. cit., pp. 18, 20.

357. Statement by Dr. Jan Tönnies, 10 March 1950—Lüneburg Trial, Vol. XII, folio 143.

358. Axel von Harnack: "Arvid und Mildred Harnack" in Die Gegenwart, 31 January 1947, p. 15.

359. Mildred Harnack's personal files—in Weisenborn's papers.

360. Gestapo Final Report, p. 11; statement by Gerhard Ranft, 7 March 1950—Lüneburg Trial, Vol. XII, folio 87.

361. Ibid.

362. Gestapo Final Report, p. 11.

363. Statement by Johannes Strübing, 18 January 1950—Lüneburg Trial, Vol. X, folio 197.

364. Statement by Alexander Kraell, 14 March 1950—Lüneburg Trial, Vol. XII, folio 112.

365. Gestapo Final Report, p. 11.

366. Instruction from Moscow to Kent, 18 October 1941; Gestapo Final Report, p. 11.

367. Statement by Alexander Kraell, 14 March 1950—Lüneburg Trial, Vol. XII, folio 112.

368. Gestapo Final Report, p. 7; statement by Johannes Strübing, 2 February 1950—Lüneburg Trial, Vol. XII, folio 1.

369. Gestapo Final Report, p. 20.

370. Ibid; statement by Alexander Kraell, 6 August 1948—Lüneburg Trial, Vol. III, folio 384.

371. Ibid.

372. W. F. Flicke: Spionagegruppe Rote Kapelle, p. 81.

373. Letter from the Lüneburg Public Prosecutor to the authorities of Hamburg, 20 January 1951, p. 4; files of the Office for Reconstruction of the Hanseatic City of Hamburg.

374. Ibid.

375. Ibid.

376. Ibid.

377. Collection of Soviet radio messages in the papers of

Wilhelm F. Flicke, p. 8 (henceforth referred to as "Flicke Collection"); private papers whose owner wishes to remain anonymous.

378. Flicke Collection, p. 10.

379. Statement by Johannes Strübing, 2 February 1950—Lüneburg Trial, Vol. XII, folio 2.

380. Ibid.

381. Flicke: op. cit., p. 81.

382. Flicke Collection, p. 3.

383. Ibid, p. 6.

384. Ibid, p. 14.

385. Ibid, p. 3.

386. Ibid, p. 9.

387. Statement by Johannes Strübing, 2 February 1950—Lüneburg Trial, Vol. XII, folio 2.

388. Gestapo Final Report, p. 7.

389. Ibid.

390. Ibid.

391. Flicke Collection, p. 14.

392. Gert Buchheit: *Der deutsche Geheimdienst*, p. 261.

393. Statement by Karl Schmauser, 9 September 1950 —Lüneburg Trial, Vol. XII, folio 188.

394. Statement by Alexander Kraell, 14 March 1950—Lüneburg Trial, Vol. III, folio 389.

395. Report by Alexander Kraell, 6 August 1948—Lüneburg Trial, Vol. III, folio 389.

396. Ibid.

397. Roeder Final Report, pp. 129–30.

398. *Junge Welt*, 22 December 1967.

399. Ibid.

400. Roeder Final Report, p. 40.

401. Ibid.

402. Flicke: op. cit., p. 59.

403. Statement by Greta Kuckhoff—Lüneburg Trial, Vol. VIII, folio 132.

404. Rote Kapelle collective report—Lüneburg Trial, Vol. VIII, folio 107.

405. Martini: op. cit. in *Die Welt*, 15 October 1966; statement by Johannes Strübing, 2 February 1950—Lüneburg Trial, Vol. XII, folio 4.

406. Report by Alexander Kraell, 6 August 1948—Lüneburg Trial, Vol. III, folio 377; Gestapo Final Report, p. 24.

407. Ibid.

408. Ibid.

409. Ibid, p. 25; Dallin: op. cit., p. 124.

410. Ibid.

411. *Für Dich*, 2 March 1968 issue.

412. Gestapo Final Report, p. 25.

413 Report by Alexander Kraell, 6 August 1948—Lüneburg Trial, Vol. III, folio 372; Gestapo Final Report, p. 11.

414. Rote Kapelle collective report—Lüneburg Trial, Vol. VIII, folio 111.

415. Ibid; Gestapo Final Report, p. 19.

416. *Pravda*, 5 July 1967.

417. Gestapo Final Report, p. 23.

418. John Nemo: *Das rote Netz*, p. 20.

419. Ibid.

420. Ibid, p. 21.

421. Letter from the counter-espionage desk in SS Headquarters [Führungshauptamt] to counter-espionage officers in SS Head Offices [Hauptämter], 17 February 1945—RFSS microfilm 17.

422. Ibid.

423. Wilhelm Bauer: *Fallschirmagenten*, p. 1.

424. Ibid, p. 8.

425. Ibid.

426. Ibid.

427. Ibid.

428. Ibid.

429. Gestapo Search Order, signed "Schmidt," 9 June 1942 —in *Der Spiegel* archives.

430. Bauer: op. cit., p. 4.

431. Ibid.

432. Ibid, p. 8; Gestapo Final Report, p. 23.

433. Ibid.

434. Statement by Greta Kuckhoff—Lüneburg Trial, Vol. VIII, folio 131; Gestapo Final Report, p. 24.

435. Statement by Reinhold Ortmann, 16 February 1950— Lüneburg Trial, Vol. XII, folio 62.

436. Statement by Heinrich Scheel, 26 November 1949— Lüneburg Trial, Vol. X, folio 65.

437. Statement by Alexander Kraell, 14 March 1950—Lüneburg Trial, Vol. XII, folio 104.

438. Statement by Hans Lautenschläger, 23 November 1949—Lüneburg Trial, Vol. X, folio 60.

439. Bauer: op. cit., p. 4.

440. Office minute dated 30 May 1942 from an unidentified Gestapo office—in *Der Spiegel* achives.

441. Circular from Gestapo office Nuremberg-Fürth, 30 May 1942—in *Der Spiegel* archives.

442. Ibid.

443. Gestapo office minute (see Note 440).

444. Bauer: op. cit., p. 4.

445. Ibid.

446. Statement by Alexander Kraell, 14 March 1950—Lüneburg Trial, Vol. XII, folio 109.

447. Rote Kapelle collective report—Lüneburg Trial, Vol. VIII, folio 102.

Chapter Five

1. Rainer Hildebrandt: *Wir sind die Letzten*, p. 157.

2. Ibid, p. 158.

3. Final Report by Dr. Finck, the Public Prosecutor, in the case against Dr. Manfred Roeder, the ex-Luftwaffe Judge Advocate (henceforth referred to as "Roeder Final Report"), p. 60.

4. "Rote Kapelle," composite report on the survivors by Günther Weisenborn—in files of Public Prosecutor of Lüneburg Provincial Court on case against Dr. Manfred Roeder (henceforth referred to as "Luneburg Trial"), Vol. VIII, folio 102.

5. Edgar E. Schulze: *Zum Gedächtnis meines Sohnes Harro*—Lüneburg Trial, Vol. XII, folio 40; Elsa Boysen: *Harro Schulze-Boysen*, p. 23.

6. Statement by Toni Graudenz, 15 November 1949— Lüneburg Trial, Vol. X, folio 48.

7. "Rote Kapelle"—Lüneburg Trial, Vol. VIII, folio 114; Günther Weisenborn: *Memorial*, p. 4.

8. Ibid.

9. Ibid.

10. Ibid.

11. Ibid.

12. Statement by Frieda Cop-

pi, 14 November 1949—Lüneburg Trial, Vol. X, folio 45.

13. Roeder Final Report, p. 373.

14. Statement by Helmut Roloff—Lüneburg Trial, Vol. X, folio 176.

15. Ibid.

16. Ibid.

17. Statement by Toni Graudenz, 15 November 1949—Lüneburg Trial, Vol. X, folio 48.

18. Statement by Hanni Weissensteiner, 24 July 1950—Lüneburg Trial, Vol. XII, folio 199.

19. Letter from Helene Heilmann to Public Prosecutor of the Berlin Supreme Court, 22 December 1966—in private Heilmann papers.

20. Verbally from Arnold Bauer, 25 May 1968.

21. Roeder Final Report, p. 60.

22. Ibid, p. 61.

23. Ibid.

24. Ibid, p. 59.

25. Ibid, p. 62.

26. *Der Spiegel* archives.

27. Roeder Final Report, p. 60.

28. Strübing's personal file in *Der Spiegel* archives.

29. Roeder Final Report, p. 62.

30. Ibid, p. 61.

31. Verbally from a military Judge Advocate; David Dallin: *Soviet Espionage*, p. 253.

32. Heinz Höhne: *The Order of the Death's Head*, p. 247.

33. Verbally from a military Judge Advocate.

34. Alexander Spoerl: *Libertas Schulze-Boysen*—Lüneburg Trial, Vol. X, folio 186; personal file on Libertas Schulze-Boysen in *Der Spiegel* archives.

35. Egmont Zechlin: *Arvid und Mildred Harnack zum Gedächtnis*, p. 2.

36. Klaus Lehmann: *Widerstandsgruppe Schulze-Boysen/Harnack*, pp. 52, 66, 38, 55; Report by Chief of Security Police and SD, IV A 2-B, No. 330/42 dated 22 December 1942 (henceforth referred to as "Gestapo Final Report"), p. 24.

37. Lehmann: op. cit., p. 69; Roeder Final Report, pp. 303, 328, 386.

38. Lehmann: op. cit., p. 83; Roeder Final Report, p. 293.

39. Lehmann: op. cit., p. 58; Weisenborn: op. cit., p. 4.

40. The first five to be arrested were Harro and Libertas Schulze-Boysen, Arvid and Mildred Harnack and Heilmann.

41. Roeder Final Report, p. 61.

42. Ibid, p. 62.

43. Aronson: op. cit., pp. 130, 307; *Der Spiegel* archives.

44. Statement by Johannes Strübing, 18 January 1950—Lüneburg Trial, Vol. X, folio 202.

45. Ibid.

46. Ibid.

47. Statement by Reinhold Ortmann, 16 February 1950—Lüneburg Trial, Vol. XII, folio 65.

48. Ibid.

49. Statement by Greta Kuckhoff—Lüneburg Trial, Vol. VIII, folio 152.

50. Dallin: op. cit., p. 167.

51. RSHA telephone directory, May 1942; files of the Personal Staff of the Reichs-

führer-SS and Chief of the German Police (henceforth referred to as "RFSS"), microfilm 232.

52. Verbally from Gertrud Hoffmann-Breiter, 23 March 1968.

53. Ibid.

54. Ibid.

55. Verbally from Dr. Hugo Buschmann, 26 June 1968.

56. Letter from Willi Weber to Public Prosecutor, Supreme Court, Berlin, 16 November 1967.

57. Verbally from Marie-Louise Schulze, 4 March 1968.

58. Statement by Johannes Strübing, 18 January 1950—Lüneburg Trial, Vol. X, folio 202 et seq.

59. Ibid, folio 198.

60. Ibid, folios 196, 198, 199.

61. Statement by Greta Kuckhoff, ibid, Vol. VIII, folio 132.

62. Report by Werner Kraus, ibid, Vol. X, folios 160, 161.

63. Letter from Cato Bontjes van Beek to her mother, 2 March 1943—in Bontjes van Beek's private papers.

64. Statement by Greta Kuckhoff—Lüneburg Trial, Vol. VIII, folio 132.

65. Statement by Ilse Schaeffer, ibid, folio 105.

66. Weisenborn: op. cit., p. 5.

67. Statement by Reinhold Ortmann, 16 February 1950—Lüneburg Trial, Vol. XII folio 62.

68. Ibid; Gestapo Final Report, p. 23.

69. Roeder Final Report, p. 65; RSHA telephone directory, May 1942.

70. Dallin: op. cit., p. 154; Gestapo Final Report, p. 3.

71. Gestapo Final Report, p. 3.

72. Heinz Schröter: *Der grosse Verrat*, p. 40; statement by Johannes Strübing, 18 January 1950—Lüneburg Trial, Vol. X, folio 220 et seq.

73. Ibid.

74. Ibid.

75. Ibid; submission by Werner Müller-Hoff to the Committee on Victims of Fascism —files of the Hamburg Municipal Authorities.

76. Statement by Johannes Strübing, 18 January 1950—Lüneburg Trial, Vol. X, folios 220 et seq.

77. Ibid.

78. Ibid.

79. Report by Werner Krauss; letter from State Attorney Lüneburg to Office for Reconstruction of the Hanseatic City of Hamburg, 20 January 1951 —in files of Hamburg municipal authorities.

80. "Rote Kapelle" composite report—Lüneburg Trial, Vol. VIII, folio 107.

81. Ibid.

82. Ibid.

83. Gestapo Final Report, pp. 18, 25; statement by Günther Weisenborn—Lüneburg Trial, Vol. VIII, folio 74.

84. *Zur Geschichte der deutschen anti-faschistischen Widerstandsbewegung*, pp. 187, 189; Gestapo Final Report, p. 25.

85. Gestapo Final Report, pp. 23, 24.

86. Lehmann: op. cit., pp. 48–9.

87. According to Roeder Final Report, pp. I–III the prisoners numbered 117, including Scheliha who was not arrested un-

til the end of October. The Gestapo Final Report (p. 26) gives a figure of 119.

88. Gestapo Final Report, p. 24.

89. Ibid, p. 8.

90. Ibid, p. 24.

91. W. Kudryavzev and K. Raspevin: "She was called 'Alta'"—*Pravda*, 5 July 1967.

92. Gestapo Final Report, p. 24.

93. Statement by Johannes Strübing, 18 January 1950—Lüneburg Trial, Vol. X, folio 200.

94. Koenen's personal file in *Der Spiegel* archives.

95. Gestapo Final Report, p. 25.

96. Verbally from Gertrud Hoffmann-Breiter.

97. Ibid.

98. Ibid.

99. Statement by Johannes Strübing, 18 January 1950—Lüneburg Trial, Vol. X, folio 202.

100. Ibid.

101. "Der braune Freund hört mit" in *Kristall*, issue No. 3 of 1951.

102. Ibid.

103. Lehmann: op. cit., p. 43.

104. Ibid, p. 81.

105. Ibid, p. 57.

106. Ibid, p. 63.

107. Günther Weisenborn: *Der lautlose Aufstand*, p. 204.

108. Report by Greta Kuckhoff, 1 February 1947.

109. Statement by Heinrich Scheel, 26 November 1949—Lüneburg Trial, Vol. X, folio 65.

110. Statement by Hanni Weissensteiner, 24 July 1950—Lüneburg Trial, Vol. XII, folio 199.

111. Statement by Isolde von Brockdorff, *née* Urban, 11 January 1967—in *Der Spiegel* archives.

112. Dallin: op. cit., p. 170.

113. Gilles Perrault: *L'Orchestre rouge*, p. 147.

114. Note by Kurt Schumacher, 2 November 1942.

115. Roeder Final Report, pp. 400–1.

116. Statement by Günther Weisenborn—Lüneburg Trial, Vol. VIII, folio 73.

117. Note by Kurt Schumacher, 2 November 1942.

118. Report by Werner Krauss —Lüneburg Trial, Vol. X, folio 161.

119. On 24 October 1942 according to a statement made by Kriminalkommissar Schwarz on 3 January 1967—in *Der Spiegel* archives.

120. On 24 October 1942 according to Kriminalkommissar Schwarz (see Note 119).

121. Statement by Manfred Roeder, 30 June 1949—Lüneburg Trial, Vol. VIII, folio 12 et seq.

122. On 4 February 1944 according to Kriminalkommissar Schwarz (Note 119 above).

123. Statement by Greta Kuckhoff, 1 February 1947—Lüneburg Trial, Vol. V, folio 628.

124. Letter from Gestapo office Berlin to Prosecutor of Peoples Court, 2 December 1942—in Willi Weber's papers.

125. Roeder Final Report, p. 66; statement by Adelheid Eidenbenz, 29 March 1950—Lüneburg Trial, Vol. XII, folio 155.

126. Lehmann: op. cit., p. 19.

127. Statement by Alexander Kraell, 14 March 1950—Lüneburg Trial, Vol. XII, folio 116.

128. Letter from Alexander Spoerl, 31 May 1968.

129. Statement by Adelheid Eidenbenz, 29 March 1950—Lüneburg Trial, Vol. XII, folio 156; Lehmann: op. cit., p. 20.

130. Lehmann: op. cit., p. 20.

131. Ibid.

132. Dallin: op. cit., p. 168.

133. In his final plea to the court; statement by Eugen Schmitt, 25 July 1949—Lüneburg Trial, Vol. VIII, folio 61.

134. Letter from Cato Bontjes van Beek to her mother, 2 March 1943.

135. Perrault: op. cit., pp. 293–4.

136. Statement by Erich Edgar Schulze, 5 December 1948—Lüneburg Trial, Vol. VI, folio 783 et seq.

137. Ibid.

138. Ibid.

139. Ibid.

140. Ibid.

141. Roeder Final Report, p. 541; statement by Johannes Strübing, 2 February 1950—Lüneburg Trial, Vol. XII, folio 3 et seq.

142. Statement by Alexander Kraell; letter from the Lüneburg Prosecutor to Office for Reconstruction of City of Hamburg, 20 January 1951.

143. Statement by Johannes Strübing, 18 January 1950—Lüneburg Trial, Vol. X, folio 200.

144. Roeder Final Report, p. 615.

145. Statement by Rudolf Lehmann, 28 September 1948—Lüneburg Trial, Vol. IV, folio 525.

146. Statement by Karl Jesko von Puttkamer, 30 September 1948—Lüneburg Trial, Vol. IV, folio 537 et seq.

147. Roeder Final Report, p. 67.

Chapter Six

1. Statement by Manfred Roeder, 30 June 1949—files of the Public Prosecutor of the Provincial Court, Lüneburg (henceforth referred to as "Lüneburg Trial"), Vol. VIII, folio 13 et seq.

2. Ibid.

3. Ibid.

4. Final Report by Dr. Finck, the Public Prosecutor, in the case against Dr. Manfred Roeder, the ex-Luftwaffe Judge Advocate (henceforth referred to as "Roeder Final Report"), p. 67.

5. Ibid.

6. Ibid, p. 68.

7. Ibid.

8. Ibid, p. 70.

9. Ibid, p. 71.

10. Ibid, p. 75; *Der Spiegel* archives.

11. Ibid, p. 74.

12. Statement by Rudolf Lehmann, 28 September 1948—Lüneburg Trial, Vol. IV, folio 527.

13. Statement by Manfred Roeder, 30 June 1949—Lüneburg Trial, Vol. VIII, folio 14.

14. Statement by Rudolf Lehmann (see Note 12).

15. Ibid.

16. Roeder Final Report, p. 68.

17. Statement by Manfred Roeder, 30 June 1949—Lüneburg Trial, Vol. VIII, folio 13 et seq.

18. Ibid.

19. Ibid.

20. Gilles Perrault: *L'Orchestre Rouge*, p. 260 et seq.

21. Ibid, p. 263.

22. Statement by Manfred Roeder (see Note 17).

23. Roeder Final Report, p. 89.

24. Ibid, p. 90.

25. Ibid, p. 89.

26. Ibid, p. 91.

27. Verbally from Marie-Louise Schulze, 4 March 1968.

28. Evidence against Roeder by Dr. Adolf Grimme, 15 September 1945; Roeder Final Report, p. 76.

29. Roeder Final Report, p. 89.

30. Ibid.

31. Ibid, p. 90.

32. Klaus Lehmann: *Die Widerstandsgruppe Schulze-Boysen/Harnack*, p. 22.

33. Roeder Final Report, p. 92.

34. Statement by Dr. Eugen Schmitt, 22 September 1948—Lüneburg Trial, Vol. III, folio 510 et seq.

35. Roeder Final Report, p. 1; *Der Spiegel* archives.

36. Ibid.

37. Report by Alexander Kraell, 25 August 1948—Lüneburg Trial, Vol. III, folio 398.

38. Statement by Alexander von Pfuhlstein, 10 March 1950—Lüneburg Trial, Vol. IX, folio 140.

39. Statement by Kurt Rheindorf, 1948.

40. Ibid.

41. Statements by Christian von Hammerstein, 22 July 1948, and Joachim-Albrecht Graf von Westarp, 9 December 1948—Lüneburg Trial, Vol. V, folio 665.

42. Roeder Final Report, p. 2.

43. Ibid, p. 3.

44. Statement by Christian von Hammerstein, 22 July 1948—Lüneburg Trial, Vol. VIII, folio 54.

45. Ibid.

46. Statement by Dr. Eugen Schmitt (see Note 34).

47. Statement by Dr. Christian von Hammerstein, 22 July 1948—Lüneburg Trial, Vol. VIII, folio 54.

48. Ibid.

49. Report by Alexander Kraell, 25 August 1948—Lüneburg Trial, Vol. III, folio 398 and report 14 March 1950, ibid, Vol. XII, folio 195.

50. Statement by Dr. Eugen Schmitt, 22 September 1948—Lüneburg Trial, Vol. III, folio 510.

51. Statement by Falk Harnack, 3 February 1947—Lüneburg Trial, Vol. V, folio 634.

52. Statement by Marie-Louise Schulze, 5 December 1948—Lüneburg Trial, Vol. VI, folio 734.

53. Statement by Elsa Boysen, 5 July 1948—Lüneburg Trial, Vol. 1, folio 109.

54. Statement by Otto Goetze, 11 October 1949—Lüneburg Trial, Vol. VIII, folio 215.

55. Statement by Joachim-Albrecht Graf von Westarp,

9 December 1948—Lüneburg Trial, Vol. VIII, folio 665.

56. Roeder Final Report, p. 230.

57. Cross-examination of Manfred Roeder, 30 June 1947—Lüneburg Trial, Vol. II, folio 262; statement by Adelheid Eidenbenz, 28 September 1948, ibid, Vol. IV, folio 543.

58. Statement by Alexander Kraell, 14 March 1950—Lüneburg Trial, Vol. XII, folio 116.

59. Information from a witness who wishes to remain anonymous, confirmed by a letter from Eva Hildebrand, Rittmeister's widow, 27 August 1968.

60. As witness the case of Anna-Margaret Hoffmann-Scholtz.

61. Letter dated 20 June 1948 from Marieluise Henniger to Dr. Heinke, State Attorney.

62. Roeder Final Report, p. 2.

63. Ibid, p. 1.

64. Verbally from Harry Piepe, 14 March 1968.

65. Statement by Alexander Kraell, 14 March 1950—Lüneburg Trial, Vol. XII, folio 99.

66. Ibid.

67. Die Reichszeitung, 1 July 1951.

68. Dr. Manfred Roeder: Die Rote Kapelle, p. 36.

69. Statement by Manfred Roeder, 30 June 1949—Lüneburg Trial, Vol. VIII, folio 13.

70. Die Reichszeitung, 1 July 1951.

71. Statement by Alexander Kraell, 14 March 1950—Lüneburg Trial, Vol. XII, folio 110.

72. Information from a source who wishes to remain anonymous.

73. Die Reichszeitung, 10 June 1951; Roeder: op. cit., p. 15.

74. Roeder: op. cit., p. 15.

75. Ibid, p. 14.

76. Kraell in his statement of 14 March 1950—Lüneburg Trial, Vol. XII, folio 98.

77. Statement by Manfred Roeder, 1 July 1949—Lüneburg Trial, Vol. VIII, folio 25.

78. Statement by Marie-Louise Schulze, 14 February 1950—Lüneburg Trial, Vol. XII, folio 57.

79. Statement by Jan Tönnies, 10 March 1950—Lüneburg Trial, Vol. XII, folio 143.

80. Roeder Final Report, p. 158.

81. Die Reichszeitung, 10 June 1951.

82. Ibid.

83. Die Reichszeitung, 1 July 1951.

84. Statement by Manfred Roeder, 1 July 1949—Lüneburg Trial, Vol. VIII, folio 25.

85. Information from a source who wishes to remain anonymous.

86. Statement by Marie-Louise Schulze, 14 February 1950—Lüneburg Trial, Vol. XII, folio 57.

87. Statement by Jan Tönnies, 10 March 1950—Lüneburg Trial, Vol. XII, folio 143.

88. Die Reichszeitung, 10 June 1951.

89. Ibid.

90. Ibid.

91. Ibid.

92. Statement by Manfred Roeder before the Provincial Court of Stade, 20 June 1957 —in Jan Bontjes van Beek's papers.

93. Ibid.

94. See statement by Kraell, 14 March 1950—Lüneburg Trial, Vol. XII, folio 96.

95. Ibid, folio 113.

96. Roeder: op. cit., p. 26.

97. Statement by Manfred Roeder, 30 June 1949—Lüneburg Trial, Vol. VIII, folio 13.

98. Report by Alexander Kraell, 10 August 1948—Lüneburg Trial, Vol. III, folio 396.

99. Text of the laws in Roeder Final Report, pp. 95 et seq.

100. Roeder Final Report, p. 7.

101. Ibid, p. 6.

102. Ibid, p. 428.

103. Ibid.

104. Statement by Adolf Grimme, 8 December 1948—Lüneburg Trial, Vol. VI, folio 791.

105. Defending counsel were Dr. Kurt Valentin, Dr. Rudolf Behse, Dr. Heinz Bergmann, Dr. Bernhard Schwarz—Lehmann: op. cit., p. 88.

106. Statement by Kurt Valentin, 14 December 1948—Lüneburg Trial, Vol. VI, folio 803.

107. Statement by Adolf Grimme (see Note 104).

108. Statement by Kurt Valentin (see Note 106).

109. Ibid.

110. Roeder Final Report, p. 75.

111. Report by Werner Krauss —Lüneburg Trial, Vol. X, folio 162.

112. Greta Kuckhoff to Finck —office minute; Roeder Final Report, p. 483.

113. Letter from Werner Müller-Hoff to the Municipal Authorities of Hamburg, 20 August 1951—in files of Hamburg Municipal Authorities.

114. Roeder Final Report, p. 7; Lehmann: op. cit., p. 22.

115. Statement by Rudolf Behse, 20 February 1950— Lüneburg Trial, Vol. XII, folio 71.

116. Statement by Gerhard Ranft, 7 March 1950—Lüneburg Trial, Vol. XII, folio 85.

117. Statement by Alexander Kraell, 14 March 1950— Lüneburg Trial, Vol. XII, folio 104.

118. Ibid.

119. Sentence of Second Chamber of Reich Court Martial in the case of Scheliha-Stöbe—in Weisenborn's papers.

120. Roeder Final Report, pp. 7, 8, 9.

121. Statement by Rudolf Behse, 20 February 1950— Lüneburg Trial, Vol. XII, folio 71.

122. Statement by Alexander Kraell, 14 March 1950— Lüneburg Trial, Vol. XII, folio 106.

123. Statement by Eugen Schmitt, 22 September 1948 —Lüneburg Trial, Vol. III, folio 510.

124. Statement by Alexander Kraell, 14 March 1950— Lüneburg Trial, Vol. XII, folio 112.

125. Statement by Rudolf Behse, 20 February 1950—Lüneburg Trial, Vol. XII, folio 72.

126. Statement by Rudolf Behse, 2 December 1948—Lüneburg Trial, Vol. VI, folio 727.

127. Roeder Final Report, pp. 8, 9.

128. Statement by Rudolf Behse, 20 February 1950—Lüneburg Trial, Vol. XII, folio 68.

129. Ibid.

130. Statement by Alexander Kraell, 14 March 1950—Lüneburg Trial, Vol. XII, folio 97.

131. See statement by Behse, 20 February 1950—Lüneburg Trial, Vol. XII, folio 69.

132. Ibid.

133. Statement by Alexander Kraell, 14 March 1950—Lüneburg Trial, Vol. XII, folio 95.

134. Ibid.

135. Roeder Final Report, p. 9.

136. Statement by Gerhard Ranft, 7 March 1950—Lüneburg Trial, Vol. XII, folio 87.

137. Report by Alexander Kraell, 6 August 1948—Lüneburg Trial, Vol. III, folio 389.

138. Ibid.

139. Statement by Rudolf Lehmann, 28 September 1948—Lüneburg Trial, Vol. IV, folio 527.

140. Ibid.

141. Roeder Final Report, p. 8; statement by Karl Jesko von Puttkamer, 30 September 1948—Lüneburg Trial, Vol. IV, folio 537.

142. Statement by Karl Schmauser, 9 September 1950—Lüneburg Trial, Vol. XII, folio 186.

143. Ibid.

144. Ibid.

145. Ibid.

146. Ibid.

147. Statement by Johannes Strübing, 18 January 1950—Lüneburg Trial, Vol. X, folio 198.

148. Roeder Final Report, pp. 8, 9.

149. Statement by Heinz Bergmann, 20 February 1951—Lüneburg Trial, Vol. XII, folio 228.

150. Ibid.

151. Statement by Alexander Kraell, 14 March 1950—Lüneburg Trial, Vol. XII, folio 97.

152. Ibid.

153. Roeder Final Report, pp. 11, 12.

154. Ibid, p. 373.

155. Statement by Hannelore Thiel, 8 December 1949—Lüneburg Trial, Vol. X, folio 93.

156. Statement by August Ohm, 7 March 1953—in Jan Bontjes van Beek's papers.

157. Statement by Kraell in judgment by Provincial Court of Stade in Bontjes van Beek's case for indemnification versus the province of Lower Saxony, 27 February 1958—in Bontjes van Beek's papers.

158. Roeder Final Report, p. 366.

159. Ibid, p. 374.

160. Statement by Alexander Kraell, 14 March 1950—Lüneburg Trial, Vol. XII, folio 97.

161. Statement by Franz Ernst, 17 March 1950—Lüne-

burg Trial, Vol. XII, folio 130.

162. Roeder Final Report, p. 283.

163. Statement by Jan Bontjes van Beek to the Provincial Court of Stade, 12 February 1958—in Bontjes van Beek's papers.

164. Letter from Cato Bontjes van Beek to her mother, 2 March 1943—in Bontjes van Beek's papers.

165. Report by Werner Krauss —Lüneburg Trial, Vol. X, folio 162.

166. Roeder Final Report, pp. 11, 12.

167. Ibid.

168. Letter from Cato Bontjes van Beek to her mother, undated—in Bontjes van Beek's papers.

169. Statement by Franz Ernst, 17 March 1950—Lüneburg Trial, Vol. XII, folio 130.

170. Statement by Alexander Kraell to Provincial Court of Stade, 12 February 1958—in Bontjes van Beek's papers.

171. Statement by Friedrich Wilhelm Neuroth, 4 August 1949—Lüneburg Trial, Vol. VIII, folio 139.

172. Statement by Alexander Kraell, 14 March 1950—Lüneburg Trial, Vol. XII, folio 94.

173. Ibid.

174. Ibid, folio 113.

175. Roeder Final Report, pp. 12, 13.

176. Ibid, p. 13; statement by Dorothea Schottmüller, 2 December 1949—Lüneburg Trial, Vol. X, folio 84.

177. Roeder Final Report, p. 13.

178. Ibid, p. 14.

179. Ibid, p. 15.

180. Ibid.

181. Ibid, p. 16.

182. Ibid.

183. Ibid, p. 17.

184. Ibid.

185. Statement by Lotte Schleif, 29 November 1949— Lüneburg Trial, Vol. X, folio 73.

186. Article by Greta Kuckhoff in *Tägliche Rundschau,* 7 March 1948.

187. Report by Werner Krauss —Lüneburg Trial, Vol. X, folio 162.

188. Ibid.

189. Statement by Alexander Kraell, 14 March 1950— Lüneburg Trial, Vol. XII, folio 115.

190. Statement by Eugen Schmitt, 22 September 1948— Lüneburg Trial, Vol. III, folio 510.

191. Statement by Kurt Valentin, 14 December 1948— Lüneburg Trial, Vol. VI, folio 803.

192. Statement by Lotte Schleif, 29 November 1949— Lüneburg Trial, Vol. X, folio 73.

193. Statement by Paul Scholz, 30 November 1949—Lüneburg Trial, Vol. X, folio 80.

194. Statement by Franz Ernst, 17 March 1950—Lüneburg Trial, Vol. XII, folio 135.

195. Statement by Alexander Kraell, 14 March 1950—Lüneburg Trial, Vol. XII, folio 113.

196. Roeder Final Report, p. 12.

197. Ibid, p. 15.

198. Statement by Greta Kuckhoff (note by Finck dated 18

November 1949)—Lüneburg Trial, Vol. X, folio 53.

199. Report by Greta Kuckhoff, 1 February 1947.

200. Statement by Alfred Eichler, 14 September 1950—Lüneburg Trial, Vol. XII, folio 183.

201. Ibid.

202. Ibid; Lehmann: op. cit., p. 23.

203. Roeder Final Report, pp. 500, 523.

204. Statement by Alfred Eichler (see Note 200).

205. Roeder Final Report, p. 522.

206. Lehmann: op. cit., p. 30.

207. Ibid, p. 35.

208. Thora zu Eulenburg: *Libertas*, p. 30.

209. Roeder Final Report, p. 500.

210. Lehmann: op. cit., p. 31.

211. Roeder Final Report, p. 500.

212. Lehmann: op. cit., p. 24.

213. Verbally from Marie-Louise Schulze, 4 March 1968.

214. Memorandum drawn up by Kriminalkommissar Schwarz on persons of the Schulze-Boysen/Harnack resistance group known on 3 January 1967 to have been executed (henceforth referred to as "Schwarz Memorandum")—in *Der Spiegel* archives.

215. Roeder Final Report, p. 9; Schwarz Memorandum.

216. Lehmann: op. cit., p. 36.

217. Schwarz Memorandum.

218. Lehmann: op. cit., p. 43.

219. Statement by August Ohm, 28 March 1950—Lüneburg Trial, Vol. XII, folio 151.

220. Schwarz Memorandum.

221. Lehmann: op. cit., p. 54.

222. Letter from Cato Bontjes van Beek to her mother, 2 March 1943.

223. Roeder Final Report, p. 19.

Chapter Seven

1. Report by Chief of Security Police and SD, IV A 2-B, No. 330/42 dated 22 December 1942 (henceforth referred to as "Gestapo Final Report"), p. 8.

2. Ibid, p. 6.

3. Ibid.

4. Ibid.

5. Ibid.

6. Ibid, p. 7.

7. Ibid, p. 6.

8. Ibid.

9. Ibid.

10. Ibid, p. 4.

11. John Nemo: *Das rote Netz*, p. 16.

12. Verbally from Harry Piepe, 14 March 1968 (henceforth referred to as "from Piepe").

13. Capitaine "Freddy": "La Vérité sur la Rote Kapelle" in *Europe-Amérique*, 2 October 1947, pp. 14, 15.

14. Ibid, p. 14.

15. Gilles Perrault: *L'Orchestre rouge*, p. 125.

16. From Piepe.

17. Nemo: op. cit., p. 11.

18. Harry Piepe: "Harburger jagte Agenten" in *Harburger Anzeiger und Nachrichten*, 11 October 1967.

19. Piepe: op. cit., 11 October 1967.

20. David Dallin: *Soviet Espionage*, p. 155.

21. Nemo: op. cit., p. 11.
22. Ibid.
23. Ibid.
24. Ibid.
25. Ibid.
26. Dallin: op. cit., p. 155.
27. Ibid.
28. Perrault: op. cit., p. 154.
29. Ibid, pp. 157-8.
30. See Gestapo Final Report, p. 4.
31. Perrault: op. cit., p. 162.
32. Piepe: op. cit., 12 October 1967.
33. Gestapo Final Report, pp. 2, 3.
34. Ibid, p. 3.
35. Ibid, p. 2.
36. Dallin: op. cit., p. 156.
37. Piepe: op. cit., 13 October 1967.
38. Ibid.
39. Ibid.
40. Perrault: op. cit., p. 162.
41. Dallin: op. cit., p. 156.
42. Gestapo Final Report, p. 4.
43. Ibid.
44. Perrault: op. cit., p. 165 et seq.
45. Ibid, p. 154.
46. Ibid, p. 165.
47. Ibid, pp. 165-6.
48. Ibid, p. 168.
49. Ibid.
50. Capitaine "Freddy": op. cit., 9 October 1947.
51. From Piepe.
52. Ibid.
53. Ibid.
54. Perrault: op. cit., p. 171.
55. Letter from Moyen to the author, 8 July 1968.
56. Perrault: op. cit., p. 172.
57. Ibid, p. 171.
58. Ibid, p. 168.
59. From Piepe.
60. Verbally from Heinrich

Reiser, 4 March 1968 (henceforth referred to as "from Reiser").
61. From Reiser.
62. Perrault: op. cit., p. 249.
63. Ibid.
64. From Piepe; Gestapo Final Report, p. 5.
65. From Piepe.
66. Ibid.
67. Ibid.
68. Ibid.
69. Ibid.
70. Perrault: op. cit., p. 253.
71. Dallin: op. cit., p. 153; Perrault: op. cit., p. 253.
72. From Piepe.
73. Perrault: op. cit., p. 259.
74. From Piepe.
75. Ibid.
76. Perrault: op. cit., p. 260.
77. Ibid.
78. From Piepe.
79. Ibid.
80. Perrault: op. cit., p. 260.
81. Ibid.
82. From Piepe.
83. Ibid.
84. Nemo: op. cit., p. 13.
85. Ibid.
86. Perrault: op. cit., p. 268 et seq.
87. Ibid, p. 270.
88. Nemo: op. cit., p. 13.
89. Ibid.
90. Perrault: op. cit., p. 275.
91. Ibid.
92. Ibid, p. 276.
93. Nemo: op. cit., p. 13.
94. Ibid.
95. Ibid.
96. Ibid.
97. From Piepe.
98. Ibid.
99. Perrault: op. cit., p. 282.
100. Dallin: op. cit., pp. 165-6; Perrault: op. cit., p. 287 et seq.

101. Nemo: op. cit., pp. 13, 14.

102. Dallin: op. cit., p. 164.

103. Perrault: op. cit., p. 331.

104. Dallin: op. cit., p. 165; Perrault: op. cit., p. 399.

105. Dallin: op. cit., p. 165; Nemo: op. cit., p. 15.

106. Nemo: op. cit., p. 16.

107. Ibid.

108. Ibid.

109. Ibid, p. 15.

110. Piepe: op. cit., 26 October 1967.

111. Report by Chief of Security Police and SD, IV A 2-B, No 330/42 to Reichsführer-SS dated 24 December 1942 —given in Wilhelm von Schramm: *Verrat im Zweiten Weltkrieg*, p. 367.

112. Ibid.

113. Perrault: op. cit., p. 289.

114. See note on p. 213.

115. From Reiser.

116. Ibid.

117. Ibid.

118. Werner Best: *Die deutsche Abwehrpolizei bis 1945*, p. 72.

119. Nemo: op. cit., p. 3.

120. Final Report by Dr. Finck, the Public Prosecutor, in the case against Dr. Manfred Roeder, the ex-Luftwaffe Judge Advocate (henceforth referred to as "Roeder Final Report"), p. 19.

121. Cross-examination of Roeder, 16 September 1948— files of investigation proceedings against Roeder.

122. Dallin: op. cit., p. 166.

123. Cross-examination of Roeder, 16 September 1948.

124. Perrault: op. cit., pp. 360-1.

125. Dallin: op. cit., p. 156.

126. Perrault: op. cit., p. 359.

127. Dallin: op. cit., p. 167; Perrault: op. cit., p. 361.

128. Cross-examination of Roeder, 16 September 1948.

129. Ibid.

130. Ibid, p. 362.

131. Perrault: op. cit., p. 362.

132. Cross-examination of Roeder, 16 September 1948.

133. Ibid.

134. Dallin: op. cit., p. 168.

135. Ibid, p. 170.

136. Ibid, p. 171.

137. Ibid.

138. From Reiser.

139. Perrault: op. cit., p. 367.

140. Ibid, p. 364.

141. Nemo: op. cit., p. 3.

142. Perrault: op. cit., p. 352.

143. Ibid.

144. Ibid, p. 346.

145. Ibid.

146. Ibid, p. 403.

147. Gestapo Final Report, p. 5.

148. From Reiser.

149. Ibid; Dallin: op. cit., p. 171 et seq.; Nemo: op. cit., p. 10 et seq.; record of conversation between Major Brandt of Military Intelligence and Kriminalkommissar Ampletzer, 9 July 1943—in Federal archives.

150. Nemo: op. cit., p. 10.

151. From Reiser.

152. Perrault: op. cit., p. 347.

153. Nemo: op. cit., p. 4.

154. Ibid.

155. See Hans Umbreit: *Der Militärbefehlshaber in Frankreich 1940 bis 1944*.

156. From Reiser; also voluminous correspondence between the Abwher and the RSHA on the subject of the Rote Kapelle "playback" games—in Federal archives.

157. Dallin: op. cit., p. 175.

158. Ibid.

159. Ibid.

160. From Reiser.

161. Collection of messages of military nature passed over the "Eifel" line during February 1943—Abwehr files in Federal archives.

162. Ibid.

163. Ibid.

164. Ibid—March 1943.

165. Ibid.

166. Ibid.

167. Ibid—messages of 17, 21 and 23 January 1943.

168. Ibid—March 1943.

169. Ibid.

170. Ibid.

171. Ibid—April-May 1943.

172. Ibid.

173. For further details see Schramm: *Verrat im Zweiten Weltkrieg.*

174. Pannwitz's personal file in *Der Spiegel* archives; also letter from Heinz Pannwitz, 26 March 1968.

175. Ibid.

176. Ibid.

177. Ibid.

178. Dallin: op. cit., p. 176.

179. Ibid.

180. Ibid.

181. Schramm: op. cit., p. 288.

182. Ibid.

183. Dallin: op. cit., p. 178.

184. Ibid, p. 179.

185. Ibid, p. 180.

186. Ibid.

187. Ibid, p. 181.

188. Letter from Chief of Security Poice and SD to Ausland/Abwehr, Section III, 2 June 1943—in Abwehr files, Federal archives.

189. Letter from Abwehr Office, France, Section F 2, 21 June 1943—in Abwehr files, Federal archives.

190. Ibid.

191. Letter from Abwehr Office, France, 25 June 1943—Abwehr files, Federal archives.

192. Ibid.

193. Ibid.

194. From Reiser.

195. Dallin: op. cit., p. 177; Perrault: op. cit., p. 415.

196. Perrault: op. sit., p. 421.

197. Dallin: op. cit., p. 176.

198. Perrault: op. cit., p 474 (Note).

199. Dallin: op. cit., p. 181.

Chapter Eight

1. David Dallin: *Soviet Espionage*, p. 148.

2. *Pubisher's Weekly*, 28 April 1969.

3. Gilles Perrault: *L'Orchestre rouge*, p. 570.

4. Günther Weisenborn: "Rede über die deutsche Widerstandsbewegung" in *Aufbau*, No. 6 of 1946, p. 576 et seq.

5. Letter from Willi Weber to the author, 5 June 1968.

6. Statement by Greta Kuckhoff—files of the Public Prosecutor of the Lüneburg Provincial Court in the case against Dr. Manfred Roeder (henceforth referred to as "Lüneburg Trial"), Vol. VIII, folio 131.

7. Günther Weisenborn in an address to the Friedrich Eberhard School in West Berlin, published in *Das Objektiv*, No 4 of 1965, p. 10.

8. *Der Reichszeitung*, 17 June 1951.

9. Manfred Roeder: *Die Rote Kapelle*, p. 36.

10. Harry Piepe: "Harburger jagte Agenten" in *Harburger Anzeiger und Nachrichten*, 10 October 1967.

11. Perraut: op. cit., p. 292.

12. *Die Reichszeitung*, 8 July 1951.

13. Verbally from Heinrich Reiser, 4 March 1968.

14. Severin Bialer: *Stalin and his Generals*, p. 212.

15. Georgi K. Zhukov: *Memoirs*, p. 227.

16. Ibid, pp. 227-8.

17. Ibid, p. 229; Bialer: op. cit., p. 213.

18. Notes in the papers of the late Captain (Dr.) Will Grosse.

19. Ibid.

20. Report by Chief of Security Poice and SD, IV A 2-B dated 22 December 1942 (henceforth referred to as "Gestapo Final Report"), p. 7.

21. Hans Umbreit: *Der Militärbefehlshaber in Frankreich 1940-1944*, p. 36.

22. See Chapter 2, p. 76 (footnote).

23. Ibid.

24. See Chapter 7.

25. Gestapo Final Report, p. 1.

26. Collection of Soviet radio messages in the papers of the late Wilhelm F. Flicke (henceforth referred to as "Flicke Collection"), p. 6.

27. Alfred Philippi and Ferdinand Heim: *Der Feldzug gegen Sowjetrussland 1941 bis 1945*, pp. 69-70.

28. Flicke Collection, p. 7.

29. Philippi & Heim: op. cit., pp. 79-80.

30. Flicke Collection, p. 7.

31. Philippi & Heim: op. cit., p. 90.

32. This is in a message of 9 December 1941 transmitted to Moscow via Dora—Flicke Collection, p. 8.

33. Wilhelm F. Flicke: *Spionagegruppe Rote Kapelle*, p. 81.

34. Philippi & Heim: op. cit., p. 95.

35. Flicke: op. cit., p. 81.

36. Bialer: op. cit., p. 603.

37. Zhukov: op. cit., p. 358.

38. Perrault: op. cit., pp. 86-7.

39. Zhukov: op. cit., p. 356.

40. Colonel-General Halder: *Kriegstagebuch*, Vol. III, pp. 401 et seq.

41. Ibid, p. 420.

42. Bialer: op. cit., p. 584.

43. Ibid, p. 588.

44. Ibid, p. 601.

45. Ibid, p. 603.

46. Ibid.

47. Ibid.

48. Ibid.

49. Roeder: op. cit., p. 19.

50. Statement by Karl Schmauser, 9 September 1950 —Lüneburg Trial, Vol. XII, folio 193.

51. Statement by Joachim Rohleder, 2 July 1950—Lüneburg Trial, Vol. XII, folio 193.

52. Günther Weisenborn: *Der lautlose Aufstand*, p. 204.

53. Ernst von Salomon: *Der Fragebogen*, p. 482.

54. Statement by Falk Harnack, 3 February 1947—Lüneburg Trial, Vol. V, folio 634.

55. Klaus Lehmann: *Wider-*

standsgruppe *Schulze-Boysen/ Harnack*, pp. 82, 84.
56. Letter from Cato Bontjes van Beek to her mother, 2 March 1943—in Bontjes van Beek's private papers.

57. Eberhard Bethge: *Dietrich Bonhoeffer*, p. 759.
58. See new account by Harold C. Deutsch in *The Conspiracy against Hitler in the Twilight War*.

Bibliography

I. *Unpublished Sources*

Bauer, Arnold: *Erinnerungen an Harro Schulze-Boysen und Horst Heilmann.* Memorandum of 1968.

Bauer, Wilhelm: *Die Tätigkeit des BB-Apparates der KPD.* Manuscript. Köln 1968.

Bauer, Wilhelm. *Fallschirmagenten.* Memorandum of 1968.

Best, Werner: *Die deutsche Abwehrpolizei bis 1945.* Memorandum of 1949.

Buschmann, Hugo: *Mein Freund Harro Schulze-Boysen.* Memorandum of 1968.

Collection of Soviet radio messages in the private papers of the late Wilhelm F. Flicke.

Files of the Personal Staff of the Reichsführer-SS and Chief of the German Police. Microfilms in the National Archives, Washington D.C. Section T–175.

Files of the Public Prosecutor of the Lüneburg Provincial Court. Case against Dr. Manfred Roeder. 15 vols.

Final report by Dr. Finck, the Public Prosecutor, on the proceedings against Dr. Manfred Roeder, the ex-Luftwaffe Judge Advocate. Reference No.: 1 Js 16/49, Lüneburg 1951.

Heimbach, Lothar: *Geheime Staatspolizei.* Memorandum of 1961 in Heimbach's private papers.

Kemp, Professor: *John F. Rittmeister zum Gedächtnis.* Memorandum of 1968.

Memorandum on persons of the Schulze-Boysen/Harnack resistance group known to have been executed, drafted by Kriminalkommissar Schwarz, West Berlin—in *Der Spiegel* archives.

Memorandum by Dr. Noack, the attorney, on the case against Keller, 8 February 1952—in Wolfgang Müller's papers.

Nemo, John: *Das rote Netz.* Undated. In *Der Spiegel* archives.

Note on important Russian organizations and agencies in Germany. Police Institute Berlin-Charlottenburg, 1933–4—in Lothar Heimbach's papers.

Prussian State Ministry, Section P: Files dealing with the communist movement, Vol. IV 1935—in Wilhelm Bauer's papers.

Schröter, Heinz: *Der grosse Verrat.* Undated. In Schröter's papers.

Schulze, Marie-Louise: *Warum ich im Jahre 1933 Parteigenossin geworden bin.* Undated note in Schulze's papers.

Vilter, W. M.: *Die Geheimschriften.* Note of 1935.

Wehner, Herbert: *Notizen.* Memorandum of 23 May 1946 in *Der Spiegel* archives.

Zechlin, Egmont: *Arvid und Mildred Harnack zum Gedächtnis.* Undated.

II. *Published Sources*

Biographic Directory of the USSR.

Halder, Colonel-General: Kriegstagebuch [Diary], Vol. III, Kohlhammer Verlag, Stuttgart 1964.

Heiber, Helmut: *Hitlers Lagebesprechungen,* Deutsche Verlagsanstalt, Stuttgart 1962.

International Military Tribunal: The Nuremberg Trial (English Version), Vol. XXXVIII, HMSO 1947–9.

Koch, Hans: 5000 Sowjetköpfe.

"Murder International Inc." Hearings before the Subcommittee to investigate the administration of the International Security Act, Washington 1953.

Who's Who in the USSR, 1961/62.

III. *Books*

Aronson, Shlomo: *Heydrich und die Anfänge des SD und der Gestapo 1931–1935,* Inaugural Dissertation of Faculty of Philosophy at the Free University of Berlin, Berlin 1967.

Balzer, Karl: *Der 20. Juli und der Landesverrat,* Göttingen 1967.

Bethge, Eberhard: *Dietrich Bonhoeffer,* Kaiser Verlag, Munich 1967.

Bialer, Seweryn: *Stalin and his Generals,* New York 1969.

Boysen, Elsa: *Harro Schulze-Boysen,* Komet Verlag, Düsseldorf 1947.

Brauer, Arthur von: *Im Dienste Bismarcks,* Mittler Verlag, Berlin 1936.

Broszat, Martin: "The Concentration Camps," translated Marian Jackson, in *Anatomy of the SS State*, Collins, London 1968.

Buchheim, Hans: *SS und Polizei im NS-Staat*, Selbstverlag der Studiengesellschaft für Zeitprobleme, Duisdorf nr Bonn 1964.

Buchheit, Gert: *Der deutsche Geheimdienst*, List Verlag, Munich 1966.

Bullock, Alan: *Hitler, A Study in Tyranny*, Odhams Press, London 1964.

Carell, Paul: *Scorched Earth*, translated Ewald Osers, Harrap, London, Toronto, Wellington and Sydney 1970.

Cookridge, E. H.: *Soviet Spy Net*, Frederick Muller, London 1955.

Dallin, Alexander: *German Rule in Russia*, Macmillan, London 1957.

Dallin, David: *Soviet Espionage*, Yale University Press, New Haven, Geoffrey Cumberledge, OUP, London 1955.

Deutsch, Harold C.: *The Conspiracy against Hitler in the Twilight War*, University of Minnesota Press, Minneapolis, Oxford University Press, London 1968.

Dulles, Allen Welsh: *Germany's Underground*, Macmillan, New York 1947.

Ehrt, Adolf: *Bewaffneter Aufstand*, Nibelungen Verlag, Berlin and Leipzig 1933.

Eulenburg, Thora zu: *Erinnerungen an Libertas*, undated.

Fischer, Ruth: *Stalin und der deutsche Kommunismus*, Verlag Frankfurter Hefte, Frankfurt 1948.

Flicke, Wilhelm F.: *Agenten funken nach Moskau*, Neptun Verlag, Munich-Wels 1954.

Flicke, Wilhelm F.: *Spionagegruppe Rote Kapelle*, Neptun Verlag, Kreuzlingen 1954.

Grimme, Adolf: *Briefe*, Schneider Verlag, Heidelberg 1967.

Hagen, Walter: *Die geheime Front*, Nibelungen Verlag, Linz & Vienna 1950.

Hart, Sir Basil Liddell (editor): *The Soviet Army*, Weidenfeld & Nicolson, London 1956.

Hassel, Ulrich von: *Vom anderen Deutschland*, Fisher Bücherei, Frankfurt & Hamburg 1964: *The von Hassel Diaries*, Hamish Hamilton, London 1948.

Heilbrunn, Otto: *The Soviet Secret Service*, Allen & Unwin, London 1956.

Heydrich, R.: *Wandlungen unseres Kampfes*, Franz Eher Verlag, Munich & Berlin 1935.

Hildebrandt, Rainer: *Wir sind die Letzten*, Michael Verlag, Berlin-Neuwied 1949.

Himmler, Heinrich: *Die Schutzstaffel als antibolshewistische Kampforganisation*, Zentralverlag der NSDAP, Franz Eher II, Munich 1936.

Höhne, Heinz: *Der Orden unter dem Totenkopf,* Sigbert Mohn Verlag, Gütersloh 1967; *The Order of the Death's Head,* translated Richard Barry, Secker & Warburg, London 1969.

Institut für Marxismus–Leninismus beim Zentralkomitee der SED: *Geschichte der deutschen Arbeiterbewegung,* Vol. V, East Berlin 1966.

Jung, Franz: *Der Weg nach unten,* Luchterhand, Neuwied 1961.

Kahn, David: *The Codebreakers,* Weidenfeld & Nicolson, London 1968.

Kalinov, Kyrill D.: *Sowjetmarschälle haben das Wort* (translated from the Russian), Hansa Verlag, Hamburg 1950.

Kennan, George F.: *Russia and the West under Lenin and Stalin,* Hutchinsons, London 1961.

Kern, Erich: *Verrat an Deutschland,* Göttingen 1963.

Koestler, Arthur: *The Invisible Writing,* Collins, London 1955.

Krivitsky, W. G.: *I was Stalin's Agent,* Hamish Hamilton, London 1939.

Laschitza, Horst & Vietzke, Siegfried: *Deutschland und die deutsche Arbeiterbewegung 1933–1945,* East Berlin 1964.

Lehmann, Klaus: *Widerstandsgruppe Schulze-Boysen/Harnack,* VVN Verlag, East Berlin 1948.

Leverkuehn, Paul: *Der geheime Nachrichtendienst der deutschen Wehrmacht im Kriege,* Athenäum Verlag, Frankfurt 1965.

Lewytzkyj, Boris: *Vom Roten Terror zur sozialistischen Gesetzlichkeit,* Nymphenburger Verlag, Munich 1961.

Neufeldt, Hans-Joachim; Huck, Jürgen; Tessin, Georg: *Zur Geschichte der Ordnungspolizei,* printed as manuscript, Koblenz 1957.

Nicolai W.: *Geheime Mächte,* Koehler, Leipzig 1924.

Nollau, Günther: *Die Internationale,* Kiepenheuer & Witsch, Köln 1959.

O'Neill, Robert J.: *The German Army and the Nazi Party,* Cassell, London 1966.

Orlov, Alexander: *The Secret History of Stalin's Crimes,* Jarrolds, London 1953.

Paetel, Karl O.: *Versuchung oder Chance?,* Musterschmidt Verlag, Göttingen 1965.

Pechel, Rudolf: *Deutscher Widerstand,* Eugen Rentsch Verlag, Zurich 1947.

Perrault, Gilles: *L'Orchestre rouge,* Fayard, Paris 1967.

Philippi, Alfred & Heim, Ferdinand: *Der Feldzug gegen Sowjetrussland 1941 bis 1945,* Kohlhammer Verlag, Stuttgart 1962.

Potyomkin, W. P.: *Geschichte der Diplomatie,* Vol. III, Moscow 1947.

Praun, Albert: *Soldat in der Telegrapher- und Nachrichtentruppe,* private publication, Würzburg 1965.

Pünter, Otto: *Der Anschluss fand nicht statt*, Hallwag, Berne & Stuttgart 1968.

Reile, Oscar: *Geheime Ostfront*, Munich-Wels 1963.

Reile, Oscar: *Geheime Westfront*, Munich-Wels 1963.

Reitlinger, Gerald: *The SS. Alibi of a Nation*, Wm. Heinemann, London, Melbourne, Toronto 1956.

Rothfels, Hans: *Die deutsche Opposition gegen Hitler*, Sherpe Verlag, Krefeld 1949.

Rowan, Richard Wilmer & Deindorfer, Robert G.: *Secret Service*, John Miles, London 1938.

Salomon, Ernst von: *Der Fragebogen*, Rowohlt Verlag, Hamburg 1951.

Schellenberg, Walter: *Memoiren*, Verlag für Politik und Wirtschaft, Köln 1956; *The Schellenberg Memoirs*, introduction Alan Bullock, translated Louis Hagen, André Deutsch, London 1961.

Schlabrendorff, Fabian von: *Offiziere gegen Hitler*, edited by Gero von Gaevernitz, Europa Verlag, Zurich 1946; *The Secret War against Hitler*, translated Hilda Simon, Hodder & Stoughton, London 1961.

Schmidt, Walter A.: *Damit Deutschland lebe*, Kongress Verlag, East Berlin 1955.

Schramm, Wilhelm von: *Verrat im Zweiten Weltkrieg*, Econ Verlag, Düsseldorf & Vienna 1967.

Schüddekopf, Otto Ernst: *Linke Leute von rechts*, Kohlhammer Verlag, Stuttgart 1960.

Schulze-Boysen, Harro: *Gegner von heute—Kampfgenossen von morgen*, W. Hoffmann, Berlin 1932.

Schwenger, Hannes (editor): *Berlin im Widerstand*, Berlin 1965.

Telpuchowski, B. S.: *Die sowjetische Geschichte des Grossen Vaterländischen Krieges*, Bernard & Graefe, Frankfurt 1961.

Tomin, Valentin & Grabowski, Stefan: *Die Helden der Berliner Illegalität* (translation from Russian), Dietz, East Berlin 1967.

Turel, Adrien: *Ecce Superhomo*, Vol. I, Adrien Turel foundation, roneoed, undated.

Umbreit, Hans: *Der Militärbefehlshaber in Frankreich 1940–1944*, Boldt Verlag, Boppard 1968.

Valtin, Jan: *Tagebuch der Hölle*, Kiepenheuer & Witsch, Köln & Berlin 1957.

Weisenborn, Günther: *Memorial*, Aufbau Verlag, Hamburg 1948.

Weisenborn, Günther: *Der lautlose Aufstand*, Rowohlt, Hamburg 1953.

Weisenborn, Günther: *Die Illegalen*, Aufbau Verlag, East Berlin 1946.

Wollenberg, Erich: *Der Apparat*, Essen 1950.

Zeutschel, Walter: *Im Dienst der kommunistischen Terror-Organisation*, J. H. W. Dietz, Berlin 1931.

Zhukov, Georgi K.: *Erinnerungen und Gedanken*, Stuttgart 1969.

Zur Geschichte der deutschen antifaschistischen Widerstandsbewegung, East Berlin 1958.

IV. *Newspaper Articles*

"Die sowjetischen Sicherheitsorgane" in *Das Parlament*, 2 December 1959.

Capitaine "Freddy": "La Vérité sur Rote Kapelle" in *Europe-Amérique*, 2 & 9 October 1947.

Harnack, Axel von: "Arvid und Mildred Harnack" in *Die Gegenwart*, Nos. 26 and 27 of 1947.

Kuckhoff, Greta: "Ein Abschnitt des deutschen Widerstandskampfes" in *Die Weltbühne*, Nos. 3 and 4 of 1948.

Martini, Winfried: "Deutsche Spionage für Moskau bis 1945" in *Die Welt*, 15–27 October 1966.

Observator: "Wir wissen alles" in *Echo der Woche*, 5 May 1950.

Piepe, Harry: "Harburger jagte Àgenten' in *Harburger Anzeiger und Nachrichten*, 30 September–31 October 1967.

Piepe, Harry: "Ich jagte rote Agenten" in *Der Mittag*, 11 February–15 March 1953.

Scheel, Heinrich: "Wesen und Wollen der Widerstandsorganisation Schulze-Boysen/Harnack" in *Neues Deutschland*, 29 June 1968.

"Aus Herbert Wehner's Akten" in *Rheinische Merkur*, 22 March 1957.

Weisenborn, Günther: "Studenten und illegale Arbeit" in *Forum*, No. 1 of January 1947.

Weisenborn, Günther: "Rede über die deutsche Widerstandsbewegung" in *Aufbau*, No. 6 of 1946, p. 576 et seq.

V. *Newspapers and Periodicals*

Der Tagesspiegel, 1948.
Die andere Zeitung, 1961.
Frankfurter Allgemeine Zeitung, 1951.
Für Dich, 1968.
Gegner, 1932 and 1933.
Heidebote, 1951.
Hamburger Tageblatt, 1941.
Junge Welt, 1967.
Kristall, 1950 and 1951.
Kölnische Zeitung, 1925.

Münchener Abendzeitung, 1959.
Neues Deutschland, 1947, 1955, 1964, 1968.
Norddeutsche Rundschau, 1951.
Pravda, 1967.
Die Reichszeitung, 1951.
Stern, 1951.
Tägliche Rundschau, 1951.

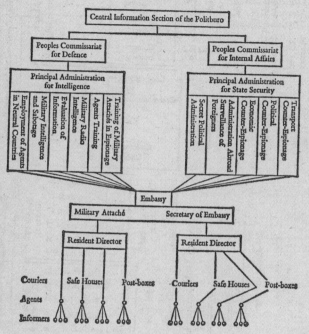

The Soviet Secret Service

Central Information Section of the Politburo

Peoples Commissariat for Defence

Peoples Commissariat for Internal Affairs

Principal Administration for Intelligence

- Employment of Agents in Neutral Countries
- Military Intelligence and Sabotage
- Evaluation of Information
- Military Radio Intelligence
- Agents Training
- Training of Military Attachés in Espionage

Principal Administration for State Security

- Secret Political Administration
- Administration Abroad
- Surveillance of Foreigners
- Economic Counter-Espionage
- Political Counter-Espionage
- Transport Counter-Espionage

Embassy

Military Attaché   Secretary of Embassy

Resident Director   Resident Director

Couriers   Safe Houses   Post-boxes   Couriers   Safe Houses   Post-boxes

Agents

Informers

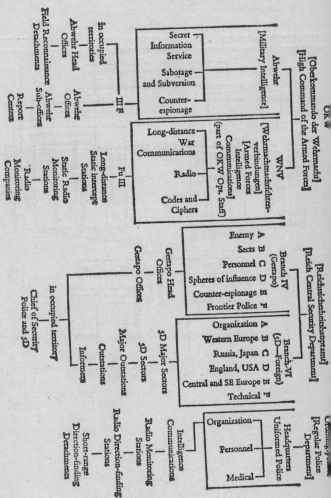

Location of Agents in the Higher Levels of the German Wehrmacht

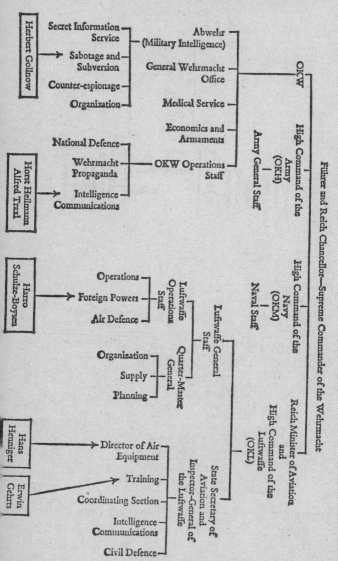

Index

Index

About the Author

Heinz Höhne was born in 1926 and grew up in Berlin. He joined the staff of the magazine *Der Spiegel* in 1955, where he specialized in foreign affairs. His first book, *The Order of the Death's Head,* was originally serialized in *Der Spiegel.* Herr Höhne is married and lives in Germany.